THE
JEWISH ENIGMA

THE
JEWISH ENIGMA
An Enduring People

Editor David Englander

The Open University

in association with

PETER HALBAN
LONDON

THE SPIRO INSTITUTE

First published in 1992 by
The Open University
Walton Hall
Milton Keynes MK7 6AA
in association with
Peter Halban Publishers Ltd
42 South Molton Street
London W1Y 1HB

This book is part of an educational project produced by the Open University
in association with the Spiro Institute for the Study of
Jewish History and Culture. The project is supported by the
Doron Foundation for Education and Welfare.

British Library Cataloguing-in-Publication Data.
A catalogue record for this book is available
from the British Library

ISBN 1 870015 44 4

Phototypeset by Computape (Pickering) Ltd, North Yorkshire
Printed in Great Britain by Ebenezer Baylis and Son Ltd, Worcester
Bound by WBC Ltd, Bridgend

Contents

In Memory of Matilda Kessler,
Member of the Council of the Open University 1974–1985

Foreword

I am glad to be able to write a foreword for *The Jewish Enigma*. When I was first asked to support the project, it seemed a far-away prospect. Now it has become a completed proposition.

The book is carefully researched and wide-ranging in the topics that it covers, all of them of importance in world history. Indeed, it can reasonably be argued that an understanding of world history is seriously incomplete unless it pays attention to these themes.

The editor has been energetic and imaginative in choosing as contributors a group of scholars of great knowledge and experience. No book is ever the last word, and this book, like all good books, not only provides information but leaves room for debate. I am delighted to have been associated with it.

Asa Briggs
Worcester College
Oxford

AUGUST 1991

Preface

Behold 'the figure of the enigmatic Jew!' George Eliot, writing in the 1870s, found Jews a puzzling people. Others, before and since, have been equally perplexed. It is not hard to see why. Stateless for more than two millenia, scattered across the four corners of the earth, living under different regimes, diverse in status, occupation, education and culture, varying in the degree of acculturation and assimilation, the Jewish people have nevertheless contrived to retain a distinct identity. How so? In this volume, seven distinguished scholars and teachers consider how a people, strangely secure, though without friend or protector, have survived the wrecks of empires and outlived oppressors from Nebuchadnezzar to the Nazis. Our contributors, experts in their fields, together create a rich and engaging portrait of an extraordinary people who have made so signal a contribution to the civilization of the modern world.

The Jewish Enigma originated in the Arts Faculty. It arose from the joint initiative of the late Matilda Kessler, member of the Council of the Open University, Dr Francis Clark, formerly head of the Religious Studies Department and Mr Robin Spiro, Director of the Spiro Institute for the Study of Jewish History and Culture. The project was taken forward within the University by Dr Michael Nathenson of the Institute of Educational Technology, and the Personal and Cultural Education Sector of the Board for Continuing Education under the direction of Geoffrey Bourne. It then returned to the Arts Faculty where it fell to me as the historian with a special interest in Jewish social history to bring the volume to its present shape. In the process many debts have been incurred. We have received expert advice and guidance from Israel Finestein QC, the Very Reverend Dr Thomas Torrance, Professor Aziz Al-Azmeh and Professor Albert Hourani. Dr Ze'ev Katz and Amitai Spitzer have been of inestimable assistance, as has Jeremy Shonfield, who has allowed us to take liberties with his time and knowledge. Charles King has been no less indulgent. His guidance on eastern Europe and Russian-language sources has helped enormously. Chimen Abramsky, Emeritus Professor of Jewish Studies at University College London, has been critical, supportive and given far more than any one has a right to expect of a special adviser. Our publishers, Peter and Martine Halban, have likewise displayed remarkable forbearance. We are grateful for the support of the Doron Foundation for

Education and Welfare. I have also been fortunate in the support received from colleagues at the Open University. Kathy Evans, Ray Munns, Andras Bereznay, Jo Beale, Andrew Coleman, John Greenwood, Beryl Ridgway and Wendy Clarke have been wonderful. Jonathan Hunt and Dr Annie Haight, through their vigilance and dedication, have saved us from numerous pitfalls. Special thanks are due to my colleagues Kate Richenburg and Dr Mark Goodwin for their dedication, sheer professionalism and considerable intellectual input, which have done so much to enhance this book. Without Matilda Kessler, too, the project might never have happened. It was her imaginaton and enthusiasm which set the wheels turning and it is to her memory that this book is dedicated.

David Englander
History Department
Arts Faculty
The Open University

Introduction

Ronald Nettler

The 'enigma' of the Jews and their history may be expressed in the following question: How did the Jews in post-biblical times, devoid of the assets of national sovereignty and independence in their own land, survive as a people, with their own religion and culture, in the lands of others? This is the nub of the question. But it grows more complex when applied to the various temporal, geographical and cultural contexts of post-biblical Jewish history. And it is only in these contexts that one can begin to fashion an answer. *The Jewish Enigma* attempts to do just that.

The genius of *The Jewish Enigma* lies in its clear presentation of the sweep of post-biblical Jewish history and in its attempt thereby to answer the 'enigma' question. Implicit as a continuous theme in the various chapters from a diversity of writers, this answer sees Jewish survival as the result of continuous interaction between the Jews and the host countries in which they lived, as opposed to another approach to the 'enigma' question which attributes to the Jews a certain stubborn singularity that ensured their survival. The book's approach locates Jewish life well within the mainstream of its historical contexts and sees Jewish survival as a part of the larger historical fabric. Jewish singularity is certainly not absent in this view, nor do those who argue from Jewish singularity usually totally disregard Jewish-Gentile historical interaction. The issue here is one of emphasis rather than one of exclusivity of approach. And the emphasis of this book is clearly on interaction as the mechanism of the 'enigmatic' Jewish survival.

I should like now briefly to introduce each chapter of the book from this point of view. Such a survey will make clear the impressive variety of periods and countries treated in the book. It will also point up, through concrete examples, the book's unified approach to the question of the 'enigma'.

Robin Spiro starts with an overview of post-biblical Jewish history, from the sixth century BCE to the eighteenth century CE. He finds in the Babylonian captivity of the sixth century a precedent and model for later post-biblical Jewish survival. Here, in 'the unique concept of a national homeland capable of existing side by side with a diaspora' Spiro sees the foundation which later 'enabled the Jews to maintain a separate existence in the face of overwhelming odds'. The model of diaspora here is clearly one of Jewish interaction with their surroundings.

Next comes a study of Jews in Islamic lands by Jacob Lassner. It surveys this history from the seventh century CE to the twentieth century, emphasizing cultural and intellectual themes of Muslim-Jewish interaction in the Middle Ages: an interaction which helped shape Jewish culture and aided its survival. Indeed, even Jewish law was affected by Islam.

In 'Jewish Emancipation in Central and Western Europe in the Eighteenth and Nineteenth Centuries' David Sorkin puts a strong emphasis on the very different kinds of social, political and cultural history which provided the contexts for Jewish-Christian relations. He clearly shows the ways in which the Jews often figured prominently in European thought. As Sorkin reminds us, there were always two participants: European society as a whole and the Jewish minority, whether involved as individuals or as entire communities.

Lionel Kochan's study of east-European Jewry since 1770 emphasizes the turbulent and quickly-changing social and political milieu in which the east-European Jews lived during this period. Examples abound of the complex inter-relationships between Jewish communities and their environment (the legacy of the arendar land leasing system being one of the most interesting). Kochan explicitly stresses the importance of the Jewish connection with the larger world history. During these times, he tells us, 'the Jews of Eastern Europe, perhaps more than any other Jewish community, were exposed to all the upheavals of the modern world'.

The focus shifts to North-American Jewry in the next section, in which Leon Jick traces this chapter in Jewish history from its inception in the Old World through its evolution in America to its present-day manifestations and predictions for the future. Throughout, Jick emphasizes the integral relationship between this Jewish community and the larger society, as exemplified by the Americanization of colonial Jews and Jewish prominence in the Arts and entertainment.

In the sixth chapter, on 'Religious and Racial Anti-Semitism and the Jewish Response', Philip Alexander traces the development of anti-Semitism from 'pagan anti-Judaism to the Holocaust'. The author's emphasis is on the history of anti-Semitic *ideas* in their social, political, theological and economic contexts.

His main argument is that we should not make too sharp a distinction between modern 'secular' anti-Semitism and pre-modern 'religious' anti-Judaism. The former is arguably simply a modernization of the latter, a mutation which has responded to the spirit of the modern age, a view which depends on the conception of Jewish history as an integral component of the various histories which have served as its environment.

In the final section, Joseph Heller discusses Jewish nationalism from early Jewish religious traditions to the PLO and Israeli Peace Initiatives of the late 1980s. Here, although the new nationalist framework of Jewish existence in Palestine and, ultimately, Israeli statehood, is different from earlier Jewish life in non-Jewish societies, the theme of interaction between Jewry and the larger world still obtains, if anything in an even more explicit, if more frankly political form.

Interaction, however, also carried risks. For in the recent post-Enlightenment and post-Emancipation periods interaction has become a threat to continued Jewish existence as well as being its support. This has happened mainly through assimila-tion, as the result of the unlimited interaction in those societies where almost all barriers to Jewish integration have been removed. In the European and English-speaking countries in particular this process has advanced so far, through inter-marriage and other mechanisms, that the Jewish communities now often see assimilation as their main problem. It would be a great irony of history if the interaction which fostered Jewish survival were now to undermine it.

The Jewish 'enigma' may not be completely resolved and perfectly understood as a result of reading this book, but for those interested in post-biblical Jewish history *The Jewish Enigma* will serve as a reliable and thought-provoking guide along the way.

1 Post-Biblical Jewish History – The Long Vista

Robin Spiro

Introduction

Post-biblical Jewish history is a relatively new subject for study. The first serious scholarship began in the nineteenth century with the German Jewish university-trained scholars who founded what became known as the 'Science of Judaism' (*Wissenschaft des Judentums*). Only in recent times have comprehensive attempts been made to research and record what happened to the Jews after the biblical period.

There were various reasons for the late recognition of post-biblical Jewish history – not least, the fact that the Jews as a people were politically powerless before the nineteenth century, with no kings or queens or major battles to be chronicled. But a far more important reason was the attitude of Christian historians, who generally regarded the Jews as an anachronism whose post-biblical existence did not merit serious attention.

To some extent the Jews felt that their history, certainly since the destruction of the Second Temple in 70 CE (Common Era), was of no great importance except in relation to the development of centres of Jewish religious learning. They considered themselves to be merely marking time until their return to the promised land in the Messianic Age – an event that could only be brought about through prayer, study and good deeds, and not by playing an active part in world affairs.

This approach to post-biblical Jewish history has now been largely superseded and the subject is widely recognized as being of great importance, both in its own right and because of its relevance to other events – from the rise and development of Christianity in the first centuries of the Common Era to the Holocaust and the creation of the State of Israel in our own century.

In fact, the post-biblical history of the Jews as a unique combination of a people and a religion has its roots in the biblical period. According to the book of Jeremiah, the Babylonians, under King Nebuchadnezzar, subjugated the kingdom of Judah and later, faced with a popular uprising, besieged Jerusalem and destroyed the First Temple. Jeremiah claimed that this devastation, which occurred in 586 BCE (Before the Common Era), was a punishment visited by God on His people for their constant lapses in religious and ethical conduct. The Babylonians took back with them as captives the royal family and the surviving members of the artisan and upper classes of the tribes of Judah and Benjamin. These captives led to the development of the Jewish community in Babylonia, which was to prove so important for Jewish survival.

Over a century earlier, in 721 BCE, most of the people of the ten tribes of the northern kingdom of Israel had likewise been taken away as captives and had disappeared from recorded history. These early dispersions are shown in Map 1. It can be imagined that when the exiles from Judah witnessed the size and power of the Babylonian kingdom they probably experienced a sense of despair in the face of this threat to their existence as a people. But the exiles in Babylonia did not disappear. Instead, they were instrumental in creating the concept of a national homeland capable of existing side by side with a 'diaspora' (a dispersion of a people outside their homeland) – the one nourishing the other. It was during the seventy-year period (586–516 BCE) from the destruction of the First Temple to the return and building of the Second Temple that the foundations were laid for a creative history that was to stretch over two and a half millennia.

This opening chapter surveys the highlights of the Jewish experience from the sixth century BCE to the eighteenth century CE and, in so doing, suggests a number of factors that may have contributed to the extraordinary survival of the Jewish people. It is not the aim of this chapter to present original, specialist findings nor to reach any definitive conclusions, but rather to set the scene for the following chapters and to provide a useful background for further reading.

The Babylonian period: the survival of the exiles as Jews

It was the prophet Jeremiah (see Plate 1), writing from Jerusalem to the exiles in Babylon, who first encouraged the Jews to maintain their separate existence as a people exiled from their homeland. He had previously tried to persuade the kings of Judah not to revolt against the far more powerful Babylonians, but rather to accept foreign domination. Jeremiah was committed to accepting a subservient national situation if this meant that Jews remained free to practise their religion and so retain their identity.

In this way, Jeremiah proved vital to Jewish survival. His great contribution was to encourage the Jewish exiles in Babylonia to believe that God had not deserted them, but had merely punished His chosen people for their sins. Provided they repented and resumed obeying God's laws, He would, in time, forgive them and restore them to their promised land.

From Jerusalem, Jeremiah wrote to the exiles:

> Thus said the Lord of Hosts, the God of Israel, to the whole community which I exiled from Jerusalem to Babylon: build houses and live in them, plant gardens and eat their fruit. Take wives and beget sons and daughters; and take wives for your sons, and give your daughters to husbands, that they may bear sons and daughters. Multiply there, do not decrease. And seek the welfare of the city to

which I have exiled you and pray to the Lord in its behalf; for in this prosperity you shall prosper ... For thus said the Lord: When Babylon's seventy years are over, I will take note of you, and I will fulfil to you My promise of favour – to bring you back to this place. For I am mindful of the plans I have made concerning you – declares the Lord – plans for your welfare, not for disaster, to give you a hopeful future. When you call Me, and come and pray to Me, I will give heed to you ... and I will bring you back to the place from which I have exiled you.[1]

Using the arguments of earlier prophets, such as Amos, Hosea and the first Isaiah, Jeremiah and others of his contemporaries presented to the exiles the idea that the God of the Jews was all-powerful, and that He was merely using the Babylonian King Nebuchadnezzar as a tool to punish His people. The justification for this punishment came directly from the covenant made on Mount Sinai between God and the Jewish people: in exchange for their being God's chosen people, the Children of Israel would undertake to obey His laws as given to Moses (the Mosaic Law). The Mosaic Law, of course, remains the cornerstone of Judaism. The Law, as set down in the Pentateuch (the Five Books of Moses) is commonly known as the Written Law or the Torah (though the word 'Torah' also has a wider meaning and can refer to the whole body of Jewish law and teachings).

The exiled Jews in Babylonia were confident of God's ultimate forgiveness and of their eventual return to the promised land. This is reflected in the words of Ezekiel during the exile (see Plate 2):

And He said to me, 'O mortal, these bones are the whole House of Israel. They say, "Our bones are dried up, our hope is gone; we are doomed". Prophesy, therefore, and say to them: Thus said the Lord God: I am going to open your graves and lift you out of the graves, O My people, and bring you to the land of Israel ... I will put My spirit into you and you shall live again, and I will set you upon your own soil. Then you shall know that I the Lord have spoken and have acted' – declares the Lord.[2]

The Persian period: exclusivity and education

In 539 BCE, the Babylonian Empire was overthrown by the Persians (see Map 2). The Persian king, Cyrus II, allowed many captive peoples to return to their homelands, in a reversal of the policy of his Babylonian predecessors. It is likely that Cyrus' motives were purely pragmatic, but the Hebrew Prophets again gave their own interpretation of the king's decision:

It is I, the Lord, who made everything, ...
who says of Cyrus, 'He is My shepherd:
He shall fulfil all My purposes.
He shall say of Jerusalem, "She shall be rebuilt,"
And to the Temple: "You shall be founded again."'[3]

Groups of returnees made their way back to Judah at various times led by priests and by members of the former royal house of Judah. However, many of the exiles remained in Babylonia.

After the return of the exiles, the rebuilding of the Temple in Jerusalem soon started, but work was disrupted and eventually came to a halt, mainly because of the opposition of the Samaritans. These people consisted of two groups: those who had originally lived in the Assyrian Empire but had been settled by the Assyrians after 721 BCE in the area of the former kingdom of Israel; and a second group comprising descendants of those members of the ten tribes who had not been exiled. They all lived in Samaria from which they took their name.

At first, the Samaritans offered their assistance in rebuilding the Temple. But although they had adopted the God of Israel, the Samaritans had also retained elements of their former religion; so, fearing the introduction of idol worship, the Jews rejected the Samaritans' offer of help.

> Thereupon the people of the land [the Samaritans] undermined the resolve of the people of Judah, and made them afraid to build ... all the years of King Cyrus of Persia and until the reign of King Darius of Persia.[4]

According to the Bible, Darius renewed permission for the Jews to rebuild their Temple. The Temple was completed three years later in 516 BCE, exactly 70 years after the destruction of the First Temple, and in fulfilment of Jeremiah's prophecy.

Although there was now a Temple in Jerusalem, the Jews in Judah once more lapsed in their religious obligations, tending to adopt the customs of the surrounding people, to intermarry, and to neglect the Mosaic Law. It was at this juncture (around 440 BCE) that two individuals, Ezra, a priest and scribe, and Nehemiah, a statesman, came to Jerusalem from Babylonia on separate missions, each armed with the authority of the Persian king. How they as Jews managed to obtain royal support is an interesting question. The answer is perhaps related to the conquest of Egypt by the Persians in 525 BCE and their need to establish a reliable regime in a 'buffer' area – namely Judah.

Whatever the purpose, the result of Ezra and Nehemiah coming to Jerusalem was the introduction and implementation of two important principles of national life that were to contribute greatly to Jewish survival: the concept of the exclusivity of the Jewish people and a widespread programme of religious education.

Ezra's first instruction was for the Jews to divorce their foreign spouses. Foreign wives were seen as a particular problem, possibly because in ancient times the wife was allowed to bring her household gods into her husband's home. (It may be that the later definition of a Jew as being the child of a Jewish mother originated at this time.)

> Then Ezra the priest ... said to them, 'You have trespassed by bringing home foreign women, thus aggravating the guilt of Israel ... separate yourselves from the people of the land and from the foreign women.'[5]

Despite considerable opposition, Ezra and Nehemiah managed to implement

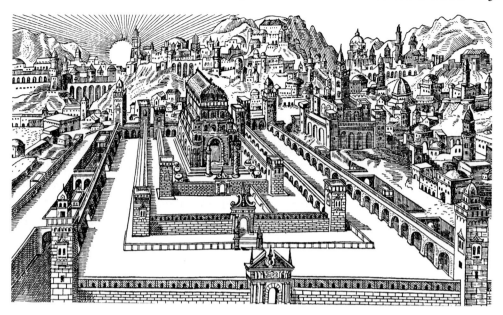

A reconstruction of the Second Temple in Jerusalem from a seventeenth-century print. For Jews, Christians and Muslims the hill on which the Temple stood is one of the most important religious sites. Here Abraham prepared to sacrifice Isaac; here Jesus drove out the moneylenders; and from here the Prophet Muhammad ascended to heaven.

this separation. The principle of exclusivity was later extended so that, for example, Jews were even forbidden to eat with Gentiles (non-Jews). By putting a cultural fence around the Jews, Ezra and Nehemiah did much to ensure their survival as a people. But this fence led to resentment in those excluded by it.

Ezra's second innovation was a result of his realizing the need to teach the Mosaic Law, not just to his fellow priests but to every Jewish household. As God's chosen people, the Jews were expected to follow the Mosaic Law and would be punished for disobeying it. Therefore, they had to be given a thorough knowledge and understanding of the Law.

> Ezra the priest brought the Teaching before the congregation, men and women and all who could listen with understanding ... and the Levites explained the Teaching to the people, while the people stood in their places. They read from the scroll of the Teaching of God, translating it and giving the sense; so they understood the reading.[6]

It should be noted that, in this passage, women are specifically included in Ezra's educational programme, despite both the Bible's main thrust and the later tradition that Jewish education was a male preserve.

In the ancient world, and indeed until relatively recent times, the idea of making education available to all classes was unique to the Jews. Ezra introduced weekly public readings, held on the Sabbath, which became a key element in his educational programme (and which still continue today). For these readings, the Five

Books of Moses were divided into weekly portions. Further texts, mainly from the Prophets, were added later.

Little is known about specific events during the last century of Persian domination in the Middle East (440–332 BCE), but the broad outlines of the period are as follows:

- The Jews in Judah developed a form of self-government and were ruled by a theocracy of priests.
- The diaspora expanded considerably.
- Jerusalem and the Temple became the focus of Jewish life for the expanding diaspora communities.

Judah no longer found itself sandwiched between warring powers: the major conflict of this period was between Persia and Greece, and not between Babylonia, Assyria and Egypt as before. This brought a long period of peace to Judah, which proved to be of great benefit because, among other things, it allowed the religious teachings of Ezra to take root.

The Greek world: Hellenism and the Hasmoneans

In 332 BCE, Alexander the Great of Macedonia and his army began their expedition against the Persian Empire and their conquest of the whole Middle East (see Map 2). After Alexander's death in 323 BCE, a war of succession broke out between his generals and resulted in the division of Alexander's vast empire into four parts. One of the generals, Seleucus, took control of the area around Mesopotamia and Syria and established the Seleucid dynasty. Another general, Ptolemy, seized Egypt and founded the Ptolemaic dynasty. For more than a century Judah was under Ptolemaic rule, but in the year 200 BCE the Seleucid king, Antiochus III, conquered the country.

The Seleucids and Ptolemies were of Greek descent and vigorously promoted Greek civilization – 'Hellenism' – in the lands they ruled. Indeed, the impact of Greek civilization on the entire ancient world was enormous. Judah, however, retained its self-government led by the High Priest and the council of Elders.

After the Seleucids arrived, the Jewish upper class, including the priestly rulers, succumbed to the attractions of Greek culture and religion. In 175 BCE, Antiochus IV carried out Hellenistic reforms in Judah; this Hellenization of the state was resented by the rest of the Jews and by a large section of the priesthood. According to the book of Maccabees:

> When ... Jason, the brother of Onias, supplanted his brother in the high priesthood [of Judah] ... he brought in new customs forbidden by the Law ... thinking the glories of the Greeks best of all.[7]

And again:

> ... they [the Hellenizing Jews] built a place of exercise [that is, a Greek gymnasium] in Jerusalem according to the laws of the Gentiles; and they made

themselves uncircumcised, and forsook the holy covenant and joined themselves to the Gentiles.[8]

In 167 BCE, Antiochus Epiphanes forbade the practice of Jewish rites in Judah and the surrounding regions. Keeping the Sabbath and circumcision were outlawed under the threat of the death penalty. Moreover, some pagan rites were imposed on the Jews and the Temple was defiled. These persecutions, which were unprecedented given the tolerant tradition of the Hellenist rulers, came after an unsuccessful revolt in 168 BCE and a substantial transfer of non-Jews into Jerusalem. Antiochus' objections to Judaism may have been due to political considerations, the Jews' monotheism being, in his opinion, the cause of their vehement rejection of Hellenization.

The enforced Hellenization and pagan rites were resisted by most Jews and it was not long before their adherence to their ancestors' religion brought them into open conflict with Seleucid rule. At first it was passive resistance only: Jews performed their religious rites in the face of the government's cruelty and suffered death for their Jewish faith. This idea of martyrdom or *kiddush ha-Shem* — that is, asserting the holiness of God's name and witnessing it by accepting death rather than committing apostasy — became a model for many Jews in future generations when confronted by demands to abandon their religion.

Passive opposition soon turned into armed resistance under the leadership of a priestly family from a place called Modiin, near the city of Lod. This family was headed by Mattathias the Hasmonean and his five sons. One of the sons was Judah the Maccabee, by whose name the family is known to history. At first the Seleucids took advantage of the Jewish reluctance to fight on the Sabbath. Mattathias the priest, however, overcame this reluctance on the grounds that in time of persecution the use of arms is allowed on the holy day. By 164 BCE, under the command of Judah the Maccabee, the Jews had regained possession of Jerusalem and the Temple. The purification and inauguration of the Temple were later commemorated in the Jewish tradition by the annual festival of Hanukkah, that is, 'Inauguration'.

Judah was now dissociated from Seleucid rule, though officially still a province in the Seleucid kingdom. The struggle continued, and in 142 BCE the independence of Judah was recognized by the Seleucids. Simon, the only remaining son of Mattathias, was established in 142 BCE by the *Knesset Gedolah*, the equivalent of a Jewish Senate, as High Priest and supreme commander of the armed forces. These offices were granted to him and his descendants who ruled Judah as the Hasmonean dynasty. John Hyrcanus (134–104 BCE), Simon's son, completed Judah's detachment from Seleucid rule and expanded the Jewish state to almost the size that David's kingdom had been in the tenth century BCE (see Map 3). He annexed Idumea to the south and forcibly converted a number of neighbouring peoples to Judaism. He conquered Samaria to the north and destroyed the monumental Samaritan Temple at Mount Gerizim. He also extended Judah's borders to include Galilee and further northern territories.

Despite their anti-Hellenistic policies, the Hasmonean family were not immune to Hellenistic influences. Already the second generation carried Greek names, such as Hyrcanus or Aristobulus. This Hellenization gained impetus through the annexation of neighbouring, already Hellenized, provinces. Judah Aristobulus proclaimed himself king in 103 BCE and added Philhellen to his name. The traditional 'Gerusia', the council of Elders, was renamed the 'Sanhedrin', the name given to the councils of Hellenistic kings. Nevertheless the Hasmoneans never denied the basic Jewish and theocratic character of their kingdom.

While the Hasmonean family became a royal dynasty, and tied itself to other prominent families to form a ruling aristocracy and priesthood, a new social phenomenon emerged. The 'Hachamim', the Sages, the learned Torah scholars, broke the priests' monopoly of interpreting the Law and became the main influence shaping the spiritual life of the people. They were the leaders of the main religious movement in Second Temple Judaism – the Pharisees.

The Pharisees gained a wide popular appeal and influence. They were the natural leaders and were recognized by most social strata. Yet the movement itself had little political power, as this remained largely with the establishment party, the Sadducees. This was so for most of the Hasmonean era, until Herod became the ruler of Judah in 30 BCE. The Pharisees' influence continued until the destruction of the Second Temple in 70 CE, on wide sections of the people, the Sanhedrin and the courts. They were mostly scribes and scholars who concentrated on studying and extending the Oral Law – the body of ideas and argument, largely preserved orally, that stemmed from interpretations of the God-given Written Law, the Torah. In particular, the Pharisees sought to demonstrate through the Oral Law that the Written Law could be humanized and adapted to new situations. Their greatest figure, Hillel the Elder, encapsulated the essence of the Torah according to Pharisee thought when a Gentile asked him to define Judaism 'while standing on one foot'. He answered: 'What is hateful to you, do not do unto your neighbour. This is the whole Law – the rest is commentary.'

From the outset, the Pharisees were opposed on several counts by the Sadducees who represented the conservative political establishment and included the higher priesthood and the aristocrats. Unlike the Pharisees, the Sadducees supported a conservative, rigid and literal interpretation of the Written Law and rejected the concept of a binding Oral Law. They disagreed with the Pharisees on various issues concerning legal matters and daily life. They believed in free will, and rejected the resurrection of the dead, which was an essential element of Pharasaic belief.

In 63 BCE, two competing Hasmonean princes, Hyrcanus and Aristobulus, asked Pompey, the Roman general who had invaded the Seleucid Empire and annexed Syria, to arbitrate between them and decide who should succeed to the crown. The result was a foregone conclusion: Pompey's legions occupied Jerusalem, Judah once again came under foreign control and the Hasmoneans lost the title of 'king'. Pompey granted the state a certain degree of self-rule and, after Julius Caesar's victory over Pompey in 48 BCE, the Idumean family of Antipater, recent converts to Judaism, came to power. Antigonus II, the last Hasmonean, was executed by the Romans in 37 BCE and Herod, Antipater's son, was crowned as king of Judea, the Roman name for Judah, in 30 BCE. Despite his unpopularity with the Jewish population, Herod managed to retain power until his death in 4 BCE; his kingdom was then divided between three of his sons. Archelaus, who inherited the region of Jerusalem, was suspended from power and exiled in 6 CE, and direct Roman rule enforced in the new province of Judea.

The Jews of the Roman Empire

The Jewish population of the world at the beginning of the Common Era has been estimated by some scholars but the numbers remain uncertain. However, many scholars believe that, by this time, the Jewish population had expanded to represent some eight per cent of the population of the Roman Empire. There were approximately two million Jews in Judea and four million lived under Roman rule elsewhere. It has been estimated that more than a million Jews lived outside the Roman Empire, mainly in Babylonia. Jewish settlements in the Roman Empire are shown in Map 4.

Shortly before the Jewish revolt against Rome in 66 CE, the Romans treated the Jews well and granted them some privileges. As early as 47 BCE, Julius Caesar confirmed Jewish religious autonomy. The Jews were allowed to send contributions to the Temple in Jerusalem, did not have to attend to civil duties on the Sabbath nor serve in the Roman army and, most important of all, were not forced to worship Roman gods or emperors. There were various reasons for these privileges, but essentially Rome, which had to govern a vast empire, recognized the Jews as a loyal, law-abiding element whose own laws were sanctioned by antiquity, an important factor as far as the Romans were concerned.

During this period of early Roman rule, Jerusalem remained the focus of the Jewish diaspora. Many Jews aspired to make a pilgrimage to the Holy City and they continued to send their sons to study in Jerusalem; they also sent regular donations to the Temple. The Romans, too, acknowledged Jerusalem as the national centre of the Jewish people. As King Agrippa I, the Roman choice as ruler of Judea (41–44 CE), wrote to the Emperor Caligula in 41 CE:

> Concerning the Holy City … [it is] the metropolis not only of the one country of Judea but also of many by reason of the colonies which it has sent out … And not only are the continents full of Jewish colonies, but also all the most celebrated islands.[9]

In 66 CE, the Jews of Judea rose up in revolt against Rome (see Map 4). The suppression of this uprising brought about the destruction of the Second Temple in 70 CE and the loss of Jerusalem, the Jewish national centre. Why did the Jews revolt? They had been granted favourable treatment by the Romans, and must have been aware of the overpowering might of the Roman Empire and the grave consequences of a failed rebellion. Josephus reported that Agrippa II tried to dissuade the Jews from rebelling:

> [God too] is ranged on the Roman side, for without God's aid, so vast an empire could not have been built up … Take pity if not on your children and wives,

then at least on your mother city and its sacred precincts. Spare the sanctuary and preserve for yourselves the Temple.[10]

But warnings, whether from Agrippa or from the Pharisees, who in effect constituted the 'peace party', proved to be of no avail.

The reasons for the uprising were spiritual and mundane. The immediate causes were the plundering of the Temple's treasures by the Roman procurator, Florus, and a ruling by Emperor Nero which exposed the Jews of Caesarea to their enemies. (The Zealot sect in Galilee, which opposed Roman rule altogether, gained influence only at a later stage in the Great Revolt.)

In the decade leading up to the revolt, the Roman procurators seem to have deliberately trampled Jewish religious feelings underfoot – they robbed the Temple, ransomed the high priest's robes, and even brought Roman legions to Jerusalem in a violation of tradition and Jewish sensitivities. The hardening of their attitude toward the Jews is illustrated by a remark made by the Emperor Nero's chief minister, the philosopher Seneca, in approximately 60 CE:

> ... the practices of the villainous race [the Jews] have become so influential that they are now accepted throughout every land. The vanquished have given laws to their victors.[11]

One possible explanation for such a radical change in the official attitude to the Jews could have been the Romans' increasing apprehension about the diffusion of Jewish humanist ideas.

Despite some initial Jewish successes, within a year Nero's Roman legions, under their general Vespasian, had overrun Galilee and most of the country north of Jerusalem. The Jewish general in Galilee was Josephus; after surrendering, Josephus changed sides, was adopted by Vespasian, added 'Flavius' to his name, and was taken to Rome where he became the most important Jewish historian on the ancient world.

From 68 to 69 CE Rome was in turmoil. The Emperor Nero committed suicide and three emperors reigned in quick succession. The situation was only resolved when Vespasian was elected emperor by the legions in July 69 CE. After Vespasian's election, his son Titus proceeded to besiege Jerusalem. This resulted in the conquest of Jerusalem and the destruction of the Second Temple in the summer of 70 CE, an event commemorated annually on the Hebrew date of 9th Av.[12] The final rebel outpost at Masada (see Plate 8) fell in 73 CE, when about a thousand Jews committed mass suicide as an act of *kiddush ha-Shem*.

The causes of the Jewish defeat included the immense military might of Rome, criticism of the revolt in some of the cities of Galilee and from parts of the Jewish political and religious elite, internal divisions and also infighting between the Jewish rebel groups – the fundamentalists and the moderates. Another major factor was the messianic expectations of some of the fighters. After the revolt, with the Temple and the national centre destroyed for the second time, the survival of the Jewish people was once more in doubt. Some began to suggest that God had finally deserted His people.

Josephus presenting a copy of his book The Jewish War *to the Roman Emperor Vespasian and his son Titus. The book, wonderful as prose and invaluable as history, remains an essential source for the modern historian and curious reader.*

As virtually all the political and priestly leaders had been either killed or enslaved during the revolt, one problem facing the survivors was a lack of leadership. A solution lay in the Pharisaic rabbis and scholars who had not been involved in the war. The head of the Pharisees, Johanan ben Zakai, managed to obtain permission from the Romans to establish a non-political religious centre at Javneh in southern Judea. Over the next two generations, Javneh became the centre of Jewish life and produced some of the most famous rabbis in Jewish history, among them Rabbi Akiba and Rabban Gamaliel.

The main preoccupation of the leadership was to keep Judaism alive. Like the Prophets after the destruction of the First Temple, the rabbis perceived the destruction of Jerusalem and the Second Temple as God's punishment for the sins of Israel. The Jewish people, now without the political entity of the state, without Jerusalem and the Temple, had to consolidate their national life on new foundations. The national entity was transformed into a society organized on a communal basis and grounded on the *Halakha* (religious law). Prayer and religious study were substituted for sacrifices and local synagogues came to replace the Temple. The belief in the return to Jerusalem, the future renewal of the Temple and of independent political life became a central feature in the lives of Jews everywhere.

Yet this time, no Cyrus appeared to fulfil Jewish aspirations. As the years turned into centuries, with still no 'return', it became ever more difficult to sustain hope throughout the far-flung Jewish world. The Jewish belief in the coming of the Messianic Era grew stronger and stronger. To bring this about the Jews were required to keep a special way of life according to commandments and prayers, and engage in perpetual study of the Torah.

In 112 CE, some forty years after the destruction of the Second Temple, the Roman Emperor Trajan set out with a vast army to conquer Persia and beyond. The resulting reduction in the number of Roman garrisons encouraged several Jewish communities in the diaspora, mainly in North Africa (Cyrenaica and Egypt) and Cyprus, to become involved in what became known as the Trajan Revolt (115–117 CE). There is little evidence as to how this revolt was organized, but it clearly had a considerable impact. Trajan was forced to halt his advance eastwards to quell the uprising, which he did in the most ruthless fashion. The Talmud describes the fate of the 'previously thriving' Egyptian Jewish community:

> In that hour, Israel's pride was cut down, and shall not grow again until the son of David [the Messiah] comes.[13]

The slaughter was dreadful wherever the Jews rebelled, and in Mesopotamia they were massacred in retaliation. But as far as later Jewish history was concerned, there was one positive result: the Romans never succeeded in conquering Babylonia. This proved to be of great importance, for it allowed the Jews of Babylonia to remain independent when Christianity became the official religion of the Roman Empire.

The Jews of Judea did not play a prominent part in the Trajan Revolt, (although some sources speak of 'the War of Quietus', after the Roman ruler of Palestine, who carried out a massacre of the Jews). In 117 CE, Trajan died and was succeeded by his adopted nephew, Hadrian. Hadrian implemented an extensive plan of development: in Judea, he created new roads across the country, expanded the urban section and elevated the status of Jerusalem to that of a colony. In 130 CE he actually proposed building a temple to Jupiter on the site of the demolished Second Temple. He also extended a previous law forbidding mutilation of the body to include circumcision. These actions, among others, provoked the Jews to take up arms against the Romans in 132 CE. Rabbi Akiba, a leading figure of the day, is said to have had a role in the rebellion, and to have anointed the Jewish general of the uprising, Simon Bar Kochba, as the people's messianic hope.[14]

By 135 CE, this third and last revolt, known as the Bar Kochba Revolt, had been crushed in a very cruel manner and with great loss of life. The final stronghold at Bethar was taken on the anniversary of the fall of the First and Second Temples – 9 Av. On this day each year, devout Jews still lament these tragedies by sitting low down, as at times of mourning, and reading Lamentations – the book of the Bible written after the fall of the First Temple.

After the so-called Bar Kochba Revolt, the Romans took steps to prevent another uprising by the Jews. Hadrian introduced a series of restrictions on the practice of Judaism and outlawed a number of Jewish commandments, as well as assemblies, public teaching and the nomination of sages. Many defied these prohibitions and paid with their lives, like the martyrs of three hundred years earlier under the Seleucid King Antiochus Epiphanes. But this time the outcome was different. The Jews were a defeated people, incapable of further armed resistance, and anyone found teaching or practising Judaism was executed. Ten leading rabbis, including Akiba, were martyred during these Hadrianic persecutions. The surviving rabbis, on whom the Jewish future would depend, found refuge in Galilee, initially around the town of Usha and thereafter in Tiberias. The death toll of the Jewish population was so devastating that the Jews were unable to recover their numbers for centuries.

In both the First Revolt and the Bar Kochba Revolt, the Jews of Galilee put up little resistance and the Romans took little punitive action. The fact that such a sanctuary was available proved crucial to the survival of the Jewish people.

Jewish settlement in Judea was totally forbidden by the Romans after 135 CE. Access to Jerusalem was only allowed on the 9th Av, when Jews were permitted to come and weep at the 'Wailing Wall' – the only remains of the Second Temple. The Romans also adopted other measures against the Jews, mainly directed at preventing the revival of a Jewish national centre and a new spiritual leadership. Thus, the *Fiscus Judaicus* was now stringently enforced. This required every Jew to contribute an annual sum for the upkeep of the Temple of Jupiter in Rome, instead of the previous half-shekel contribution to the Temple in Jerusalem. The Romans also wiped the name of Judea from their maps and called the land Palestine.

The Talmud (*Mishnah* and *Gemara*) in Palestine and Babylonia

The persecutions ended after the death of Hadrian in 138 CE and the appointment of Emperor Antoninus Pius. One of the first edicts then introduced by the rabbis was a law forbidding Jews to fight – because of the demographic losses suffered by the Jewish people over the previous two or three generations and the threat these losses posed to Jewish survival. In addition, many thousands of Jewish survivors of the revolts had been transported to distant places through the Roman slave markets and had lost contact with Jewish communities and Jewish life.

In an attempt to ensure the continued physical existence of the people, no Jew would henceforth be allowed, in ordinary circumstances, to risk his or her life except to avoid breaking three biblical laws, namely those against forced adultery, idol worship and the shedding of innocent blood. All forms of oppression not involving such sins had to be accepted; accordingly, other religious laws could be transgressed in order to avoid the risk of death. Only in certain special situations, notably during times of persecution, was adherence to all aspects of Jewish law required; in these circumstances, a Jew was expected, if necessary, to lay down his or her life as an act of *kiddush ha-Shem* to set an example of religious steadfastness to the rest of the community.

In such trying times, the rabbis stressed even more that the real key to Jewish survival was religious learning and, in particular, the development of religious laws.

Their attitude is well described in the following passage:

> Rabbi [Judah the Prince] sent R. Assi and R. Ammi on a mission to organize [religious education in] the cities of the land of Israel. They came to a city and said to the people, 'bring us the guardians of the city'. They fetched the captain of the guard and the magistrate. The rabbis exclaimed, 'These are the guardians of the city? They are its destroyers!' The people enquired, 'Who, then, are its guardians?' And they answered, 'The instructors in Bible and *Mishnah*, who meditate upon, teach and preserve the Torah day and night.'[15]

Within a generation, the Romans, for political and administrative reasons, re-established a Jewish leadership in Palestine; they created the position of Patriarch or Nasi, an hereditary office with wide-ranging powers. This position was held by the descendants of Hillel, an outstanding religious leader and Pharisaic sage in Judea in the first century BCE.

At the end of the second century CE, a descendant of Hillel, Rabbi Judah ha Nasi (the Prince), who held court in Tiberias, succeeded to the position of Patriarch and introduced a revolutionary innovation into Jewish life, again as part of the effort to ensure a Jewish future. Until then, there had been the Written Law, contained in the Hebrew Bible, and an Oral Law. The Pharisees and their heirs, the rabbis, had developed this Oral Law to explain the divinely-given Written Law and, if necessary, to adapt it to the changing conditions of life, always basing their decisions on passages and principles from the Written Law. They maintained that the Oral Law was, in fact, contained within the Written Law and was just as sacred . It merely had to be extracted from the Written Law by proper interpretation. According to this belief, the Oral Law, as much as the Written Law, had been given to Moses on Mount Sinai.

The rabbis had refused to commit the Oral Law to writing as they thought that this might diminish the sanctity of the Written Law. But around the year 200 CE, with so many scholars having been killed in various revolts and persecutions, the danger of the Oral Law being lost was realized. It was, therefore, thought prudent to have the Oral Law committed to writing in the form of the *Mishnah*. This was done by rabbis and scholars working in Tiberias.

As the Oral Law was the very *raison d'être* of rabbinic Judaism or rabbinism, which came to be the one accepted form of Judaism, it is important to have some understanding of its workings. Take, for example, the biblical injunction:

> 'On the seventh day you shall have a Sabbath of complete rest, holy to the Lord; ... You shall kindle no fire throughout your settlements on the Sabbath day.'[16]

If followed literally, this law could have prevented Jews from staying warm in winter on the Sabbath, especially in the colder climates of the diaspora, and from eating hot food on the Sabbath. Yet the Sabbath was given as a day of rest, to be enjoyed by the whole community, even by 'the stranger within thy gates'. Therefore, through the Oral Law, the rabbis sought to present a biblical justification for a Sabbath fire, as the *Mishnah* shows:

Since it says 'In ploughing time and in harvest thou shalt rest' (Ex. 34:21) [which means] ... that one must refrain from ploughing in the sixth year for the sabbatical year ... one might think that in like manner a person should rest on Friday from work to be done for the Sabbath. Therefore Scripture says: 'Ye shall kindle no fire in your dwelling-places on the Sabbath day.' On the Sabbath day itself you may not kindle a fire, but you may on Friday kindle a fire [to remain alight] for the Sabbath.[17]

In this way, the *Mishnah* provided reasoned arguments, based on biblical passages, that could be used to adapt the Written Law to people's changing circumstances. Within a short time, the *Mishnah* was accepted as the code for all Jews to live by, both in Palestine and throughout the diaspora.

It was soon realized, however, that even the *Mishnah* left many questions unanswered. Take the famous biblical law: 'an eye for an eye and a tooth for a tooth'. The *Mishnah* readily defines liability and the basis of compensation for personal injury. But why should one pay compensation in the first place, rather than simply follow the clear biblical injunction of 'an eye for an eye'? To answer such questions and, in effect, to explain the *Mishnah*, an additional body of work was developed. This supplementary text is known as the *Gemara*. The *Mishnah* and *Gemara* together are called the Talmud. Like the *Mishnah*, the *Gemara* bases its arguments on verses from the Bible:

Why [pay compensation]? Does the Divine Law not say 'Eye for eye' (Ex. 24:24)? Why not take this literally to mean ... where he put out his eye, the offender's eye should be put out, etc ... [but] it is stated 'Moreover, ye shall take no ransom for the life of a murderer that is guilty of death' (Num. 35:31), implying that it is only for the life of a murderer that you may not take 'satisfaction' [that is, a ransom that would release him from capital punishment] whereas you may take 'satisfaction' for the principal limbs, though these cannot be restored.[18]

There were two versions of the *Gemara*: one was produced in Tiberias and when combined with the *Mishnah*, became known as the Jerusalem Talmud; the other was compiled in Babylonia, and became known as the Babylonian Talmud (from which the above quotation is taken). The Babylonian Talmud, edited by Rabbi Ashi, was written in Aramaic with some Hebrew, unlike the *Mishnah* which was written entirely in Hebrew, and it became the basis for normative Judaism to the present day.

As far as the Jerusalem Talmud is concerned, it only covers four sections of the *Mishnah*: the *Zeraim* (seeds), *Moed* (festivals), *Washim* (laws relating to women) and *Nezikin* (torts). The rest is lost except for quotations found in early commentaries.

The rise and development of Christian anti-Judaism

The first Christians were virtually all Jews, most of whom considered themselves to be devout and still within the general body of the Jewish people. Indeed, Christianity must be seen as one of the many sects followed by the Jews in Palestine at the time. Despite some contradictory and apparently anti-Jewish passages in the New Testament, Jesus seemed to make this clear:

> Do not suppose that I have come to abolish the Law and the Prophets; I did not come to abolish, but to complete. I tell you this: so long as heaven and earth endure, not a letter, not a stroke, will disappear from the Law until all that must happen has happened. If any man therefore sets aside even the least of the Law's demands, and teaches others to do the same, he will have the lowest place in the Kingdom of Heaven. Whereas anyone who keeps the Law and teaches others so will stand high in the Kingdom of Heaven.[19]

Jesus even suggested that his mission was largely restricted to the Jews:

> And a Canaanite woman came ... crying out [to Jesus], 'Sir! have pity on me, Son of David; my daughter is tormented by a devil.' But he said not a word in reply. His disciples came and urged him: 'Send her away; see how she comes shouting after us.' Jesus replied, 'I was sent to the lost sheep of the house of Israel, and to them alone.' But the woman came and fell at his feet and cried, 'Help me, Sir.' To this Jesus replied: 'It is not right to take the children's bread and throw it to the dogs.' 'True, Sir,' she answered: 'and yet the dogs eat the scraps that fall from their masters' table.' Hearing this Jesus replied: 'Woman, what faith you have! Be it as you wish!' And from that moment her daughter was restored to health.[20]

Christianity began to spread from about 40 CE, mainly through the evangelizing missions of Paul, and these passages provide some insight into a disagreement between Paul and the Jewish-Christian leadership in Jerusalem. Many of the local leaders insisted that converts to Christianity had to become Jews first, whereas Paul wished to dispense with Jewish ritual in order to spread the Christian message as widely as possible. After the destruction of Jerusalem in 70 CE, little more is heard of the Jewish-Christian leadership. Thereafter the leadership of the Christian movement was taken over by non-Jews living in centres such as Antioch and Alexandria, who had little connection with, or sympathy for, the Jewish background of Christianity.

The four Christian Gospels were probably written around this time (60–110 CE). Notwithstanding certain pro-Jewish, even chauvinistic, passages like those already mentioned, and the fact that many of the early Christians were Jews, a number of anti-Jewish passages do appear in the New Testament. These may have been more in the nature of polemics, but they include specific accusations concerning, among other things, the Jewish people's collective responsibility for the death of Jesus:

> ... the Jews, who killed the Lord Jesus and the Prophets and drove us out, the Jews who are heedless of God's will.[21]

They also include the suggestion that the Jews are the children of the devil, rather than the children of God:

Your Father is the devil and you choose to carry out your Father's desires ...
You are not God's children.[22]

These accusations, when combined with the claim that the Old Testament had
prophesied the coming of Jesus, and that God had deserted the Jews, thereby
allowing the Christians to take over the role of the 'chosen people', became an
integral part of church doctrine and fuelled Christian anti-Judaism. The early
Christians began to distance themselves from the Jews, and were seen by the
Romans as an ever more troublesome and subversive group. Steps were taken to
curb their activities and Christians were subject to mounting and systematic
persecution from the time of Emperor Trajan (98–117 CE) onwards. The Jews, by
and large, fared much better than the Christians at the hands of the Romans, and
retained the majority of their special privileges in the aftermath of the Trajan and
Bar Kochba Revolts.

Although attacks on the Christians continued unabated under successive
emperors, reaching a climax under Emperor Diocletian at the end of the third
century, Christianity survived. It spread through the Roman Empire, though its
followers still probably represented no more than ten per cent of the Empire's
population. But the fortunes of the Christian movement changed dramatically when
Diocletian's successor, Constantine, converted to Christianity in 312 CE. Soon
after, in 313 CE, Constantine legalized Christianity, and by 379 CE it had made
such progress that it was declared the official religion of the Roman Empire.

From the outset, orthodox church doctrine maintained that Christianity was the
one true way to salvation. Its basic aim, therefore, was to save every soul, pagan and
especially Jewish, through conversion. It is not surprising that the newly-won power
of the Christian Church lead to difficulties for Judaism, particularly as Judaism
continued to represent a competing religion. In 325 CE, the Christian Church
Council of Nicea passed the following laws designed to separate Christian from
Jew:

- The date of Passover was henceforth never allowed to coincide with Easter.
- No Christian was allowed to eat *matzah* (unleavened bread) at Passover.
- Christians were forbidden to visit synagogues.
- The Christian day of rest was changed from Saturday to Sunday.

From an early date, the rabbis refused to accept Christians as a legitimate group
within Judaism, in contrast to their reaction to other sects: they rejected the
Christian belief that the Messiah had already come and that all prophecies in the
Bible had been fulfilled.

Shortly before the recognition of Christianity as the official Roman religion, the
Roman Empire voluntarily split into two parts: West and East. The western capital
remained Rome, where later the Roman Catholic form of Christianity was to
develop. The eastern capital was established at Byzantium – renamed Constantinople by the Emperor Constantine – where the Greek or Orthodox form of
Christianity emerged.

Notwithstanding its new-found power, Christianity failed to eliminate Judaism in the Roman Empire. Within a few years of the division of the Roman Empire, tribes from the north overran the Western Empire and initially adopted a unitarian form of Christianity known as Arianism which was more accommodating towards the Jews. When the Arian kings of Spain became Roman Catholics, pressure was placed on the Jews to convert to Christianity. From the sixth century to the Muslim conquest of Spain in 711 CE, the Jews were persecuted. Outside Spain, they survived in small communities scattered throughout central and western Europe.

In the Eastern Empire the Christian Church remained all-powerful but the Jews found themselves 'protected' by what became known as St Augustine's Doctrine. Later, the Doctrine was also adopted by the Roman Catholic Church. St Augustine (354–430 CE), a leading church theologian from Hippo in North Africa, then part of Christendom, argued that the Jews should not be destroyed, but instead should be dispersed and allowed to exist, albeit in an oppressed condition, as living witnesses to the truth of Christianity. (This argument was based on a Christian interpretation of Psalm 59.)

Christianity becoming the official religion did affect the legal status of the Jews in the Roman Empire, yet their peaceful existence was ensured by the old pagan Roman law. Their lives were occasionally disturbed in the Eastern Empire by skirmishes between local communities and, rarely, by armed force. Occasionally, synagogues were set on fire. Yet the state persisted in defending those civil rights and privileges of Jews acknowledged by the law. Considerable Jewish communities continued to exist around the Mediterranean, in Egypt, North Africa, Spain and the Middle East. There were also very large communities in Syria and elsewhere.

There is little evidence about Jewish life in Europe in the sixth and seventh centuries CE. However, but for the Jewish centre in Babylonia, which was capable of succouring Jewish life and hope during this period, it is doubtful whether Judaism would have survived.

The Jewish centre in Babylonia

The first Jewish settlement in Babylonia occurred when Nebuchadnezzar took back captives from Judah after the destruction of the First Temple in 586 BCE. The Bible also reports that, within a generation, Jehoiachin, king of Judah, was released from prison and given a place of honour at the court. Late in the second century CE, a Jewish Exilarch – *Rosh Golah*[23] – is known to have been the recognized leader of the Babylonian Jewry. He had a similar role to that of the Jewish Patriarch – the Nasi – in Judea, and, like him, claimed to be a descendant of the House of David.

In the time of the Second Temple, two Jewish centres emerged, one in the north of Mesopotamia, the other to the south, in Nippur and ancient Babylonia. By the first century CE, it is estimated that there were over a million Jews in Babylonia, but the community did not yet act as an international Jewish centre in its own right. The Babylonian Jews continued to look to the Holy Land – by going on pilgrimages there, by sending many of their sons, such as Hillel and Rav, to learn and sometimes settle there, and of course by contributing funds to the Temple in Jerusalem.

Towards the end of the Second Temple period, Babylonia begins to appear as a place of learning and the teaching of the Law. During the first and second centuries CE there was some contact between the sages in the Holy Land and those in Babylonia. The foundations of learning in Babylonia were laid by these contacts and by visiting scholars from Palestine, after the first and third revolts.

It was from the beginning of the third century CE, with the return in 219 CE from Tiberias to Babylonia of Judah ha Nasi's favourite pupil, called Rav, that the Jewish community in Babylonia began to assume a new role as a centre of learning. Initially, this was achieved by Rav founding a *yeshivah* (a school for religious study) in a town called Sura on the banks of the Euphrates. This school complemented one already in existence at nearby Nehardea which was subsequently transferred to Pumbeditha, and headed by another outstanding scholar, Samuel. From the end of the sixth century CE, the heads of the academies held the title of 'gaon', the supreme, and until the eleventh century CE these academies remained the most important institutions in the Jewish world. Along with the academies in Tiberias and elsewhere in Palestine, they provided stability and a centre of religious knowledge that kept the diaspora alive. The period from the end of the sixth century to the eleventh century CE is named after the heads of the academies, 'the age of geonim'.

From around 220 CE, the Babylonian schools began compiling a *Gemara*. Unlike the Tiberian school, however, the Babylonian academies were free from the economic, political and religious problems that prevailed in Palestine, and were thus able to develop a far more comprehensive body of work. The Babylonian Talmud, which was largely written in Aramaic, was completed around 500 CE and, from the ninth century, became accepted by Jews throughout the diaspora as the code for Jewish living. The significance of the Aramaic language should be noted: it became sanctified and a number of important prayers were recited in Aramaic, including the three versions of the *Kaddish* (The Prayer for the Dead). From the eighth and ninth centuries CE, Jews in the east and in parts of Spain wrote in Hebrew, Aramaic and Judaeo-Arabic (Arabic with some Hebrew, written in Hebrew characters).

By the middle of the seventh century CE, Babylonia, like virtually all of the Middle East, had been conquered by Islam (see Map 5). (The history of the Jews in Islamic lands is discussed in more detail in Chapter 2.) This religion, which originated in the Arabian Peninsula in the seventh century CE, became a world power within 100 years.

The authority of the Babylonian academies was extended to the rest of the Jewish communities under Islamic rule – as far as Spain. Knowledge of the Talmud was further spread and augmented at this time through a system of questions and answers, termed *responsa* (known in Hebrew as *She'elot U'teshuvot*).

Local communities in the diaspora would send messengers to Babylonia with money, requesting answers to questions that had arisen and for which decisions were needed from the acknowledged Babylonian rabbinical authorities. The answers, which the rabbis discussed publicly in their schools, were then sent back to the communities: the name *responsa* is derived from these replies. One of the most famous examples is that of Rav Amram, the Gaon of Sura in the ninth century, who was asked by the head of the Barcelona Jewish community to set out the Order of Prayers in the *Siddur* (prayer book). Thereafter the *Siddur* as laid down by Rav Amram became the universally accepted version.

The *responsa* were usually transmitted by Jewish traders who operated a wide network of international commerce during these centuries. They travelled in caravans, and their passage was made easier by the infrastructure, cohesion and additional security that developed when much of the Jewish world became part of the new Islamic empire in the seventh century CE.

In the eighth century CE, the capital of the by-then vast Islamic empire was established in Baghdad. Thereafter it was clearly of political interest for the Muslim rulers to encourage the Jewish world, both within and without the Islamic domain, to look to neighbouring Sura and Pumbeditha as its own quasi-political centre. This desired cohesion was very much facilitated by the *responsa*. So, the Babylonian Talmud gradually became the authoritative version in western Muslim countries, a process which took several centuries. In addition to the *responsa*, Jews frequently paid for copies of the Babylonian Talmud to be sent to them in communities as far apart as Cologne (one of the Rhine communities), Barcelona and the North African community of Fez.

When Jerusalem was taken over by the Muslims in 640 CE, laws were laid down governing Christians and Jews. The Pact or Covenant of Umar, as these laws became known, effectively reduced the position of Christians and Jews ('People of the Book') to second-class, though protected, status in all Islamic countries.

Karaite cemetery. The Karaites are regarded by many as the Protestants of Judaism because of their insistence on the authority of biblical law.

Around the middle of the eighth century CE, a break away movement sprang up within the Babylonian community and threatened the unity of the Jewish people. This movement represented a social and intellectual revolt; a call for a return to the Bible and a movement away from rabbinism and the authority of the Oral Law, the interpretations of the *Mishnah* and *Gemara* introduced over the centuries by the rabbis and their academies. The movement started under the leadership of one Anan ben David, a disappointed potential exilarch, and was called Karaism (perhaps from the Hebrew 'to read', thus 'Champions of Scripture'). The Karaites maintained that the Hebrew Bible was there for all Jews to read and thereby decide for themselves how to interpret biblical law, without reference to the rabbis.

The movement received considerable support, and for some time there was a struggle between the geonim and the Karaites. In the ninth century CE, however, the conflict was resolved in favour of the geonim, mainly through the intervention of an outstanding scholar, Saadiah Gaon. Saadiah, born in Egypt and the only non-Babylonian who ever became head of the academy at Sura, was able to help stop the spread of Karaism by making it clear that, without a central, legal authority, chaos would ensue. The Karaites were thereafter excluded from the Jewish fold. Rabbinism became universally accepted as the one legitimate form of Judaism, at least until the rise of the reform movement in the nineteenth century. Despite their defeat and exclusion, the Karaites, as a small sect, continued to exist in Egypt, Turkey, the Crimea and a few small towns in Lithuania, and have survived to modern times.

By the eleventh century CE, Baghdad was no longer the capital of a unified Islamic empire. The empire had begun to fragment in the tenth century and several major centres, such as Cordoba, Cairo and Kairouan (in today's Tunis) had come to prominence. Although these changes contributed to the decline of Jewish Babylonia, they coincided with the rise of new Jewish centres in Europe. Before moving on to discuss the European centres, we shall first examine the fate of the Jewish communities in the Byzantine Empire.

The Byzantine Empire

The Eastern Roman Empire, which came to be called the Byzantine empire, with its capital Constantinople – the ancient city of Byzantium – managed to withstand the invasions of the various tribes from northern and eastern Europe who overran the Western Roman Empire in the fifth century CE. For a thousand years, the Christian Byzantine Empire continued to maintain its independence, at times expanding, at times contracting, before finally falling to the Muslim Ottoman Turks in 1453 CE. The Empire's greatest expansion occurred in the sixth century CE, when the Emperor Justinian and his general Belisarius succeeded in retaking North Africa, the southern tip of Spain, Sicily and much of Italy from the nomadic tribes.

With regard to the Jews, their position in the Byzantine Empire varied considerably during the Christian period. Justinian, for example, passed a series of anti-Jewish laws that were not at all in keeping with St Augustine's Doctrine. He forbade the study of the Talmud, prohibited some Jewish rituals and even introduced forced conversion in some of the conquered territories of North Africa, where the Jewish population was accused of assisting the Vandal enemy.

In the seventh century CE, with the rise of Islam, the Eastern Empire was forced to relinquish much of its territory but managed to retain Asia Minor and the Balkans. During the succeeding centuries, the Jews in Christian Byzantium suffered oppression which could have brought about their ultimate extinction.

It has been suggested that one factor which may have contributed to the continuation of Jewish existence in eastern Europe was the nearby Khazar kingdom. This kingdom occupied an enormous area in what is today southern Russia. It was situated to the north of the Islamic heartlands and to the east of the Byzantine Empire (see Map 6).

The Khazars were pagans of Turkic-Mongol origin. In 740 CE the Khazar king, Bulan, decided to adopt Judaism. This enabled him to remain 'religiously' independent of his two powerful neighbours, the Islamic and Byzantine empires, and also reinforced his political independence. From the eighth century CE to the end of the tenth century CE, the Khazar kingdom afforded Jews from elsewhere a haven.

> The king of the Khazars had ... become a Jew ... and was joined by Jews from all the lands of Islam and the Country of the Greeks [Byzantium]. Indeed, the king of the Greeks at the present time [943–4 CE] has converted the Jews in his kingdom to Christianity by coercion ... Thus many Jews took flight from the country of the Greeks to Khazaria.[24]

The actual power of the Khazars is well illustrated by the Byzantine Emperor Constantine VIII (913–959 CE), who had it recorded as court protocol that a seal of three gold *solidii* should be affixed to a letter to the Khazar king, whereas letters to the Pope and the Holy Roman Emperor were only to receive a seal of two gold *solidii*.[25]

Judaism in Khazaria was chiefly restricted to the court and to the immigrant Jews. The majority of the native population remained a mixture of pagans, Christians and Muslims. While there was little apparent contact between the Khazars and the thriving Jewish centres in Babylonia, the Khazar king managed to maintain a Jewish identity. At the end of the tenth century CE the Khazars were defeated by the Slav forces under the command of the prince of Kiev. This probably resulted in an exodus of some of the Khazar Jewish population to the neighbouring lands of eastern Europe.

The European experience: an overview

Until the tenth century the most important events of Jewish history had taken place in the Middle East. Thereafter, however, Jewish settlement spread further afield and, by the end of the eighteenth century, 75 per cent of world Jewry was living on the continent of Europe. The continuing history of Jewish communities in the Middle East and North Africa will be covered in Chapter 2. The rest of this chapter will concentrate on the history of the Jews in Europe.

Although small Jewish trading communities had existed in Europe for hundreds of years, it was not until the tenth century that any important centres appeared. However, a common pattern soon emerged. Jewish communities would be encouraged by a local ruler to settle in his territory and act as his agents. They would frequently prosper, but their very prosperity ultimately led to attacks. It mattered little whether such attacks were motivated by religion or economic resentment or were merely the result of the Jews no longer being of use to the ruler. The end result was often the same: the destruction of the community and migration.

Yet, when one such centre collapsed another would often arise elsewhere. The decline of Babylonia around 1000 CE coincided with the rise of the great medieval European centres of Jewish learning: the Sephardi in Spain, and the Ashkenazi along the Rhine in Germany. (Spain and Germany are named in Hebrew after the biblical names of *Sepharad* and *Ashkenaz* respectively.) In the later Middle Ages, both these communities were themselves destroyed. However, these cultures were so developed and so strong that, when their communities were dispersed, they became dominant in the new place of settlement. The Jewish world of today remains roughly divided into the Sephardi and Ashkenazi traditions.

Jews were already living in Spain by the end of the first century CE, and a large Jewish presence is recorded by the fourth century. Evidence of Jewish communities in the Visigothic period (418–711 CE) is abundant. Yet it was not until the tenth century CE, under the Muslims, that the Jews began to flourish – and in fields both secular and religious. After experiencing periods of prosperity and creativity as well as decline over the next 500 years, under first Muslim and then Christian masters (see the next section), this important community came to an end in 1492 through a combination of conversion and expulsion.

Expulsion was likewise the fate of many Ashkenazi Jewish communities in western and central Europe during this period, especially when they ceased to be of economic value to the ruler. England provided the earliest example. William the Conqueror invited Jews from France to settle in England. Some two centuries later, in 1290, the Jews, having been impoverished by the kings' taxes, were expelled. Southern Italy followed in 1288–94 and France in 1306. Jewish life in France was devastated by the massacres of 1348. These communities represented, among other things, a highly advanced model of Jewish education and social welfare, as developed in the Rhine communities by scholars such as Rashi. It was these Rhine communities that bore the worst of the anti-Jewish excesses which soon became part of medieval European life.

Starting with the First Crusade in 1096, attacks against Jews began to be commonplace. Based on a variety of false accusations, from poisoning of wells to ritual murder, these attacks continued into the sixteenth century and beyond. The Reformation in the sixteenth century, and the religious wars between Catholics and Protestants that followed, relieved the Jewish population of much of the previous physical persecution. Nevertheless, the oppressive legal and social measures against Jews adopted by both sides continued in central Europe, in some cases well into the nineteenth century.

In western Europe, where from the thirteenth to the fifteenth century the Jews had been subjected to wholesale expulsions, Jewish centres began to be re-established from the seventeenth century onwards. This resettlement, for example in London and Amsterdam (see Plate 7), was largely effected through the migration from Spain and Portugal of Marranos, or secret Jews, who had managed to escape the terrors of the Spanish Inquisition and had retained their clandestine Judaism, frequently over many generations.

One country from which Jews were not expelled, and which maintained an unbroken Jewish presence for more than two millennia, was Italy – first during the Roman Republic, and then through the Empire and in various of its successor states. In the nearby Balkan Peninsula, also a site of ancient Jewish settlement, the Jews suffered periodic oppression and expulsion as under Byzantine rule. As far as the Balkan hinterland was concerned, Jewish settlement developed later and mainly to accommodate Jews fleeing from other countries.

The last major area of Jewish settlement, eastern Europe, held something like 60 per cent of world Jewry by the end of the eighteenth century. Beginning in the fourteenth century and continuing to the seventeenth century, economic prosperity allowed the Jews in eastern Europe to create a centre of learning which some claim outshone even Babylonia. But as will be seen, this centre too was attacked in 1648 by Ukrainian Cossacks rising up against their Polish landlords and the Jews. Over the next century, the Polish Commonwalth gradually weakened and by the end of the eighteenth century its territories were partitioned between its stronger neighbours. Various parts, together with their resident and increasingly vulnerable Jewish populations, were incorporated into Prussia, Austria and Tsarist Russia.

The Jews of Spain: to the expulsion of 1492

The first substantial Jewish population probably arrived in Roman Spain as slaves after the Jewish revolts against Rome. Such slaves were often freed by the existing local Jewish community; Jewish tradition has always held that redemption of captives is a great *mitzvah* (a religious or ethical obligation or privilege). Over the next few centuries, Jewish life was comparatively peaceful and prosperous, even after the conquest of Spain early in the fifth century CE by the barbarian Visigoths, who adopted the Arian form of Christianity.

By the end of the sixth century CE, however, the Visigothic king had adopted Roman Catholicism, probably for political reasons, and the Spanish Jews began to be persecuted by the church-dominated monarchy. Many anti-Jewish laws were introduced. These involved the kidnapping of Jewish children and the forced baptism or enslavement of those Jews who would not accept Christianity. For the next century, life became progressively more difficult, and when the Muslims invaded the country in 711 CE they were welcomed by the Jews.

The Muslims, under their general El-Tariq, crossed into Spain from North Africa and forced the Christian Visigoths northwards. The majority of the Iberian Peninsula remained in Muslim hands until the thirteenth century, when the Christians succeeded in reconquering most of the country. The Muslim domination of Spain thus lasted for some 500 years (711–1212), the later part the

This representation of a family sitting down to the Passover meal (Seder) is taken from a fourteenth-century Barcelona Haggadah, the prayerbook for the Passover.

so-called Golden Age of Spanish Jewry. This fascinating and important period in Jewish history is covered in more detail in Chapter 2.

Although there are very few records detailing the first two centuries of Jewish history in Muslim Spain, there is some indication that the Jews were treated well and proved useful in establishing the state of Cordoba as one of the most powerful states in Europe by the tenth century. Cordoba emerged as an important entity under a branch of the Umayyad dynasty. The Umayyads had ruled the Islamic Empire from Damascus until overthrown by the Abbasids in the eighth century: a surviving Umayyad had then escaped to Spain, and by the middle of the tenth century, one of his descendants, Abd al-Rachman III, was sufficiently powerful to declare a Caliphate of Cordoba, independent of the Islamic capital in Baghdad. Rachman III's court physician and finance minister was a Jew – Hasdai ibn Shaprut.

At the beginning of the eleventh century, the Caliphate of Cordoba was conquered by various Muslim Berber tribes from North Africa, and this resulted in the creation of a number of smaller Islamic emirates. The Jews continued to hold positions of influence in each of these lesser states throughout the eleventh and twelfth centuries: cultural, political, social and financial, with Jewish prime ministers (viziers), diplomats, astrologers, finance ministers and physicians. Such Jewish prominence was not, however, always to the satisfaction of Muslims:

> In Granada I saw that the Jews hold leading positions ... they have divided the capital and the provinces among themselves. Everywhere one of this accursed race stands at the head of the government.[26]

During these centuries, Spain also became a centre of Jewish learning; again, it was Hasdai ibn Shaprut who was instrumental in initiating this development.

In the latter part of the eleventh century, just before the First Crusade, the Christian kingdoms in the north of Spain – Leon, Castile and Aragon – launched their own crusade to reconquer Spain for Christendom, the 'Reconquista'. By 1085 they had advanced as far as Toledo. The Muslim emirates then sought assistance from the Almoravids, a North African dynasty supported by Muslim Berber tribesmen, and with their help the Christian advance was halted in 1086 at the Battle of Zallaka. Legend has it that not only were Jews fighting on both sides in this battle, but that because of the three religions involved, it was decided that the battle could not be fought on Friday, Saturday or Sunday, and had to take place on the Monday.

Although the Christian armies had been defeated, the Muslim emirates were unable to consolidate their position. In 1148 they suffered another invasion from North Africa, this time by the Almohads, followers of a Muslim movement for religious reform. The Almohads showed little religious toleration, and insisted that both Christians and Jews should convert to Islam, even by force, and should no longer be allowed a separate existence as originally permitted by the Covenant of Umar, established some five hundred years earlier.

Many Jews then fled from Muslim Spain to the Christian north. Some, including the family of Moses Maimonides (1135 or 1138–1204), the great Jewish scholar and philosopher, escaped to the city of Fez in Morocco. Some did make a show of accepting Islam while secretly remaining loyal to Judaism. In 1165 Maimonides and his family moved to Egypt. In 1177 he was appointed leader of the Jewish community in Fustat (Cairo). In 1185 Maimonides became physician to the vizier of the famous Sultan Saladin. His works on the *Halakha* and Jewish *mitzvoth*, as well as on philosophy (for example, his celebrated book *Guide to the Perplexed*) confirmed him as one of the great authorities on Jewish Law and philosophy.

In the Christian kingdoms of Spain during this period, the Jews were comparatively well treated and many achieved high positions in the Christian courts. This situation continued as long as there was a major Muslim presence in the Iberian Peninsula. However, by the latter part of the thirteenth century, most of Spain and Portugal had come under Christian rule. Only the small emirate of Granada in the far south remained in Muslim hands.

It was during the thirteenth century that the Christians turned their attention to the Jews, not just because of the removal of the Muslim threat, but also because Christian Europe as a whole now acted as a collection of religious states, propagating religious social policies. One way to exert pressure on the Jews to convert was through forced religious disputations, public as well as private. This procedure had been used for several centuries. But in the thirteenth century it became an instrument of conversion by the state. The most famous disputation in Christian Spain occurred in 1263 in Barcelona. The Jewish religious leader at the time, Moses ben Nachman (Nachmanides), was forced to take part in a public 'debate' on the merits of Judaism; his opponent was an apostate, the Dominican monk Pablo Christiani. The 'trial', for in effect Judaism was on trial, was held before King James of Aragon.

Over the next century, life became increasingly difficult for the Jewish population, and in 1391 there were forced conversions and church-inspired physical attacks on Jews throughout Spain. Thousands of Jews died in these attacks and thousands more accepted baptism to escape being killed. Of the forcibly-baptized Jews, many secretly retained their Judaism and continued to intermarry with fellow 'New Christians'. They proved extremely successful in various fields, and resentment against them often developed into hatred. The result was further attacks by the indigenous population – this time not against Jews, but against New Christians.

In 1469 the marriage of Ferdinand of Aragon and Isabella of Castile brought about the unification of Spain under one Christian monarchy. In 1481 the Queen's confessor, the Dominican monk Torquemada, persuaded these zealous Catholic monarchs to fulfil Isabella's promise to make Spain a Christian country. He introduced the Spanish Inquisition to root out Christian heretics and, specifically, any New Christians who remained loyal to Judaism. One of the peculiar features of the Spanish Inquisition, as compared with the Papal Inquisition – which it far surpassed in both scope and intensity – was that the goods belonging to anyone found guilty, as well as any assets their successors might have inherited, went directly to the Spanish Crown. This was undoubtedly a major factor in encouraging the monarchy to perpetuate the dreaded institution.

The Spanish Inquisition soon identified many New Christians who, it main-

A sixteenth-century woodcut of a public disputation between Jewish scholars and Christian clergy. These were more often trials than debates and were held from the eleventh century to the sixteenth century across Europe. In general, they generated more heat than light.

tained, were being encouraged in their clandestine Judaism by the existing Jewish community. In March 1492 a decision was taken to expel the Jews from Spain; significantly enough, only two months after the last Muslim stronghold of Granada had fallen to the Christians. The expulsion took place on 2 August 1492, 9 Av in the Hebrew calendar – the date of the two destructions of the Temple in Jerusalem.

It is broadly estimated that of a Spanish Jewish population totalling some 400,000 at that time, almost half accepted baptism, and many thousands sought refuge abroad – mainly in Muslim countries bordering the eastern Mediterranean. The remainder moved, with their families and whatever belongings they could carry, over the border into Portugal. Unfortunately for this last group, it was not long before they once again found themselves subjected to persecution. In 1497, the Portuguese King Manuel had to agree to the expulsion of the Jews from his country as a precondition of his marrying the daughter of Ferdinand and Isabella. As the time limit given to leave the country was only a matter of months, the vast majority of Jews remained and were compelled to be baptized as Christians. The secret Jews or Marranos of Portugal, nevertheless, retained their allegiance to Judaism over the years. Those who left Portugal were largely responsible for establishing the new Jewish centres in western Europe and the New World.

The Jews of central and western Europe (outside Spain)

During the early Middle Ages (from the fifth to tenth centuries), in the remainder of what had been the Western Roman Empire, small Jewish settlements continued to be established throughout France, central Europe and Italy. The question could well be asked: why and how did Jewish communities settle and develop in such 'inhospitable' places?

As to 'why', two of the most important features of being Jewish must be kept in mind. First, being of a different religion within a society organized on a religious – Christian or Muslim – way of life and on religious ideas, Jews were unable to become an integral part of such a society and always remained distinct from it. Being independent of the local religious and social institutions, the Jews found it easier to move from one place to another and to migrate. On the other hand, it was easier for the political and ecclesiastical authorities to insist on the Jews leaving. Thus, the Jews did not always have the option of choosing their place of dwelling. However, as a minority religious community, the Jews were allowed to arrange for their own religious and communal needs. This often meant moving to places where such services already existed – services such as synagogues, courts and rabbis.

Outside Europe the large Jewish communities lived on the land, working in agriculture and in crafts rather than in trade. Likewise in Palestine and in Babylonia. Yet they were always connected with commerce. They took part in the trade across the Mediterranean, and in the land routes from central Asia across eastern and central Europe to Spain in the west. In Europe, land ownership or farming were usually, but definitely not always, closed to the Jews, as they were not part of the original local population, nor part of the conquering forces. The spread of Jewish settlements, often across the trade routes, and the family and religious connections between distant settlements, facilitated long-distance trade. The lack of land or property led to an involvement in local trade. And not least, the religious prohibition on Christians to trade in money left this occupation open to the Jews.

As to 'how', it is clear that Jews originally established settlements in Europe either as traders, following the expansion of the Roman Empire, or as freed Roman slaves. Despite church opposition, these communities were often encouraged to expand by local secular rulers; for the Jews' ability to establish trade and other connections, especially with Jews in other countries, was of considerable benefit to the secular power. For example, Charlemagne employed Jews in both trade and diplomacy with the Islamic world and the east.

In the European feudal society of the day, in which all members of the population owed fealty to their superior in the feudal pyramid, it gradually became law that the Jews and their possessions belonged to the king. This situation brought with it both advantages and disadvantages: on the one hand, it meant obtaining protection from him in times of trouble; on the other hand, the Jews were often made to act as the ruler's financial 'sponge' and were sometimes squeezed out of economic existence. A classic example of this occurred in England.

The first Jews were brought to England from Normandy by William the Conqueror, specifically to act as his bankers and tax collectors. For over a century,

A caricature of English Jews from Norwich Castle dated 1233. Staring down is the bearded Isaac of Norwich, the wealthiest Jew of the time. He wears the crown of Henry III to demonstrate his status as the king's property.

and with the support of successive kings, the Jews prospered and settled in about ninety towns throughout the country. They brought with them their rich cultural, religious and artistic traditions and produced many great works of a spiritual and artistic nature. But in 1186, when Henry II decided to expropriate the whole estate of the rich Aaron of Lincoln after his death, rather than merely tax it, the writing was on the wall.

At the coronation of Richard I, three years later, the Jews of London were attacked. This was quickly followed by similar outbreaks elsewhere, culminating in the massacre at York in 1190, when virtually the whole Jewish community committed *kiddush ha-Shem* rather than fall into the hands of the Christians.

For the next hundred years, the position became worse, with the monarchs growing more rapacious and introducing increasingly heavy taxes on the Jews. Thus a petition from the leaders of English Jewry to Henry III in 1250 prayed for a safe passage out of the country: 'The King [takes] from us those things we cannot give him, although he would pull out our eyes, or cut our throats, when he had first pulled off our skins.'

Forty years later their plea was granted, when the whole, impoverished Jewish community was expelled from England by Edward I in November 1290. This was to be the first of many such expulsions that the Jews of Europe were to suffer.

By the tenth century, before any Jews had ever reached England, a new and important Jewish centre of learning had been established in the Rhine communities of Cologne, Mainz, Worms and, later, Speyer. This centre was instrumental in developing a separate Ashkenazi religious culture, as distinct from the Sephardi tradition being developed in Spain. Great scholars emerged, such as Rabbi Kalonymus, Rabbenu Gershom (called the Light of the Exile), and Rashi (Rabbi Shelo-moh Itzhaki) and his family. Apart from their important contributions to the interpretation of the Torah and Talmud and the development of Jewish law and study, the academies of the Rhine communities introduced some structure and cohesion into Ashkenazi Jewish life. This proved crucial later, when the Jews of central and western Europe began to suffer widespread attacks, starting with the First Crusade in 1096.

The crusades and the increase in Christian anti-Jewish activities

Jews had been established in small communities throughout Europe for hundreds of years, and in some places even since Roman times. During this long period, they had lived alongside their Christian neighbours and had rarely suffered persecution, apart from the later Visigothic period in seventh-century Spain. However, in the eleventh century, with the advent of the crusades, the climate changed dramatically.

We have mentioned elsewhere that there was frequent tension between the secular rulers of Europe and the leaders of the church. By the end of the eleventh century, the popes had succeeded in establishing their authority over most of their secular opponents. This situation coincided with a plea to Rome from the Byzantine emperor, who had recently been defeated in battle by the Seljuk Turks (1078). One result of this defeat directly affected Christians in the west: pilgrimages to the Holy Land were henceforth forbidden by the Turks. In order to assert his newly won authority, and to recapture the Holy Land from the 'infidel' Muslim, Pope Urban II convened a council of European leaders in 1095 and called for a popular crusade – a mass military expedition to the Holy Land involving all classes of feudal society. Absolution for past sins was offered to those who joined.

The religious fervour stirred up by the Pope's call brought dire consequences for the Jews, not only in the Holy Land but in the many European Jewish communities on the crusaders' route to Palestine. In 1096, the first crusading masses on their way to the Mediterranean Sea attacked and destroyed Jewish communities in the Rhineland and massacred large numbers of Jews. The cru-saders' argument was that, before they went to fight the Muslims abroad, they ought to deal with the infidels in their midst. The local lay and ecclesiastical rulers usually tried to prevent the assaults and to protect the Jews but, in most cases, it was impossible to resist the fanaticism of the crusaders or the intervention came too late.

Now that the church had become dominant, the preaching of the newly formed monastic orders began to reach the masses and fuelled anti-Jewish feeling. Hence-forth, the Jew, as an alien element in Christendom, was subject to continual and varied forms of oppression and attack.

In England, in 1144, an accusation was made that the Jews of Norwich had killed a Christian child (William of Norwich) for ritual purposes. His blood was allegedly used in making the *matzah* for the Jewish Passover. Although the English Jews were then protected by the king, this preposterous charge, later known as the blood libel, soon gained wide credence. Since then, such libels have been repeated over the centuries, in various countries, and have resulted in attacks on the Jews. These attacks usually, but not always, took place at Easter.

In 1179, the Third Lateran Church Council, following the biblical injunction, forbade Christians to lend money at interest. The dubious and often risky occupation of money-lending was thus handed over to the Jews. The Jews themselves at this time were permitted by their rabbis to engage in usury as a matter of practical necessity. Before, Jews had been restricted to a handful of despised occupations, such as peddling and trade in second-hand goods. As usurers, they inevitably became vulnerable to attack. This resulted in many voluntary ghettos being created for purposes of security; compulsory ghettos were only formally introduced in the sixteenth century.

By enacting that Jews should wear a distinctive badge in order to be recognized by the Christian population, the Fourth Lateran Church Council (1215) made

Jews at work in medieval Europe. The occupations open to the Jews included usury (lending money at interest) and the distillation of wines and spirits.

them more vulnerable to attack. The council also formally introduced the Christian doctrine of transubstantiation, whereby the wine drunk and the wafer eaten during Mass was taken to represent the literal blood and body of Jesus. This doctrine was indirectly responsible for another form of anti-Jewish attack. Wafers stored in damp churches frequently formed brown patches resembling dried blood. Jews were accused of stealing the wafers and pricking them with pins to draw the blood from Jesus' body, or of destroying them in some other way, often involving a Satanic-type ritual. The painting by Uccello reproduced in Plates 3 and 4 provides a graphic representation of an accusation which was responsible for many attacks and the deaths of many Jews over the centuries.

At about the same time as the Fourth Lateran Church Council, Pope Innocent III decided to root out any form of non-orthodox Christianity in Europe. The Christian Albigenses in the south of France, for example, were slaughtered as heretics in 1219. The Pope was assisted in this battle against heresy by the new Dominican monastic order, referred to by him as 'the pugilists of the faith', and also to some extent by the Franciscans. These two orders were put in charge of the Papal Inquisition when it was established in 1233.

Although the Inquisition was officially only concerned with Christian heresy, and indeed many Christians were condemned to death by the Inquisition, the zeal of the monks soon found a way to reach the Jews. In 1233 the Dominicans persuaded the French king to put the Talmud on trial at a public disputation in Paris. Twenty-four cartloads of Jewish religious books were subsequently condemned to be burnt in a Paris square. The destruction of these manuscripts, in an age before printing, had a disastrous impact on Jewish cultural and religious life in central and western Europe for centuries. Other public disputations, such as the Barcelona Disputation of 1263 already mentioned, continued to be held over the centuries with the basic intention of putting Judaism on trial.

In the fourteenth century, the medieval belief that the Jews were connected with the devil, and therefore necessarily at war with Christendom, led to a frightening new accusation. As the bubonic plague (the Black Death) swept through Europe in 1348, Jews were forced, under torture, to 'admit' that they had poisoned Christian wells. A contemporary chronicler reported:

> In the matter of this plague the Jews throughout the world were reviled and accused in all lands as having caused it through the poison which they are said to have put into the water and wells ... and for this reason the Jews were burnt all the way from the Mediterranean into Germany, but not in Avignon, for the pope protected them there.[27]

These vicious attacks, in addition to the expulsions from western and central Europe – England in 1290, France in 1306 and 1344, Spain in 1492 and Portugal in 1497 – had weakened and reduced the populations of many Jewish communities by the end of the fifteenth century. At this time, the only substantial Jewish communities remaining in western or central Europe were in Italy and in the German states, where the lack of unified regimes permitted Jewish settlement. But even in these areas, local rulers frequently had to be bribed to accept Jewish refugees and would often only allow settlement for temporary periods. As a result, some of the survivors began to look for a refuge in eastern Europe (see Map 7).

The Christian rationale for attacks on Jews

The anti-Jewish activities described in the preceding section continued unabated for hundreds of years. It is worth drawing a comparison with life for the Jews under Islam during these centuries, where, despite their second-class status, they fared measurably better than in most places in Christendom. It was not until the Protestant Reformation in the sixteenth century that the Christian persecution of the Jews eased to any meaningful extent. The question could well be asked: why was it that the Jewish people were made to suffer so much and for so long, when, on the face of it, they had done little to deserve such treatment?

It was suggested earlier in this chapter that the insistence on Jewish exclusivity since the first return to Zion gave rise to an inevitable resentment against the Jews. With the rise and development of Christianity, a number of new factors aggravated this resentment of the Jews. From the beginning, Christianity found itself in some competition with Judaism. In the fourth century a new claim appeared against the Jews: that only one generation after Jesus' death, God had deserted the Jews by allowing their Temple to be destroyed and His people to be defeated and scattered. This appeared to support the Christians' claim to be God's chosen people. This claim was further reinforced over the centuries as Christianity became universally triumphant in Europe and the Jews remained powerless.

In the Middle Ages, there was a widespread belief that a continuous struggle existed between good and evil, heaven and hell, God and the Devil, and that in this fight the Jews were on the side of the Devil. After all, the Jews refused to acknowledge the Messiah, the promised Redeemer, Jesus Christ. It was thus evident that the New Testament's inferences about the culprit Jews and their satanic tendencies were correct. This idea, which was portrayed annually at Easter in popular passion plays, was enhanced by the fact that the Jews insisted on following 'strange' customs and keeping themselves apart.

The Christian claim to be the one true religion could, of course, be challenged by the very refusal of the Jews to accept Christianity. But this refusal was used by St Augustine to prove the truth of Christianity – for the misery of the Jewish condition was a living proof of their rejection by a God who had transferred their privilege as chosen people to successful Christianity. Nevertheless, St Augustine's doctrine enabled the Jews to survive during the first millennium of Christianity. In addition, Roman law, which prevailed throughout Europe during the whole medieval period and up to the modern age, supplied the Christian countries with a legal framework which allowed the retention of the Jews within society.

However, in the thirteenth century, Christianity became supreme in Europe and the ground-rules were changed. The new monastic orders claimed that the Talmud had altered and corrupted the very nature of the Jew in the period since St Augustine. They used this claim to justify coercing the Jews who were then the only people in Europe refusing to convert to Christianity. In 1244, Pope Innocent IV described the new situation:

> Christian piety allows [the Jews] to live among them through pity ... [but] they, display no shame for their guilt nor reverence for the honour of the Christian faith; they throw away and despise the Law of Moses and the Prophets and follow certain traditions of their elders ... In traditions of this sort [the Talmud], they rear and nurture their children ... They fear that, if the truth which is found in the Law and the Prophets – indicating that the only begotten son of God is to appear in the flesh – be furnished, these children would be converted to the Christian faith.[28]

This new attitude coincided with both the introduction of the Inquisition and the various disputations which placed the Talmud, and hence Judaism, on trial. Material factors also contributed to anti-Jewish feeling. One such factor was the number of Jews acting as money lenders. As Jacob von Konigshofen wrote, when discussing the massacres of Jews which followed the Black Death (1348):

> The money was indeed the thing that killed the Jews. If they had been poor and if the feudal lords had not been in debt to them, they would not have been burnt.[29]

The Protestant Reformation

A major factor in relieving the pressure on the Jews of central Europe was the Protestant Reformation, which began in the sixteenth century. In bringing about an inter-Christian conflict, the Reformation and the wars that followed resulted in a legitimizing of differences in belief which, in time, led to the toleration of other religions.

Although there had been earlier attempts to reform the Roman Catholic Church, the true Reformation started in 1517, when a German Benedictine monk, Martin Luther, led a revolt protesting against what he claimed was the all-powerful and corrupt hand of Rome and its priests. For political as well as theological reasons, a number of secular rulers supported Luther. This led to a series of horrendous wars throughout much of Europe: the population of the German states, at the centre of the conflicts, was halved through slaughter, famine and sickness. The Peace of Augsburg in 1555 decreed that the religion of each state in Germany should be that of its ruler. Yet, it took another century before the Peace of Westphalia (1648) finally decided the lines of religious division in Europe.

In his early writings, Luther expressed great sympathy for the Jews, clearly in the hope of persuading them to become Protestants:

> Popes, bishops, sophists and monks dealt with the Jews as if they were dogs and not human beings ... How can we expect them to improve if we forbid them to work among us and to have social intercourse with us, and so force them into usury?
> We must deal with them not according to the law of the pope, but according

to the law of Christian charity ... so that they may have a good reason to be with us and among us and an opportunity to witness Christian life and doctrine; and if some remain obstinate, what of it?[30]

Twenty years later, with the Jews still refusing to convert, Luther's attitude had clearly changed:

What then shall we Christians do with this damned, rejected race of Jews?
First, their synagogues or churches should be set on fire.
Secondly, their homes should likewise be broken down and destroyed ...
They ought to be put under one roof or in a stable, like gypsies.
Thirdly, they should be deprived of their prayer-books and Talmuds.
Fourthly, their rabbis must be forbidden under threat of death to teach any more.
Fifthly, passport and travelling privileges should be absolutely forbidden to the Jews.
Sixthly, they ought to be stopped from usury. All their cash and valuables of silver and gold ought to be taken from them.
Seventhly, let the young and strong Jews and Jewesses be given the flail, the axe, the hoe, the spade, the distaff, and spindle, and let them earn their bread by the sweat of their noses.[31]

Such sentiments, emanating from the founder of Lutheranism, undoubtedly contributed to later German Protestant anti-Semitism. Julius Streicher, editor of the notorious anti-Semitic newspaper *Der Sturmer*, who was sentenced to death at the Nuremberg trials, claimed that he and his fellow Nazis were merely carrying out Luther's instructions.

The Catholic Church, reacting against the rise of Protestantism, also blamed the Jews for initially influencing Luther. Already, in previous centuries, reformers of Catholic Christianity and their followers had been put on trial for 'becoming Jews'. Now, with the Reformation gaining pace, these accusations were reinforced. In order to restrict any Jewish influence, a papal edict of 1555 declared that Jewish settlement in Catholic states should henceforth be confined to a restricted, walled area to be locked at night; this area became known as a ghetto. The name originated in Venice, which had introduced a similar system for its Jews as early as 1516.

Within a short time, several Protestant states also introduced ghettos, as if both sides had agreed to keep the Jews a segregated race. There is a tendency to think that prior to emancipation all Jews were ghetto-dwellers, but in fact only a very few 'closed' ghettos were ever established outside Italy, the German states and Austria.

The Jews of central Europe in the pre-emancipation period

Emancipation and the granting of equal rights did not reach the Jews of Europe until the eighteenth and nineteenth centuries. This process will be covered in more detail in Chapter 3. During the preceding two hundred years, the Jews remained

A caricature of 'Jew Süss', the able financial minister to the Duke of Württemburg. A victim of court jealousy, he was placed in an iron cage, exhibited in the city square and subsequently hanged.

very much outside the mainstream of western European life. Although physical attacks had more or less ceased, Jewish day-to-day existence continued to be subject to severe restrictions. The only exception to the pattern of oppression was the institution of the court Jew.

Many of the rulers of central Europe were finding themselves in need of money – in the first instance, to pay for their ever-warring armies and then, in the post-war period, to satisfy their newly acquired taste for emulating the extravagant lifestyles of courts such as Louis XIV's in France. To raise the finance a rich Jew attached to the court (*Hofjude*) was frequently appointed as finance minister; perhaps the most famous was 'Jew Süss' of Württemberg. Such individuals were allowed to live at court and were often permitted to have a limited number of fellow Jews from the ghetto join them as employees and servants. At the time, most of these states had no educated middle class. The land-owning aristocracy, traditionally despising trade and commerce, had little alternative but to rely on the Jews for financial expertise. Moreover, the Jews rarely presented a political threat. As far as the local Jewish community was concerned, the court Jew was of vital importance: his intercession was frequently their only protection against arbitrary expulsion or oppression.

The vast majority of Jews, however, continued to be treated very much as second-class citizens. As can be seen from the edict quoted below, they were subject to stringent limitations on residence, occupation and demographic expansion. Thus, for example, in addition to classifying 'forbidden increase' on a par with 'fraud' and 'cheating', there were laws permitting only one child in any family to marry and remain living in the parents' town.

After the massacres in the Ukraine in 1648, the Jewish problem was compounded by refugees fleeing westwards into the various central European states. This resulted in even harsher legislation to curtail Jewish settlement. As late as 1750, an edict of Frederick the Great, relating to the Jews of Berlin, showed the nature of these laws, and described the invidious creation by the state of different classes of Jews:

> We, Frederick, by God's grace, King of Prussia ... establish that
>
> I.   No other Jews are to be tolerated except those named in the lists that are attached to the end of these regulations ...
>
> V.   A distinction is to be made between Regular Protected Jews and Special Protected Jews who are merely tolerated in their life time.
>
> Foreign [non-Prussian] Jews are not allowed to settle in our land at all. However, if one should really have a fortune of ten thousand Reichstaler, and bring the same into the country and furnish authentic evidence of the fact, then we are to be asked about this and concerning the fee he is to pay.
>
> In order that in the future all fraud, cheating and secret and forbidden increase of the number of families may be more carefully avoided, no Jew shall be allowed to marry, nor will he receive permission to settle, in any manner, nor will he be believed, until a careful investigation has been made by the War and Domains Office together with the aid of the Treasury.
>
> Male and female servants and other domestics, however, are not allowed to marry. Should they attempt to do this they are not to be tolerated any longer.
>
> VII. No Protected Jew can stay away from home for more than a year without authorization; otherwise his place will be given to another.
>
> XI.   The Jews must not pursue any manual trade ... Particularly are they enjoined not to brew beer nor to distil spirits. However, they are allowed to undertake the distilling of spirits for the nobility, government officials, etc.
>
> XXIV. The Jews must watch one another and pay attention carefully when they find any of their people on the wrong road and immediately report such a person to the proper authorities.[32]

These restrictions, imposed on the Jews in the eighteenth century, appear extreme, especially in an age which prided itself on being 'enlightened'. On the other hand, it can be argued that the host society had to deal with what appeared to be an alien group – one which refused to mix with the local population and often did not even wish to learn the language of the host country. Whatever the rights or wrongs, it is clear that those who would fight for Jewish emancipation in Germany (which was granted a little over a century later) would have to overcome a long history of mistrust and misunderstanding on both sides (see Chapter 3).

The Jews in south-eastern Europe

Although both Joel and Isaiah refer to Jews living in Greece, the earliest evidence of their presence is a tombstone inscription of around 300–250 BCE discovered at Oropus, near Athens. In I Maccabees 5:9, Areus I, king of Sparta, is said to have sent a letter of friendship to the High Priest Onias I. In 168 BCE Jason, the Hellenistic High Priest of Jerusalem, escaped to Sparta, while the Hasmonean ruler, Jonathan, renewed the friendship with the Greeks that dated from the time of Areus. Furthermore, during the Maccabean uprising, it is more than likely that the Jewish communities in Greece expanded as slaves were brought in from Judah. The first Greek writer to deal expressly with the Jews was Theophrastus (372–288/7 BCE), a pupil of Aristotle. His contemporary, Hecataeus of Abdera, also wrote about Jewish history, religion and political institutions.

Many Greek Jewish communities are mentioned in the New Testament and there was a large Jewish population in Cyprus at the start of the Trajan Revolt in 112 CE. After the triumph of Christianity in the fourth century CE and the establishment of the Eastern Roman Empire, the Jews' position in society changed. In 393 CE their religious ceremonies were disturbed and the Emperor Theodosius I came to their assistance. However, legally, they began to lose ground through the new legislation laid down in the Code of Theodosius II in 438 CE.

Over the next thousand years, until the Muslim Ottomans conquered Constantinople and the Byzantine Empire came to an end (1453 CE), the Jews of Greece suffered periodic persecutions and expulsions, which gave them little opportunity to develop a centre of Jewish learning.

The Ottoman Empire, which extended over vast areas and many countries of Europe, Asia and Africa, was a Muslim state. The religion of Islam informed every aspect of its legal and administrative structure. Jews, as one of the 'People of the Book', enjoyed a measure of toleration; their persons and property were protected and they were free to practise their faith. At the same time, they were required to pay a special tax and not dress like Muslims. Although there had been a Jewish presence in the territories of the Empire since the Byzantine period, the Jewish population rose dramatically following the expulsion of the Jews of Spain and Portugal. The Ottoman state welcomed the Jews, who brought with them commercial, technical and scientific skills that were an asset to a dynamic and expansionist imperial power. Bayazid II (1481–1512), the Ottoman ruler, teased Ferdinand, the king of Portugal, for impoverishing his own kingdom and enriching the Ottoman Empire through the expulsion of the Jews. Throughout the sixteenth century the Jews continued to arrive and Iberian immigrants transformed the Jewish community in Istanbul. In 1478, it had a population of 10,000 Jews; in 1550 its 30,000 souls made Istanbul the world's largest Jewish community. Salonika, where the Marranos outnumbered the Jewish and non-Jewish populations, became a Jewish city; Safed and Smyrna also grew in population.

Safed, a centre of kabbalistic[33] learning, was the source of a peculiar combination of mysticism and messianism that was to convulse the Jewish world in the second half of the seventeenth century. Smyrna was the birthplace of its leader, Shabbetai Zevi. Shabbateanism, one of the largest and most extraordinary events in Jewish history after the destruction of the Temple and the Bar Kochba Revolt, underscored the strength and vitality of the Jewish religious tradition with its emphasis upon political and spiritual redemption. That is why it was to have such tremendous appeal in the Ottoman-ruled communities, which were comparatively free from oppression as well as in those parts of the diaspora where Jews were actively persecuted.

The Jews of eastern Europe

Eastern Europe developed much later than the rest of the continent, partly because it remained far from the civilizing influence of the Roman Empire. The people of eastern Europe were also subject to frequent invasions by marauding tribes from the east. It was not until the thirteenth century that a degree of stability was achieved with the introduction of a centralized and effective system of law and order.

In 1264 the king of Poland, Boleslaw V the Pious, issued a charter known as the Statute of Kalisz which gave protection and some freedoms to the new settlers, including the Jews, who came to colonize his lands. The privileges and rights of this Statute were expanded by Casimir (III) the Great in 1344, so as to encourage Jews to settle in his territories which had, once again, been devastated by tribesmen from the east.

After the Black Death massacres of 1348, many Jewish survivors, in particular those from Bohemia, Austria and Germany, but also many from Italy and Turkey, took advantage of Casimir's offer and began to settle in the combined Kingdom of Poland and Lithuania (the two states merged at the end of the fourteenth century).

Why was greater tolerance shown to the Jews in medieval Poland and Lithuania as against those in the rest of Europe? In the eastern provinces, the need for a constant flow of fresh settlers to maintain the domains newly acquired by the nobility, as well as the need to colonize the recently deforested territories in Poland, compelled the rulers to attract one of the more mobile sections of European society – the Jews. They, therefore, offered the Jews specific guarantees of safety and of free religious practice, as well as protection against the persecution of the kind familiar to them in central Europe. In the Statute of Kalisz, for example, it was forbidden to charge Jews with ritual murder. If such charges were pressed by Christians, they had to produce at least six reliable witnesses to the alleged crime, three of them Jews! It is also interesting to note that the Black Death, which struck Europe in 1348–9, inexplicably affected Poland far less than elsewhere. The Jews came to Poland, which was generally backward and on the perimeter of Europe, from the highly developed European countries to the west; they were educated, skilled, knowledgeable in trade and languages, with a network of connections and families in their countries of origin. Thus they were capable of contributing to the development of Poland, to its linking up with Europe, and to strengthening the central power of the king *vis-à-vis* the might of the nobles.

Over the next 300 years the combined kingdom of Poland and Lithuania became extremely powerful and was the largest state in Europe after the colonization of territories to the east, including the Ukraine: it came to be known as the Polish Commonwealth. Until the Khmelnitskii uprising in 1648, the Jewish community, despite some anti-Jewish activities, prospered economically and developed into a uniquely successful cultural and religious centre. As Nathan of Hanover wrote in the 1640s:

> In no country was the study of the Torah so widespread among the Jews as in the Kingdom of Poland. Every Jewish community maintained a *yeshivah*, paying its president a large salary, so as to enable him to conduct the institution without worry and to devote himself entirely to the pursuit of learning. Moreover every Jewish community supported college students (*bahurim*) giving them a certain amount of money per week. Every one of the *bahurim* was made to instruct at least two boys, for the purpose of deepening his own studies and gaining some experience in Talmudic discussions. The poor boys obtained their food either from the charity fund or from the public kitchen.[33]

The Jewish population under Polish rule increased dramatically, especially when compared to the rest of Europe over the same period. Figures provided by the *Encyclopaedia Judaica* estimate that there were 30,000 Jews in Poland and Lithuania in 1490, and it is generally accepted that the Jewish population in the mid-seventeenth century was well over 300,000.

In the fifteenth century, anti-Jewish activities began to increase, often encouraged by German burghers, who had also settled there and were the continuing rivals of the Jews. A serious outbreak of violence took place in Cracow in 1407 during Easter week when a mob of looters, incited by the German traders and a local priest, destroyed the Jewish quarter and killed all the Jews that would not accept baptism. It was also at this time that the centralized power of the king was reduced by the rise of the feudal barons, many of whom allied themselves with both the church and the German burghers against the commercial activities of the Jews.

The greatest conflict arose in the competition for the monopoly leasing of operations such as the mint, salt mines, customs and tax farming: these were known as 'Great Arendas'. From the fourteenth century it had been the custom of the Royal Prerogative to grant such monopolies to Jews. During the sixteenth century, however, the Polish nobility, through the Sejm or parliament, tried to prohibit the leasing of such royal revenues to Jews.

Nevertheless, it suited the Polish nobles to grant leases on their own estates and allow the Jews to administer their economic affairs. These were known as 'Agricultural Arendas'. The Jewish lessee and his family and fellow-Jews would then deal with the local peasant population, collect and market the local agricultural products, and be responsible for activities such as the running of local breweries and taverns. The greatest expansion of these Agricultural Arendas took place in the Ukraine during the colonization period up to 1648.

The Jew from feudal times had, as in other parts of Europe, belonged to the king. They were therefore treated as a separate group and allowed to develop their own way of life, language, culture and even dress, which tended to isolate them from their Christian countrymen. The cultural, physical and, to a large extent, economic separation of the Jews from outside society had a unifying effect on the Jews themselves, and a very distinct and rich culture developed. Much of this culture emanated from the Ashkenazi rites, liturgy and religious customs established by the Rhine communities and transported by refugees from the west. An essential element was, of course, the development of the Yiddish language, which ultimately produced a colourful and valuable literature in the nineteenth and early twentieth centuries. This language, which originally evolved among the Jews of Germany, spread among the Jewish communities, not only in Poland and Lithuania, but also in Austria, Bohemia and Hungary. Yiddish thus became the *lingua franca* which bound together Jews from anywhere in eastern and central Europe.

The Polish rulers, with the sanction of the Church, found it sensible to encourage such isolation and to grant local self-government and autonomy to the Jewish community through the institution of the *kahal* or community board. Jewish autonomy also helped ease the work of tax collection. The height of such self-rule was reached in the year 1564, when the Jews were given their own parliament known as the Council of Four Lands: the four lands being Lesser Poland, Greater Poland, Red Russia (that is, East Galicia) and Volhynia (see Map 7).

This period of general peace and prosperity came to an end for the Jews in 1648 when the Greek Orthodox Ukrainians, under the Cossack leader Bogdan Khmelnitskii, rebelled against their Roman Catholic Polish overlords. During the Cossacks' advance the Jews, who were identified with the Poles, suffered terribly. It is estimated that some 100,000 Jews were killed and many communities and centres of learning were destroyed. Over the next century or so, internal conflicts combined with external pressures from the adjoining states brought about the gradual disintegration of the Polish Commonwealth. As far as the Jews were concerned, their dreadful experiences at the hands of both the Cossacks and the Poles in the seventeenth century left a feeling of insecurity which was carried down into later generations. This insecurity was made worse during the first half of the eighteenth century, as peasant rebels called Haidamaks rose up and attacked the Jews and others without mercy at a time when the central government was unable to exercise any form of effective control.

In 1772, three powers – Russia, Prussia and Austria – began to divide Polish territory; after the third partition, in 1795, the independent Polish state ceased to exist. The Jewish population, by this time totalling some one and a half million, now found itself distributed between the three conquering states, with the majority now in Russia. The period of Polish decline was accompanied by a collapse of the rule of law and increasing numbers of attacks on the Jews. Shortly before the partitions, in 1764, certain Jewish self-governing agencies, notably the Council of Four Lands, were abolished. The instinct of the Jewish masses had always been to turn to religion for consolation, but for many Polish Jews, this now presented a problem.

Jewish tradition had always insisted that learning was a major part of religious life. Yet due to the continuing chaos, *yeshivot* in the Ukraine and southern Poland had not been re-established since their destruction by the Cossacks in the middle of the seventeenth century. The rabbis and scholars of Lithuania and northern Poland, an area that had escaped much of the destruction, formed a kind of intellectual aristocracy that tended to despise the unlearned Jew. In these northern *yeshivot*, the learning was often characterized by the sophistry of *pilpul*, an intricate dialectical technique for reconciling contradictory texts.

In the middle of the seventeenth century, differences within the Polish-Lithuanian Jewish communities and economic hardships exacerbated the divisions in Jewish society between the learned and rich, and the poor, ordinary people. The institutions of self-government lost much of their control over the community, and corruption became the rule rather than the exception.

Hasidism

For most Jews learning was out of reach, and the communal institutions did not serve them satisfactorily. They had, in fact, no leadership at a time when leadership was particularly needed. More Jews began to turn to mysticism. In the Kabbalah[34], which encouraged the individual to attempt divine communication and seek inner secret meanings, many Jews found a new outlook on religion and social conduct. The Kabbalah, combined with the popular traditions of ecstasy and mass enthusiasm, supplied the basis for the close-knit groups and charismatic leaders from which Hasidism as a popular movement was to grow.

It was at this time that a powerful spiritual figure appeared in south-east Poland. Israel ben Eliezer, the *Ba'al Shem Tov*, known as the Besht (1700–1760), was a faith healer with little formal Jewish education. Although he left very little in writing, his ideas were passed on by his disciples through simple folk-tales, parables and homilies. He preached to the depressed Polish Jews a new doctrine, which later became known as Hasidism. This was a doctrine of hope and joy rather than of mortification and learning. God could be reached by devotion, by simple, heartfelt prayers and even by singing and dancing; it was not necessary to study to be a good Jew. This last claim was, of course, anathema to most rabbis and scholars.

The followers of the Besht also created a new type of Jewish religious leader called the *Zaddik*, the Just, who, according to Hasidic thought, was closer to God than ordinary men. He served as a mediator between the believer and God. A special attachment to his community made it the *Zaddik*'s responsibility to mix with the common people in order to lift them up to his own exalted spiritual level. In return, they were expected to obey him in both spiritual and temporal matters and to support him financially. The Hasidim believed that the *Zaddik*'s powers could be inherited by his sons or even his sons-in-law, and dynasties of *Zaddikim* were formed which have survived to modern times.

The new movement expanded rapidly, establishing its own places of worship in many hundreds of Jewish communities in eastern Europe. In those areas where Jewish centres of study had been maintained, notably Lithuania, Hasidism encountered resistance. To counter this resistance, one of the Hasidic leaders, Rabbi Schneur Zalman of Lyady in Lithuania (1745–1813), evolved a school of

Hasidic thought known as *Habad*, which placed greater emphasis on the intellect than on the emotions and restricted the *Zaddik*'s role to spiritual matters. The well-known Lubavitch branch of *Habad*, one of the few evangelizing Jewish movements, is a direct descendant of *Habad*.

A campaign against Hasidism was led in Lithuania by Rabbi Elijah, known as the Gaon of Vilna (1720–1797). His followers, known as *mitnagdim*, violently objected to the concept of the *Zaddik*. They claimed that it was non-Jewish, inherently corrupt – coming close to the worship of man – and that the *Zaddik*'s intermediary role between individuals and God was similar to the Roman Catholic/ Greek Orthodox practices of communicating with God through a 'Holy Man'.

The *mitnagdim* tried everything, including excommunication, to break up the new Hasidic movement but failed. The fight between the two sects continued into the nineteenth century, and was only partly resolved when a common enemy arose in the shape of the Haskalah, or Jewish Enlightenment. This development is discussed in Chapters 3 and 4. In some ways the opposition between Hasidim and their *mitnagdic* opponents continues today.

Despite this rapprochement, east European Jews confronted the nineteenth century in a weakened position. Although they were to display enormous resilience and powers of recuperation, their autonomy and prosperity had been seriously undermined.

The Jewish demographic situation at the end of the eighteenth century

During the period covered by this chapter, Jewish demography changed dramatically. Before the destruction of the First Temple in 586 BCE, the vast majority of Jews lived in the kingdom of Judah, an estimated Jewish population of around 150,000. There was a very small diaspora in Babylonia and Egypt. By 1800 CE, some 2,400 years later, out of a total world Jewish population of some three million, 83 per cent lived in Europe. The main reasons for this radical movement have been covered in this chapter. Table 1 presents the demographic situation at the end of the eighteenth century. It shows how the size and distribution of the world Jewish population changed from 1300 CE to 1800 CE. It also presents the corresponding figures for the general population. There are a number of points arising from this table that are worth highlighting.

• The total for the Jewish population in Europe in 1800 of over two million hides the extraordinary geographical movements that had taken place since the fourteenth century. A virtually non-existent Jewish community in eastern Europe had now become by far the largest in the world, whereas the Jews of western Europe had been reduced from some 30 per cent of world Jewry to less than 4 per cent.
• While the Jewish population of eastern Europe increased from about 5,000 to about 1·5 million during these five centuries, the size of the general population only increased from some 20 million to just over 50 million. The enormous disparity can be explained by migrations from both the west and the south-east, and by both a higher rate of birth and a lower rate of child mortality.

• In 1300 a world Jewish population of approximately 950,000 was made up of about half a million living in Islamic countries in the Middle East and about 450,000 in Europe. In 1800, while the European Jewish population had increased to nearly 2.5 million, the number of Jews in the Middle East had remained static at about 500,000.

Table 1: Jewish demographic situation – 1300 CE and 1800 CE[35]

	1300			1800		
	Jewish population		General population	Jewish population		General population
	(thousands)	%	(millions)	(thousands)	%	(millions)
Western Europe						
Spain	150	16.0	7.50	Nil	–	11.50
Portugal	40	4.0	1.25	Nil	–	2.75
France	100	10.5	16.00	40	1.5	29.00
The Netherlands	5	0.5	0.80	45	1.5	2.00
England	Nil	–	3.75	20	0.5	9.25
Total	**295**	**31.0**	**29.30**	**105**	**3.5**	**54.50**
Central and Southern Europe						
Germany/Austria	95	10.0	11.00	200	7.0	21.00
Hungary/Romania/ Balkans	5	0.5	7.75	500	17.0	3.25
Italy	50	5.0	10.00	25	1.0	19.00
Total	**150**	**15.5**	**28.75**	**725**	**25.0**	**43.25**
Eastern Europe Poland/Lithuania/ Russia	5	0.5	19.50	1500	51.0	51.00
European total	450	47.0	78.0	2410	82.5	164.00
Middle East	500	53.0	?	500	17.0	695.00
North and South America	Nil	–	?	10	0.5	24.00
Estimated total world population	**950**	**100.0**	**?**	**2920**	**100.0**	**883.00**

Percentage figures show per cent of total world Jewish population. Figures are given to the nearest 0.5 per cent.

Conclusion

In the introduction to this first chapter of *The Jewish Enigma*, the following question was posed: how have the Jews been able to survive as a people for well over two and a half millennia – much of that time dispersed, without a land and often beset by enemies determined to oppress, if not destroy, them? It is perhaps worth reviewing some of the factors that have already been mentioned to see whether any clues suggest themselves. Needless to say, no definitive answers can be given to such a profound and complex question within the context of such a brief historical review.

Until recent times, it was acknowledged that, first and foremost, rabbis and scholars who knew and could interpret Jewish law were an integral component of the community's leadership. Jews were taught that the guardians of a city were not the soldiers or magistrates, but those who taught the Bible and *Mishnah* and instructed in *Halakha*. This implied a certain set of priorities.

Until the emancipation, the Jewish community was recognized as a separate legal entity by the state's ruler, and thereby had the authority to compel its members to obey. Yet the mechanisms of enforcement, the harshest being the *Herem*, the Ban of Excommunication, were very rarely used. The main means of coercion were public opinion and communal pressure. As long as the king acknowledged the community's right to self-government, its members complied with its rulings as if there were a local government. The rabbis, being both the instructors and the judges of the community, exerted a very strong influence. Yet in most communities the public and the lay leadership – usually the well-off members – were able to restrain the more extremist rabbis and prevent them from unpopular *Halakhic* decisions.

Again, rabbinical leaders could emerge from any social background, for religious education was available to all boys, and the rigid class distinctions of other societies were less in evidence. The Jewish religious practices and public prayers maintained an intensive communal life. This was not just a question of Jewish tradition, but was also partly a result of the precariousness of Jewish existence as a religious minority and an ethnic group.

The value placed on human life by Jews in different circumstances is itself worthy of note. On the one hand, in times of persecution Jewish tradition expected that every man, woman and child be prepared to accept death rather than conversion. On the other hand, one of the most crucial decisions made by the rabbis was the edict preventing unnecessary loss of life after the slaughter of Jews during the revolts against Rome. Jews were obliged to risk their lives in cases of idol worshipping, the shedding of blood and sexual promiscuity. This law ensured the survival of the Jewish community beyond the period of persecutions. Jews were aware of the importance of their remaining alive to practise Judaism and pass it on to their children. As the Psalmist wrote: 'The dead cannot praise the Lord, nor any who go down into silence.'[36]

Judaism did hold the promise of the hereafter for every pious Jew. But it also always encouraged the struggle to improve life in this world, coupled with a determination not to accept the 'status quo' if existing conditions inhibited social progress. In this connection, it should be realized that Jewish communities became highly organized, not only for education but also for social welfare. The less fortunate – the widow, the orphan, and the sick – all became the responsibility of relevant local communities. Communal bodies looked after the various needs of their members and provided help for the needy, burial and, of course, education.

Social cohesion and mutual support were encouraged, and it was considered a sin for a Jew, however poor, to refuse to help a fellow Jew.

Education was also significant. Since the time of Ezra there has been an insistence in Jewish life on widespread literacy and constant practical religious study. Jews were not only taught to read the Hebrew Bible, and later the Talmud and its commentaries, but were also encouraged to use these books as a guide to daily living. Their content provided the justification for Jewish survival; a belief that it was the responsibility of the Jewish people to maintain the ethical monotheism of the Prophets. Judaism was never just a religion; it was a total way of life. On the other hand, it was this legal, ethical and social system which preserved the Jews united and conscious of their allegiance to their religious fellows, to their ancestors in the past and to their descendants in the future.

Throughout much of Jewish history, the value placed by Jews on learning was in sharp contrast with the attitude of outside society. This was particularly true in pre-modern times, when education was often restricted to the clergy and the vast majority of the population were illiterate peasants tied to a local lord who could barely read or write.

The Jewish stress on learning put it in very high esteem. It was not unusual, for example, for a Jewish man to spend his evening hours studying in the *yeshivah* (academy) or the synagogue after, or even before, returning home from a hard working day. Again, when arranging a marriage a family would seek a scholar for their daughter or the daughter of a scholar for their son. Learning was often appreciated more than economic success.

Another element was the family. In the family, the woman played a very important role. Although to modern observers her role may seem subservient , with no life of her own, her duty was to raise children, to maintain a proper Jewish home, and to enable her husband to continue his religious learning; yet she was always accorded respect both by law and custom.

The factors mentioned so far have mostly been positive. Many would claim, however, that it was the negative factor of anti-Semitism which, more than any other, was responsible for the survival of the Jewish people. In other words, continuing anti-Jewish pressure has kept the Jews together. Jean-Paul Sartre claimed that the Jews maintained their affiliation to their religious communities and Jewish consciousness only because they were always reminded of it by an anti-Semitic world. There have been, however, periods and places in which the Jews have not been subjected to oppression or attack. Yet during such periods the Jews did not assimilate, but created new centres for a creative and rich Jewish life.

Vital though each of the above factors may have been for the process of survival, there still had to be an underlying determination to resist either blandishments or threats to convert on the one hand, and oppression and anti-Semitism on the other. A basic conviction shared by the majority of Jews is the need for the continued separate and distinct existence of Judaism and the Jewish people – at no matter what cost to the individual.

Historians, rabbis and thinkers have provided a number of answers to the question: the feeling of being a 'chosen people', and the messianic hope, the Jewish religion and the purity of Jewish monotheism, the uniqueness of the Jewish spirit, an inborn and unique talent for survival, an ability for adaptation and for rebuilding national and religious centres beyond the original homeland, the ever-strong attachment to that original homeland, and other similar factors. It has not been our intention here to authenticate any of these explanatory theses, but rather to review the varied historical conditions of Jewish survival. The survival itself is a fact. The central role of religion until emancipation is also indisputable. But in the post-emancipation period, many Jewish movements and communities were non-religious altogether. Is there a valid explanation of Jewish survival or does it remain the Jewish enigma?

2 Jews in Islamic Lands

Jacob Lassner

An overview

During the seventh century CE, conquering Arab armies traversed the frontiers separating the Arabian Peninsula from the lands beyond. This action set in motion a complex historical process that was to lead to the creation of an Islamic state which rivalled the old Roman Empire in size. Within ten years, the Arab conquerors – at best a relatively small fighting force – managed to destroy various opposing armies in Palestine, Syria and Mesopotamia, and bring about the capitulation of Egypt. To the east, Arab forces crossed into Iraq[1] (then part of the Sasanian Empire[2]), decimated the Sasanian defenders and their allies, and obliged the Sasanian Emperor to retreat hastily. Within another decade, Arab armies had extended Muslim rule to North Africa and vast regions of Iran, while a Muslim naval force threatened Constantinople itself. So, by the second quarter of the eighth century the Abode of Islam extended from Central Asia to Spain (see Map 6).

At first the Arab victors forsook the great urban centres of the classical world. The conquerors of Ctesiphon, Antioch, Alexandria, Jerusalem and the like kept themselves at arm's length from the variegated life of these sophisticated and time-honoured cities. They chose instead to create settlements of their own – the garrison colonies of Fustat in Egypt, Ramleh in Palestine, Kairouan in North Africa, and Basrah and Kufah in Iraq. These settlements were soon infiltrated by non-Arab merchants and tradesmen, and thus cultural forces were introduced that ended the isolation of the Arabs and exposed them to the fantastically rich intellectual and artistic heritage of late antiquity. In due course this cultural mingling led to the descendants of the Arab conquerors becoming patrons of arts and letters themselves; it was they who preserved Greek science and philosophy through Arabic translations, and who also safeguarded numerous less well-known cultural artifacts from ill-defined regions to the east. The evolving Islamic civilization enjoyed a material culture comparable to that of Rome, and it displayed an intellectual vitality that made it a cultural bridge from the ancient world to the Renaissance.

Along the route of the Arab conquests were the venerable Jewish communities of Babylonia, ancient Palestine,[3] the Levant and Egypt, as well as many lesser settlements of Jews. So the vast majority of world Jewry now came under Muslim rule, and the Jews found their condition much altered by the tide of historical events. Jewish society became increasingly urbanized and showed remarkable adaptation to the economic transformations of the times. As a result the Jews were able to contribute much to the expanding world economy. They also played a key role in the flourishing intellectual life of the day; they mastered the Arabic language and served as an important, if not unique, conduit in transmitting Islamic culture to the Latin West. Indeed, there is much in the Jewish civilization of modern times that was forged in the heyday of Islam. As one scholar observed: 'The Babylonian Talmud gradually became the constitutional foundation of Diaspora Judaism; the synagogue service and the prayerbook text took on their familiar form; Jewish theology was systematized; Jewish law codified; and Hebrew language and litera-ture underwent [their] greatest revival prior to [their] rebirth in modern times'.[4] Many of these achievements reflect the influence of Islamic scholarship and literary advances, as well as a spirit of free inquiry which was nourished under Muslim rule.

In recent years, considerable scholarly interest has been devoted to what is sometimes termed 'Judeo-Islamic civilization';[5] a new coterie of scholars, acquainted with both Islamic and Jewish sources, have focused attention on one of the most fascinating and important chapters in the long and checkered history of the Jews.

Some terms defined

In speaking of 'Islam', Western scholars are using a specific term that denotes adherence to the religion of the Prophet Muhammad by surrender, submission or resignation to God. The word 'islam' is itself a verbal noun from the Arabic 'aslama' which basically means 'to give up or deliver something to someone'. The active participle of that verb is 'muslim', and in a religious context a Muslim is one who gives up or delivers him or herself to God.[6] All of these usages are to be found in the public utterances of the Prophet Muhammad, which are enshrined in the Quran, the book that Muslims regard as revealed scripture. Not surprisingly, the passages of the Quran that encompass these terms have given rise to considerable theological discussion and exegesis. In the Muslim commentaries that explain and interpret the text of the Quran, the term 'islam' is invested with a meaning that transcends the act of doing something and has become synonymous with a system of beliefs and practices, thus denoting a formal religion (din). In that sense, 'islam' becomes 'Islam', and 'muslim' takes on the meaning of 'Muslim'.

As regards the adjective, 'Islamic' relates to 'Islam', broadly speaking, as 'Judaic' relates to 'Judaism'. In a narrow, formal sense, 'Islamic' is used to describe that which pertains directly to the religion of Islam or to the dominions of Muslim rulers. More generally, the adjective 'Islamic' is applied to the culture and civili-zation that evolved under the aegis of Muslim rule. It may also be applied to the culture and civilization of lands where there is a significant population of Muslims, and it is this last use of 'Islamic' that causes confusion. How, for instance, would one describe the culture of the various religious minorities within the Islamic world, the Jews among them?

In an effort to be more precise, some Western scholars have adopted a term coined in the 1970s: by analogy with 'Christendom' they speak of 'Islamdom'. This term refers to the lands and civilization of the hegemonic culture, but it also embraces the cultural and social artifacts of the various subject peoples.[7] The new terminology includes the adjective 'Islamicate', a term that has no analogue but which is intended to describe something that is not necessarily derived from Islam though is part of the shared milieu. As a rule, scholars have tended to retain the older convention and so use the word 'Islamic', however imprecise the term. Some scholars prefer to use 'Muslim' as an adjective when referring specifically to 'Islam', and 'Islamic' when referring to a broader cultural context; it is this usage that is followed here.

It is important to be aware of other terms that still find currency in Western literature on Islam: 'Muhammadan' or 'Mohammedan' is sometimes used to mean 'Muslim' or 'Islamic' and, by extension, 'Mohammedanism' is used in place of 'Islam': the analogue here is the derivation of 'Christian' and 'Christianity' from 'Christ'. However, the formulation is quite erroneous and offensive to Muslims as it imputes to Muhammad a divine stature that they themselves deny to him, and indeed deny to Christ as well. This convention, which enjoyed wide use in the nineteenth century, is used less and less and is gradually being replaced by the preferred terminology of 'Muslim' (or 'Moslem' which is the anglicized version), 'Islamic' and 'Islam'.

The rise of Islam

The proponents of Islam adhere to the beliefs and practices advanced by the Prophet Muhammad and his followers. The Prophet was born around the year 570 CE in Mecca, a town in western Arabia (see Map 6). Mecca had originally developed as the site of a shrine, but by the time of Muhammad it had become a centre of commerce and trade. In a few generations the main inhabitants of Mecca – the Prophet's tribe, the Quraysh – were transformed from a nomadic clan into sophisticated entrepreneurs. Muhammad himself reputedly escorted caravans to Syria, and this would have given him access to the heartland of the monotheist religions, Judaism and Christianity. The rapid changes in Mecca occasioned new political forms and social behaviour. Although the Meccans were, on the whole, content with their lot, a certain spiritual malaise seems to have affected some of the Quraysh as traditional tribal values which stressed interdependence and collective responsibility clashed with a new emphasis on the individual and the smaller family unit. It was against the background of these changes that Muhammad began his mission in about 610 CE.

The initial phase of the Prophet's activity revolved around his preaching in Mecca and lasted until 622 CE. Over the years in Mecca it became increasingly clear that the Prophet would not succeed in converting his kinsmen to his mono-theist faith. On religious matters his views were in conflict with those of his fellow

Quraysh who had much invested in their pagan sanctuary and its pilgrimage – the pilgrimage being an event of considerable economic and political importance to the Quraysh. Furthermore, complex political realities isolated Muhammad and his small following. So, for the group to survive, let alone prosper, a move to a new location was judged necessary.

After serious negotiations, Muhammad and his followers migrated to Medina in 622 CE – an event known in Arabic as the *Hijrah*. This move was not the flight depicted in some Western textbooks: it was, rather, a migration that followed at least two series of complex negotiations, the details of which still remain unclear. However, the situation in Medina at the time, which was a key factor, is better known.

Medina was an oasis settlement with a diverse population. Its inhabitants consisted of the three major Jewish tribes that had originally settled the area, namely the Nadir, the Qurayzah and the Qaynuqa, as well as various scattered smaller groups of Jews, and the Aws and the Khazraj – Arab tribesmen who had migrated into the vacant lands of Medina, initially as the clients of the Jews. The origins of the Jewish tribes in Medina (and of the other Jews of Arabia) are obscure; it is not even clear whether they were Jewish settlers or indigenous Arab tribesmen who had been converted to Judaism. They may have been descended from Jews who had come to the Arabian Peninsula either as a result of the exiles after the destruction of the Temples, or as refugees from the Hadrianic persecutions.

Whatever their origins, the Jewish tribes were well established in Medina: the Nadir and the Qurayzah were noted for their advanced techniques of agriculture and had fertile plantations, mainly of dates, while the Qaynuqa were famous as goldsmiths. These tribes also held the majority of the forts in the oasis of Medina and could, if called upon, each mobilize several hundred fighting men. Moreover, the Jewish tribes, at times at odds with one another, were linked with various Arab tribesmen by informal contractual arrangements.

In the early seventh century, Medina was wracked by serious conflict that completely disrupted the rhythm of economic life. All the tribal units, the Jews included, became involved in fighting. There was an uneasy truce, and Muhammad came to Medina in 622 CE at the invitation of the Aws and the Khazraj, who sought an arbitrator for their own dispute which, of necessity, had involved their Jewish allies. Early in his stay, Muhammad drew up a covenant that established his primacy as the arbitrator of all internal disputes in Medina; the covenant also defined the obligations of the inhabitants, including the Jews, and subjected them to some measure of political control. Even before his arrival in Medina, Muhammad had won adherents among the Aws and the Khazraj. Once he was in Medina his following grew as did his political power. Within five years he had consolidated his position locally, exiled or killed his enemies (and potential enemies) and taken to the field against the Meccans.

The move to Medina marked a dramatic change in the character of Muhammad's activities and of his message. In Mecca he was without marked influence or following. In Medina he stood at the head of a distinct Muslim community that attracted religious adherents and political clients. His pronouncements in Mecca were characterized by abstract religious pleadings, sprinkled with references to biblical themes concerning those who arrogantly contented themselves with material gain; in addition, there were warnings of a terrifying day of judgement for those who failed to recognize Allah, the one true God. In Medina the Prophet's pronouncements were much longer and were increasingly about practical matters: the internal governance of the Muslim community, the efforts to consolidate Muslim influence over the entire population of Medina, and the drive to dislodge the Meccans and Mecca as the linchpins of political and economic influence in western Arabia. In Mecca, Muhammad was a preacher; in Medina he also became a conqueror and a statesman. By 630 CE the Prophet felt his position was sufficiently strong for him to confront the Meccans in Mecca itself, and he managed to force their capitulation without conflict. By the time of his death two years later, Islam had become the dominant force in the entire Arabian Peninsula – a triumph accomplished at the expense of the Jews of Medina and of other Jews in north-western Arabia, for Muhammad had defeated all the major Jewish tribes of the region and made them accept degrading conditions of surrender.

The development of Islamic attitudes towards the Jews

The *Hijrah*, a watershed in the Prophet's career, had brought Muhammad into direct and sustained contact with the local Jewish tribes of Medina and its environs. At first, Muhammad made direct overtures to his fellow monotheists. Asserting that the Jews and his followers had a common heritage, Muhammad established a clearly marked place for the Jewish tribes in the political affairs of his new home. He also adopted the fast of the Jewish Day of Atonement (Yom Kippur), fixed the orientation of prayer towards Jerusalem, and stressed a number of other practices familiar to Jews. Some of these practices may have been adopted by him even before he came to Medina.

Be that as it may, the Jews, who had initially cooperated with Muhammad the political leader, rejected his spiritual guidance and his claims to prophethood. With a time-honoured religious tradition of their own, they remained loyal to their faith and presumably steadfast in their religious observance. That can be inferred from Muhammad's later contentious attitude towards them.

For the Jews, some aspects of Muhammad's teachings would have been perplexing. His stories of biblical personalities and events must have seemed incongruous to those Jews who were familiar with the traditional Jewish sources: there are, for instance, substantive differences between the Quran's treatment of the ancient Israelites and the versions in biblical and post-biblical Jewish literature. In addition, certain elements of Muslim practice (for example, the consumption of meat from horses and camels) would have been at odds with the dictates of Jewish law, making the Prophet's overtures even more problematic.

The crisis in relations occasioned by the Jews' rejection of Muhammad's teachings is reflected in the Quranic texts from the Medina period. Invoking images of Moses and the Israelites, Muhammad compared the Jews of his day to the stiff-necked, wayward followers of Moses. At the same time, he claimed that he was linked to Moses and the other Israelite prophets of the past in a line of divine messengers. In theory, Islam had an ancient history – it was not just the creation of an Arabian prophet of the seventh century, as Westerners maintain. For Muslims, Muhammad's mission was the culmination of many such missions: Muhammad was the last or 'Seal' of God's prophets, a messenger preceded by a number of well-known figures. Among these earlier Muslim prophets were figures who appear in the Hebrew Bible and the New Testament and in rabbinic and patristic sources: they included the likes of Moses and Jesus, Solomon and David, Ezekiel (see Plate 2), Jonah, John the Baptist, Job and others, though in the Quran and its commentaries the names are Arabicized and the descriptions of people and events are different from those in more familiar texts. These earlier figures received revelations and were, each in turn, enjoined to reveal the future coming of Muhammad to their followers. So, if the Jews rejected Muhammad's message, it was not for lack of having been informed of its legitimacy – their own scriptures contain many references to the emergence of God's quintessential messenger.

From a Muslim perspective, any dissonance claimed by the Jews between their scriptures and God's word as revealed to Muhammad sprang from falsification and distortion on the part of the Jews. Jewish recalcitrance was, therefore, rooted in a rejection of their very own teaching. Put differently, to deny Muhammad, as the

Jews in traditional attire are told of the coming of Muhammad, the 'Lord and Seal of the Prophets', by an aged Jewish sage in Damascus. From a sixteenth-century Turkish manuscript. As the scene signifies, the interaction of the monotheistic faiths was a dominant theological preoccupation of the period.

Jews did, was to deny Moses and all the monotheist prophets of the past who had heralded the Muslim prophet and his future calling. Those Jews who rejected Muhammad were even likened to the recalcitrant Israelites who had earlier rejected Moses.

In theory, similar criticisms could be levelled against the Christians and, in fact, they were. The Quran admonishes Christians for false theological beliefs, principally belief in the Holy Trinity which was seen as compromising the oneness of God. It is, however, the Jews who bear the brunt of Muslim criticism, for unlike the Christians, who are blamed only for theological error, the Jews resisted Muhammad's prophethood and also played a central role in the political arena at the time of the birth of Islam. According to Muslim tradition, the Jews did not support the Prophet in his campaigns. Worse yet, there are accusations that the Jewish Qurayzah tribe actively assisted Muhammad's enemies who were led by his kinsmen, the Quraysh. At the very least, the Qurayzah could be accused of holding talks with the opponents of Islam. It is likely that they also supplied the Quraysh and their allies with food. Furthermore, there is evidence of links between the Jewish tribes of Medina and the so-called *munafiqun* or hypocrites, backsliders who had accepted Islam but were grudging in acknowledging the political authority of the Prophet. This association with Muhammad's opponents and, above all, with his most dangerous enemies represented a breach of faith on the part of the Jews and earned for them, and their co-religionists everywhere, an unshakable reputation for treachery.

In response to the religious and political rejection by the Jews, Muhammad changed the orientation of prayer to Mecca, made the fast of the Day of Atonement secondary to the month-long fast of Ramadan, and even initiated physical attacks upon the Jews. In 624 CE the fortresses of the Jewish Qaynuqa tribe were besieged after an alleged prank led to bloodshed. The Qaynuqa surrendered and were forced into exile, leaving behind their tools and non-movable property. The following year, the Nadir tribe suffered the same fate. Finally, the Qurayzah were besieged and, after an unconditional surrender, all their men were executed. The former Jewish lands were then settled by the growing community of Muslims, which had developed in Medina since the *Hijrah*. In 628 CE, Muhammad turned his attention to the Jewish oasis of Khaybar, where many of the Medinese exiles had gone, and after fierce fighting it succumbed to Muslim control. With the defeat of the Jews at Khaybar, the smaller Jewish settlements all became subservient to Muslim rule and the Jews ceased to be a political factor in Islamic lands until the twentieth century.

The expanding Islamic world and the status of the Jews: 632–1250 CE

Following the death of the Prophet in 632 CE, the entire Arabian Peninsula was plunged into conflict. The end of this conflict saw the consolidation of Muslim control in Arabia and the expansion of Islam beyond the Arabian borders. Leadership of the Muslim community now rested with Muhammad's successors. The succession, at times hotly contested, gave rise to a line of leaders, which stretched through the Middle Ages. They adopted the title 'Commander of the Faithful', though the term 'caliph' (from *khalifah*, the Arabic for 'successor') came to be widely used. Generally recognized as the successor to the authority of the Prophet but without a prophetic function (Muhammad having been the last of the Prophets), the caliph wielded enormous power. However, he did not usually enjoy the same right as Muhammad to formulate law and doctrine. That right belonged to a body of religious scholars who provided spiritual guidance. So the caliph was essentially a political leader – the ruler of the Islamic domain.

The first four caliphs were drawn from Muhammad's immediate circle and were, in fact, related to him (two of his fathers-in-law and two sons-in-law); they held office over the period 632–661 CE and were based in the Prophet's city, Medina. These caliphs are characterized in Muslim sources as the righteous or rightly-guided caliphs, and it was they who laid the early foundations of the administrative and judicial structure of the Muslim community. They also success-fully carried forward the policy of expanding Islam into new territories (see Map 6), thus establishing the groundwork for a vast Islamic empire.

However, in 661 CE, in the wake of growing internecine strife which culmi-nated in armed confrontation, the position of caliph was appropriated by a member of the Umayyad family – a branch of the Quraysh that had initially opposed Muhammad. The new caliph was a former governor of Syria and was backed by a highly disciplined Syrian army. This transfer of power marked the start of the Umayyad dynasty of caliphs. Syria was their powerbase and from their capital, Damascus, they presided over the ever-expanding Islamic domain for nearly a hundred years until ousted by Muhammad's kinsmen, the Abbasids, in 750 CE.

The Umayyad regime resonated to Arab tribal sensibilities; indeed, the organi-zational structure of the Islamic state under the Umayyads was essentially tribal in character. A cohesive factor was the commitment to military conquest: the regime geared itself accordingly, and while the Umayyads held sway, Muslim forces conquered territory from eastern Iran to North Africa and Spain (see Map 6). So, within a century of the Prophet's death, a vast swathe of the then-known world had come under Islam, and the venerable Jewish communities of Babylonia, ancient Palestine, the Levant, Egypt, North Africa and Spain, which all lay in the path of the conquests, found themselves under Muslim rule.

As the Muslims were only a minority in their vast dominions, they introduced various regulations for dealing with the local populace. What then was the position of the Jews under Muslim rule? In the Quran, the Jews, along with the Christians and others who possess a divinely revealed scripture, are defined as 'People of the Book'. In the Islamic state those in this favoured category of non-believers were tolerated and were not compelled to accept Islam; moreover, they were afforded a special protected status provided they acknowledged the supremacy of Islamic rule, obeyed an assortment of regulations and paid a capitation tax called the *jizyah*. The Quran itself, while recognizing that belief cannot be imposed, stipulates that non-believers should be humbled bearers of tribute, hence the *jizyah*.

On account of their status, the Jews and other People of the Book were referred to as *dhimmis* (the protected). Certain important rights were safeguarded for them, notably religious freedom was assured and the security of life and property were guaranteed. Yet they were also subject to numerous restrictions which, along with the *jizyah*, were part of the price paid for protection.

Much of the discriminatory legislation imposed on the Jews and other *dhimmis* was set out in the so-called Covenant of Umar, named after Umar, the second caliph, who held office from 634 to 644 CE. Among the conditions listed, *dhimmis* were required to wear distinctive clothing and not imitate Muslim fashions. Furthermore, they were not permitted to use saddles or carry arms, and they had to show particular deference when Muslims approached. *Dhimmis* were even obliged to open their gates to Muslim strangers and to provide them with food and lodging for up to three days, but were bound to deny shelter to the enemies of Islam. They were forbidden to offer instruction in the Quran and were prohibited from holding public religious celebrations; ceremonies such as funerals had to be marked by quiet decorum and conducted away from Muslim view. There were also restrictions on building new religious edifices and on restoring older religious structures that had fallen into ruin or were located in Muslim quarters. In addition, non-Muslims were not allowed to employ Muslims, and government service was closed to non-believers. Many other discriminatory practices were in evidence. Muslim law gave special advantages to Muslims in economic transactions, while in litigation involving *dhimmis* and Muslims, testimony was weighted towards the Muslim. Punishments were also weighted differently, and in the legal system generally, there were numerous minor imbalances.

There was, however, a reverse side to this coin. Although Muslim jurists devoted considerable attention to the Covenant of Umar and other legislation, the edicts were rarely invoked. When invoked they were, more often than not, applied with moderation. On the whole, Jewish sources originating in the Islamic world are free of references to the physical degradation of the Jews, whereas such references are all too common in the record of the Jewish communities of Christendom. Despite lingering memories of Muhammad's conflicts with the Jews, the notion of the recalcitrant Jew did not vex Muslim religious leaders as it did the Christian theologians of the West: the Muslim view of Jews and Judaism was not so directly or heavily invested with anti-Jewish concerns as was the theology of the Church. It was accepted that by legal right the Jews were, for all time, a distinct and protected community and were entitled to share a homeland with their Muslim neighbours.

Nevertheless, the memory of active Jewish opposition to Muhammad was indelibly etched in the historical consciousness of Muslim peoples and could not be dismissed. Even at times when the Muslim authorities were most benign in their treatment of the Jews, the constant repetition of anti-Jewish traditions must have had a subliminal effect on Muslim attitudes. The retelling of these popular traditions in the mosques and in the streets was bound to have a more potent effect than the dry fare of formal theological polemics. In this way the popular accounts helped to create a mind set that gave rise to rigid and intolerant attitudes whenever the self-confidence of Muslim society was shaken, either by internal crisis or by outside forces that seemingly threatened the equilibrium of traditional Islamic life.

In times of tension, religion often became a weapon to be turned against certain elements of society, including its minorities, in order to preserve the religious foundations of Islam and its political and social structures. Such a reaction was precipitated by the Crusades, by the penetration of Western political influence and culture, and more recently by the rise of the State of Israel.

The organization of the Jewish community in Islamic lands in the medieval period

In the lands conquered by the Arabs, the far-flung Jewish communities adjusted more easily to Muslim rule than did the Christians: the Jews had long been accustomed to minority status, whereas the Christians were the absolute majority in most regions and had held power prior to the advent of Islam. Past experience had taught the Jews the realities of living in dispersion without a territory of their own. Guided by pragmatism, they simply adapted to the latest political upheavals and carefully maintained a low profile. In light of a long history of failed rebellions and difficult experiences under so many previous regimes, stability seemed preferable to activism.

Everywhere that the Muslims declared their sovereignty, the Jews co-operated and behaved according to well-defined and mutually accepted rules. Jewish communal institutions were, therefore, geared not only to internal concerns but to negotiating with the dominant political authority. Foremost among the spokesmen for the Jews under Muslim rule was the exilarch (*resh galutha*), a hereditary Jewish leader based in Babylonia. In theory, the exilarch could trace his descent back to King David, a claim that went uncontested, so the institution continued, for the most part without interruption, until the eleventh century. The exilarch had been the representative of the Jewish community to the pre-Islamic Sasanian authorities, and after the advent of Islam he simply carried on as before – a prince among public servants, able to intervene at the highest levels on behalf of his flock.

As the intermediary between the government and the Jews, the exilarch was responsible for collecting the taxes levied against his brethren. Within the Jewish community he exercised great power. He was in charge of judicial appointments and was the supreme judge for all civil and criminal cases involving Jews; he could even issue writs of excommunication. The exilarch was also responsible for the internal security of his community and, in addition, was invested with the authority of the Islamic *muhtasib*, an official who was charged with licensing commerce, regulating weights and measures and, more generally, enforcing public morality; in this role the exilarch could initiate fines, imprisonments and floggings.

This concentration of power in the hands of a public official, moreover a hereditary one, could and did lead to excesses. There are reports of intrigues and corruption, as well as of disputes with the rabbinical authorities based in the great Babylonian centres of Jewish learning at Sura and Pumbeditha. A major issue was the authority to appoint judges and, related to that, misuse of the courts. Significantly, there are documents which indicate that, in certain circumstances, Jews preferred to take their disputes to Muslim judges rather than have them adjudicated by Jewish officials.

In the middle of the eighth century there was a major change in power in the Islamic world. The Umayyad dynasty, which had held the caliphate for nearly a hundred years, was beset by mounting insurrection and tribal strife. After a military struggle, the Umayyads were overthrown in 750 CE by the Abbasids, who were descendants of Muhammad's uncle, Abbas, and who, after half a century of clandestine revolutionary activity, had surfaced in Iraq, supported by a large tribal army from Iran. Thus the Abbasid dynasty of caliphs came to power, and from their newly founded capital, Baghdad, they created a sophisticated state on truly imperial lines, stretching from Central Asia to North Africa. However, by the middle of the ninth century, local petty dynastics, nominally under Abbasid rule, had begun to sap the vitality of the centralized regime. In time, rival caliphates were established – by the Fatimids in Egypt and North Africa, and by an Umayyad survivor in Spain. But the demise of Abbasid power was gradual, and the Abbasid caliphate persisted until 1258 when the Mongols sacked Baghdad and murdered the caliph.

The Abbasids were more universal in outlook and less preoccupied with tribal sensibilities than their predecessors, the Umayyads. Furthermore, they seem to have had enlightened economic views which brought prosperity and growing urbanization. Consequently, there was greater freedom of movement, and Jewish communities previously isolated from one another became more closely linked. The establishment of a highly centralized regime in Iraq under the Abbasids therefore strengthened the influence of the great Babylonian academies of Jewish learning, and by the ninth century, Jewish leadership in the Muslim world was increasingly represented by the geonim, the heads of these academies. Emissaries from the geonim took up residence in a wide variety of locations, serving as legal experts, community leaders and also as fundraisers for the academies that trained them. And so the centres of Jewish learning, with their emphasis on the study of Jewish law, continued to thrive and exert influence.

Jewish law encompassed every aspect of life and was the cement that held the world Jewish community together and gave it an identity. The fact that geonim and their students were immersed in the study of the law meant that they were able to provide guidance and leadership in all areas of Jewish life – their knowledge was not some arcane irrelevance. The leadership of the geonim rested on claims that they had inherited the interpretive legitimacy of a chain of authorities going back to Moses himself. The most recent links in that chain were their rabbinic predecessors who had been responsible for compiling the Talmud, the great compendium of Jewish legal materials from antiquity. In effect, the Babylonian academies supplied the far-flung Jewish communities with licensed authorities who could interpret the law. Questions that required further study were forwarded to the geonim, who considered the issues and then responded in writing. In this way a body of literature known as *responsa* was built up – it is concerned with every aspect of Jewish law and ritual, and is a mine of information on daily life.

Not all Jews followed the dictates of the geonim. Small breakaway groups influenced by Islamic sectarians established themselves in the far regions of the Abbasid caliphate, notably in eastern Iran. Little is known of these Jews; they seem to disappear from history almost as soon as they appear. More significant was the

Karaite schism of the ninth and tenth centuries. The Karaite movement began in the latter half of the eighth century when Anan ben David, an ascetic Babylonian sage, propagated views that rejected the Oral Law – the very foundation of rabbinic Judaism. Instead, he based all authority on the text of the Hebrew Bible alone. As a result of these heretical tendencies he was passed over as a candidate for exilarch. Anan ben David would appear to have had only a few followers, known as Ananites, but in the next century his general views were embraced by a more substantial number of co-religionists.

At first, Karaism lacked homogeneity, and the Karaites did not have a uniform view or leadership. On the fringes there were various Karaite sects strongly influenced by Islamic eschatology. These groups soon splintered and disappeared as the Karaite movement consolidated its following and established a more uniform and rigorously intellectual doctrine, although disagreements remained among its leading theoreticians.

At the heart of Karaism was the rejection of rabbinic principles of interpretation and authority, with free and individual study of the scripture being substituted. The Karaite analysis of texts was strongly influenced by intellectual trends among Muslim thinkers. Brilliant Karaite scholars like Benjamin al-Nehawandi (died c. 860 CE) possessed a formidable intellectual arsenal drawn from the Jewish and Muslim traditions, and thus armed they engaged the traditionalist followers of rabbinic Judaism or rabbinism, whom the Karaites referred to as Rabbinites. The leading Rabbinite authorities were then forced to do battle on their adversaries' terms.

Karaite communities spread far and wide, but by the eleventh century the movement was fading in the lands of Islam. By then it had charted a new path that took it to the Byzantine Empire and later to Europe. Only a small trace of Karaism remains today, for the very success of the Karaites in attracting practising Jews led to the ultimate failure of the movement. When it came to actual observance, many Karaites could not bring themselves to abandon the laws and customs of rabbinic Judaism: given that inconsistency, Karaism was destined to fail. The Karaites, in effect, betrayed their own principles and created only confusion by accepting much of rabbinic Judaism as part of religious practice while rejecting it in a theoretical context. Nevertheless, the legacy of the Karaites was far-reaching. Forced to engage their rivals, the Rabbinites became better acquainted with the intellectual trends of the Islamic milieu and incorporated some aspects into Rabbinite Jewish discourse. In this respect, the Karaite schism might be seen as a force that rejuvenated Judaism.

In the tenth century, as Abbasid power waned, the authority of both the exilarch and the Babylonian geonim over the Jewish communities in Islamic lands began to be seriously eroded. The Abbasid caliphate faced increasing challenges and relinquished effective control over many parts of the Islamic world; various local dynasts then assumed autonomy for their regions or even declared full independence, and regional centres of power developed. At the same time the economy of Iraq declined, so large numbers of Jews migrated in search of new opportunities. With Jews ever more dispersed and with the loosening of centralized Islamic rule,

A Karaite manuscript of the tenth century, written in Hebrew but with Arabic characters, highlighting the close cultural connections between Arabs and Jews at the time. It is particularly interesting that the vowel points of Hebrew have been retained.

Jewish leadership also became devolved. The centrally located exilarch in Baghdad was slowly displaced by new, more locally based Jewish communal leaders known as 'princes' (*nasi* or *nagid* in Hebrew). The prince was installed by the local ruler to serve as the representative of the Jews of the region – a role akin to that of the exilarch. Given the dispersion of the Jews, there were princes in such diverse places as Spain, North Africa, Egypt and the Yemen.

The influence of the Babylonian academies also decreased as the Jewish communities in the various territories sought to develop their own hierarchies and institutional structures. Local rabbinical academies were established, independent of the institutions in Sura and Pumbeditha. So it was that in Egypt under Fatimid rule in the tenth century the highest Jewish legal authority was a representative of the Palestinian academy, while in North Africa there was not just one major Jewish institution of higher learning, but two.

Jewish economic and social activity in the medieval Islamic world

The Arab conquests and the later creation of an Islamic empire under the Umayyads and then under the Abbasids effected many changes in the economic life of medieval Near-Eastern Jewry. The early conquerors settled in military encampments that soon attracted a host of non-Arabs drawn from the surrounding towns and villages. Merchants, artisans, craftsmen and unskilled casual labourers alike were attracted to the evolving garrison towns which afforded ample opportunities for material gain.

The establishment of the great Abbasid capital at Baghdad in 750 CE and the founding of a second imperial city at Samarra the following century completely changed the demographic profile of medieval Iraq (which included the lands of ancient Babylonia, still the centre of world Jewry). The very construction of these cities, each covering more than twenty square miles, required an immense labour force, as well as merchants and artisans to provide supplies and services. The urban population of Baghdad, although difficult to estimate, may have been upwards of half a million people in the latter half of the eighth century when the city was in its heyday.

With such unprecedented growth, distinctions between the urban and the rural became blurred. There is reason to believe that the great urban centres of the Islamic empire had more in common with the metropolitan areas of modern times than we are wont to imagine. Cities such as Baghdad and Fustat (now Cairo) were more akin to the sprawling urban corridors of today than to the small, tightly-knit provincial towns of antiquity and the Middle Ages. Generally speaking, the Muslim rulers encouraged and invested in urban development, promoted commerce and trade, and taxed heavily the new sources of wealth whose creation they openly supported.

Jews previously engaged in agriculture and traditional crafts must have been drawn from small towns and villages to the growing urban environment, not only in Iraq but throughout the Islamic world. In all likelihood, whole areas of the countryside were denuded of population as streams of migrants poured into the towns and cities. The two great capitals of the Abbasids – Baghdad and Samarra – alone accounted for almost 90% of all settlement in central Iraq.

When economic conditions in Iraq deteriorated in the tenth century, many Jews moved to new locations, and so the great Babylonian Jewish community provided immigrants to Egypt, North Africa and more distant lands. That path was made easier by the tolerance of the Fatimid caliphs who presided over North Africa and, later, Egypt, holding power from 909 to 1171 CE. Their dynasty having been founded by a Shiite refugee from Iraq, the Fatimids claimed descent from Fatimah and Ali, the daughter and son-in-law of Muhammad. They had achieved supremacy with the support of various Berber tribesmen, dislodging the Abbasids from control of the lands to the south of the Mediterranean. The early Fatimids were on the whole extremely tolerant of religious minorities and ran a prosperous state. This tolerance was reflected in the appointment of Jews to the Fatimid court in Cairo and the relaxation of discriminatory tariffs against Jews. Interestingly, Ubaydallah al-Mahdi, the first of the Fatimid rulers, was accused by his opponents of being Jewish, a canard that was used on occasion to denigrate the legitimacy of Shiite claimants to rule.

Under the successive Islamic regimes the Jews increasingly established their pre-eminence in commerce and trade. Although business was not the archetypal Jewish profession it was a metier to which the Jews readily adapted, and with their communities dispersed throughout the Islamic world they were ideally placed to create an effective commercial network.

By the ninth century, a vigorous Jewish merchant class had developed and was playing a significant role in international trade. The merchants, called Radhanites after a district in the vicinity of Baghdad, traded from China to the Iberian Peninsula, plying both land and sea. They might sail to India and China, or go overland via Iran; with them they would take merchandize such as damask and furs and other luxury goods, as well as swords from the workshops of the renowned Arab armourers. The Radhanites would return from the East with spices, camphor and other wares. Then, from Mediterranean or Black Sea ports, they would set off overland, even penetrating to the Khazar Kingdom and the Kingdom of the Franks, going as far as the Frankish capital, Aachen. The Radhanites were unusual in that their trading activities encompassed Europe as well as the East. Being part of a minority without military or political power, and with their magnificent linguistic skills (it seems that they mastered not only Arabic and Persian, but also the languages of the Byzantines, Franks, Iberians and Slavs), they no doubt had access to places and individuals beyond the reach of European Christians and Near-Eastern Muslims. However, by the tenth century, traders from the merchant republics of the Italian city-states had displaced the Jewish Radhanites from many places. By then, the economic transformation of Near-Eastern Jewry into a commercial and artisan class was all but complete.

The scope of Jewish commercial activity is revealed in a remarkable treasure trove of documents that came to light in the nineteenth century. Hundreds of thousands of manuscripts and fragments of manuscripts, mostly dating from between the tenth and thirteenth centuries, were discovered in the *geniza* of the old synagogue of Fustat in Egypt. In general a *geniza* was a storeroom for obsolete texts and artifacts that bore the name of God; under Jewish law, such items could not be destroyed. The collection of materials found in Fustat has come to be called the Geniza (or, more precisely, the Cairo Geniza from the modern name for Fustat). It is now being mined by an increasing number of scholars, as it provides a remarkable window on the private and public lives of Jews of the period. In personal correspondence, court records, the paperwork of commercial transactions, and the miscellaneous 'laundry lists' of daily life, the Geniza reveals the workings of a medieval Mediterranean society composed of Muslims, Christians and Jews.

From the Geniza one learns of Jewish entrepreneurs who fitted out cargo ships and even owned what were, in effect, long-distance haulage and shipping companies. The Geniza also furnishes details of the voyages and activities of Jewish merchants. It seems that they would usually travel with companions and would act as agents for those providing capital for the venture – given the risks, few would undertake a voyage without financial partners. In many cases the merchants would take with them orders and letters from business associates, so even modest entrepreneurs were given access to long-distance trade.

The Geniza shows that business relationships were often family affairs as wandering Jews took wives in distant places, thereby extending and consolidating their networks for commercial activities. Merchants also established their own native synagogues and inns among the Jewish communities that dotted the trade routes. Moreover, in many waystations they had non-Jewish intermediaries who knew the local customs and language and could successfully intervene with the local

The riches of the Cairo Geniza. The discovery in 1896 of a huge cache of manuscripts, that had been practically undisturbed for 900 years in the storeroom of the Fustat synagogue, has transformed our understanding of Jewish history. The photograph shows the great Semitic scholar, Solomon Schechter, surrounded by the 100,000 fragments that he had shipped to Cambridge for further study.

authorities or even ransom the merchants should they be taken captive. These agents often owned warehouses in which the merchants stored goods; they also served as emergency bankers and held letters and commercial documents. When Jewish clients were shipwrecked or died while travelling, the agents would look after their assets. Agency was not infrequently transmitted from father to son, and this strengthened the sense of trust between business associates. Overall, the increased travel which was made possible and indeed encouraged by the Muslim authorities had the effect of shrinking the Jewish world and creating a greater sense of Jewish unity and self-confidence – factors which are reflected in the sophisticated mercantile operations detailed in the records of the Geniza.

There were literally hundreds of professions in which Jews were involved according to the Geniza. Certain branches of trade and commerce were heavily populated with Jews: in particular, they were tanners, goldsmiths, silversmiths, jewellery craftsmen, and manufacturers of metal vessels and implements. Jewish traders were prominent in dealing in metals, primarily exporting copper and lead and importing iron and steel. They also handled much of the trade in pearls and coral, and dealt in a wide range of other commodities, including spices and medicinal herbs. There were hardly any areas of medieval commerce in which Jews did not engage.

The picture that emerges from the material in the Geniza is supported by other historical sources. For instance, there is evidence that the Jews were particularly well represented in banking in the mercantile centres of the Islamic world, at times serving as silent partners for those (such as Muslims and Christians) who were prohibited by law from collecting interest. It should be emphasized that banking was not just a matter of moneylending. First and foremost, a banker acted as a clearinghouse for payments and as a moneychanger: diverse currencies were in circulation, so coins had to be weighed and their fitness assessed – a task demanding great expertise. In general, banking involved complex business procedures at which Jews learned to excel.

In the tenth century a number of Christian and Jewish bankers were employed at the court of the Abbasid caliphs in Baghdad. Two of them, Joseph ben Phineas and Aaron ben Amram, are repeatedly mentioned in contemporary sources where they are described as the bankers of the province of Ahwaz and also as the bankers of the court. The two, who like many businessmen seem to have formed a joint company, were entrusted with managing the personal fortunes of local officials who feared that their funds might be lost in one of the periodic state confiscations. At the time it was common for those in positions of power to have money invested with private bankers. The Abbasid caliph himself made use of Ben Phineas and Ben Amram to obtain credit for the state. Since the employment of Jews in an administrative capacity was expressly forbidden by the Covenant of Umar, a special edict was required to give formal legitimacy to their service. One might ask to what extent the activities of these two Iraqi Jewish bankers had parallels elsewhere in the Islamic world. Interestingly, the tenth-century Muslim geographer, al-Muqaddasi, reported that most of the bankers and moneychangers in Egypt were Jews. However, the broad picture of Jewish involvement in finance has yet to be fully researched.

The extraordinary documents of the Geniza, along with the geonic *responsa* and other contemporary materials, also provide a detailed picture of the social organization of the Jewish community. Whereas the Talmud, when it addresses legal matters, is largely concerned with jurisprudence, the Geniza contains a vast number of actual court records. Marriage contracts are highly informative; descriptions of bridal dowries contain information about the dress and domestic life of the times. Other documents detail the social and charitable services: not all Jews enjoyed the prosperity of a flourishing mercantile society – there were the poor, the widowed and the orphaned who required care. Among the multitude of documents so far uncovered in the Geniza are numerous texts that refer to women, including more than a hundred letters apparently dictated to scribes by women themselves.

Here then is a record that illuminates a daily life hitherto known largely from literary and juridical sources. Although a number of the documents, in particular the proceedings of the courts, indicate a wide variety of practices, some of which were at variance with rabbinic legislation, the Jewish communities of Islamic lands were deeply rooted in Talmudic Judaism and tended, on the whole, to reflect traditional values and norms.

Spain and the concept of the 'Golden Age' of Jewry

Among the various Jewish communities of Islamic lands, none has elicited greater attention and admiration than the Jewish community of Spain. Oddly enough, the Jewish experience in the Iberian Peninsula is often cited as typical of the Jewish experience everywhere in the Islamic world. But scholars who focus more narrowly on the world of the Muslims have come to appreciate how different Islamic Spain was from the other parts of the Islamic domain.

In the nineteenth century, Jewish scholars, particularly those in western Europe, spoke of the Jewish experience in Spain as the 'Golden Age'. Measured by any yardstick the literary and scholarly achievements of Spanish Jewry, which reflected an ability to assimilate the best of Muslim culture, were outstanding: in this respect, Spain certainly equalled if not surpassed the other major centres of diaspora Jewry.

However, the accolade of 'Golden Age', in effect, amounted to high praise for cultural assimilation and for the innovative literary forms and philosophical thought to which it gave rise; the term, in fact, reflected the aspirations of nineteenth-century European Jewry, which had entered its own age of enlightenment. The achievements of Spanish Jewry were, therefore, much valued by the first generation of Jewish scholars. Their preference was for intellectual history, which at the time was far better known than the social condition of Spanish Jewry, and this tended to leave them with a somewhat skewed picture, for all was not benign in Spain: one has only to recall that the great Moses Maimonides, the outstanding Jewish mind of the Middle Ages, was forced to leave Spain for North Africa in about 1160 CE because of a wave of persecution. In truth, the experiences of Spanish Jewry add up to a complex picture of unprecedented political and cultural advances marred by periods of great uncertainty and danger.

Jewish settlements dotted the Iberian Peninsula even before the Muslim conquest of Spain in 711 CE. When the Muslims crossed the Mediterranean and seized the land they were to call al-Andalus (Andalusia), they encountered a highly diverse and polyglot population. Unlike the Byzantine and Sasanian territories conquered earlier by the Arab armies, Spain was an isolated provincial enclave with no distinct cultural traditions of its own. The Jews, who had suffered under the previous rulers, the Visigothic kings, rallied to the side of the Muslims and were settled by them in a series of garrison towns. These towns were later to become the flourishing cosmopolitan cities of Cordoba, Toledo, Granada and Seville. There, the Spanish Jews were joined by co-religionists who migrated from North Africa, including some who had previously fled from Spain to escape persecution by the Visigoths. Although at no time were the Jews more than a small fraction of the total population of Andalusia, they represented between 5 and 10 per cent of the urban population and may have accounted for as much as 15–20 per cent in some cities. As in the Islamic lands in the east, the Jews were transformed into city dwellers.

In the eighth century the Umayyad family, which had ruled as Islam's first dynasty, was defeated by the Abbasids. One of the few survivers of the Umayyads made his way to southern Spain and in 756 CE established rule at Cordoba,

I. The first destruction of Jewish independence and the early dispersions 722-586BCE

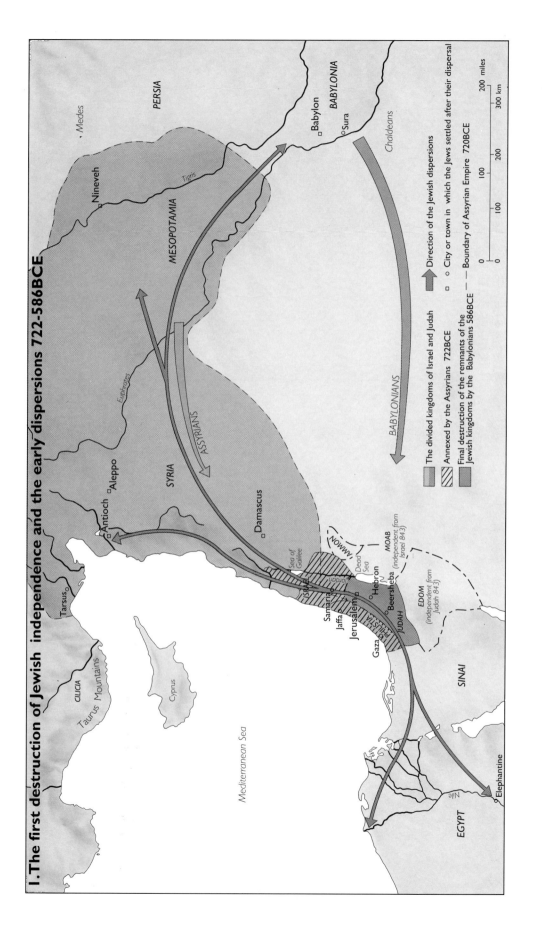

PERSIA

Medes

Babylon □
BABYLONIA

Sura □

Chaldeans

Nineveh □

Tigris

MESOPOTAMIA

200 miles

300 km

100

200

100

→ Direction of the Jewish dispersions

○ City or town in which the Jews settled after their dispersal

☐ Boundary of Assyrian Empire 720BCE

Euphrates

ASSYRIANS

BABYLONIANS

The divided kingdoms of Israel and Judah

Annexed by the Assyrians 722BCE

Final destruction of the remnants of the
Jewish kingdoms by the Babylonians 586BCE

Aleppo □

□ Antioch

Tarsus ○

CILICIA

Taurus Mountains

Cyprus

SYRIA

Damascus □

Sea of
Galilee

AMMON

*Dead
Sea*

MOAB
*(independent from
Israel 843)*

ISRAEL

Samaria ○

Jaffa ○

Hebron ○

Beersheba ○

EDOM
*(independent from
Judah 843)*

Jerusalem ○

PHILISTIA

JUDAH

Gaza ○

Mediterranean Sea

SINAI

Elephantine ○

Nile

EGYPT

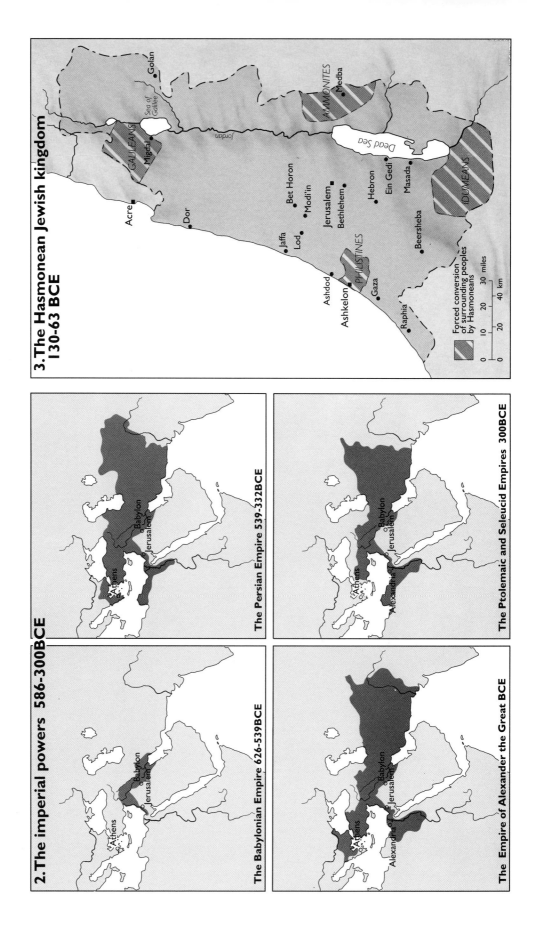

2. The imperial powers 586-300BCE

The Babylonian Empire 626-539BCE

The Persian Empire 539-332BCE

The Ptolemaic and Seleucid Empires 300BCE

The Empire of Alexander the Great BCE

3. The Hasmonean Jewish kingdom 130-63 BCE

Forced conversion of surrounding peoples by Hasmoneans

Acre
Dor
Jaffa
Lod
Ashdod
Ashkelon
PHILISTINES
Gaza
Raphia
Beersheba
Bethlehem
Jerusalem
Modi'in
Bet Horon
Hebron
Ein Gedi
Masada
Dead Sea
IDUMEANS
AMMONITES
Medba
Jordan
GALILEANS
Migdal
Sea of Galilee
Golan

0   10   20   30 miles
0   20   40 km

4. The Jews of the Roman Empire 100-300

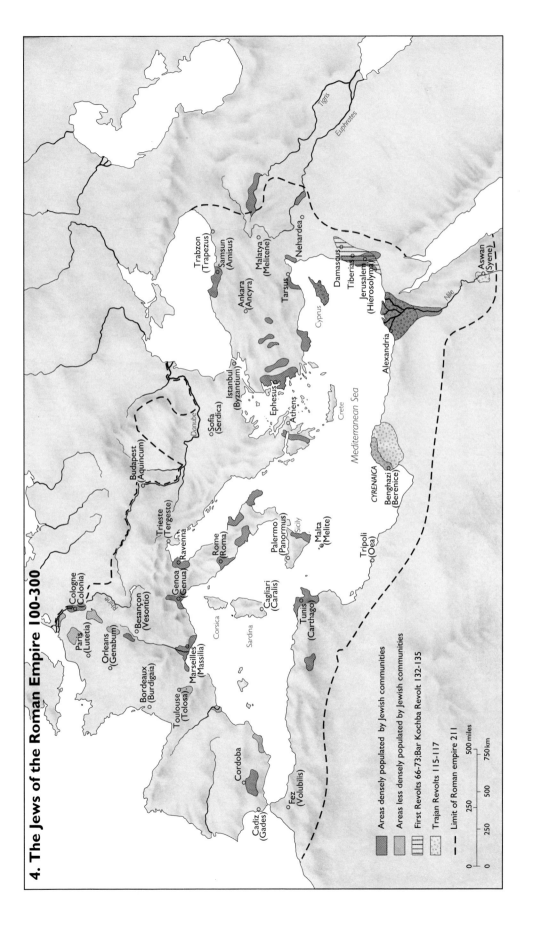

Cologne (Colonia)
Paris (Lutetia)
Orleans (Genabum)
Bordeaux (Burdigaia)
Toulouse (Tolosa)
Marseilles (Massilia)
Besançon (Vesontio)
Cadiz (Gades)
Cordoba
Fez (Volubilis)
Tunis (Carthago)
Cagliari (Caralis)
Corsica
Sardina
Genoa (Genua)
Ravenna
Rome (Roma)
Trieste (Tergeste)
Budapest (Aquincum)
Palermo (Panormus)
Sicily
Malta (Melite)
Tripoli (Oea)
Sofia (Serdica)
Ephesus
Athens
Crete
Istanbul (Byzantium)
Mediterranean Sea
CYRENAICA
Benghazi (Berenice)
Trabzon (Trapezus)
Samsun (Amisus)
Ankara (Ancyra)
Malatya (Melitene)
Tarsus
Cyprus
Nehardea
Damascus
Tiberias
Jerusalem (Hierosolyma)
Alexandria
Aswan (Syene)
Nile
Tigris
Euphrates
Danube
Rhine

Areas densely populated by Jewish communities
Areas less densely populated by Jewish communities
First Revolts 66-73:Bar Kochba Revolt 132-135
Trajan Revolts 115-117
Limit of Roman empire 211

0   250   500   750km
0   250   500 miles

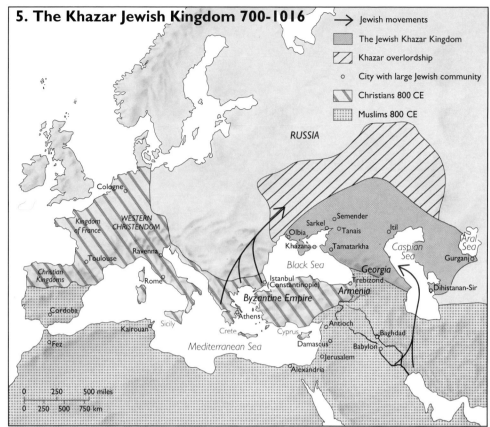

5. The Khazar Jewish Kingdom 700-1016

→ Jewish movements

The Jewish Khazar Kingdom

Khazar overlordship

○ City with large Jewish community

Christians 800 CE

Muslims 800 CE

RUSSIA

Cologne

Kingdom of France

WESTERN CHRISTENDOM

Ravenna

Toulouse

Christian Kingdoms

Rome

Cordoba

Fez

Kairouan

Sicily

Crete

Cyprus

Mediterranean Sea

Athens

Istanbul (Constantinople)

Byzantine Empire

Olbia

Khazana

Sarkel

Tanais

Semender

Tamatarkha

Black Sea

Itil

Caspian Sea

Aral Sea

Gurganj

Georgia

Trebizond

Armenia

Dihistanan-Sir

Antioch

Damascus

Jerusalem

Babylon

Baghdad

Alexandria

0   250   500 miles

0 250 500 750 km

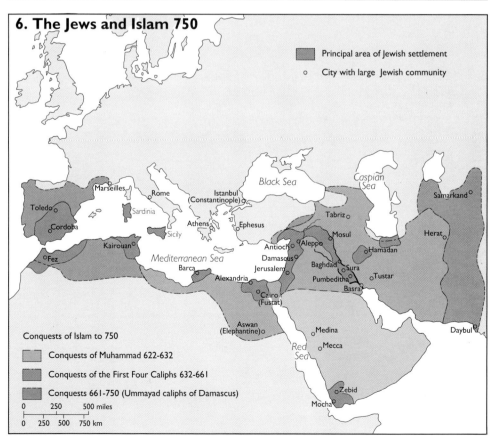

6. The Jews and Islam 750

Principal area of Jewish settlement

○ City with large Jewish community

Black Sea

Caspian Sea

Marseilles

Rome

Istanbul (Constantinople)

Toledo

Cordoba

Sardinia

Sicily

Athens

Ephesus

Kairouan

Mediterranean Sea

Fez

Barca

Alexandria

Antioch

Damascus

Jerusalem

Cairo (Fustat)

Aswan (Elephantine)

Aleppo

Baghdad

Pumbeditha

Basra

Sura

Tustar

Tabriz

Mosul

Hamadan

Samarkand

Herat

Medina

Mecca

Red Sea

Daybul

Zebid

Mocha

Conquests of Islam to 750

Conquests of Muhammad 622-632

Conquests of the First Four Caliphs 632-661

Conquests 661-750 (Ummayad caliphs of Damascus)

0   250   500 miles

0 250 500 750 km

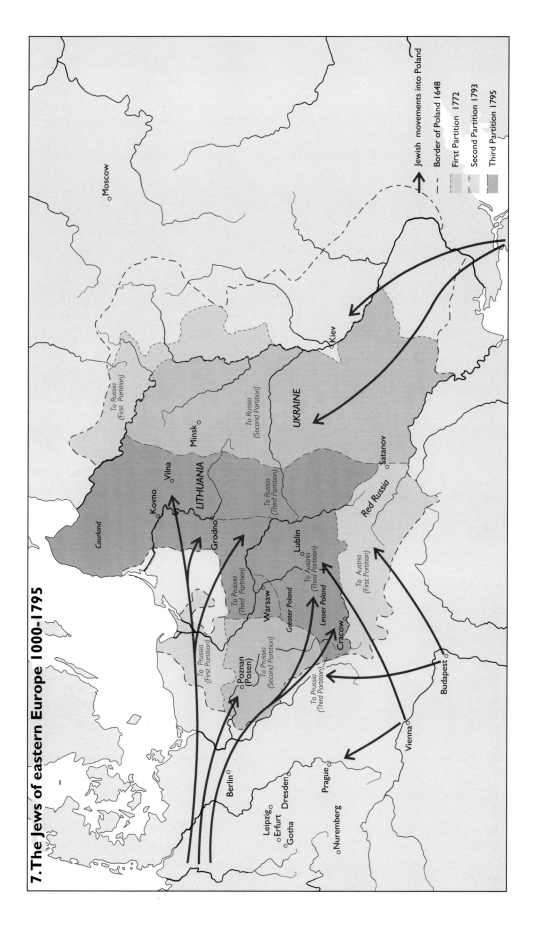

7. The Jews of eastern Europe 1000-1795

Moscow

Courland

Kovno○
Vilna○ LITHUANIA
Grodno○
Minsk○

*To Russia
(First Partition)*

*To Russia
(Second Partition)*

*To Russia
(Third Partition)*

UKRAINE

Kiev○

Satanov○

Red Russia

Berlin○
Leipzig○
Erfurt○
Gotha○
Dresden○

Nuremberg○

Prague○

Poznan○
(Posen)

*To Prussia
(First Partition)*

*To Prussia
(Second Partition)*

*To Prussia
(Third Partition)*

Warsaw

Greater Poland

Lesser Poland
Cracow○

Lublin○

*To Austria
(Third Partition)*

*To Austria
(First Partition)*

*To Prussia
(Third Partition)*

Vienna○

Budapest○

Jewish movements into Poland

-- Border of Poland 1648

First Partition 1772

Second Partition 1793

Third Partition 1795

8. The Jews of eastern Europe 1795-1917

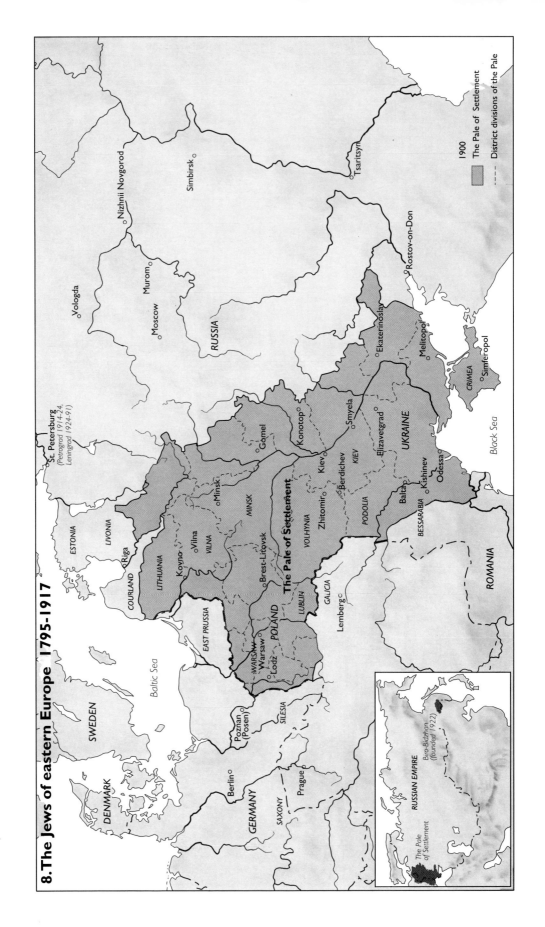

The Pale of Settlement

1900

The Pale of Settlement

District divisions of the Pale

SWEDEN

DENMARK

Baltic Sea

GERMANY

SAXONY

Prague

Berlin

SILESIA

Poznan (Posen)

EAST PRUSSIA

COURLAND

ESTONIA

LIVONIA

Riga

LITHUANIA

Kovno

VILNA

Vilna

Minsk

MINSK

St. Petersburg
(Petrograd 1914-24,
Leningrad 1924-91)

Vologda

Nizhnii Novgorod

Murom

Moscow

Simbirsk

RUSSIA

Gomel

Brest-Litovsk

POLAND

WARSAW

Warsaw

Łódź

LUBLIN

GALICIA

Lemberg

VOLHYNIA

Zhitomir

PODOLIA

Konotop

Berdichev

KIEV

Kiev

Smyela

Elizavetgrad

UKRAINE

Ekaterinoslav

Melitopol

Balta

BESSARABIA

Kishinev

Odessa

Simferopol

CRIMEA

ROMANIA

Black Sea

Tsaritsyn

Rostov-on-Don

RUSSIAN EMPIRE

The Pale
of Settlement

Biro-Bidzhan
(founded 1922)

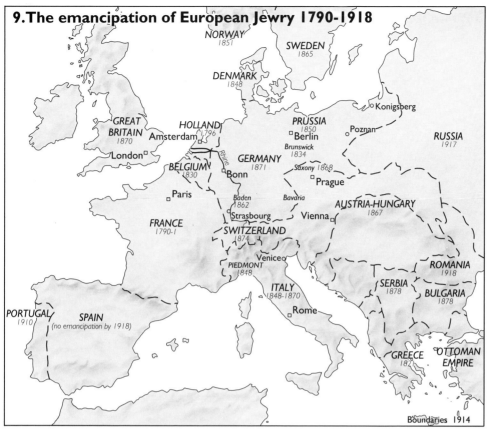

9. The emancipation of European Jewry 1790-1918

NORWAY
1851

SWEDEN
1865

DENMARK
1848

Konigsberg

GREAT
BRITAIN
1870

HOLLAND
1796
Amsterdam

PRUSSIA
1850
Berlin

Poznan

RUSSIA
1917

London

Rhine

GERMANY
1871

Brunswick
1834

Saxony *1868*

BELGIUM
1830
Bonn

Prague

Paris

Baden
1862

Bavaria

AUSTRIA-HUNGARY
1867

FRANCE
1790-1

Strasbourg

Vienna

SWITZERLAND
1874

Venice

PIEDMONT
1848

ROMANIA
1918

ITALY
1848-1870

SERBIA
1878

BULGARIA
1878

PORTUGAL
1910

SPAIN
(no emancipation by 1918)

Rome

GREECE
182

OTTOMAN
EMPIRE

Boundaries 1914

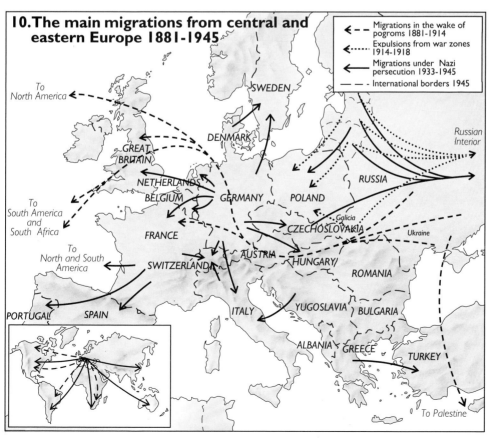

10. The main migrations from central and eastern Europe 1881-1945

- ← − − Migrations in the wake of pogroms 1881-1914
- ←······ Expulsions from war zones 1914-1918
- ← Migrations under Nazi persecution 1933-1945
- − − − International borders 1945

To
North America

SWEDEN

DENMARK

GREAT
BRITAIN

Russian
Interior

RUSSIA

NETHERLANDS

BELGIUM

GERMANY

POLAND

To
South America
and
South Africa

FRANCE

Galicia

CZECHOSLOVAKIA

Ukraine

To
North and South
America

SWITZERLAND

AUSTRIA

HUNGARY

ROMANIA

PORTUGAL

SPAIN

ITALY

YUGOSLAVIA

BULGARIA

ALBANIA

GREECE

TURKEY

To Palestine

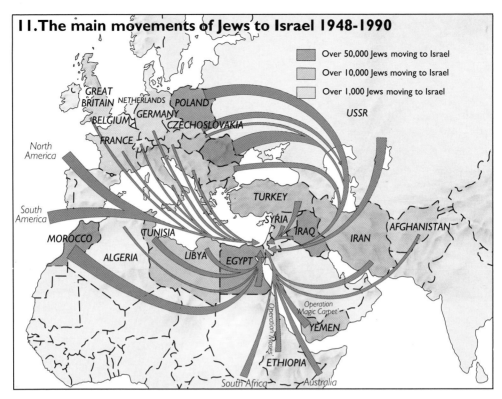

11. The main movements of Jews to Israel 1948-1990

Over 50,000 Jews moving to Israel
Over 10,000 Jews moving to Israel
Over 1,000 Jews moving to Israel

GREAT BRITAIN
NETHERLANDS
POLAND
BELGIUM
GERMANY
CZECHOSLOVAKIA
FRANCE
USSR
North America
South America
TURKEY
SYRIA
IRAQ
IRAN
AFGHANISTAN
MOROCCO
TUNISIA
ALGERIA
LIBYA
EGYPT
Operation 'Magic Carpet'
Operation Moses
YEMEN
ETHIOPIA
South Africa
Australia

12. Israel today

LEBANON
SYRIA
Acre
Haifa
Sea of Galilee
Golan Heights
As Suwayda
Nazareth
Jenin
Hadera
Netanya
Nablus
West Bank
Mediterranean Sea
Tel Aviv
Jordan
Amman
Ashdod
Jerusalem
Ashkelon
ISRAEL
Bethlehem
Gaza Strip
Gaza
Hebron
Dead Sea
Khan Yunis
Rafah
Beersheba
Karak
El Arish
JORDAN
Isma'iliya
Ma'an
EGYPT
Suez
Sinai Peninsula
Red Sea
Eilat
Gulf of Aquaba
SAUDI ARABIA

becoming Abd al-Rahman I – a remnant of Umayyad power in an Islamic world then dominated by the Abbasids. Umayyad rule was, on the whole, enlightened and the economy of Andalusia prospered. The Jews were represented in a wide variety of occupations; they also established close contacts with Jewish communities in North Africa and Egypt, as well as with those in the Fertile Crescent (the arc of land extending from Palestine in the west, through Syria, to Iraq in the east). Moreover, there was an active correspondence between the local rabbinical authorities and the Babylonian geonim.

The tenth century brought significant changes. Throughout the Islamic world there were moves toward regional independence as the Abbasid caliphate faltered. In this climate, the Umayyad, Abd al-Rahman III, declared an independent caliphate in Cordoba in 928 CE. The emergence of an Andalusian identity gave rise to a distinctive Jewish culture and afforded scope for considerable Jewish influence, not least in the political arena. Given the heterogeneity of the Andalusian population, discriminatory legislation of the sort detailed in the Covenant of Umar, which might have barred Jews from government service, had little if any impact. Thus Hasdai ibn Shaprut (c. 915–c. 970 CE), the court physician who was Jewish, was able to serve as the caliph's ambassador in delicate negotiations and to preside over the customs service. At the same time, he held the title of *nasi* or 'prince', signifying his leadership of the Jewish community in Andalusia. His appointment as prince marked the growing independence of Spanish Jewry.

As regional centres of power were established, so the authority of the Babylonian geonim declined. In Spain the fortuitous arrival in the 950s of Moses ben Hanokh, the alleged survivor of a shipwreck, provided an opportunity for the Jews of Andalusia to strike out on their own in rabbinical matters. Ben Hanokh, who is believed to have come from southern Italy, was very learned. At the instigation of the powerful Hasdai ibn Shaprut, he was installed as the chief rabbi of a newly established academy in Cordoba, so making the Jews of Andalusia completely independent of the Babylonian geonim. Indeed, Spain became a hub of Jewish activity as contacts were extended well beyond its frontiers, and foreign scholars were encouraged to visit and take up residence. Ibn Shaprut's agenda was nothing short of establishing pre-eminence for Spanish Jewry. Concurrent with the rise of traditional Jewish learning, leading Jewish scholars, influenced by their Muslim peers, engaged in new disciplines such as the development of Hebrew grammatical theory, a discipline that was to revolutionize biblical exegesis.

The independent Umayyad caliphate in Spain did not last. In 1009 CE, Berber tribesmen from the Atlas Mountains of North Africa conquered Cordoba, setting in motion a series of events that shattered the unity of the peninsula and that of Spanish Jewry. The caliphate was replaced by a series of petty kingdoms under a succession of provincial rulers representing the heterogeneous population. The supremacy of Cordoba came to an end, and there was considerable movement to other cities. The Jews, like others, migrated from place to place. However, the local rulers proved to be extremely tolerant, as the Umayyads had been, and they were also patrons of culture and learning like their predecessors. Jews were again sought out as public officials, advisors and courtiers. As before, learned Jews continued to pursue a combination of traditional scholarship and those disciplines that the Arabs called the philosophical sciences.

The various provincial rulers vied with one another, assisted by talented Jewish courtiers and financiers. Unlike the occasional Jew who rose to a position of prominence in the court of the Abbasid or Fatimid caliphs, Jewish administrators were now to be found in all the major centres of power in Spain. The most noteworthy of these was Samuel ibn Naghrela (993–1055 CE), otherwise known as ha-Nagid, 'The Prince'. A refugee from Cordoba, he settled in the Berber state of Granada in about 1013 and rose to the rank of vizier – in effect, the chief minister and the centre of executive power. He held that position for some three decades until his death. More remarkable were his military exploits, which are recorded in both Jewish and Muslim sources. Obviously, the notion of a Jewish warrior serving an Islamic state was at odds with the Muslim concept of the *dhimmi*, and it points to the very different nature of the Spanish Islamic domain. By any standard, Ibn Naghrela was a man of many parts: the warrior-statesman was also an accomplished talmudist and one of the greatest Hebrew poets ever.

Direct involvement in affairs of state aroused enmity. Ibn Naghrela's son Joseph, who succeeded his father as vizier, was assassinated by Muslims in 1066. Not content with murdering the Jewish vizier, raging mobs hung his torso from the city gate, and rampaged through the Jewish quarter of Granada, killing many inhabitants and causing enormous damage.

The prominence of the Jews in the political and cultural life of Spain also occasioned an intellectual response from Muslim scholars. The eleventh century saw the development of an extensive polemical literature directed against the 'People of the Book' – Jews, Christians and others with a divinely revealed scripture – but most especially against the Jews. The leading figure in this enterprise was the great Muslim scholar Ali ibn Hazm who harboured a particular animosity towards Ibn Naghrela whom he accused of debasing Islam. The polemics were informed by great intelligence and learning: Ibn Hazm was familiar with the Bible, which he read in Arabic translation, though he was considerably less well acquainted with post-biblical sources. One gains the impression that the polemics were the product of intellectual inquiries that had taken a particularly aggressive turn. The polemics were not limited to philosophical considerations and the interpretation of scripture: there were references to Jewish opposition to Muhammad and more generally to flawed Jewish behaviour in many spheres, with the prime target being the Jewish viziers of Granada. The volatile nature of Andalusian politics and society which opened doors for Jews could, in times of stress, lead to attacks on them.

The loss of Toledo to the Christians in 1086 shook the foundations of Muslim rule. In an effort to stem the Christian reconquest, the ruler of Seville was forced to seek support from abroad and so made an alliance with the Almoravids – a Muslim dynasty which had its origins among Berber tribesmen from the fringes of the Sahara and which now ruled Morocco and neighbouring territories. Thus the Almoravids came to Muslim Spain, and by 1090 they had become the dominant political power there, remaining as such until the end of the 1140s. The introduction of this intolerant dynasty to Spain dramatically changed the general condition of the Jews. Having defeated the Christians of Castile, the Almoravids, flushed with victory, attempted to convert the Jews of Lucena by force – an act that was totally inconsistent with traditional Muslim attitudes and law, going against the notion of the *dhimmi* – the protected monotheist. At Lucena, however, the payment of a large tribute caused the Almoravid leader to rescind his decree. Almoravid aggression carried over from the frontline with the Christians into Muslim-controlled regions: Granada, where the Jewish community had re-established itself after the riots of 1066, was sacked in 1090, and the Jewish quarter was destroyed yet again with considerable loss of life.

The period of Almoravid dominance coincided with relentless pressure on Muslim territory from the Christians to the north and this led to increasing religious intolerance. The tolerant attitudes that reflected the heterogeneity of Andalusian society gave way to sharply defined religious sensibilities. In short, there was a growing polarization between the threatened Muslims and their erstwhile allies, the Jews. The number of Jews in government service declined noticeably; certainly there were none wielding power like 'the Prince', Samuel ibn Naghrela, and his son. And yet, the intellectual vitality of Jewish life continued as before. Rabbinic scholarship, philosophy and poetry flourished. The uncertainty of the times created anxiety among the Jewish community which contributed to the sporadic manifestations of messianic yearning, an historic indication of Jewish unease in troubled times. Nevertheless, most Jews continued to prefer life in Spain, little realizing the dangerous period that lay ahead.

More serious in disrupting Jewish life than the arrival of the Almoravids was the invasion of Andalusia by the Almohads. This intolerant Muslim dynasty began as a religious movement rooted in the Atlas Mountains of Morocco and organized by the Berber, Ibn Tumart (died 1130), who had returned to Morocco from his studies in Damascus and Baghdad filled with asceticism and reforming zeal. Obtaining the support of his Berber kinsmen, he declared himself the Mahdi, that is, a messiah-like figure. Having overthrown the Almoravids in Morocco, the Almohads invaded Spain in 1148. The Almoravids were then ousted from the Iberian Peninsula, and by 1172 the Mahdi's lieutenant, Abd al-Mu'min, controlled most of the region, establishing Almohad rule. The power of the Almohads in Spain was eventually broken by their defeat by the Christians in 1212.

The Almohads carried out the systematic persecution of non-Muslims to an extent never seen in the Muslim East. The flourishing Jewish communities of Andalusia were decimated. Jews were forbidden to practise their religion openly; houses of worship and academies of learning were closed; and many Jews were compelled to embrace Islam. The persecution by the Almohads resulted in widespread migration. Many Jews moved north into the Christian enclaves of Castile and Aragon where Jewish communities enjoyed the protection of the Christian rulers, and individual Jews even rose to prominent positions at court. Others, like the great philosopher Maimonides, moved first to North Africa and then to Egypt. Still others remained behind, converting to Islam but secretly retaining their Jewish faith.

Despite the efforts of the Almoravids and the Almohads, the slow, grinding Christian reconquest of Muslim Spain continued. It brought significant benefits to the Jews: not only were the Christian areas a haven for Jewish refugees from the Muslim south, but they were places where Jews might truly prosper. When territories were won from the Muslims, the new Christian rulers often sought out the Jewish inhabitants, encouraged them to stay and employed them in a wide variety of jobs – a marked contrast to the Christian attitude towards the indigenous Muslim population. However, this preferential treatment did not mean that the Jews were put on an equal footing with the Christians. Although the Jewish communities were granted autonomy, a wide variety of discriminatory practices were instigated: Jews and Christians were forbidden to occupy the same house; Jews were not permitted to hold positions that would give them authority over Christians; limits were placed on the size and number of Jewish houses of worship; and the Jews were obliged to wear distinctive badges, emblematic of their faith. By the thirteenth century, the Christians began to display increasing intolerance, so when in 1492 the last Muslim enclave fell in the south, the Jewish community in Spain had long since lost its political freedom and intellectual vitality.

Cross-cultural relations: the Jewish–Muslim symbiosis

From the very outset of Islam, Muslims were much interested in Jewish themes. It was noted earlier that the Quran contains many stories of biblical characters and happenings. Later works, commenting directly on the Quranic text, amplify greatly the material found in Jewish and Christian scripture. Arab historians were fascinated by these stories and the commentary that they engendered. Anthologies giving prominence to these and other themes from ancient sources were published, and the Muslim versions of the Jewish past became the recurrent focus of sermons in the mosque and the basis of popular homilies in the street. The literature was known collectively as *Isra'iliyyat*, that is, the tales of the Israelites.

Aware that Jewish scripture and lore had penetrated their own tradition, the Muslim authorities engaged in a lively discussion about the potential impact of this borrowing. There were those who maintained that the text of the Hebrew Bible should not be cited because, as the Quran indicates, it had been inaccurately transmitted and deliberately falsified. This view, which eventually prevailed, was favoured by active polemicists. On the other side, there were those Muslims who regarded the Torah revered by the Jews as an authentic document of God's revelation – a Hebrew version of scripture, comparable to the Quran. This second school argued that the benefits of citing Hebrew scripture were significant. For instance, the Torah was perceived as foretelling Muhammad's mission; it even contained a description of Muhammad and indicated that Moses had instructed the Israelites to obey him. Similarly, the Psalms were said to address the future mission of the Prophet.

The transmission of non-scriptural Jewish material was also a source of discussion among the Muslim authorities and was looked upon with greater favour, even by the Prophet himself. Properly understood, the non-scriptural Jewish material was said to predict the coming of Muhammad, as did the Hebrew Bible, and also to foretell the events of later Islamic history. In fact, the learned Jew was often seen as a sage character who interpreted mysterious apocalyptic texts of his own tradition and predicted future happenings in the world of Islam with great accuracy. To read about the Israelites was therefore desirable as well as licit. In any event, whether or not Muslim authors actually read Jewish texts, they certainly cited them; moreover, Jewish themes appear in Muslim writings without any indication of their origin.

The process by which this material became available to Muslims is anything but clear. The most likely avenue was through Jewish and perhaps Christian converts to Islam who had access to Jewish sources. Muslim scholars were familiar with the Hebrew Bible through translations into Arabic, but there is no indication that they had the linguistic proficiency to handle the vast range of rabbinic materials.

One should be clear about the Muslim concern with the Jewish past: the interest that the Muslims had in Jews and Judaism was linked to a passionate involvement with their own religion and society. No doubt, they were inquisitive about their fellow monotheists and read the *Isra'iliyyat* out of curiosity as well as for enjoyment. But, for Muslims, the main reason to reflect on this literature was to elaborate on the meaning of their own traditions and to reaffirm the truth of their religion while rejecting as false the claims of others.

For their part the Jews were intrigued by Islam and Islamic writings. Learned Jewish scholars were familiar with the Quran and with a wide range of other Muslim religious texts. They also had access to what might loosely be called the 'secular' branches of Islamic learning, namely, grammar, poetry and philosophy. In addition, titbits of Muslim history and folk tales found their way into Jewish texts and oral traditions through a shared folklore.

The acquisition and absorption of Muslim culture by the Jews was made easier by the existence of a common language – Arabic. Although the Arabs represented but a fraction of the population in the lands that they conquered, and in many ways they assimilated the indigenous cultures, in the area of language they gained remarkable hegemony with the widespread diffusion of Arabic. The importance of this linguistic phenomenon should not be underestimated: throughout the Fertile Crescent, Egypt, North Africa and Spain, Arabic became the dominant language of social intercourse and, very often, of scholarly writing. By the year 1000 CE the dominance of Arabic was complete. Only in the eastern regions of the Islamic world did the older linguistic traditions prove resilient, but even there, they were much affected by Arabic terminology and linguistic structures.

Aside from the scattered Jewish communities of Kurdistan and Armenia which retained their Aramaic dialect, the Jews of Islamic lands all adapted to the language of their conquerors. However, by utilizing Arabic, the Jews did not become Arabs. The notion that the speaker of a particular language somehow assumes a wider identity and belongs to a larger community is a modern notion. During the formative periods of Judeo-Islamic civilization, the term 'Arab' referred specifically to a bedouin or more widely to someone affiliated in some manner with an Arab tribe. Even today, one can generally distinguish between Arabs and other speakers of Arabic by their private and/or liturgical language.

A dialect of Arabic written in Hebrew characters, known as Judeo-Arabic, was the main vehicle, alongside Hebrew, for religious and scholarly discourse among learned Jews. It was also the language of social intercourse and business, and was therefore commonly used to record the minutiae of daily transactions. As the vernacular of the Jews, Judeo-Arabic was much more closely linked to the Arabic of the Muslims than the Jewish vernaculars of today are to the languages of their host countries.

With regard to the Jewish use of Arabic, it is important to appreciate that the Jews did not simply resort to Arabic out of pragmatism; they also looked to it as the key to Muslim civilization and culture. Jews were intellectually stimulated by developments in Muslim scholarly and literary circles. A wide range of medieval Muslim writings thus influenced the Jewish intellectual agenda, be it in the growth of Jewish philosophy and mysticism, the creation of Hebrew poetry, the study of the natural and physical sciences, and not least, the development of Hebrew grammar and philology, which was crucial to biblical exegesis. Even the application of Jewish law was affected by Islam. The fascination with Islamic materials was essentially directed toward Jewish concerns though Islamic learning was of great interest in and of itself. There was, in short, a widespread and persistent encroachment of Muslim influence.

With the general diffusion of Arabic among Jews, it is not surprising that the Hebrew Bible was translated into that language, as it had been translated into Greek and Aramaic in earlier times. In fact, Arabic became more accessible than Hebrew or Aramaic. The most famous translation was that of Saadiah al-Fayyumi (died 942 CE), the renowned Egyptian scholar who was a gaon. Al-Fayyumi was typical of the great Jewish luminaries of the Judeo-Islamic world: he was, first and foremost, a great legal scholar but he was also an outstanding philosopher, linguist and poet.

Philology and grammar, disciplines developed by Muslim scholars, attracted wide interest in Jewish circles. Using models borrowed from Arab grammarians, Jews plunged into the rigorous study of the Hebrew language. The point of the exercise was to give more certain readings to difficult passages in traditional Hebrew sources. The pronunciation, grammar and vocabulary of biblical and post-biblical Hebrew came under serious investigation for the first time. The lexical aids and grammatical tomes that were produced are models of linguistic inquiry. Given that learned Jews knew three Semitic languages – Hebrew, Arabic and Aramaic – the range of their philological insights was vast and served ultimately to lay the foundations for modern comparative Semitics.

The systematic study of Hebrew permitted major breakthroughs in understanding not only the language of the Hebrew Bible but the meaning of obscure and hitherto misunderstood passages. The midrashic commentary of Talmudic times was supplemented by a highly sophisticated exegesis that stripped numerous biblical passages of fantastic interpretations and made them more understandable. In many respects this linguistic analysis provided some of the groundwork for modern biblical criticism. Here as well, Jewish exegetes and Muslim commentators on the Quran can be seen using comparable methods, each stemming from a common interest in language.

This fascination with language found its highest expression in the development

בעל הבית ונ״ע ביינו שאומרים ההגדה

The Passover service conducted in a fourteenth-century Spanish synagogue. From the Golden Haggadah, *Spain, fourteenth century. Jewish acculturation depends in no small part on the character of the dominant or host society. The impact of the environment on Jewish worship is evident from the Arabic influences depicted in this illustration: note the lamps and Arabesque decor.*

of Hebrew poetry, not only for liturgical and other religious needs but for secular purposes as well. Hebrew religious poetry was well established long before the rise of Islam and had an honoured place in the Jewish prayerbook. Secular poetry also reportedly existed in pre-Islamic times but nothing compares with the brilliance of the Jewish poetry written in Islamic lands in the Middle Ages. With Arabic models of form and metre, Jewish poets turned to the biblical text for vocabulary and produced a meticulous and disciplined literary œuvre on a wide variety of themes. At first, Hebrew poetry tended to be derivative of the Arabic in form and theme, but in the eleventh century, Jewish poets in Spain broke free and experimented, developing a flair and style of their own.

The field in which Jewish and Muslim scholars most commonly shared discourse was probably philosophy. In the Islamic world the philosophers were the most eminent guardians of 'high culture'. Among them there was a general consensus as to the issues of the times, and Jewish and Muslim philosophers alike focused on these matters. Whether or not they actually read each other's works in the original, they were clearly familiar with the intricacies of the argumentation. For Jews and Muslims, the basis of this philosophical discourse lay in Greek science and thought. In this respect, Judeo-Islamic philosophy was a bridge between Hellenistic civilization and the philosophical activity that has continued to this day. The first major effort was to preserve what was then known of Greek thought, which existed in texts usually obtained from digests of philosophical works that were themselves translations of the original. This process of absorbing the legacy of Hellenistic culture was completed, by and large, by the end of the tenth century. It was not, however, the purpose of Jewish philosophers to study Greek works just to preserve the legacy of the ancient world; rather, they sought to reconcile the challenging concepts of philosophical thought with their world of traditional Judaism. In this they had a delicate role: the survival of the Jewish community was rooted in a system of beliefs and practices which had been recognized as axiomatic to the Jewish existence but which could have been compromised by infusions of abstract ideas. So whatever doubts might be raised, they were best discussed among the philosophers themselves and in a language that was not likely to be understood by the uninitiated. The philosophers were certainly not about to overturn traditional Jewish observance.

On the whole, the philosophers succeeded in keeping their discourse within the mainstream of Jewish thought and, in so doing, developed new approaches to the larger questions in Judaism and Jewish life. Their writings, later translated from Arabic into Hebrew, found an eager audience outside the Islamic world and among non-Jews as well. There was an enormous variety of ways in which individual philosophers reconciled Greek–Muslim thought on the one hand with the world of traditional Judaism on the other: the philosophical enterprise of Jews in Islamic lands is yet another indication of the resourcefulness with which Jewry in the orbit of Islam managed to conduct its activities.

The Islamic influence on Jewish popular culture is more difficult to measure, given the distance that separates us from medieval Judaism and Islam. But the evidence, such as it is, indicates that even distinctively Muslim cultural artifacts were adopted by the Jews. How else can one explain Jewish folklore about the Caliph Harun al-Rashid? It would appear that the stuff of *The Thousand and One Nights* was relished by a Jewish audience receptive to the delight of it all.

The waning of the Middle Ages and the concurrent breakdown of order in the world of Islam fundamentally changed the vibrant intellectual life of Jewry in the lands of Islam, as indeed it marked a watershed in Jewish–Muslim relations.

The decline of Judeo-Islamic civilization and the Ottoman Empire

Slowly but perceptibly the condition of Jewry throughout the Abode of Islam began to change for the worse from the twelfth century onwards. There were occasional peaks to go with the increasing number of troughs, but a process had begun that was irreversible. That process was conditioned by an apparent decline in self-confidence among the Muslims themselves. The invasions of the Crusaders and the consequent establishment of a non-Muslim enclave in the Abode of Islam, the relentless Christian reconquest of Spain, the dissolution of the Fatimid caliphate which was beset by internal disorder, and the progressive weakening of the Abbasid caliphate, one of the longest-lasting family dynasties in the history of the region – all these created tensions which disturbed the tranquillity of Muslim society and impinged upon its self-confidence.

There were further blows: military dynasties replaced civilian regimes in Egypt, Palestine and Syria; a wide variety of Iranian and Turcic groups established petty dynasties to the east; and the Mongols, in effect, put an end to the caliphs of the Prophet's line when they murdered the last Abbasid caliph in Baghdad in 1258 – an event that Muslims liken to the destruction of the Temple in Jerusalem. Finally, the Ottoman Turks swept through the lands of Islam, establishing dominions that extended from North Africa to the Balkans. The cumulative effect of these events on a once tolerant and intellectually curious Islamic society was devastating.

As a leading modern scholar stated: 'The secular and humanistic tendencies of Hellenism, which until this period [of decline] had been the predominant cultural forces in Islamic society began to wane; at the same time the Islamic religious element in its most rigid form began to wax even stronger.'[8] The changed climate even affected Jewish scholarship and letters. Concurrently, the economy, which had brought great prosperity to Jews and Muslims alike, suffered shocks induced by political instability, as well as by debased currency, repressive regulation, mismanagement and short-sighted policies that encouraged immediate relief at the expense of long-term progress.

The slow process of Islamization ran its course through the fourteenth and fifteenth centuries. The Muslims were the dominant majority in regions that once had sizeable populations of Jews and, more particularly, Christians. Local dynasts relied heavily on the Muslim religious authorities to produce a quiescent populace and so gave these authorities the licence to legislate and enforce morality and religious orthodoxy. The Muslim populace, frustrated and uneasy, was susceptible to pleadings to turn against the *dhimmis*, the protected minorities. More generally, there was much greater reliance on discriminatory legislation which had rarely been invoked in the past. Even when the Jews managed to prosper economically, they suffered great indignities, if not pariah status.

With the establishment of the Ottoman Empire in 1517, diverse regions of a fragmented Islamic world were united once again – Syria, Palestine, Egypt, parts of the Arabian Peninsula and North Africa, and many other territories were all drawn together. For the Jews, this marked a change for the better. As in the Arab lands of

Femme Juive

*An etching from the album by
M. de Ferriol,* Receuil de cent
estampes représentant
différentes nations du Levant
*(Paris, 1714), after a drawing by
Jean-Baptiste Vanmour. It depicts
a Jewish woman bringing her
merchandize of cloth to sell to the
women of the harem who, of course,
were not permitted to go out. In the
Ottoman Empire, Jews were
pre-eminent in the textile trade.*

the Near East and in the Iberian Peninsula, the fortunes of the Jewish communities of the Ottoman Empire reflected political developments taking place within the Muslim state and its provinces. Challenges to central authority tended to create difficulties for local Jewry, especially as the Jews had often been placed in positions of trust by the authorities and were therefore identified with them. Don Joseph Nasi, a prominent Jew of the sixteenth century, was made the ruler of Naxos and other Cycliade islands and was given various concessions in Palestine where he became the great patron of the Jewish community. Similarly, his contemporary, Don Solomon ibn Yaish, became the Duke of Myteline.

The expansion of the Ottoman realm put Jews in a favoured position. They had retained their widespread international contacts with other Jewish communities, which proved most useful to the Ottomans, and, as always, they could conduct themselves in a variety of languages. They were heavily relied upon in banking and commerce, and secured an important place in Levantine trade. In many respects the Ottoman Jews owed their position to their political weakness which was, paradoxically, a source of strength: they had no meaningful links to the Christian powers and, given their small numbers relative to the hegemonic Muslim community, they were at all times susceptible to pressures, so they were regarded as extraordinarily trustworthy and loyal. They were entrusted with handling the finances of leading Ottomans, with delicate diplomatic missions, and with tax farming. By the late eighteenth century, various Jews were serving as intermediaries between the Ottoman Empire and the Christian states of Europe.

There is much evidence of the vital role played by Jews in the economic life of the Empire. They were particularly active in all aspects of textile production and in the manufacture of clothing. Whereas the Ottomans had previously relied on imports, they could now turn to the great textile centres of Safed in Palestine and Salonika in what is now Greece. Jews were also involved in the leather trade, exporting raw hides to Europe and producing leather for local use. The traditional Jewish trades of the Near East were practised as before, and so Jews were noted for a wide range of activities related to the skilled crafts – they were especially famed as goldsmiths, silversmiths and dealers in gems. Given the nature of Muslim dietary laws (which are similar in certain respects to Jewish ones), Jews supplied Muslims with cheese that was free of rennet, thus distinguishing it from the prohibited food of the Christians. In time, however, the Jews faced fierce commercial competition from other minorities, principally the Armenians and the Greeks. By the end of the Ottoman Empire, the commercial role of the Jews had declined greatly.

The internal organization of the Jewish community followed a familiar pattern. A Jewish official was recognized by the Ottomans to serve as the intermediary between the community and the central authorities. At first, this responsibility fell to an officially recognized Chief Rabbi. But the migration of Spanish and Portuguese Jews to the Ottoman lands in the late fifteenth century and thereafter tended

A Levantine Jew of the Ottoman Empire who appears prosperous. From the Ferriol album. In general, Jewish society prospered under Ottoman rule.

to fragment the Jewish community, as each group of new arrivals sought to establish its own synagogue and other communal institutions. Furthermore, the different groups were registered and taxed separately. The office of the Chief Rabbi therefore gave way to different secular authorities which bore the responsibility of coordinating the various communal functions, including raising funds for the charitable institutions that served the poor, the sick, and those generally unable to care for themselves. Meanwhile the religious administration handled the appointment of rabbis and judges, as well as that of teachers in the religious schools. The task of negotiating communal affairs was no simple matter, given the division of the community into discrete congregations with their own customs and means of conducting communal business.

The cultural life of Ottoman Jewry was particularly rich. The influx of Spanish and Portuguese Jews soon made the Ottoman Empire a centre of rabbinical learning. But the Jews there also experimented with forms of religion that were off the beaten track of normative Judaism. The town of Safed in Palestine became the centre of Jewish mysticism which spread throughout the Ottoman domains and beyond. Nevertheless, the mystics, despite their beliefs, remained rooted in traditional Judaism. A more dangerous threat to the Jewish community was messianic striving. The apocalyptical tradition is deeply embedded in Jewish thought, and at different times and places from the Middle Ages up to the emancipation of European Jewry it gave rise to local messianic pretenders. The resulting disillusionment was generally restricted to the narrow community affected, though the situation was different with the Shabbatean movement of the seventeenth century, as noted earlier (see Chapter 1).

In the end, the fate of Ottoman Jewry was linked to that of the Empire itself. The failure of the regime to control its various regions had dire consequences for local Jewish communities, whose leaders were often associated with the central authorities. Any perceived breakdown in traditional Muslim society was strongly felt by the vulnerable Jewish minorities. When the Ottoman Empire became the 'sick man' of the nineteenth century, the Jews were subjected to a wide variety of pressures including anti-Jewish sentiments that had been implanted as a result of Christian influence from Europe.

Ultimately, it was the encroachment of the West and, more particularly, the creation of the state of Israel in 1948 that was to alter, perhaps irrevocably, the condition of the Jews in Islamic lands. The threat to traditional Islamic values presented by westernization has created enormous tension and instability. It has also shaken the foundations of Muslim regimes and has given rise to an Islamic religious revival. The creation of the Jewish state of Israel only served to reinforce self-doubt in a proud and at one time self-confident culture. The decisive military victories over the Arab armies were incongruous to the Muslims who recalled the Jews as *dhimmis* – a protected minority in their midst.

Following the establishment of the Jewish state, an enormous exodus of Jews from Islamic lands took place. In the more than forty years that the state of Israel has existed, entire countries in the Islamic domain have become denuded of their ancient Jewish populations. The once-great Jewish centres of Iraq, Egypt and the

Yemen no longer contain viable communities, and Syria and the Lebanon have just a few Jews left. The great majority of Jews migrating from Islamic countries have settled in Israel, where in recent years they have expressed renewed pride in their Near-Eastern heritage.

3 Jewish Emancipation in Central and Western Europe in the Eighteenth and Nineteenth Centuries

David Sorkin

Introduction

The story of how the Jews were 'emancipated', gaining equal civil and political rights in central and western Europe, is not simple. Emancipation resulted from a momentous transformation of Europe in the eighteenth and nineteenth centuries, a change that affected all aspects of society from science and philosophy to politics and population. The process of emancipation was similarly complex, involving the creation of new images and changing ideas, and the formation of new political institutions and social structures. To grasp its complexity we must consider the very different kinds of social, political and cultural history that unfolded during this period. In addition, we must remember that there were always two participants: European society as a whole and the Jewish minority – whether involved as individuals or entire communities. Map 9 shows the dates of Jewish emancipation throughout Europe between 1790 and 1918.

The significance of the European Enlightenment

The Enlightenment marked a turning point in European culture by inspiring a new confidence in the ability of human beings to understand and control the world. The scientific revolution of the seventeenth century, and especially Newton's physics, appeared to have reduced the workings of the physical universe to a set of laws. This triumph of human reason, celebrated in Alexander Pope's famous passage,

> Nature, and Nature's laws lay hid in night:
> God said, *Let Newton be!* and all was light.[1]

was based on the application of mathematics to empirical data, and inspired a philosophical revolution as well. If Newton could understand nature through observation and mathematics, then philosophers could do the same for humankind. John Locke explained the workings of the human mind entirely on the basis of experience, without appeal to a set of pre-existing or innate ideas. The Enlightenment thus seemed to promise a new era in which human beings would understand the world and themselves exclusively through their own reason. Human reason,

critical, probing and honest, was to be the new authority in human affairs, supplant-
ing any other authority, whether of tradition or revelation.

This new confidence in human reason altered the balance within European
culture by elevating science and philosophy at the expense of religion. This is not to
say that the Enlightenment was incompatible with religion or religious belief. In fact
only its most radical exponents could be said to have held this view. What the
Enlightenment aimed at was a religion in accord with reason: one that had been
purged of superstition, falsehood and legend. Yet the Enlightenment was inherently
at odds with the domination of all other forms of thought and life by religion.
Exponents of the Enlightenment could not accept the subordination of all forms of
human knowledge to theology – and especially a theology that was ultimately based
on Aristotle. So, they challenged the pre-eminence of theology among the human
sciences and attempted to recast religion in a rational mould. Moreover, they
questioned the ability of church or religion to govern or influence human affairs. If
humanity could penetrate the truths of physics, and plumb the depths of the mind,
then it should also be able to manage the affairs of state and society in a rational and
orderly manner. The Enlightenment became, in the course of time, an ideology:
beginning with physics and then with philosophy, it went on to develop ideas about
how all human affairs should be conducted. Thus the pertinence of the philosopher
Immanuel Kant's definition of Enlightenment as 'man's release from his self-
inflicted minority'[2]: through the use of reason, humankind was to assume responsibility for itself, and 'man', as a reasonable creature, was to serve as a new ideal.

However, it would be misguided to ignore the historical setting that engendered
the Enlightenment. It emerged in the last decades of the seventeenth century in a
Europe weary of religious war. In the sixteenth century, the Reformation had
resulted in over a century of war that had brought unprecedented destruction. In
central Europe, for example, the flourishing urban culture of the Renaissance was
virtually destroyed by the contending armies. The devastation was so great that on
the site of previously important towns the inquiring traveller could now find only
wolves. Europe, in other words, had good cause to want to find a substitute for
religion as humanity's guiding light, since religion seemed peculiarly well equipped
to breed hatred, strife and destruction. The Enlightenment emerged in the period
of relative peace that prevailed from the middle of the seventeenth century (around
1648) until the beginning of the French Revolution (1789) – a period that was
punctuated by frequent wars, but nothing on the scale of the wars of religion
(1560–1648) that followed the Reformation.

It was hardly surprising that instead of religious war the Enlightenment proposed religious toleration. Such toleration presupposed a fundamental compromise: it assumed that neither Protestants nor Catholics could rule Europe, but that
each would have to accept the other's existence. This meant accepting both
Protestant and Catholic states, and tolerating the presence within any state of
members of the other faith (and, in the case of Protestantism, members of
competing Protestant sects).

This idea of religious toleration seemed to achieve fruition first in England,
which was famous for its innumerable Protestant sects. After a religiously inspired

civil war (1642–1646), the execution of Charles I and the founding of a religious Commonwealth in 1649, and the deposition of another king (James II, a Catholic), in 1689 England achieved a modicum of toleration that soon inspired the rest of Europe. As Voltaire put it, with a characteristic mordant twist, 'If there were only one religion in England one would have to be afraid of despotism. If there were two they would cut each other's throats. But there are thirty, and they live happily in peace.'[3]

The Enlightenment endeavoured to provide a basis for toleration by appealing to reason. Previously it had been thought that without a common religion, society would lack the necessary moral and political cement. Enlightenment thinkers proposed the idea of a 'natural religion'. All those who subscribed to three key ideas (the existence of God, the immortality of the soul, and God's government through the reward of good and the punishment of evil in the hereafter) would be acceptable to society since it could be assumed that they would comply with the dictates of morality. In other words, the Enlightenment aspired to a universal morality, one common to all Christians despite the sectarian differences that separated them.

Enlightenment thinkers offered a similar notion in the realm of politics. The idea of 'natural law' posited that all people should be governed by laws that were discoverable by reason. These laws prescribed an individual's rights and duties, obligations and privileges, irrespective of religion or beliefs. What the Enlightenment hoped was that even if Protestants and Catholics, or Anglicans and Presbyterians, or Lutherans and Calvinists, could not marry or worship together, on the basis of ideas such as natural religion and natural law they might be able to live together in peace.

Enlightenment thinkers' efforts to find a new conceptual basis for toleration and peace were matched by the efforts of the rulers and statesmen of the period. The upheaval of war had disrupted, if not destroyed, economies and administrations. Peace, in contrast, held the undeniable attractions of prosperity and power. Without the heavy cost of wars, and the burden of foreign troops wreaking havoc, farmers could harvest crops, artisans could produce goods and, of increasing importance in the eighteenth century, merchants could trade and bring hard currency into their countries. In addition, peace and prosperity would allow governments to consolidate rule through consistent taxation and the erection of efficient bureaucracies. It should not be forgotten that the Enlightenment coincided with the growth of states and of state absolutism. 'Enlightened absolutism' (or as it used to be known, 'enlightened despotism') was the result of a convergence of intellectual developments and political interests. The Enlightenment seemed suited to promote the best interests of the state (*raison d'état*) through mercantilism – the broad set of policies that protected home industries by levying tariffs, promoted trade via monopolies and accumulated bullion.

But how did all this relate to the Jews? Did the Enlightenment include them in its scheme of toleration? Were they to be governed by natural religion and natural law? Were Jews capable of discovering reason and following its light? And finally, did states interested in prosperity and taxation want to admit Jews? The intellectual and political shift that the Enlightenment represented did ultimately come to include Jews and, by incorporating them into European culture and society, radically transformed them. Where Jews became equal citizens they did so because the heritage of the Enlightenment, whether changed more or less by time and circumstances, had become the political norm. Yet this process, which in the nineteenth century came to be known as 'emancipation' (drawing on the idea of the emancipation of the Catholics in England), was nowhere straightforward or simple, painless or automatic. It would be unreasonable to expect any great social or political transformation to be so. And freeing the Jews from their late medieval or early modern status was, in fact, part of a great transformation.

The reasons for the tortuous nature of the change are not difficult to find. As we saw in Chapter 1, Jews in Europe had been subjected to special laws and restrictions since the time of the Roman Empire. There had been no Jews (officially at least) in England and France since the medieval expulsions. Central Europe had witnessed a wave of expulsions in the Reformation and post-Reformation period so great that it had virtually emptied the German states of Jews. The seventeenth century, however, had brought a virtual resettlement of Jews in central and western Europe. During the Thirty Years War (1618–1648), Jews found their way back into many German territories under the protection of invading armies. After the conclusion of the war, they were often invited back by princes wanting to rebuild their states, especially where rulers thought the Jews could help them break the power of the local estates which depended on closed, guild economies. Cromwell *de facto* allowed Jews back into England without any decree, though here religious motives – the hope of bringing the millennium – were as strong as economic ones. In France during the last decades of the seventeenth century, the Marranos who had gathered in the southern towns of Bayonne and Bordeaux under the guise of Portuguese merchants gradually emerged into public as Jews. The larger communities of Ashkenazi Jews in Alsace were acquired with that territory by France in 1648.

While this demographic shift brought the Jews economic advantage, it did not fundamentally alter their status; they did not become equal citizens of the kingdoms, cities or towns in which they resided, but remained a separate group on the periphery. Except in England, where the medieval laws on the statute books were not applied, Jews remained subject to special restrictions and disabilities, though they also enjoyed certain special privileges. In short, the policy of *raison d'état* or mercantilism might gain the Jews admission and economic privilege, but it did not change their status as outsiders and inferiors.

Nor did the Enlightenment immediately affect that status. In part this was due to European culture's profound ambivalence toward Jews. The Enlightenment notion of 'utility' as the basic criterion for the reshaping of society certainly encouraged the tendency to appreciate the Jews' economic usefulness. Yet while this image could and did promote the need (at least in theory) to accept the Jews as human beings and thus to extend toleration to them, it did not necessarily do so. Rather, the Jews' relationship to commerce and money became part of a deeply held conviction that Jews remained inferior, though not in the traditional terms of theology. The Enlightenment converted the Christian conception of the Jews' religious inferiority into the secular doctrine of their moral inferiority. Jews were thought to be incapable of subscribing to natural religion or complying with natural law because of their ritualistic religion, national character or economic situation which, separately or together, prevented them from being moral. Enlightenment thinkers almost without exception subscribed to this image of Jewish inferiority.

But this consensus held only for the image; it broke down on the consequences to be drawn from it. Some thought the inferiority innate and immutable, and thus despaired (or rejoiced) that Jews could never become part of the new society the Enlightenment envisaged. This view tended to emerge among the most vehement critics of established Christianity, such as the Deists in England or the most radical thinkers, such as Voltaire, Diderot and D'Holbach in France. The Jews were the stick they used to beat the church. They expatiated on every instance of immorality in the Old Testament in order to discredit Christianity: if the church's foundation was a morally rotten Judaism, how could the upper storey be different? Voltaire, for example, revived the image of a debased Jewry found in classical literature.

That the Jews could become an element in the struggle between established Christianity and its critics or reformers is also evident in the work of the paramount philosopher of the Enlightenment in Germany, Immanuel Kant. Kant wanted to purge Christianity of its legalistic and ritualistic aspects in order to base it instead on the autonomous reason of each individual. He saw Judaism as the archetype of a religion based on law and thus not only wanted to cleanse Christianity of any remaining Jewish elements, but even went so far as to deny that Judaism was a religion, seeing it instead as a political constitution.

Other Enlightenment thinkers believed that the Jews' inferiority could be remedied. They attributed this inferiority not to Jews themselves, but to the laws that restricted their occupations and settlement and to the contempt they met in the Gentile world. Change the laws and remove the contempt and the Jews would be as capable of morality as other people. This meliorative tradition usually found its exponents among advocates of legal and economic *raison d'état* who were not locked in battle with the established church. In France, for example, the satirist and early sociologist Montesquieu linked this notion to a broader conception of cultural relativism: the Jews might have their relative merits and deficiencies, but they still deserved toleration.

For the thinkers so far mentioned, the Jews were a subject of passing interest. Only in the last three decades of the eighteenth century did they suddenly become a subject to be considered in its own right. The Jews emerged as an issue of concern because the *ancien régime* societies that had kept them marginal were being reformed. The Enlightenment's theoretical concern thus quickly became a practical political and administrative one. Joseph II's 1781 Edict of Toleration granted Protestants religious toleration, though not the right of public worship, in the predominantly Catholic Habsburg Empire. It also extended limited toleration to Jews, though not uniformly throughout the Empire. Yet hand in hand with toleration went provisions for the Jews' 'regeneration' (that is, social rehabilitation, including such things as occupational restructuring, use of the vernacular language, and changes in manners and morals), especially through education. The absolutist state accepted the task of legislating the Jews' 'improvement'.

In Prussia, Christian Wilhelm Dohm, a civil servant and journalist, published a treatise in 1782, *On the Amelioration of the Jews' Civil Status*, in which he argued that by removing the discriminatory laws that had perverted the Jews, the state could regenerate them. 'The Jew is more a man than a Jew', he asserted, and thus would be capable of moral improvement if certain occupational and pedagogical changes were instated. In 1787, the Academy of Metz in eastern France, where the poor Ashkenazi Jews were concentrated, announced a prize for the best essay on the topic 'How to Make the Jews Happy and Useful'. The prize-winning essay, by the Abbé Grégoire, a Jesuit priest who consistently advocated rights for the Jews, urged that freedom and equality would make the Jews both more 'enlightened' and more 'useful'.

By the closing decades of the eighteenth century, the question of the Jews' place in society was high on the agenda in central and western Europe. This was a result of the tensions between the Enlightenment and the *ancien régime*. But because of the Enlightenment's profound ambivalence towards the Jews, the prospect of equality always brought with it the demand for 'regeneration'. Thus emancipation became a 'contract' in which regeneration was exchanged for rights. In large part, it was this contract that was to determine the shape of Jewish emancipation in Europe.

The role of Moses Mendelssohn in Jewish emancipation

Moses Mendelssohn was a seminal figure for Jewish emancipation because he gave the lie to the notion that Jews were inferior; or, stated more positively, his life and achievements demonstrated that a Jew could be a paragon of the Enlightenment in all respects. He subsequently became a symbol of the age of emancipation, proof that a Jew could be all, and indeed more, than the emancipation contract of regeneration for rights asked.

Yet we should not mistake the symbol for the reality. Older accounts of Jewish emancipation (beginning as early as the first biography of Mendelssohn, by Isaac Euchel, published in 1788), made precisely this mistake, turning Mendelssohn into the solitary embodiment of the modern Jew and the single-handed creator of modern Judaism. Mendelssohn did not migrate from atrophied ghetto Judaism to cosmopolitan European culture and society in the way that this view would indicate. Rather, he was the foremost representative – one among many – of the eighteenth-century renaissance of Jewish culture that culminated in the Jewish Enlightenment or Haskalah.

An exaggerated view of Mendelssohn's accomplishments rests on the assumption that Jews lived in a cultural as well as physical ghetto until freed by emancipation. The Jews of central Europe were, in fact, culturally isolated during the post-Reformation wars. But this situation was something of an anomaly in Jewish history, and pained the most sensitive members of the rabbinical and intellectual elite. They thought it a disgrace that Jews were less educated than their Christian neighbours and thus less prepared to defend their faith.

A mezzotint of Moses Mendelssohn, after a portrait of Anton Graff, c. 1722. Mendelssohn, a renowned philosopher, was a leading figure in the Jewish Enlightenment or Haskalah, and he was also prominent in the wider intellectual life of Berlin. He made his living as a silk merchant, despite a considerable physical disability stemming from a childhood illness.

The great Rabbi Judah Loew of Prague felt that the entire system of Jewish education, with its narrow concentration on the Talmud, stood in need of reform and suggested including the Bible and Mishnah also. Other rabbis later echoed his complaints and suggestions. For example, in 1707 Tobias Cohn, a doctor trained at Frankfurt-an-der-Oder, published a handbook of science and medicine to combat widespread ignorance and restore belief. This sense of dissatisfaction was encouraged by the model of Sephardi education in places such as Amsterdam, Livorno and Bordeaux, where secular subjects, including mathematics, geography and languages, were studied alongside Jewish ones, especially the Bible and Hebrew. A tradition of internal criticism existed at that time and, eventually, informed the efforts of Mendelssohn and the early *maskilim* (followers of the Haskalah).

These cultural developments should be seen against the social background of a Jewish community in flux. In the 120 or so years from the Peace of Westphalia (1648) – which put an end to Europe's wars of religion – until the emergence of the Haskalah in the 1770s and 1780s, the nature of Jewish communal life changed markedly. The very pattern of resettlement was significant: Jews settled in smaller groups in numerous areas, in many cases fanning out into the countryside. These small settlements were less disposed to strict religious control, especially since they often could not afford a rabbi. At the same time as their religious supervision decreased, however, their ties to secular authorities increased. As we have seen, rulers admitted Jews into their territories for economic purposes. In many cases a community developed around a court Jew, a wealthy individual who helped the ruler financially and promoted commerce and industry, and who, because of this direct access to the ruler, was very influential within his community. While some court Jews used their position to benefit their communities, others undoubtedly became petty despots, just like so many of the Christian heads of the German states during this period. In any case, because of this link to the state, the Jews had to accept increasing interference in their internal affairs: the rulers who were consolidating their political power in this era of relative peace wanted to bring the Jews within their administration as well.

The combined result of these trends was the beginning of the deterioration of the 'autonomous' Jewish community that had existed in medieval Europe, in which, in exchange for paying taxes, the Jews were granted autonomy in matters of law, religion, education and social life. During and after the Enlightenment, the Jews were increasingly integrated into the administrative and fiscal structures of the state, a trend that paved the way for emancipation, though inadvertently, since the absolutist rulers had no intention of removing the Jews' legal disabilities. These social developments combined with, and indeed reinforced, the Jews' dissatisfaction with their education and isolation from European culture to create a situation ripe for revival and reform, just at the time when Moses Mendelssohn became active.

Born in 1729 in Dessau (in what is now Germany), a community founded in the 1680s by a court Jew, Mendelssohn received the predominantly talmudic education typical of his time. Yet before his bar mitzvah, he had also begun to lay the foundation of his later interests – aesthetics, literature and metaphysics – through a study of the Bible, Hebrew grammar and the medieval Jewish philosopher Maimonides. When he followed his teacher to Berlin in 1743, he continued to study the Talmud, but also joined a circle of young Jews who, educating themselves in Jewish and general culture, helped him to learn classical and modern languages and to continue his philosophical studies. He concentrated on the pillars of the Enlightenment in central Europe – Leibniz, Locke and Wolff – and the great dissident Jewish philosopher Baruch Spinoza.

Where did these other 'enlightened' Jewish students come from? They were of two types. In the course of the eighteenth century, some 470 Jewish students were admitted to the various German universities, especially in the medical faculty. Most of them came from wealthy urban families (court Jews) in Berlin, Königsberg, Breslau and Halberstadt, and had been taught by private tutors. There were also poor students who, like Mendelssohn, were self-taught. Some of these, like Mendelssohn again, came from one of the German states, but others, for example, Solomon Maimon and Israel Zamosc, came from eastern Europe and gathered in Berlin or Königsberg. It is against this varied background that Mendelssohn's own career should be seen.

Mendelssohn was not exceptional in studying philosophy and adhering to Enlightenment ideals. What singled him out was that he became one of the most important philosophers and noted personalities of the German Enlightenment while remaining a practising Jew. In numerous works (for example, *Letters on the Sentiments*, 1755, and *Philosophical Writings*, 1761) he contributed to contemporary aesthetics. His *Treatise on Evidence in Metaphysical Sciences* won him first prize in the Prussian Royal Academy of Science competition in 1763 (Kant won second prize).

His platonic dialogue on the immortality of the soul, *Phaedon* (1767), gained him a European reputation.

Mendelssohn consequently became a Berlin landmark – the German and Jewish Socrates, whose wit, charm and penetrating intelligence attracted dignitaries, intellectuals and the curious from all over Europe. In fact, early on, Mendelssohn became a close friend of the leading lights of the Berlin Enlightenment, especially Friedrich Nicolai, a bookseller, editor, publisher and writer, and Gotthold Ephraim Lessing, the foremost writer and critic of the German Enlightenment. His friendship with Lessing became something of a symbol of the kind of social relationship that was possible between Jew and Christian within the context of the Enlightenment.

While Mendelssohn gained a European reputation with his German works, he also wrote in Hebrew. His Hebrew works are entirely consistent with the German ones and reveal an attempt to revive the Hebrew language (as in *Preacher of Morals*, 1758, the first modern journal in Hebrew, modelled on those of the early German Enlightenment) and the tradition of Hebrew philosophy (as in *Logical Terms*, 1769, a commentary on a treatise of Maimonides).

He also carried on a learned correspondence with leading rabbis of the time. His best known work for a Jewish audience was his translation of the first five books of the Bible into German, printed in Hebrew letters, with a Hebrew commentary that drew on the medieval rationalist tradition (the book was generally known at the time by its title in Hebrew, *Biur*, which means 'commentary'). In part, Mendelssohn undertook the translation because of a nervous debility that prevented more demanding philosophical study, but also because changing circumstances in Germany persuaded him that a climate more favourable to Jews and the possibility of Jewish emancipation might develop. In his correspondence, Mendelssohn called his translation a 'first step toward culture'. He did not envisage, as has often been thought, that it would direct Jews to German and European culture and thus to the abandonment of Judaism, but rather he hoped to foster a renaissance of Jewish culture based on the Hebrew language and the Bible.

This effort was joined by groups of young intellectuals in Berlin and Königsberg who first formed a Society for the Propagation of the Hebrew Language (1783). They then renewed Mendelssohn's efforts of the 1750s by issuing a Hebrew journal (*The Gatherer*, 1784) devoted to education and culture which included, for example, articles on the Bible, the Talmud, famous Jews, the Hebrew language and moral issues. In 1782, N. H. Wessely, a Berlin *maskil* who worked closely with Mendelssohn, published a tract, *Words of Peace and Truth*, in response to Joseph II's Edict of Toleration. Wessely advocated a reform of Jewish education which showed the influence of Judah Loew of Prague and his successors in recommending the study of the Bible and *Mishnah*, and the influence of the Sephardim in its proposals for secular studies.

As a prominent philosopher and a practising Jew, Mendelssohn became a spokesman for Jews and Judaism. In 1769–70, he deflected the conversionary challenge of a Swiss theologian, Johann Kaspar Lavater, who found it hard to believe that a Jew who acknowledged Jesus to have been a great teacher was not ripe for conversion. Mendelssohn constantly interceded on behalf of Jewish communities (for example, Schwerin 1772, Switzerland in 1775 and Dresden in 1777) with authorities whom he had often met at his Berlin home. He also served the Prussian government in 1778 and 1782 as a consultant on Jewish law.

The changing situation of the 1780s helped shape Mendelssohn's position. A call for aid from Alsatian Jewry led Mendelssohn to persuade Dohm to write his treatise, *On the Amelioration of the Jews' Civil Status*. Yet Mendelssohn found that he disagreed with some of Dohm's views: for example, Dohm thought the Jews could retain autonomy in legal matters once they had been granted rights. Mendelssohn took issue with Dohm on this question. Mendelssohn's opinions, in turn, elicited an anonymous response (1782) which he thought had been written by an important Viennese statesman, Joseph Sonnenfels, accusing him of inconsistency in not converting to Christianity.

Mendelssohn's reply, *Jerusalem, or On Religious Power and Judaism* (1783), is a classic theory of Jewish emancipation and of Judaism. Mendelssohn analysed church–state relations in a 'secular' society in the Enlightenment natural law tradition. He argued for a strict separation of church and state, asserting that all coercive power belonged to the state, since only the state was based on a contract. Religion, in contrast, should be viewed as a voluntary association that has only persuasion and admonition at its disposal. Judaism, in other words, should be divested of all the corporate characteristics it had acquired in medieval and early modern Europe (the 'autonomous community'). Mendelssohn offered a definition of Judaism that showed it to be perfectly compatible with such a programme. Judaism was a 'revealed legislation' based on the precepts of natural religion. It did not claim to possess revealed truth, but rather prescribed a set of actions (the Commandments).

Mendelssohn not only became the very symbol of the 'enlightened' Jew, but also generated a theory of Jewish emancipation and a new definition of Judaism. Although he was but one representative of the revival of Jewish culture in the eighteenth century, it was his work and, perhaps more, his life, that were to serve as touchstones for the Jews of Europe during their struggle for emancipation. The Haskalah, of which Mendelssohn was the foremost representative, seemed to suggest that there were good reasons for the Jews to accept the emancipation contract of rights for regeneration. The old Jewish life was in disrepair; reform was necessary for internal reasons alone. With the coming of emancipation, the argument would seem ever more compelling.

The significance of the French Revolution for Jewish emancipation

As we have seen, there were a number of developments in the eighteenth century that were paving the way for the emancipation of the Jews. With its emphasis on the rational individual, expressed in the ideas of natural law, natural religion and toleration, and its notion of an exchange of regeneration for rights, the Enlightenment offered the theoretical basis for the equality of the Jews. By integrating Jews into its administrative and fiscal mechanisms, and thus undermining Jewish communal autonomy, the absolutist state provided the practical basis for Jewish inclusion. And in the Haskalah's revival of Hebrew language and culture, readiness to acquire secular skills, and redefinition of Judaism (embodied in Mendelssohn's *Jerusalem*), the Jews, or at least the new intelligentsia, seemed willing to assume the burden of regeneration that was part of the emancipation contract.

The 1780s seemed heavy with the possibility of emancipation. Yet the time proved too short for a full gestation and a natural birth. Emancipation was rushed into the world, premature and howling, by the French Revolution. And thus a pattern was established. From that time on, Jewish emancipation was not to proceed slowly and in isolation, but instead was to be impelled along by the great upheavals of political revolution and the restructuring of states. However much the Jews desired emancipation, when it finally came it was out of their control.

The immediate cause of the French Revolution was a fiscal crisis. Because Louis XVI lacked funds and had no idea how to raise them, in May 1789 he convened the legislative body known as the Estates General, which had not met since 1614. This body was composed of nobility, clergy and commoners. The nobility quickly reached a deadlock with the crown over reforms in return for taxation, and the commoners, assisted by liberal nobles and clergy, soon transformed the Estates General into the National Assembly. Soon after, the mob in Paris stormed the Bastille (14 July 1789), feudalism was abolished (4 August) and the Rights of Man were decreed (26 August). With the Enlightenment's idea of equality now enacted into law, the emancipation of the Jews would have seemed the next logical step. But events were not to be so simple. While the logic of revolution and the reordering of France required Jewish emancipation, the Enlightenment's own image of Jewish inferiority – backed by traditional Christian notions – combined with the actual situation of the Jews in France to create a more complicated scenario.

The 40,000 or so Jews in France on the eve of the Revolution fell into two main groups. The Ashkenazim, accounting for almost 85 per cent, lived in the north-east, in Alsace. This community had essentially the same legal and economic profile as the Jewish communities of the German states, which is not surprising considering that this area became part of France only in the seventeenth century. The Jews enjoyed autonomy in matters of law, religion, education and social welfare, in exchange for fixed taxes. Alsatian Jews were restricted in their occupations, engaging primarily in petty trade and credit; but there was a handful of wealthy court Jews who, as in the German states, benefited from political access and consequently played a greater role in communal affairs. The Jews' occupations brought them into conflict with the guilds on the one side and the peasants on the other, and feelings of enmity ran high. It should be remembered that it was the tension over peasant debts to Jewish creditors in Alsace in the 1770s that had resulted in the community turning to Mendelssohn for aid, which he provided by encouraging Dohm to produce his treatise.

The much smaller Sephardi community of south-west France, concentrated in Bayonne and Bordeaux, contrasted sharply with the Ashkenazim in the north-east.

Its earliest members had been Marranos fleeing the Iberian peninsula in the 1550s. The community's rights and privileges were thus those of a corporation of merchants; it had no religious character. The Sephardim survived an expulsion order of 1615 and the revocation of toleration of Protestants (in the Edict of Nantes in 1685), and by the end of the seventeenth century were beginning to emerge as Jews. By the 1690s, for example, they had stopped having their children baptized; and in 1711, they ceased having a priest officiate at marriages. This community of wealthy merchants managed to have its privileges confirmed in the 1720s, and, while remaining Jews, gradually fell in step with the enlightened eighteenth century. The Sephardim limited the rabbi to religious functions alone, depriving him of juridical powers; and their schools taught the Bible and Psalms, but not the Talmud. In contrast to the Ashkenazi Jews of Alsace, the acculturated and wealthy Jews of Bordeaux and Bayonne were well integrated into the broader French society.

These differences between the two communities were to have lasting consequences, and revealed both the working of the emancipation contract and the different expectations each group held of the Revolution. The Ashkenazim of Alsace wanted an end to economic and residential restrictions, while retaining communal autonomy, at least in juridical and fiscal matters. The Sephardim, in contrast, wanted to be confirmed as full and equal French citizens. There was nothing in their community they could not maintain on an entirely voluntary basis.

The issue of Jewish emancipation came before the National Assembly because the Declaration of the Rights of Man, which promised equality to members of all religions, was found to be deficient. The Assembly was asked whether the Declaration applied to Protestants, and a new decree had to be issued to admit them to the civic oath and the National Guard. The same question was raised for the Jews in three sessions in December 1789. The Jews of Alsace, that is, the Ashkenazim, were the centre of attention, and the chief proponent of emancipation, the orator and statesman Mirabeau, had the motion shelved because he knew he did not have enough votes to carry it. Why was this so? In this debate Count Clermont-Tonnere made his justly famous statement, 'The Jews should be denied everything as a nation, but granted everything as individuals. They must be citizens.' The Jews had to give up all forms of separatism, aside from religion, and become French citizens. But the force of this argument did not carry the day. The opponents, especially the Bishop of Nancy, Henry de la Fare, and the Abbé Maury, prevailed. Together they argued – invoking Voltaire – not only that the Jews were alien to France by virtue of their religion, but that they inevitably aroused the wrath of the Alsatians with their incorrigible business practices. Were the Jews to be granted rights by the National Assembly, the mob would attack them without remorse, as it had already threatened to do in the first days of the Revolution.

This first debate persuaded the leaders of the Sephardim in Paris that they must separate themselves from the Ashkenazi Jews. They consequently argued that their legal privileges dating back two centuries separated them from the Jews of Alsace. This gambit succeeded. On 28 January 1790, a separate decree was enacted granting Sephardi Jews (and those of Avignon, a formal papal territory) complete equality. The National Assembly had little problem this time, since this wealthy,

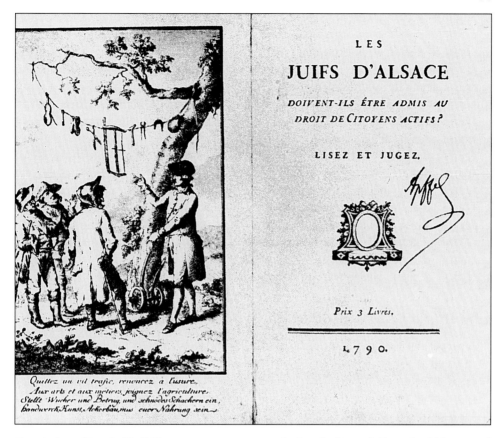

LES

JUIFS D'ALSACE

DOIVENT-ILS ÊTRE ADMIS AU
DROIT DE CITOYENS ACTIFS?

LISEZ ET JUGEZ.

Prix 3 Livres.

1790.

Quittez un vil trafic, renoncez a l'usure.
Aux arts et aux metiers joignez l'agriculture.
Stellt Wucher und Betrug, und schnödes Schachern ein,
Handwerk Kunst, Ackerbau, muss euer Nahrung sein.

Frontispiece of Les Juifs d'Alsace, *1790, a tract on whether the Jews of Alsace should be granted full French citizenship. The illustration shows a Frenchman exhorting a group of Jews to renounce usury and take up more worthy occupations: the arts, the professions, and agriculture—all symbolized by the items strung from the tree.*

acculturated community which enjoyed the respect of the local French population already complied with the emancipation contract. The future statesman and diplomat Talleyrand, who sponsored the measure, was quick to point this out.

In the meantime, the Ashkenazim attempted to remedy their situation. They not only renounced their claims to limited autonomy, but also argued that they already showed signs of the required regeneration, in that some of them were serving in the National Guard and so on. These efforts fell short of the mark, however, because of the worsening situation in Alsace. Resentment against Jewish creditors and middlemen, as part of the general release of grievances triggered by the Revolution, flared into rioting and pillaging. In April 1790, the National Assembly was forced to adopt special laws to protect the Ashkenazim. The reality of Jewish life in Alsace seemed to vitiate any argument that the Jews could be regenerated or easily accepted by the French. Were the issue to be argued again on the merits of the Ashkenazim alone, it was doubtful that rights would be granted.

Fortunately for the Ashkenazim, the Revolution took a more radical turn with the adoption of a constitution on 14 September 1791, which offered grounds for the equality of the Jews. On 27 September 1791, the Jacobin (or radical democratic) delegate Duport rose to argue that the Revolution remained incomplete so long as the Jews of Alsace were excluded from equal rights. Duport argued solely for the logic and integrity of the Revolution – he did not discuss the Ashkenazim or the prospects for their regeneration. So long as the Jews were willing to take the oath of citizenship, they must be granted equality before the law. Therefore, on 27 September 1791, the Ashkenazim gained rights; the issue of regeneration went unmentioned and unresolved.

But the issue of whether the Ashkenazim were capable of fulfilling their side of the emancipation contract was not entirely lost. The next day, 28 September, the opponents of the amendment, especially those hailing from Alsace, tried to qualify it. They succeeded in adding a clause stipulating that the Jews' oath be considered a 'renunciation of their special privileges', that is, the right to autonomous administration and courts. In addition, they persuaded the Assembly to pass a special law against Jewish usurers. These qualifications, however, did not put an end to matters. The same issues were to reappear with the rise to power of Napoleon.

The impact of Napoleon on the Jews in France

The success of emancipation in revolutionary France seemed to herald a new era for European Jewry. The promise of the Enlightenment was now fulfilled. There were, to be sure, occasional infringements, such as the persecution of Jews for religious observance when all traditional religion was under attack in 1793–4, but the achievement seemed secure not only in France but everywhere that the Revolution spread. Jewish emancipation travelled along with the other ideas of 1789 in the baggage trains of the revolutionary armies. When French troops entered the Rhineland in 1792, the commanding general (Custine) announced that the Jews would be granted rights, and this occurred in 1797 when an independent republic, the so-called Cisrhenane Republic, was created there. The revolutionary 'Batavian' republic in the Netherlands, helped into being by the French army, extended rights to the Jews as individuals, but not as a group, in 1796 – thus following the principle enunciated by Clermont-Tonnere. And in 1796–8, the conquest of northern and central Italy by a French general named Napoleon Bonaparte resulted in the physical destruction of ghetto walls and the granting of legal equality. Napoleon was hailed as the liberator of the Jews.

It was all the more disconcerting when this same Napoleon, who had become first consul in 1799, consul for life in 1802 and emperor in 1804, decided to reopen the issue of the Jews' status in 1806. But an astute observer could have predicted the trouble ahead. Napoleon's entire effort in domestic affairs was directed at retaining the essentials of the revolutionary heritage (for example, individual rights) within a system of efficient, orderly and despotic state centralism. His reform of the legal code, for instance, demonstrated that he did not want unresolved issues and untidy administration.

The Revolution had left many loose ends, and nowhere were they looser than with regard to the Jews. First and foremost, the issues of Jewish communal debt remained. Before the Revolution, the Jewish community of Alsace had been heavily in debt, in part because of an economic downturn, but in larger part because of the manipulation of taxes by the community's leaders, who made sure that the bulk fell not on themselves, but on the community's poorest members. With emancipation in 1791, the official *kehillah* (community) was abolished, but the debts were not. The Revolution's normal procedure of selling religious property to pay the debts was not used for the Jews. The *kehillah* was revived in the guise of a 'Commission in Charge of Liquidation of the Debts', but it had no power of taxation, so its brief, understandably, went unfulfilled.

Secondly, the organization of the Jews as a religious group had not been resolved. They now constituted merely a voluntary society, with none of the legal recognition that had been accorded to Catholics and Protestants in 1801. In 1804, the Jews of Metz requested what amounted to a reinstatement of the old corporation with a right to levy taxes and fines. In 1805–6, more progressive leaders submitted a blueprint for a reorganization in which the rabbi would be a spiritual leader – but not a judge – and the French language would be used. Whatever the proposal, both the Jews and the government realized that some solution was required.

Finally, the tension between Jewish creditors and French peasants had been exacerbated by the massive sale of church lands. In Alsace, the Jews were virtually the only source of credit. Peasants who had arranged credit in order to buy church lands had trouble meeting their debts, since purchase prices had often been inflated by Christian speculators. Jewish creditors resorted to the law courts with increasing frequency, and the number of seizures and forced sales of peasant property rose dramatically in the first years of the new century. (It should be noted that in provinces where there were Christian creditors, the peasants fared no better.)

These problems were brought to Napoleon's attention in the audiences he held when he passed through Strasbourg on 23–4 January 1806. In addition, Napoleon was familiar with the tract of a vehement opponent of Jewish emancipation, who argued that emancipation should have been made conditional upon the resolution of the problem of usury, since it was Judaism, and not legal discrimination, that was responsible for the Jews' reprehensible way of life. These influences, along with his desire for tidy administration, and possibly his own opinions of the Jews, prompted Napoleon to conclude that the National Assembly's grant of rights in 1790–1 had been an act of 'unwise generosity'. He therefore decided to convene an Assembly of Jewish Notables to redress the balance between rights and regeneration.

Napoleon's commissioners presented the laymen and rabbis who comprised the Assembly of Notables with twelve questions designed to ascertain whether Judaism prevented the Jews from complying with France's laws and civic morality. These twelve questions fell into five main categories:

- Do Jews allow bigamy, divorce and intermarriage?
- Do Jews consider Frenchmen to be brethren, and will Jews obey the laws of France?
- What powers do the rabbis have, who appoints them, and are their powers sanctioned by law or custom?

- Can Jews practise all professions?
- Does Jewish law permit Jews to charge interest on loans only to Gentiles, or to Jews and Gentiles equally?

An ultimatum accompanied the questions: 'The wish of his Majesty is that you should be Frenchmen; it remains with you to accept the proffered title, without forgetting that, to prove unworthy of it, would be renouncing it altogether.'[4]

This ultimatum did not succeed in compromising the deputies' integrity. Convinced that Judaism did not preclude social regeneration, they discussed the questions with remarkable candour and managed to formulate answers that virtually all of them could accept. Such widespread agreement represented a considerable achievement, given the Assembly's diversity. The deputies were drawn not only from the two very different communities of Ashkenazim and Sephardim, but also from parts of Italy. Yet neither a traditional Ashkenazi rabbi like David Sintzheim, the guiding light for all issues touching on rabbinic law, nor a Sephardi enlightener like Abraham Furtado, the President of the Assembly, felt compromised. Sintzheim, in particular, corresponded with other rabbinic authorities in Europe throughout the proceedings and justifiably believed that he had remained faithful to Jewish law (*Halakha*).

The Assembly's answers to the twelve questions did show that the emancipation contract entailed a redefinition of Judaism and its relationship to the nation state and civil society. The answers were thus to be of lasting significance in formulating the central tenets of an ideology of emancipation. First, Judaism was defined as a religion alone. The rabbi was merely a spiritual leader rather than, as in the *ancien régime*, the arbiter of a corporation's laws. Secondly, the Jews subordinated themselves entirely to the authority of the state. The deputies made repeated and profuse professions of their loyalty to the Emperor of France. The Assembly also recognized the superiority of civil over religious law, asserting, for example, that while rabbis could refuse to give religious sanction to a mixed marriage, they were obliged to recognize that it was legally binding in civil law. Thirdly, the Jews recognized the equality in Jewish law of their French fellow citizens. This meant seeing Christians as righteous people who subscribed to natural religion – that is, to universal standards of morality – and who therefore deserved the same treatment as fellow Jews (in the Middle Ages Jews, like Christians, accorded adherents of other religions inferior treatment). The Assembly's 'ideology of emancipation' satisfied both the deputies' consciences and Napoleon.

In 1807, Napoleon summoned a body composed primarily of rabbis to give religious sanction to the Assembly's answers, and in a characteristically grandiose gesture, gave it the title of 'Sanhedrin', after the supreme Jewish court at Jerusalem from the second century BCE to the first century CE. In so doing, he claimed the messianic role attached to renewing a religious institution that had not functioned for eighteen centuries. As he put it, he wanted the Jews to 'find Jerusalem in France'. Many Jews did hail Napoleon as the new liberator, though subsequent events showed how mistaken this optimism was.

Having assured himself of the Jews' loyalty, Napoleon went on to achieve two

The Great Sanhedrin convened by Napoleon in Paris in 1807. This assembly had seventy members drawn from France and other parts of the Napoleonic empire, and was presided over by Rabbi David Sintzheim of Strasbourg, a great authority on Jewish law.

further aims. His commissioners proposed an institutional framework to sustain the new 'religion' of Judaism and also to pay outstanding communal debts. Judaism was reorganized as a 'consistory' (literally: council), following the model of the French churches. Relying on the Catholic idea of a clerical hierarchy, the consistory made Judaism a rabbi-centred religion. The rabbi was to teach Jewish doctrine in accordance with the decisions of the Sanhedrin. Yet he and the consistory had another range of duties as well: they were also functionaries of the state, responsible for the Jews' military service and occupations. The consistorial system subjected them to the same comprehensive supervision and control as the rest of French society. Napoleon's goal of despotic state centralism had been achieved.

Napoleon had convened the Assembly in search of a pretext for discrimination. During the final sessions of the Assembly, his commissioners pushed through a motion requesting that the government adopt measures to ensure the Jews' regeneration. Using the legal fiction of the motion, on 17 March 1808 Napoleon's government issued the so-called 'Infamous Decrees' which regulated the Ashkenazim of Alsace, especially their economic activities and residential rights, for a period of ten years.

The deputies to the Assembly and the representatives at the Sanhedrin felt betrayed, but there was nothing they could do. The principle of legal equality adopted by the National Assembly in 1791 had now been violated, and the Ashkenazim justifiably felt themselves demoted to the status of second-class citizens.

The effects of the Infamous Decrees were, however, not lasting. When they expired in 1818, the restored Bourbons (the ruling family of France from 1589–1793 and 1814–48) did not renew them. Jewish emancipation was confirmed by the French parliament in 1831, when Judaism was accorded equality with the Christian churches and the state assumed responsibility for the salaries of its officials. Napoleon had called Jewish emancipation into question, but the state was never to do so again. After 1818, the far-reaching emancipation the Revolution had granted was secure, and the issue of regeneration no longer concerned the state. When it arose, it was as a political or social issue to be thrashed out among citizens and parties. In central Europe, by contrast, emancipation was to take a very different course.

Turning back the clock on Jewish emancipation: the Congress of Vienna

The Congress of Vienna (1815) made it clear that central European Jews were not going to enjoy emancipation as quickly as those in France. Emancipation had arrived in the German states either directly with the French armies, or indirectly, in reaction to the French model. French occupation brought emancipation in the Rhineland (1797–8), and the ghetto walls were dismantled in Mainz and Bonn. In the newly created kingdom of Westphalia, King Jerome (Napoleon's brother) issued a decree emancipating the Jews in January 1808. In 1811, the Jews of Frankfurt-am-Main were granted civil equality (though they paid a large indemnity – the equivalent of twenty years of the special tax they had been required to pay the city until that time). After the French occupied Hamburg, the Jews gained rights in 1811. Among the states to react to the French precedent were Württemberg (1807), Baden (1809) and Prussia (1811). The new Baden constitution (1807), designed to unify the recently enlarged state, extended certain rights of education and occupation in 1809, and also reorganized the community along the lines of the consistory.

When Napoleon defeated the Prussians at Jena in 1806, the Prussian state was on the point of collapse. As part of an overall reform designed to rouse the citizenry from torpor through the extension of rights, the Jews were granted almost complete civil rights and certain political ones (1812). But in Prussia, as in Baden, the emancipation contract passed into law: not only were the Jews expected to assume 'equal duties' in exchange for 'equal rights' – including military service – but they were also expected to regenerate themselves by acquiring education and training and shifting out of peddling and usury into more 'useful' and 'healthy' occupations. Moreover, equality meant that all vestiges of Jewish communal autonomy (for example, taxation and courts) were also abolished.

Whether directly or indirectly, then, the French precedent succeeded in bringing emancipation to Jews in the most important of the German states and free cities (Bavaria was an exception in passing harsh laws together with liberating ones in 1813). But whereas in France Napoleon's fall and the restoration of a traditional monarchy brought a reconfirmation of rights, in Germany the opposite occurred. The Congress of Vienna was convened in 1814 to determine Europe's future, and

Germany was at the centre. Napoleon had dissolved the 800-year-old Holy Roman Empire and redrawn political boundaries. Would Germany remain politically fragmented or would it be unified? Jewish leaders and German statesmen correctly thought that Jewish rights depended on unity. A unified state or confederation of states would at worst confirm the rights already attained; at best, it would extend full and equal rights uniformly. In contrast, the failure to achieve unity would send the issue back to individual states. In that case the outcome was unpredictable, but the prospects for improvement slight.

At first, the advocates of unification and Jewish emancipation had the upper hand. The Prussian statesmen Karl August von Hardenberg and Wilhelm von Humboldt and the Austrian statesman Prince Klemens von Metternich favoured a uniform solution to the problem of Jewish rights. They hoped not only to ensure the rights gained under Napoleonic auspices, but also to use Prussia's legislation as a model for all the other German states. They introduced such an article into the statutes of the proposed Confederation. The measure immediately found opponents in the cities of Frankfurt, Hamburg, Bremen and Lübeck – all wanting to rescind the rights the French had introduced. Bavaria and Hanover joined the opposition to Jewish rights and also, not surprisingly, opposed unification.

Napoleon's return from Elba resolved the conflict. Austria and Prussia sacrificed the cause of a far-reaching political unity, and with it Jewish rights, for the sake of a lesser one that would both galvanize the German states for renewed warfare and be guaranteed by the European powers. Hardenberg's and Humboldt's proposed statute underwent so many revisions that its original intent was ultimately reversed. Rather than conferring full rights, their first compromise proposal deferred the issue until the Confederation convened in Frankfurt; in the meantime, the legal status quo was maintained. Yet even that minimum proposal was eroded when the statute's wording was amended from decreeing the rights 'in the states' (thus including those gained under French rule) to the rights accorded 'by the states' (meaning only those given by the states' own sovereign institutions). The legal status quo was not maintained, as the states gained a free hand to rescind the legislation enacted under French domination. The Confederation never seriously considered the issue once it met in Frankfurt.

The Congress of Vienna made Jewish rights a domestic issue of the sovereign states, and thus subject to the varying political tendencies of the era (1815–48). The issue confronting the states was what they now would do with the liberal ideas of 1789 – natural rights, popular sovereignty and Jewish emancipation – in the changed climate of the Napoleonic era. Not only had all external pressure to adopt those ideas been removed, but the alliance of Austria, Prussia and Russia increasingly exerted pressure in favour of the principle of legitimacy (the hereditary right of sovereigns to rule).

Jews fared worst in Prussia, where the edict of 1812 was gradually restricted by bureaucratic practice. In 1817, it was decided that the new laws did not extend to Posen, the western portion of Poland that Prussia had acquired in the partition of 1793. In 1818, Napoleon's Infamous Decrees were renewed in the territories along the Rhine. And in 1822, the Prussian Ministry of Education decided that Jews did not have the right to teach in secondary schools and universities.

The smaller south German states, in contrast, gave the emancipation contract a new twist, asking for regeneration and equal duties without granting equal rights. This was especially the case in Baden and Württemberg which, unlike Prussia, had a form of limited parliamentary government. In these states, the issue of Jewish emancipation was debated numerous times in the 1820s and 1830s and the question of the Jews' 'regeneration' was always pre-eminent.

The fact that emancipation remained incomplete in the German states resulted in continuous ferment among the Jews. First, there was the tension between the Jews' rising socio-economic status and their rights. The basis of German Jewry's economic ascent was laid in the Napoleonic and immediate post-Napoleonic period. The new bourgeoisie felt the strain between their new prosperity and their continuing lack of rights, so that with each failure to gain emancipation or each major setback there were conversions to Christianity. These conversions were disturbing not because they involved large numbers, but because the apostates came from the élites of the community. In the 1790s, for example, this tension had led to the anonymous offer of the *maskil* David Friedlander to lead the foremost heads of houses in Berlin into a deistic Christianity. This offer, made in a moment of despair, was rejected by Christian theologians and Friedlander remained an active member of Berlin Jewry until his death in 1834.

Another factor causing dissatisfaction among German Jews was the continuous pressure for 'regeneration'. This resulted in a kind of ideological hothouse in which new movements and ideas sprouted and took root. It is not surprising that many of the major phenomena associated with the modern Jewish experience – reform, positive historical and neo-orthodox Judaism, as well as the academic study of Judaism – emerged in the German states in the years between the start of the Congress of Vienna in 1814 and the Revolution of 1848.

Yet it would be wrong to forget that these developments were built on the ideas of the Haskalah. The Haskalah had advocated changes that would make Jewish practice and belief compatible with the Enlightenment. Moderate *maskilim* like Isaac Euchel, the publicist and biographer of Mendelssohn and Wessley, wanted to do away with the casuistic (*pilpul*) and mystical (kabbalistic) methods of studying Jewish texts in favour of a more literal approach. They advocated the study of the Bible and Hebrew language, and an end to the medieval liturgical poetry. In short, they espoused certain minor reforms that were entirely in keeping with Jewish law. Radical *maskilim* like David Friedlander and Lazarus Ben-David proposed reforms without regard to *Halakha* (Jewish law) and rabbinic authority.

In what came to be known as the reform movement (later known as reform Judaism) the moderates at first held sway. The earliest reforms were introduced in the kingdom of Westphalia as part of the new consistory under French auspices (1808). The former court Jew of Brunswick, Israel Jacobson, was appointed head of the consistory and he recruited *maskilim* from throughout Germany for key positions. Jacobson ushered in religious reforms as part of a larger programme of re-education and occupational restructuring. The reforms were limited to the decorum and solemnity of the liturgical service, and did not directly challenge *Halakha*:

the liturgical poetry (*piyutim*) was eliminated, the service became more frontal (the reader's platform was moved from the centre to the front of the synagogue) and a German-language sermon and an organ were introduced. Similar reforms of this limited type were introduced in Berlin in private synagogues prior to 1815.

Only after the Congress of Vienna did a more radical spirit gain control of the reform movement. In 1817, a group of local notables in Hamburg opened a 'temple' independent of the organized religious community, which challenged rabbinic authority: the prayer book was printed from left to right with some prayers in German; there were an organ, a choir and a sermon in German; some prayers were revised to give them a universal cast; and the prayer '*Aleinu*' (which praises God for making the Jews superior) was deleted. The Hamburg rabbinical court issued a ban against the 'temple' and solicited support for their action from eminent rabbis throughout Europe, whose letters were published in a volume entitled *These are the Words of the Covenant*.

Hamburg was exceptional until the 1840s. Most communities fought not over extreme reform, but over whether to introduce secular studies into the primary school or to hire a preacher to give sermons in German. The programme of social regeneration and the agenda of religious reform spread via the institutions of the sermon and the school. Jewish schools with mixed secular and religious curricula appeared during the revolutionary and Napoleonic eras and developed in significant numbers in the 1820s and 1830s. The schools taught a version of Judaism that centred on morality and introduced new ceremonies like 'confirmation', whose aim was to demonstrate publicly that the students had learned moral precepts. The moralizing sermon in German also became a major vehicle for the programme of regeneration, including reform; the sermon became a permanent feature of Jewish worship in most urban and small town communities.

Of enduring significance for the rethinking of Judaism was the invention of the academic study of Judaism (*Wissenschaft des Judentums*). The Haskalah had advocated a rationalist and literal approach to Jewish texts. A group of Jewish students at the new University of Berlin, dismayed by the Congress of Vienna and the Hep Hep riots (protests against Jewish emancipation, which began in Würzburg in 1819 and spread elsewhere in the German states), attempted to enlist the humanist disciplines such as philology and philosophy to the cause of Jewish emancipation. They thought that the philosophical and philological study of Judaism would prove its equality with Christianity and thus pave the way for the equality of Jews with Christians, and that past neglect of the academic study of Judaism was intricately bound up with the Jews' civic degradation.

In addition, the founders of this movement thought that the academic study of Judaism would be an invaluable tool in the struggle for the reform of Judaism, which they also thought integral to the emancipation process. The students formed the Society for the Academic Study of Judaism and published a journal. Although this institution was short-lived, and two of its best-known founding members, Eduard Gans and Heinrich Heine, ultimately converted, the discipline itself lasted, and became a form of authority in competition with Jewish law.

Taken together, the reforms of Jewish institutions and the founding of the academic study of Judaism led to a new image of the rabbi. The rabbi was no longer to be the talmudically learned judge of an observant community, but rather an academically trained teacher, preacher and minister to souls. In the 1830s, a new cohort of rabbis educated in universities as well as in *yeshivot* began to appear. These men attempted to wrest control of the movement for reform from lay leaders by convening a series of rabbinical conferences in the 1840s. One dissenter from these conferences, Zacharias Frankel, became the founder of 'positive-historical' (or what is known today as 'conservative') Judaism. Frankel succeeded in founding the first modern rabbinical seminary in Breslau in 1854.

Orthodoxy was not oblivious to these developments. Indeed 'orthodoxy' first emerged as a distinctive strand of Judaism as a result of the controversy with the reformers. In the 1830s, Samson Raphael Hirsch, the founder of neo-orthodoxy, attempted to revive orthodoxy by using some of the central ideas of the reformers, thus combining adherence to Jewish religious law and practice with modern culture and education. This trend continued, and by mid-century the orthodox had also turned to, among other things, the German-language sermon.

The protracted nature of the emancipation process meant that German Jews

Hepp! Hepp!

An early-nineteenth Frankfurt print depicting a scene from the Hep Hep riots of 1819, when Jews and their property were attacked by the local populace fired by resentment of Jewish emancipation and its economic consequences. The origins of the Hep Hep slogan are unclear, but it may come from the rallying cry of the Crusades: 'Hierosolyma est perdita' ('Jerusalem is lost').

became the creators of the various new ideologies of Judaism in the nineteenth century. While these ideologies influenced communities in Europe and elsewhere, nowhere else did a similar combination of circumstances emerge to create an ideological hothouse. For instance, in the Habsburg Empire there was little pressure for regeneration between the death of Joseph II in 1790 and the revolution of 1848. The Viennese Jewish community became a centre of moderate reform and Prague a centre of moderate Haskalah. In turning back the clock on Jewish emancipation, the Congress of Vienna paradoxically advanced the history of Jewish self-understanding.

Jewish involvement in liberal and national movements

If there had ever been any doubts about who the friends of Jewish emancipation were, they were dispelled during the years from the Congress of Vienna until 1848. In those decades, the alliance of the Jews with liberalism was firmly cemented. Jewish emancipation not only became an item on liberalism's agenda, but Jews also participated in the liberal politics of the period.

The rights that had been extended to the Jews – even where these rights had been limited (as in the German states) – made it possible for them to enter into the political life of their countries. This is not to say that Jews had not been politically active previously. The autonomous communities had always had an intercessor ('shtadlan'), the court Jew in the eighteenth century, who negotiated with the ruler for the community's well-being. But his activity belonged to the court politics of an estate society. In the early stages of the emancipation process, similar figures used their influence to push for rights. The Berlin maskil and court Jew David Fried-lander, for example, submitted numerous memoranda to the Prussian government (between 1786 and 1792) detailing the advantages that would accrue from removing disabilities. But again, such efforts represented the court politics of a notable dealing with an enlightened absolutist government. In contrast, after 1815, but especially after the July revolution in 1830, Jewish intellectuals participated in the new public, liberal politics on behalf of Jewish rights and general issues.

In the German states the most prominent Jewish political figure was Gabriel Riesser. Trained as a lawyer, Riesser campaigned for Jewish rights by using the available means of liberal politics: pamphlets, petitions and the press. He rejected the emancipation contract of rights for regeneration, arguing that on the basis of natural law the contract should be one of rights for duties. And since the Jews were already fulfilling their duties, it was legally inconsistent for the states to deprive them of their rights. Although based in Hamburg, Riesser reached an audience throughout the German states and was to play a prominent role in the Revolution of 1848. Another figure in the German states who made his entrance into politics in the 1830s with the issue of Jewish rights was Johann Jacoby. By the 1840s he had become one of the most prominent politicians of Prussia, widely known for his militant liberalism.

In France, Adolphe Crémieux began his eminent political career with a suc-cessful campaign to remove one of the last vestiges of Jewish inequality, the oath *more judaico.* (Since the Middle Ages, Jews involved in lawsuits with non-Jews had been forced to swear this special oath. It was virtually a self-imposed curse, in which the deponent detailed the punishments that would befall him if his oath was falsely sworn. The oath shows the degree of distrust Christians had for Jews, and the ceremony that accompanied it was usually both humiliating and degrading.) Crémieux subsequently graduated to the general liberal movement, serving as a minister of state, yet nonetheless remained committed to Jewish issues. He accompanied Sir Moses Montefiore, perhaps the most important Jewish philanthropist of the age, to the Middle East during the Damascus affair (1840), and later served as first president of the Alliance Israélite Universelle (1864), an organization devoted to the education and defence of less-fortunate Jews.

In addition, Jews became involved in politics not only at the national level, but also locally, playing an active role in the German states, for example, in municipal politics and local chambers of commerce. The careers of Riesser, Jacoby and Crémieux show the continuity between the cause of Jewish emancipation and the general cause of liberalism. In the German states, where it was incomplete, Jewish emancipation became part of the larger liberal agenda; indeed, the concept of 'emancipation' was applied not only to the Jews but to the middle classes, the economy, society and indeed to humanity as a whole.

The broadening of the definition of Jewish emancipation was of great significance: it meant that liberals essentially accepted Riesser's argument that the original emancipation contract was no longer valid. Jews were to be granted rights according to the same criteria as everyone else and not in return for a special variety of 'regeneration'. Of course, the existence of men like Riesser and Jacoby encouraged such a view. Liberalism was the politics of the middle classes. In the years after 1815, a German Jewish urban middle class began to emerge. To a large extent it shared the education, social organization and political outlook of the German middle class – and thus a growing social basis existed for an alliance between the two.

Yet not all liberal politicians were in favour of this alliance. Some still subscribed to the emancipation contract of rights for regeneration. Some even turned the new slogan of emancipation on its head, asserting that the Jews first had to 'emancipate' themselves before they could be emancipated by society. Other liberal politicians adopted aspects of the conservative ideology of the Christian state. They felt that granting the Jews full rights entailed a secularization that would deprive the state of its moral foundation.

Nonetheless, the logic of emancipation was compelling and gradually won the hearts and minds of most liberal thinkers and politicians. In the German states, and in Austria and England, it was the liberals, as heirs of the Enlightenment, who championed the cause of Jewish rights against its conservative opponents.

Given their liberal affiliations, it was not at all surprising that Jews were actively engaged in the Revolution of 1848. The Revolution began in Paris, but quickly spread to Vienna, Berlin and Milan. The reactionary, legitimist settlement imposed upon Europe crumbled within a matter of days. Everywhere there were demands for constitutional government and, especially in central Europe, the independence and unification of national groups. It was also to be expected that in the German states and Austria the emancipation of the Jews was in the offing. In the 1840s, the growing militancy of liberals had led to resolutions in favour of Jewish equality in a number of the German states (for example, in the Rhine in 1843), and in 1847 Prussia passed a new law removing some of the barriers in existence since 1812.

Perhaps the most striking aspect of the early days of the Revolution was the extent of Jewish political participation. In Germany, there were Jews among the activists on the barricades as well as among the victims of the fighting. The public funeral of the victims of the first violence of the Revolution held on 20 March 1848, which was addressed by priests and rabbis, turned into a demonstration for the removal of religious distinctions. Six Jews were named to the non-elective pre-parliament in Frankfurt and five were elected to represent Germany at the actual German National Assembly: Johann Jacoby, Gabriel Riesser, Moritz Veit, Luwig Bamberger and F. W. Levysohn. Riesser played an especially prominent role: he sat on the Constitutional Committee, was elected second vice-president (October 1848) and was a member of the deputation that unsuccessfully invited the king of Prussia to become German emperor (April 1847).

Jews were also elected to the assemblies or parliaments of a number of German states for the first time: Bavaria, Saxony-Anhalt, Hesse-Homburg and Prussia (where Johann Jacoby was one leader of the democratic faction), and the free cities of Frankfurt, Hamburg and Lübeck. In Austria, Jews were on the barricades in Vienna, and here, too, the funeral for the victims (17 March) became a protest of fraternity. When the imperial government in Vienna collapsed, a young Jewish doctor, Adolf Fischhof, became head of the Committee of Security. A number of Jews were delegates at the Austrian National Assembly, including Fischhof, Joseph Goldmark, Joseph Unger, Rabbi Mannheimer of Vienna and Rabbi Meisels of Cracow, and two Jews were among the Austrian representatives to the German National Assembly (Ignaz Kuranda and Moritz Hartmann). In France, the new government included two Jewish ministers, Crémieux holding the portfolio for Justice and Goudchaux that for Finance.

But the Revolution of 1848 did not immediately bear fruit. As with the French Revolution, emancipation was neither automatic nor unambiguous. Prussia's 'Decree on the Foundations of the Future Constitution' (April 1848) merely anticipated the basis of equality of rights. Equality itself was not granted until the restored government imposed a constitution in December 1848. Similarly, in Bavaria the Revolution granted Jews political rights, but left harsh restrictions intact (June 1848); the post-revolutionary government enacted rights in May 1849. In the Frankfurt National Assembly, Riesser pushed through a provision for equality without serious debate, though misgivings were voiced in committee. In Austria, as well, the Revolution did not unequivocally proclaim rights: as early as 25 April 1848, the equality of religions was declared, but Jewish disabilities were not removed. Here again, the government that suppressed the Revolution granted Jewish rights (March 1849).

Yet, in keeping with the earlier German experience, the failure of the Revolution of 1848 brought the repeal of emancipation. Within a few years even the equivocal gains were lost. In August 1851, the Act that Riesser had sponsored was formally repealed. While Prussia confirmed the Jews' equal status in the revised constitution (31 January 1850), its force was attenuated by another clause that proclaimed Christianity to be the state religion. In 1851, Austria repealed the constitution of March 1849, leaving the matter of Jewish rights entirely unresolved.

The Revolution of 1848 was enough of an upheaval to beget emancipation – albeit with great difficulty – but not to sustain it. The restored governments disowned this ill-begotten offspring as soon as possible, and were often applauded for so doing. As in 1789, the 1848 Revolution had been accompanied by anti-Jewish disturbances. These disturbances were worst in Alsace and Baden (areas where Jews were creditors), and were at their height in the early days of the Revolution (March–April). The new governments and the liberals had immediately suppressed them. But these outbreaks represented an opposition to Jews and to emancipation that also found ideological expression: it was during the ferment of the 1840s and the subsequent Revolution that Jews were first made symbols of capitalism's excesses, being turned from the oppressed into the oppressors.

In 1848, emancipation failed because the liberals were not sufficiently strong to retain power. The opposition had considerable support. But 1848 did succeed in establishing Jewish emancipation as a principle of liberalism, and the next upheaval that brought liberalism to power would also establish Jewish emancipation.

The achievement of full emancipation in central and western Europe

Throughout its history, European liberalism had been linked to nationalism. Liberals had assumed that the freedom of the individual depended upon the freedom of the nation. A German or Italian could only be free when his or her country was united and self-governing. In central Europe, as in Italy, liberalism seemed to achieve its greatest triumph when it succeeded in establishing unified states based on individual rights. This occurred in the 1860s and 1870s in a number of countries, and it was this triumph that brought full emancipation to the Jews. If the Revolution of 1848 had made emancipation a key principle of liberalism, national unification made it a reality. This time around there was no talk of the emancipation contract. The principles of natural law and individual freedom prevailed.

After the failure of the 1848 Revolution, a wave of reaction washed over Europe. Its greatest symbol was probably Napoleon III, a lesser version of the original despot. But this reaction did not last for long. Liberals everywhere recovered their confidence and began pressing the old issues. Within two decades of the Revolution, their cause was triumphant.

In Germany, Bismarck forged the German Empire out of 'blood and iron': national unification could only be achieved by defeating the opponents of a united Germany on the battlefield, first the Habsburg Empire and then Napoleon III. Most liberals enthusiastically supported Bismarck. When he triumphed over Austria in 1866 and created the North German Confederation, liberal measures were legislated, including a ban on religious discrimination (1867); and in July 1869 'all existent restrictions on civil and political rights derived from the difference in religious confession' were repealed. Political and public offices in particular were opened to Jews. When the new German Empire was declared in 1871, these laws were extended to the remaining territories (especially Bavaria).

In the Habsburg Empire, the defeat by Bismarck in 1866 led to a restructuring of the Empire. Such a restructuring had been on the agenda since 1848, but the crisis of 1866 made it unavoidable. The Habsburg Empire became a dual monarchy, with Austria and Hungary as equal partners. The constitution of 1867, which embodied liberal principles, extended full rights to the Jews in Austria.

National unification in Italy also brought emancipation. The kingdom of Sardinia, which led the effort at unification (known as the *Risorgimento*) had granted rights to its own Jews in 1850, and subsequently extended rights to Jews in the territories that came into its possession in the process of unification. This process was completed in 1870 when the Papal territories became part of a new unified Italy and the Jews of Rome, representing the oldest continuous Jewish settlement in Europe, were emancipated.

English Jews were also 'emancipated' at this time, but the process was piecemeal and its meaning different. 'Emancipation' designated merely the ability to hold political office, since Jews had long been eligible for citizenship by being born in the country. An attempt to legislate full Jewish emancipation (1830) in the wake of Catholic emancipation (1829) had failed. The political liberals, or Whigs, succeeded in getting the bill passed in the Commons (1833), but it was blocked by the Lords with the backing of the King.

Instead of a frontal attack, English Jewry's leaders tried a step-by-step flanking manoeuvre. In 1833, Jews were allowed to be called to the bar. In 1835, David Salomons (1797–1873), a member of the Stock Exchange and a Lloyds underwriter, was elected Sheriff of London, parliament passing a special bill to allow a non-Christian to hold that office. In 1845, parliament opened all municipal offices to Jews. Thus all restrictions except on the ability to sit in parliament had been lifted. In 1847, Baron Lionel de Rothschild, scion of the famous banking family, was elected to parliament to represent the City of London. He was unable to take his seat because of the oath which contained the words 'on the true faith of a Christian'. The Prime Minister, Lord Russell, tried to put through a bill that would abolish this piece of discrimination, but once again the Lords blocked it. Rothschild was re-elected numerous times, and in 1851 Sir David Salomons was also elected, but was obliged by order of the Speaker to leave the chamber before he could take his seat. A compromise was finally reached between the two Houses in 1858, allowing each one to determine its own oath.

In just under two hundred years, the Enlightenment and liberalism had succeeded in establishing the legal equality of the Jews in most of central and western Europe. This triumph was part of the general success of liberalism, which in turn depended upon the transformation of society (from estates based on corporate privilege to a civil society based on individual rights) and the unification of states. Jews could only be included when notions of their inferiority (whether religious,

BARON ROTHSCHILD AT THE TABLE OF THE HOUSE OF COMMONS—TAKING THE OATHS.

Baron Lionel de Rothschild being sworn in as the first Jew in the House of Commons on 26 July 1858, as depicted in the Illustrated London News *of 28 July 1858. Although he was prevented from taking his seat in 1847, the City of London had continued to elect him to the Commons until a compromise was reached over the oath.*

moral or pedagogical) were discarded and the emancipation contract of rights for regeneration – so prominent from the late eighteenth century until 1848 – could give way to an unequivocal demand for rights on the basis of natural law. The inclusion of the Jews in liberalism's triumphant vision opened a new era in Jewish history.

Yet the triumph did not go unchallenged. This was true of liberalism in general and of Jewish emancipation in particular. Old opponents looked back to a pre-liberal order, and new opponents looked forward to a new illiberal one. In Germany, the alliance of liberalism and nationalism soon split apart as Bismarck shunned his erstwhile allies in order to be able to pursue repressive, undemocratic policies. Anti-Semitism as an organized political movement emerged within a decade of 1871 and, though it did not gain victory at the polls, it did legitimate anti-Semitism as a form of political thinking and as an attitude in social behaviour. In the Austro-Hungarian Empire, the Jews became identified with the state, which was now attacked by the numerous national minorities (for example, Czechs, Slovaks and so on) striving for self-determination. The position of Lord Mayor of Vienna, the highest elected office in the Austro-Hungarian Empire, was won by Karl Lueger on an openly anti-Semitic platform in 1895. In France, the Dreyfus affair in the 1890s (see Chapter 6) called into question the ideas of 1789 and the possibility of a secular state. In England, the Marconi affair (1912), in which four government ministers, two of whom were Jews, were accused of attempting to gain financially from a government contract with the Marconi company, similarly gave rise to anti-Semitic sentiments.

Despite these challenges, emancipation held until fascism repudiated liberalism and with it, Jewish emancipation. In the twelve ghastly years from 1933 to 1945, millions of Jews were deprived first of their rights and possessions and then of their lives. Although the losses of those years were beyond imagination or repair, emancipation was reinstated after 1945, and Jews continue to enjoy its benefits today.

4 East European Jewry Since 1770

Lionel Kochan

Introduction

From the Middle Ages to the late eighteenth century, the vast majority of east European[1] Jews lived under Polish rule. Indeed, the Polish Commonwealth,[2] which comprised Poland, Lithuania, the Ukraine and various other territories, had the largest Jewish population of any state in Europe (see Chapter 1 and Map 7). With the break-up of that Commonwealth, starting in the early 1770s, there began a long period of enormous change. Since 1770, the Jews of eastern Europe have probably been subjected to more upheavals than any other Jewish community in the world. They experienced changes of nationality as Polish territory was partitioned between Russia, Austria and Prussia in the late eighteenth century, and subsequently those under Russian rule were confined to an area known as the Pale of Settlement. They suffered from anti-Jewish legislation and were the victims of pogroms – anti-Jewish attacks by the general populace. As a result, at the end of the nineteenth and beginning of the twentieth centuries, they emigrated *en masse*, primarily to the United States, and changed the Jewish world map.

Those who remained within the Russian Empire found themselves in the front line during the First World War, and in 1917 they were caught up in the Russian Revolution, with many Jews playing an active part. The collapse of that empire resulted in another change of nationality for some and life under Soviet rule for others. With the Second World War came the German invasion and the tragedy of the Holocaust, which was responsible for the deaths of almost five million east European Jews. Remarkably, the post-war period has witnessed the reassertion of Jewish identity in eastern Europe; there has also been increased emigration, particularly to Israel but, on the darker side, there has been an alarming resurgence of anti-Semitism. Now, with the fall of communist regimes and the rise of latent nationalisms in the former Soviet bloc, yet more changes seem likely for east European Jewry.

The position of the Jews in the Russian Empire after the Polish partitions

The Jewish panorama of growth, suffering and achievement in eastern Europe had its roots in Poland, where most east European Jews lived. As Chapter 1 indicated, the Jewish community in Poland and its territories grew and prospered from the fourteenth century until the middle of the seventeenth century despite constant undercurrents of repression, discrimination and persecution. The Khmelnitskii massacre in 1648 signalled a major reverse in the fortunes of Jews within the Polish Commonwealth. Attacks on Jews gathered pace as the Polish state succumbed to internal and external pressures, and began to crumble: the disintegration of Jewish society paralleled that of Polish society in general.

In the three partitions of 1772, 1793 and 1795, the Polish Commonwealth was carved up among its powerful neighbours – Russia, Austria and Prussia – and ceased to exist as a political entity (see Map 7). The majority of Polish Jews (over half a million people) thus found themselves under Russian rule just as the Enlightenment was making its mark on European thinking and attitudes. So, from the late eighteenth century the greater part of east European Jewry came within the Russian Empire.

The acquisition of a large number of Jewish subjects in the course of the Polish partitions created something of a dilemma for the Russian ruler, Empress Catherine the Great, who reigned from 1762 to 1796. In Russia there had been a long history of discrimination against the Jews. Indeed, much of the time they had been prohibited from entering the country, hence the Jewish population had remained small. Ultimately, in 1742, the Jews had been expelled outright, and so when the first Polish partition took place in 1772 there were virtually no Jews living in Russia itself. Yet Catherine was a devotee of the Enlightenment and was inclined to tolerance; therefore, in the years following the first partition of Poland, her government apparently made every effort to treat the Jews in the annexed Polish territories as a religious minority entitled to the same rights as Christians of similar social status. Accordingly, they were allowed to retain their livelihoods, property and traditions, and their conditions improved overall.

While Catherine was content to leave the Jews to continue their way of life in the former Polish territories, she was more circumspect about allowing Jews into Russia itself. Despite her liberal inclinations, she intentionally put off making a decision on whether to readmit Jews officially to Russia, since she was keenly aware of the likely opposition to such a move, especially from the clergy. But, at the same time, she made it possible for Jews to enter unofficially, and a number of Jewish merchants and traders made their way to Russia to take advantage of business opportunities.

Catherine even surreptitiously encouraged Jews from the former Polish Commonwealth and elsewhere to come and settle in certain parts of her empire. Her reasons for doing this were economic as much as enlightened: sparsely inhabited tracts of land in southern Russia around the Black Sea had been acquired during the recent wars with the Ottoman Empire and needed to be colonized; the Jews, with their noted business acumen, were seen as good candidates to develop trade and resources there.

Because of Catherine's benign attitude, conditions for Jews under Russian rule were generally more favourable than for Jews in most of western Europe. Unfortunately, this situation did not last. There were two main reasons for the change: first, with the start of the French Revolution in 1789, Catherine's enthusiasm for the Enlightenment waned and she became committed to the status quo; secondly, the notion of equality for the Jews was highly unpopular, particularly with the native Poles in the provinces annexed by Russia and also with the Russian merchants, who feared the competition of their Jewish counterparts.

By the time of the final partitions of Poland in the 1790s, Russian policy was already turning firmly against the Jews. Some of the measures that had been devised by Catherine to ensure rights and opportunities for the Jewish population were set aside, and restrictions were once more imposed. A prime objective now was to prevent the Jews from spreading throughout the Russian Empire. With this aim, imperial decrees were issued in 1791 and 1794, placing restrictions on Jewish civil rights and merchant activity in areas outside the former Polish and Ottoman territories. These territories were left open to Jews because, in the case of the Polish lands, Jews were an inextricable part of the fabric of society, while in the erstwhile Ottoman territory they served as useful colonizing agents. The decrees effectively limited Jewish settlement to these areas. (The area open to settlement was extended to cover Polish Jews who became Russian subjects after the final partition of Poland in 1795.)

At first these measures seemed to have only minor importance since the overwhelming majority of Jews were already living in the designated provinces, which constituted a vast area, and in any event, Russians generally were not free to live wherever they wanted. But, later, in the nineteenth century, the full implications became evident and the area came to be known as the Pale of Settlement (see Map 8).

Russian policy toward the Jews in the nineteenth century

As the influence of the Enlightenment waned, long-standing anti-Jewish prejudices came more and more to the fore. Throughout the nineteenth century, the Jews in the Russian Empire were regarded as parasites and exploiters from whose depredations the population, especially the peasants, had to be protected. This attitude was partly rooted in the resentment and moral condemnation engendered by the Jews' prominent role in the alcohol trade (as innkeepers, retailers and producers) – a role that had originated under the arenda system in the late Middle Ages (see Chapter 1). So, whenever the general population fell victim to hardship or distress, the Jews were held responsible: they became the scapegoats for the social stresses and strains within Russian society as a whole.

Yet the policy of the state toward the Jews was ambivalent: it veered between harsh repression and quasi-benevolent attempts at making the Jews a more integral part of Russian society and maybe effecting their assimilation. However, there were a number of themes that recurred in the policy throughout the nineteenth century – first and foremost, the containment of the Jews. The existence of the Pale of Settlement – an area to which the Jews were confined – was a fundamental part of this policy. In the nineteenth century, while the majority of people were enjoying greater liberty and increased freedom of movement, most Jews were compelled to stay within the Pale, thereby preventing their participation in the economically developing regions of the Russian interior. Although in the 1860s certain favoured categories of wealthy and skilled Jews were allowed to leave the Pale, it remained in existence until the Russian Revolution of February 1917, its extent changing several times and the regulations governing residence there being enforced with varying degrees of rigour depending on the prevailing political mood.

Other recurrent themes in tsarist policy toward the Jews were concerned with trying to decrease the Jewish identity: for instance, there were several moves to suppress the use of Hebrew and Yiddish, and there were also frequent attempts to divert Jews from their traditional occupations (as traders, brokers, innkeepers etc.) into agriculture – seen as a more beneficial activity.

One attempt by the government to assimilate the Jews involved reducing the autonomy of Jewish communities. Traditionally, Jewish society was organized on self-governing lines, and this independence had long been officially accepted. Each local community was largely responsible for running its own affairs, with the main mechanism of self-government being the *kahal* – a 'board' or assembly of prominent community members. The *kahal* exercised control over many aspects of community life: religious, social and economic. For instance, it oversaw schools, synagogues and cemeteries, had a judicial role, and also had extensive charitable and welfare responsibilities; in addition, it was used by the government to collect the various special taxes and levies imposed on the Jews. The new imperial Jewish policy, introduced in 1804 by Tsar Alexander I, sought to promote the integration of Russian Jews by, among other things, reducing the influence of the *kahal* and thus weakening the community structure.

The so-called Jewish Statute of 1804 nominally confirmed the authority of the *kahal* within a community, but limited the legal powers of its officials and of the rabbis, and prohibited the use of Yiddish or Hebrew in official transactions. The *kahal* was still allowed to maintain its own schools, financed from public funds, though these schools now had to adopt the curricula and language of instruction of the other public schools, with the study of Russian, Polish or German being made obligatory in Jewish schools. Moreover, older pupils were ordered to abandon their traditional Jewish clothing. At the same time, the 1804 statute opened Russian elementary schools, secondary schools and universities to Jewish students, so encouraging assimilation.

The statute also contained some far more drastic measures: it provided for the forced evacuation of Jews from villages in certain areas, and it prohibited Jews from dealing in alcoholic beverages in villages or leasing commercial enterprises there. Under the arenda system several centuries earlier, Jews had been granted special rights as innkeepers and as liquor merchants and producers, and the alcohol trade had become the traditional mainstay of the Jewish rural economy, so the latter provision of the statute had severe implications. Instead, the government set up agricultural colonies and encouraged migration to the cities, thereby hastening the demise of long-established Jewish communities. Additionally, the Pale of Settlement was extended by the statute to include Astrakhan and the Caucasus.

In the end, the wide-ranging 1804 reforms were largely frustrated by disagreements between Alexander's advisers and by the exigencies of the Napoleonic Wars (1805–15). There was, in fact, concern that the Jews might be so disaffected by the measures that they would support the French in the wars, but in general they showed great loyalty to the tsarist regime, and many Jews in the western part of the Empire (notably in Belorussia) actively supported Russian troops against Napoleon's forces in 1812.

Alexander's somewhat ambivalent attempts to integrate Russian Jewry were radically transformed for the worse during the reign of his successor, Nicholas I, who ascended the throne in 1825. Nicholas and his advisers saw the extent to which the Jews had been assimilated into west European society and aimed to achieve the same in Russia. They wanted Jews to be educated in the Russian language and culture, to play a productive role in the economy, and to practise an 'enlightened' form of Judaism leading, perhaps, to conversion to Christianity. In western Europe this policy had been accomplished on the basis of gradual Jewish emancipation; in Russia the government attempted to achieve the same end through a policy of discrimination and coercion that began in the late 1820s and lasted throughout the 1830s and 1840s.

For the Jews, by far the most harsh and most damaging of the measures introduced by Nicholas was his notorious conscription policy which served as an instrument for assimilation. In 1827, Nicholas imposed conscription on Russian Jews, breaking with the policy initiated by Catherine the Great of exacting monetary payment from them in lieu of military service. Among the non-Jewish population a quota of men between the ages of eighteen and twenty-five was called up every two years, whereas a separate quota of Jewish men was called up every year. Furthermore, Jews could be conscripted when they were only twelve years old: conscripted Jewish boys were placed in special units ('cantons') for pre-military training, and when they reached the age of eighteen they were transferred to the regular service for the standard term of twenty-five years; Jews, therefore, were often required to serve up to six years longer than non-Jews. But what made this policy particularly invidious was the pressure put on the Jewish conscripts – many of whom were mere children – to convert to Christianity. They were forbidden to speak Yiddish, denied contact with their relatives or with Jews in the vicinity of their camps, and all their religious requisites were confiscated. In many cases the Jewish conscripts were subjected to torture and physical maltreatment to force them to convert. Altogether about 70,000 Jews were conscripted in this way between the late-1820s and the mid-1850s when the policy was discontinued by Nicholas' successor, Alexander II; about 50,000 were aged below eighteen, and at least half of these underwent baptism, while a considerable proportion of the adults were also converted.

An important indirect casualty of the conscription policy was the traditional Jewish leadership. The policy made the community leaders responsible for supplying the designated quota of recruits. If there were not enough adult males to meet the quota, then the leaders had to turn to minors under the age of eighteen. As it was often the case that an adult male aged between eighteen and twenty-five was already married and the father of a family, the leaders tended to choose those males without family responsibilities, even if they were just children (sometimes below the minimum age of twelve). Although the burden of conscription should have been distributed equally across a community, it was not: the community leaders frequently rigged the recruitment registers to favour the wealthy at the expense of those without money or influence. The inevitable consequences were the weakening of the solidarity that had hitherto characterized Jewish society, and a distinct loss of confidence in the leadership, as well as a profound bitterness amongst the poor.

In the course of Nicholas' thirty-year reign, numerous measures relating to the Jews were brought in, the centrepiece of the legislation being a set of ordinances known as the Jewish Regulations, introduced in 1835. These regulations were designed to bring order to the often-conflicting laws concerning the Jewish population. They distinguished the Jews as a separate social group on the basis of religion, customs and place of residence, and, among other things, enforced traditional prohibitions on the employment of Christian servants by Jews and on the building of synagogues next to churches. Furthermore, the legislation now decreased the size of the Pale of Settlement.

Of the barrage of measures directed at the Jews by Nicholas, several were intended to reduce obvious manifestations of the Jewish identity and hasten the process of russification. For example, in 1827, Jews were required to adopt fixed family names (in effect, surnames) like the bulk of the Russian population, rather than use patronymics; under an 1836 statute, all Hebrew printing presses were closed down (except for one in Vilna and another in Zhitomir); and in the late 1840s, Jews were ordered to give up their traditional garments and wear European dress.

As in the past, there were intermittent expulsions of Jews from some areas, and there were also renewed attempts to get Jews to abandon their traditional roles as traders (especially in alcohol) and brokers, and to take up agriculture; agricultural settlements were established on government lands, and Jews who chose to work on the land were automatically exempted from military service. In 1844, special schools for Jews were set up under the aegis of the government, with the aid of 'enlightened' Jewish educationalists from Germany, the emphasis being on a more secular education. In the same year, Nicholas dissolved the institution of the autonomous *kahal* – the mainspring of Jewish community self-government – and placed the Jews under the control of the police and the municipal authorities, though a limited communal organization was retained to oversee the collection of taxes and the filling of conscription quotas.

There was even some talk in official circles of classifying Jews as 'useful' and 'non-useful': those employed as agricultural workers, clerics, artisans and merchants would be classed as useful; the rest – that is, the vast majority of the Jewish population – would be deemed 'non-useful' and would be subject to harsh repression. Even though this particular policy was never implemented, Nicholas' other repressive moves prompted personal appeals from the British Jewish philanthropist Sir Moses Montefiore in 1844 and 1846. However, apart from conscription, the measures introduced by Nicholas had surprisingly little success – Jews resolutely kept up their own institutions, adhered to their own system of justice and boycotted

Sir Moses Montefiore, leader of Anglo-Jewry and financial adviser to Queen Victoria, delivering a personal memorandum to Tsar Nicholas I during a visit to St Petersburg in 1846. In particular, Montefiore pressed for the abolition of the hated 'cantonist' conscription system.

the state-run schools. It is indicative of the difficulty of implementing these policies that between 1848 and 1853 the government handed down no fewer than three separate prohibitions on the wearing of traditional Jewish dress.

Tsar Nicholas I died in 1855 and was succeeded by his son, Alexander II. The new tsar soon found himself faced with two major problems: social unrest throughout the Empire, and the effects of the humiliating Russian defeat in the Crimean War in 1856, which highlighted the need to modernize Russian society. To address the demands of both liberal reformers and the peasantry, and to embark on modernization, Alexander II, the so-called Tsar-Liberator, adopted many policies that were far more liberal than those of his father: in the 1860s and 1870s he emancipated the serfs, removed many of the barriers to foreign travel, established regular courts of law, facilitated the formation of an independent professional judiciary, and permitted freer expression of public opinion in the press and elsewhere. As far as the Jews were concerned, his most important reforms were the abolition of juvenile conscription, the repeal of a law barring Jews from government service, and the granting of permission for wealthier Jewish merchants, graduates of institutions of higher education, and skilled artisans to leave the Pale of Settlement. A small number of Jews were thus able to move into the mainstream of Russian life, and influential Jewish communities developed outside the Pale, notably in Moscow and St Petersburg.

While statutes, regulations and reforms were imposed on Russian Jews by successive tsarist governments as the nineteenth century progressed, Jewish society itself was undergoing internal changes. Like Russian society in general, Jewish society was in a state of transformation, and no institution was left untouched. Many of the changes arose as a result of tensions between traditionalists and reformers in east European Jewry: while great Talmudic academies still flourished in Lithuania, and Hasidic rabbis continued to dominate in the Ukraine and in other parts of the old Polish Commonwealth, an important reform-oriented movement was gaining momentum among the Jews of eastern Europe from the 1820s onward – this was the Haskalah, or Jewish Enlightenment (see Chapter 3).

The Haskalah had its origins in Berlin in the 1770s and 1780s, guided by Moses Mendelssohn. The movement sought to reshape Jewish life to embrace the ideals of the European Enlightenment. Like the European Enlightenment, the Haskalah looked both to the future and to the past: the movement aimed to prepare Jews for a full, emancipated role in the modern world, but at the same time it encouraged the preservation and revival of certain aspects of Jewish culture.

The adherents of the Haskalah, known as *maskilim*, set out to broaden the traditional educational curriculum of Jewish elementary schools and *yeshivot* and to promote an interest in the Hebrew language. In addition, the *maskilim* endeavoured to widen the occupational base of Jews from a narrow concentration on commerce to include agriculture and crafts – interestingly, the occupations of Jews in ancient times. Also on the agenda was the overhaul of the Jewish community structure, as well as the reform of Judaism itself in order to bring about a return to the 'true religion of Moses'.

The Haskalah spread from Berlin to Galicia, reaching Russia about fifty years after its appearance in the West. In Russia the Haskalah is perhaps best represented by the writings of one of its leaders, Isaac Baer Levinsohn. In *Testimony in Israel* (*Te'udah be Yisrael*), published in 1828, Levinsohn advocated the establishment of schools for impoverished Jewish children where crafts and trades would be taught alongside traditional subjects; he also supported earlier attempts to steer Jews toward agriculture by advocating that the government should transfer one-third of the Russian Jews into agricultural occupations. In general, Levinsohn, like most *maskilim*, espoused a reform of Jewish society, religious life and communal organization, in the belief that this would enable Russian Jews to participate in the world of European culture and society while retaining their Jewish identity. Levinsohn's suggestions received a certain amount of official backing: the Russian government, eager to encourage Jewish assimilation into wider Russian society, was receptive to a number of the proposals of the *maskilim*. For instance, the government established special 'enlightened' Jewish schools in 1844, and made recurrent attempts to direct Jews into agriculture.

Although the *maskilim* remained a tiny minority, they were very influential and were active on many fronts; among other things, they revived the Jewish press, and Odessa and Vilna became the centres of Jewish publishing, with works printed in both Russian and Hebrew despite continuing censorship. A special Society for the Promotion of Culture Among the Jews of Russia (*Obshchestvo dlia Rasprostraneniia Prosveshcheniia mezhdu Evreiami v Rossii*) came into existence in 1863 to further the aims of the *maskilim*. Its founders and leaders were a group of wealthy and powerful Jews in St Petersburg – members of the millionaire Günzburg family and other *maskilim*.

The broad aim of the Society was to bring culture and education to the Jewish masses of Russia, with an emphasis on the learning of Russian. To this end, the Society subsidized the publication of journals and books in Russian (as well as some in Hebrew), encouraged the development of Jewish literature, supported poor

Jewish university students and, later, school pupils within the state education system as well as in 'enlightened' schools. The Society also augmented teachers' pensions. Its membership never reached more than about 750 in the nineteenth century, yet its influence was enduring. The Society even had some measure of success in broadening the curriculum of Jewish elementary schools, especially in the 1870s, so that it included not only traditional subjects, such as Hebrew and biblical studies, but also secular subjects, such as Russian, mathematics and geography. It was in this spirit that the poet Judah Lev Gordon had sent his famous call to Russian Jews in 1863, exhorting them to 'awake', learn Russian and draw closer to the Russians. Gordon appealed to his fellow Jews to 'be a brother to your countrymen and a servant to your king'.[3]

However, the problems of Russian Jewry could not be solved by the reforming philosophy of the Haskalah, certainly not in the short term, nor even by the liberalizing measures that had been introduced by Alexander II in the 1860s and 1870s. While these measures, together with increasing industrialization, did create unprecedented opportunities for some Jews, the benefits were distributed very unevenly. A small number of Jews achieved great prominence and wealth – as railway-builders, exporters, bankers and industrialists. Easier access to universities also produced a Jewish professional class composed mainly of doctors and lawyers, and in the 1870s the number of Jewish university students increased dramatically. Unfortunately, what made some Jews wealthy or successful undermined the livelihoods of others. For example, the birth of the railways resulted in a multitude of Jewish workers – innkeepers, carters and coachmen, in particular – losing their jobs. The railways also led to the decay of various centres in the Pale, such as Berdichev, and to the rise of others, such as Odessa.

There was an enormous natural increase in the Jewish population at this time (a consequence of early marriages, the emphasis on large families, and lower infant mortality probably attributable to good Jewish maternal care). This, plus the forced relocation of Jews into the Pale of Settlement and internal migration from north to south within the Pale, resulted in poverty and social strain among Russian Jews. Between 1820 and 1880 the number of Jews in the Russian Empire rose from an estimated 1.6 million to about 4 million, an increase of 150 per cent, compared with an increase of about 90 per cent in the general population over the same period. Moreover, the increase in the Jewish population was disproportionately concentrated in certain urban areas of the Pale in southern Russia; for instance, in the southern provinces of New Russia, between 1844 and 1880, the Jewish population increased by more than 300 per cent, mainly due to migration. Migration was particularly marked after 1869, when harvest failures, food shortages and an outbreak of typhus in the northwestern provinces of the Pale drove masses of impoverished Jews to the south. Odessa, with its already thriving Jewish community, was a favourite resettlement destination, and its Jewish population of 17,000 in 1854 roughly tripled to 52,000 (out of a total population of 193,000) by 1873. The city became notorious for poverty, congestion and the general misery of many of its Jewish inhabitants.

The average Jewish employee in the Pale worked fourteen to sixteen hours a

Jews in Odessa, 1837. Located on the Black Sea, Odessa became a crossroads for Jews from many different traditions and geographic regions. A centre of Jewish culture, the city was also a focus of anti-Semitism: pogroms killed hundreds of Jews in Odessa in 1881 and 1905.

day, six days a week, in return for a pittance – the Jewish working classes were employed primarily in the food, tobacco, textile and wood processing industries, where wages were extremely poor and the demand for labour was subject to great fluctuations. The factories in which they worked were small and primitive, and were often owned by other Jews whose standard of living was scarcely better than that of their employees. It is, therefore, understandable that the health of the Jews in the Pale of Settlement was, in general, markedly inferior to that of their Christian neighbours. Ultimately, these grim conditions led to the emergence of a Jewish proletariat and to the development of Jewish political and cultural activism – key elements in the strategy for survival as the nineteenth century drew to a close.

Growing anti-Semitism and the Jewish response

In March 1881, matters worsened considerably for the Jews: the period of comparative liberalism came to an end when Alexander II was assassinated by members of the revolutionary People's Will Party (*Narodnaia Volia*). A significant proportion of the members of this group were Jews, and one of those directly implicated in the assassination plot was a young Jewish woman, Hessia Helfman.[4] Six weeks later, anti-Jewish attacks – pogroms – broke out in Elizavetgrad in southern Russia. During the next few weeks, similar pogroms occurred throughout the Ukraine and in other parts of the Russian Empire – not only in minor Jewish centres, but also in major cities such as Kiev and Odessa (and even in Warsaw in December 1881). Although the government probably did not instigate these pogroms, it certainly did not discourage them – at least not until 1882 when the new Minister of the Interior, Dmitrii A. Tolstoi, alarmed by the scope of these rampages, emphatically refused to tolerate any further outbreaks.

The pogroms were an expression of the widespread anti-Jewish feeling that had developed in Russian society in the nineteenth century. The authorities argued that the pogroms were simply popular retribution for the Jews' ruthless exploitation of the Russian peasantry – a view that could, in part, be traced back to the role of the Jews in the arenda system in Poland several centuries earlier (see Chapter 1). Between 1903 and 1905, further anti-Jewish attacks took place, largely organized by the League of the Russian People (*Soiuz Ruskogo Naroda*), more commonly known as the 'Black Hundreds' – a paramilitary alliance of extreme Russian nationalists. Attacks in 1903 claimed the lives of over forty Jews in Kishinev, the capital of Bessarabia. In Odessa, in 1905 more than 300 Jews were killed, thousands were injured and countless others lost their means of livelihood.

Government policy toward the Jews was also essentially hostile and was succinctly expressed in the notorious formula attributed to Konstantin Pobedonostsev, who was the chief adviser to Alexander III, tsar from 1881: a third of the Jews will die, a third will be converted, and a third will emigrate, and thus the Jewish question in Russia will be solved. Accordingly, between 1881 and 1914 the government initiated a series of anti-Jewish policies which affected most aspects of Jewish life. In May 1882 several 'Temporary Regulations' concerning the Jews were issued by Alexander III. These 'May Laws', as they came to be known, were a direct response to the pogroms: it was felt that if the Jews were less of an 'aggravation' to the general populace, the attacks would stop. The aim then was to restrict and contain the Jews still further by limiting them to urban areas. So the May Laws effectively prohibited Jews from settling outside the cities and towns, and Jewish ownership of land and property in the countryside was annulled. One of the most economically damaging provisions of the May Laws was the banning of Jews from the alcohol trade in the villages: the production and sale of alcoholic beverages had traditionally been central to the Jewish rural economy, but the May Laws virtually destroyed these sources of income and thereby accelerated the move to the cities and towns. Other acts passed under Alexander III limited educational opportunities by introducing percentage quotas, the so-called *numerus clausus*, for Jewish students at Russian secondary schools and universities. The number of Jews allowed to become physicians in the Russian army was also restricted. The area of the Pale of Settlement was further decreased, and efforts to restrict Jewish habitation to the Pale were stepped up; to this end, about 30,000 Jews were expelled from Moscow (two-thirds of the Jewish community) during Passover in 1891.

The reign of Nicholas II, who became tsar upon his father's death in 1894, was also characterized by continuing official anti-Jewish attitudes. The 'blood libels', based on the medieval belief that Jews ritually murdered young Christian boys and used their blood in Passover rites, once again drew wide public attention. In the most sensational of these cases, Mendel Beiliss, a Jewish employee at a brick kiln in

Kiev, was arrested on a charge of stabbing to death a twelve-year-old Christian boy in March 1911. After an international outcry, the evidence against Beiliss was exposed as false with the Russian government implicated in its production, and Beiliss was acquitted. The government's role in the case, particularly the hand of the Minister of Justice in providing 'experts' to verify the existence of ritual Jewish murder, illustrated the state's attitude toward the Jews.

A powerful element in the anti-Semitic ideology of this period was a bizarre work known as the *Protocols of the Elders of Zion (Protokoly Sionskikh Mudretsov)*. Originally appearing in St Petersburg in the last decade of the nineteenth century, the *Protocols* outlined what purported to be a plan by the leaders of international Jewry to conquer the world. In 1905 this fabrication was reprinted by the official government press and distributed by the imperial army staff in the St Petersburg region. Anti-Semitic propaganda now depicted the Jews as part of a vast international conspiracy.

The unrelenting violence, discrimination and propaganda drove many Jews to flee Russia; indeed, mass emigration was a major Jewish response to the pogroms and their aftermath. Roughly 12,500 Jews emigrated annually between 1881 and 1886, and between 1906 and 1910 the annual figure averaged 82,000. By 1914, emigration from Russia had changed the world map of Jewry: nearly two million Jews had left. Most entered the United States, though significant numbers also went to Great Britain, Canada, Argentina, South Africa and countries in western Europe (see Map 10).

Those Jews who remained in the Russian Empire were faced with ongoing violence and anti-Jewish sentiment. In addition, social conditions within the Pale of Settlement remained appalling; overcrowding was as serious a problem as ever, with natural population increase outstripping emigration. Yet the established leaders of Russian Jewry, rabbinical and lay, offered no positive solutions to these problems. Moreover, they opposed emigration, the solution increasingly favoured by hundreds of thousands of Russian Jews. The leadership, therefore, seemed powerless and out of touch with popular concerns; as a result, its authority was severely diminished.

The violence and repression led not only to Jewish emigration from the Russian Empire and to the growing gulf between the established leaders and the Jewish populace, but also to the increasing radicalization of young Jewish intellectuals. In the 1860s and 1870s, Russian universities had provided fertile soil for the growth of radical political philosophies – ranging from agrarian populism to socialism. These new ideas, coupled with the quotas imposed on Jewish students (their representation amongst all Russian university students dropped from 14 per cent in 1886 to 7 per cent in 1902), resulted in frustration with the existing political system, so young Jewish activists began to press for the reform of all existing conditions – by violence if need be. This new generation was to form the core of a virtual revolution in Russian Jewish political life.

There were two important elements in this 'revolution': the formation of Jewish Marxist parties and the emergence of Zionism. By far the most significant Jewish Marxist party was the Bund, established in 1897. Its full title, adopted in 1901 at its fourth congress, was the General Jewish Workers' Union in Lithuania, Poland and

Russia (*Algemeyner Yidisher Arbeter Bund in Lite, Poyln un Rusland*). By 1905, when the Bund reached the zenith of its pre-revolutionary influence, it had a membership of about 30,000 and a much larger number of sympathizers – it far exceeded the other Russian social democratic parties of the period in size and influence. The Bund's programme called for equal rights for Jews in a future socialist era, though it later modified this to a call for immediate equal national rights for Jews, to include not only citizenship but also the right of Jews to enjoy their own institutions, courts, and means of cultural expression. The Bund was active in organizing strikes and demonstrations amongst the Jewish workers in the Pale, and after the Kishinev pogrom of 1903 it formed defence squads to protect Jews.

A second element in the Jewish political 'revolution' was the emergence of Zionism, first formulated by Leon Pinsker, whose own social and political development mirrored that of many Jewish activists of his generation. A graduate in medicine of the University of Moscow and decorated for service in the Crimean War, Pinsker had previously been a supporter of the Haskalah and of the Society for the Promotion of Culture Among the Jews of Russia. However, the pogroms of the early 1880s convinced him that anti-Semitism was ineradicable as long as the Jews lacked a country of their own. Pinsker articulated this view in his famous pamphlet of 1882, *Autoemancipation* (*Autoemanzipation*), in which he wrote:

> The Jews are not a living nation; they are everywhere aliens, therefore they are despised ... The proper, the only, remedy would be the creation of a Jewish nationality, of a people living upon its own soil, the auto-emancipation of the Jews; their emancipation as a nation among nations by acquisition of a home of their own.[5]

Pinsker emphasized that the 'home' did not have to be Palestine: 'the goal of our present endeavours must be not the "Holy Land", but a land of our own'.[6] Nevertheless, because his analysis of anti-Semitism so closely matched that of those who advocated migration to Palestine, Pinsker gladly became associated with them. In Russia the Zionist movement initially appealed most to middle-class Jews; then in 1906 a socialist-Zionist movement came into existence and, with it, the beginning of mass emigration to Palestine. Between 1881 and 1914, about 50,000 Jews, mainly young socialist-minded pioneers, left tsarist Russia to work in Palestine.

Bundism and Zionism did not exhaust the political effervescence of the turn of the century. In 1906 the small but influential Jewish People's Party (*Volkspartei*) was formed by the historian Simon Dubnov; its aim was Jewish autonomy within a future liberalized Russia. When the Duma (the quasi-parliament extorted by the Russian Revolution of 1905) came into existence in 1906, it provided a platform for a range of Russian Jewish liberals to add their own criticism of the tsarist regime, and some of these Jews later became prominent in the leadership of the liberal Constitutional Democratic (*Kadet*) party, which formed the majority in the first two Dumas.

Fierce controversy raged among the various movements. The religious groups, especially the Hasidim, assailed the Bundists for their atheism and criticized the Zionists for trying to usurp God's authority – God alone could restore the Jews to their land. The Bundists accused the liberals of being allies of the discredited old leadership and denounced Zionism not merely as a Utopian movement, but also as an obstacle to the development of class consciousness among the Jewish proletariat. The Zionists responded by arguing that the Bundists utterly failed to grasp the strength of anti-Semitism and that any talk of the unity of the working class was a deceptive myth. But the outbreak of war in 1914 fundamentally altered the whole context of these controversies. It created a situation that had not been anticipated by any of the participants and brought to power one of the smallest of the revolutionary groupings in Russia – the Bolsheviks.

The First World War and the Russian Revolution

The First World War created unprecedented hardship and suffering for Russian Jewry. On the eastern front, Russia engaged the Central Powers (Germany and Austria), and the war was waged in the Pale of Settlement – precisely those territories where the bulk of east European Jewry lived; consequently, the Jews were in the front line. The fate of the ancient Jewish centre of Vilna provides a telling example of the turmoil generated by war and its aftermath. It was captured by the Germans in September 1915. In 1918 it became the capital of the recently restored independent state of Lithuania. In January 1919 it fell into Soviet hands, only to fall to the army of newly independent Poland later in the year. In 1920 the Poles lost Vilna to the Red Army, but by the end of the year, Vilna, renamed Wilno, became a part of the Polish state.

When the First World War broke out, a Jewish deputy in the Duma, Naphtali Friedman, declared that 'nothing could ever alienate the Jews from Russia, their native land', and that they would 'rally to the defence of their country'.[7] Indeed, this proved to be the case: it is estimated that by 1917 as many as 600,000 Jews were serving in the Russian army. One reason for the Jews' patriotism, despite their history of persecution, was the hope that Russia's wartime alliance with the western powers would give them a status similar to that enjoyed by Jews in Britain and France. But these hopes were never realized.

The actual experience of war proved to be an unmitigated catastrophe for the Jews of the Pale. In addition to the inevitable hardships of war, they were subjected to the anti-Semitic policies of the Russian High Command – they were branded as disloyal by the military authorities and made the scapegoats for the army's failures. As a result, they were forcibly expelled *en masse* from their homes in the war zones, first from Galicia in 1914–15 and then from the northwestern front in Lithuania (see Map 10). In June 1915 the authorities expelled some 200,000 Jews from the provinces of Kovno and Courland. In all, perhaps as many as 600,000 Jews were uprooted by the tsarist government during the course of the war, with very few able to take their possessions with them. These hundreds of thousands of refugees fled to the Russian interior and to the large cities of the Polish provinces: at one point in the war there were more than 80,000 Jewish refugees in Warsaw alone. Serious food shortages then ensued as these areas were overwhelmed by refugees.

Although there were attempts by prominent Russian Jews and certain tsarist ministers to intervene and halt the policy of expulsion, they were of no avail. However, the effects of the expulsions were not all negative – there were two far-reaching positive consequences. The first was the virtual abolition of the Pale of Settlement. In August 1915 the Minister of the Interior, Prince Shcherbatov, told his colleagues that they would have to allow forcibly evacuated Jews to reside in areas beyond the Pale of Settlement, at least temporarily. He informed all Russian provincial governors that 'in view of the extraordinary wartime situation and until the review of the laws governing the Jews, I am . . . granting permission to Jews to reside in all urban communities',[8] though this permission did not apply to Moscow or Petrograd (the name given to St Petersburg during the war[9]), or to some minor areas.

The second positive consequence of the expulsions was the birth of the Central Jewish Committee for the Relief of Victims of War (*Evreiskii Komitet Pomoshchi*), generally known by the initials EKOPO. It functioned not only as a privately funded relief body but also as an agent for political mobilization. Under EKOPO, relief to stricken Jewish communities throughout Russia, and above all to the many refugees, was provided by Jewish physicians, nurses, teachers, sanitation experts and other professionals, as well as by thousands of unskilled volunteers. Their expertise, material resources and grassroots involvement gave them an influence over the new refugee communities of the interior that far surpassed the power exercised by the Jewish elites of Moscow and Petrograd. So the vacuum of authority created by the disruption of war was filled by an entirely new social force, one that was eager for change. Many of the young relief workers came from the left-wing Zionist movement and the Bund, and although they were hostile to one another (in fact, Zionists tended to support Russia's role in the war, while Bundists advocated withdrawal), they worked side by side in EKOPO. Significantly, in the course of providing aid, they were able to take their various political ideologies to masses of Jews who had previously been beyond their reach, and thus they greatly increased Jewish political awareness.

War, mobilization and the accompanying hardships and upheavals served to bring about a new political consciousness in the entire Russian population. This awakening manifested itself dramatically in February 1917 with the collapse of the tsarist regime. After two and a half years of war which had brought the regime very little military success and had exposed its incompetence and corruption, Tsar Nicholas II was forced to abdicate and the Russian Empire collapsed. The power vacuum was filled by the hastily formed Provisional Government, composed of party leaders from the Duma. Alongside the Provisional Government in Petrograd there arose what was, in effect, a second governing body – the Petrograd Soviet. A soviet was a popularly elected council representing the workers, soldiers and peasants, and thousands of soviets sprang up across Russia to challenge and eventually topple the Provisional Government.

All the organized Jewish political bodies, whatever their differences, welcomed the fall of tsarism and the formation of the Provisional Government. Together with the vast majority of their fellow Russians, the Jews prepared to exercise the political freedom that the new system proclaimed. This freedom was particularly significant for the Jews because one of the first acts of the Provisional Government was to remove at a stroke the whole apparatus of tsarist anti-Jewish legislation. In 1917 a decree pronounced: 'All the limitations on the rights of Russian citizens imposed by hitherto existing laws on the basis of religion, creed or nationality are hereby revoked.'[10]

This decree, in conjunction with the wider political freedom enjoyed in 1917, enabled Jews to participate fully in the hectic political manoeuvrings of those months between the February Revolution and the Bolshevik October Revolution.[11] Not only were there Jews serving as political secretaries to ministers in the Provisional Government, but they were also to be found in the leadership and in the rank and file of all the political parties, with the exception of the extreme right. In particular, by mid-1917 there were six Jews on the twenty-one-member Bolshevik Central Committee, including Leon Bronstein (better known as Trotsky) after he returned from exile abroad. As Lenin's closest collaborator, and later as Commissar for War, Trotsky assumed a crucial role in the victory of the Bolsheviks and the establishment of the Soviet state. It is interesting that many of the politically radical Jews did not come from the mainstream of Russian Jewry; rather, they hailed from outside the Pale of Settlement and had lost all ties with the Jewish community.

The traditional Jewish parties were also active. The Jewish deputies in the Duma relished the opportunities that now existed for solving the serious problems facing Russian Jewry. The Zionists sought to combine their work for Palestine with action in Russia itself aimed at securing the defence of Jewish civil and national rights, to include the recognition of Yiddish and Hebrew as Jewish national languages. The Bund saw the beginning of a new stage in the history of the Russian people and, above all, of the Jewish working class; for the Bund, the Revolution, with the backing of the entire Russian proletariat, had at last brought freedom to the Jewish people. The traditional Jewish parties were joined by newly formed religious parties (for example, Tradition and Freedom, known by its Hebrew name *Masoret Veherut*), whose programmes called for Jewish national autonomy and government financial aid for Jewish communities, as well as the guarantee of Saturday as a day of rest.

There was general agreement among the Jewish parties that they should try to present a common front to the authorities. Appeals were therefore issued for the convocation of an all-Russian Jewish congress that would develop a plan for Jewish autonomy:

> Citizens, Jews! The Jewish people in Russia now face an event which has no parallel in Jewish history for two thousand years. Not only has the Jew as an individual, as a citizen, acquired equality of rights – which has also happened in other countries – but the Jewish nation looks forward to the possibility of securing national rights. Never and nowhere have the Jews lived through such a serious, responsible moment as the present – responsible to the present and the future generations.[12]

In late 1917, elections for the proposed congress were held. The result was an overwhelming majority for the Zionist parties, which received 60 per cent of the votes.

Given the differences between the parties, it is extremely doubtful whether they would ever have succeeded in presenting a united front. But plans were overtaken by events: in October 1917 the Bolsheviks seized power in Russia, fundamentally altering the whole course of Russian life, and the kind of autonomy that had been envisioned by the Jews proved to be impossible under the new circumstances.

Between the World Wars

The national affiliations of east European Jews were fundamentally transformed at the end of the First World War. Whereas most Jews in eastern Europe had been Russian subjects before the war, with the dissolution of the Russian Empire many became subjects of the various successor states that took advantage of the tsarist collapse to declare their independence. Poland was the most important of these new states; others included Lithuania, Latvia and Estonia. As a result, out of the approximately six million Jews who had been under Russian rule, only about two and a half million remained within the redrawn borders of Russia, while approximately three million found themselves in the newly created state of Poland and the remainder mostly became citizens of Lithuania, Latvia and Estonia.

The corpses of Jews murdered in the Ukraine and wrapped in prayer shawls, 1919. During the civil war which followed the Bolshevik Revolution, Jews were attacked from all sides – by Bolsheviks, Whites and nationalist groups alike.

The fate of the Jews in the inter-war period varied considerably depending on where they happened to be living. As far as the Soviet Union was concerned, the early years of the new regime were marked by the most terrible massacres of Jews in Belorussia and the Ukraine. An independent Ukrainian republic had been proclaimed in 1917, but it soon succumbed to the turmoil of civil war and counter-revolution before Soviet authority was finally consolidated there in 1921. The Ukrainians had a long history of hostility to the Jews, as exemplified by the Khmelnitskii massacre of 1648 (see Chapter 1). They now identified the Jews with Bolshevism and made them the scapegoats for frustrated Ukrainian nationalism. More than 1,000 separate outrages took place in the Ukraine in 1919 alone, leaving at least 60,000 Jews dead and thousands wounded, widowed or orphaned. Although detachments of the Red Army often contributed to these atrocities, there were instances when the Red Army came to the Jews' rescue; this was an important factor in helping to reconcile the Jewish population of the Ukraine to Bolshevik rule. The ambivalent feelings of the Jews in the Ukraine toward the Bolsheviks, in fact, mirrored the attitude of Russian Jewry as a whole – an attitude graphically summed up by Gedali, the elderly Jew in the short story by the Russian Jewish author Isaac Babel: 'But the Pole, kind sir, shot because he was the counter-revolution. You shoot because you are the revolution ... How is Gedali to know who is the revolution and who is the counter-revolution?'[13]

At the time, the only political choice was, in effect, between the Bolsheviks on the one hand and assorted White generals, Ukrainian nationalists and various counter-revolutionaries on the other – groups that made even less of an attempt to curb the anti-Semitic outrages of their followers than did the Bolsheviks. The Bolsheviks at least made anti-Semitism a criminal offence and were often successful in repressing its overt expression.

In general, the Bolsheviks' policy toward the Jews was decidedly ambiguous. Their approach was largely determined by the pre-war debates between Lenin and the leaders of the Bund. Lenin believed that the idea of a Jewish nationality was 'definitely reactionary' and a threat to the unity of the proletariat; on these grounds, all manifestations of separate Jewish aspirations came under increasing attack by the Bolsheviks. The Bund was suppressed, and in 1922 its pre-war leaders were forced into exile abroad. The Zionist parties were subjected to the same treatment, although more gradually, and in the 1920s the Zionist Central Committee went underground in order to survive and continue to provide support for local Zionist groups. Despite the professed atheism of the regime, the Soviet government moved more cautiously in its assault on the Jewish religion – to act openly against Judaism would have been altogether too reminiscent of tsarist policy. Nevertheless, in the 1920s, moves against Judaism did gather pace with the harassment of rabbis and other religious officials, followed by show trials, prohibitions on printing prayerbooks in Hebrew, and the forcible closure of synagogues and religious classes.

Cultural activities in Hebrew also came under attack because of the link between Hebrew and Judaism. In the years immediately following the Revolution there was a wide range of creative work in Hebrew – both in the literary field (periodicals and *belles lettres*, as well as scholarly books) and in the performing arts, where the great Moscow-based Jewish theatre company, Habimah, was pre-eminent. But with the moves against the Jewish religion came the suppression of Hebrew work. Hebrew writers were persecuted, and in the late 1920s and in the 1930s their publications were more or less completely suppressed. (Jewish material in Russian also suffered, though less severely.) In 1926 the Habimah theatre company, despite the support of leading Soviet intellectuals, was so threatened and constrained that it did not return to the Soviet Union after a foreign tour. Just how far-reaching the onslaught on Hebrew was is shown by the fact that spelling reforms were introduced into the Yiddish language in order to sever the link with Hebrew; these changes also served to distance Soviet Jews from Jewish communities in other parts of Europe.

However, in parallel with the attacks on the Jewish religion, the Bolsheviks used the Communist Party's Jewish section, known as Evsektsiia, to bring Bolshevism 'to the Jewish street' and to create a secular Yiddish culture – a proletarian culture – in place of the traditional Judaic culture. A certain degree of success was achieved. For example, many synagogues were converted into local secular 'cultural centres' by Evsektsiia officials (several of whom were former Bund members). Yiddish schools were opened, and Yiddish theatre groups sprang up, with the Jewish State Theatre the most prestigious. Soviet Yiddish literature also flourished, and important research into Yiddish language, literature and folklore was carried out at academic institutions in Kiev, Moscow, Minsk and Odessa. Between 1925 and 1932, on average almost 350 books in Yiddish were published each year, and there were more than forty Yiddish newspapers and periodicals.

Unlike Hebrew work, Yiddish culture itself did not come under attack in the 1920s and early 1930s, though some of its proponents fell foul of the moves against other aspects of Jewish culture, and in the 1930s a number of Yiddish writers, including Perets Markish and Samuel Halkin, were accused of 'nationalist deviations'. But by the late 1930s, Yiddish output had begun to decline in the face of ideological pressures, growing Jewish assimilation and waning official backing, and it was then further inhibited by the upheavals of the Second World War.

Along with the assault on Jewish religion and culture, as the 1930s progressed there was a drive against Jews prominent in public life, culminating in the show trials of the late 1930s in which leading Jewish figures in Soviet politics and diplomacy – among them Zinoviev, Kamenev and Radek – were purged by Stalin. There is some evidence to suggest that Stalin exploited the latent anti-Semitism of his supporters in the struggle against his enemies.

Politically, the status of the Jews proved, as ever, to be extremely complicated and even contradictory. On the one hand, they were considered a nationality on the way to assimilation; on the other hand, they lacked a territory, one of the conditions of nationhood (Stalin once argued that the Jews were 'a nation whose existence and future [were] open to doubt'[14]). The result was an awkward compromise that led in 1928 to the creation of the Jewish national area of Biro-Bidzhan (which became the Jewish Autonomous Region in 1934). Located along the northern border with China (see inset in Map 8), Biro-Bidzhan was intended as an area for the settlement

A concert by young musicians in Biro-Bidzhan, 1973. The map at the rear of the stage shows the 'Jewish Autonomous Region', located thousands of kilometres away from traditional areas of Jewish settlement in the Soviet Union: Biro-Bidzhan is roughly 8000 km from Odessa – but only 1500 km from Beijing.

of Jewish workers, primarily in agricultural colonies. It was hoped that the establishment of this region would help to solve the problem of Jewish pauperization which had arisen in the wake of the Bolshevik Revolution. The decline in the economic status of the Jews had been caused mainly by the Soviet nationalization of the means of production and distribution, which had destroyed the livelihoods of thousands of Jewish traders and small manufacturers in the former Pale; moreover, growing industrialization had undermined the position of the many Jewish craftsmen. The Biro-Bidzhan experiment was never a real success and, according to the census of 1979, only about 10,000 Jews were living there (roughly 7 per cent of the region's population and about 0.55 per cent of the total Soviet Jewish population).

In fact, the general tendency of Jews in the post-revolutionary years was to offset the loss of their traditional occupations by seeking new forms of employment in the major cities, where the development of Soviet industry and bureaucracy had created new openings. Many Jews went to Moscow and Petrograd/Leningrad – cities from which they had been largely excluded before 1917 – and by 1923, according to a survey by the USSR Central Statistical Administration, Jews formed the second- and third-largest ethnic groups, respectively, in these cities. In terms of employment, it is estimated that by 1939, 30 per cent of the Soviet Jewish workforce were manual or industrial workers, 41 per cent had administrative or professional jobs (clerks, accountants, teachers, doctors etc.), 20 per cent were craftsmen or artisans, and 9 per cent made their living in other ways (including agriculture). In the pre-revolutionary era, trade and crafts had predominated, with fewer than 10 per cent of Jews in the professional and administrative category. Like Soviet society at large, the Jewish population thus experienced both increasing urbanizaton and a growth in the industrial labour force as people sought to take advantage of the opportunities provided by the industrialization drives of the 1920s and 1930s.

Besides the Soviet Union, the other principal home of east European Jewry after the First World War was the state of Poland, which was recognized in 1919 under the policy of national self-determination adopted at the Versailles Peace Conference. Yet in Poland, as in much of central and eastern Europe, the mixture of different groups of people was too divergent to permit a 'pure' Polish state. Independent Poland's population of roughly thirty million included more than four and a half million Ukrainians, three million Jews and 700,000 Germans – each of these groups benefiting from the protection of the so-called minority clauses in the Treaty of Versailles. In the case of the Jews, these clauses guaranteed them equal civil, political and legal rights, as well as control over their own education system; a further provision in the Treaty ensured the inviolability of the Jewish Sabbath.

In reality the status of the Jews was determined by the actual conditions existing in the country where they lived, rather than by the specific minority rights set out in the Treaty of Versailles but lacking the machinery for enforcement. In Poland, conditions were dominated by the country's prevailing economic stagnation. As a result of the loss of export markets in Russia, the widespread destruction of the war period and the consequent collapse of the agricultural sector, Poland suffered disproportionately from the economic depression of the inter-war years. Once again the Jews were blamed, and anti-Semitism found expression in many areas of everyday life: educational restrictions were imposed on Jews (notably, limits on the numbers of Jewish university students); occupational barriers were erected, with Jews being excluded from employment by the state (both in the civil service and in the state-run industries); and economic discrimination was stepped up, with, among other things, boycotts of Jewish businesses. Most alarmingly, there were renewed pogroms.

At this time there were three main Jewish political groupings in Poland: General Zionist, Agudat Israel (the orthodox religious party) and the Bund. Their prime objectives were very different: the Zionists, who constituted the major Jewish party, sought to promote the *aliyah*, or the return to Palestine, whereas Agudat Israel stressed the importance of preserving traditional Jewish culture and religion within the diaspora. The Bund, on the other hand, focused on the interests of the Jewish working class and the development of a secular Yiddish culture. In their separate ways, these groups each attempted to put pressure on the Polish parliament – the Sejm – in order to achieve their objectives. Despite considerable dissension within their ranks, the Zionists tried to form a parliamentary bloc with the other minority groups in Poland. The Agudat Israel, which rejected Zionist militancy and secularization, pursued a policy of discreet intervention with the authorities, combined with the utmost loyalty to the Polish state and its political objectives. The Bund, a revolutionary Marxist party, rejected the policies of both the Zionists and the Agudat Israel, and instead favoured co-operation with the Polish Socialist Party, the largest of the workers' parties. None of these strategies had any lasting success. The Polish Jews remained without political allies and, therefore, without political influence; consequently, their economic and social position relative to the non-Jewish population continued to deteriorate.

Nevertheless, Polish Jewry flourished intellectually, and the country remained a centre of Jewish learning and scholarship as it had been since the Middle Ages: Polish rabbinical training schools enjoyed world repute, and Warsaw continued to be a centre of literary creativity. Not least, Poland made remarkable contributions to Yiddish literature – in 1928 alone, 622 Yiddish works were published in Poland, and in 1930 there were 180 Jewish periodical publications, mostly in Yiddish but including 28 in Polish and 16 in Hebrew. So, against a backdrop of oppression, Polish Jews retained their culture and their identity.

In Lithuania, another of the new states, the initial approach taken to the Jews was quite different from and much more positive than that in Poland. Shortly after declaring independence in February 1918, the Lithuanian government created a Ministry of Jewish Affairs and instituted an extensive system of Jewish self-government; this system, which encompassed education and social security, was presided over by an elected Jewish National Council empowered to raise its own taxes. However, early 1923 saw the erosion of the autonomy of Lithuanian Jews. Powerful clerics and nationalist groups forced the Constituent Assembly to remove the clauses providing for separate ministries for national minorities from the draft constitution. Funds for the Ministry of Jewish Affairs were not included in the 1924 budget, and the new cabinet formed in April 1924 had no Jewish Affairs minister.

The rise of extreme nationalists in Lithuania caused a further deterioration in Jewish rights. After a *coup d'état* in December 1926, the rightist political faction Tautininkai dissolved parliament and established an authoritarian regime. Thus, the Lithuanian experiment with Jewish national autonomy in a modern nation-state proved to be short-lived.

The Second World War

Even in the late 1930s, when the rise of the Nazis and their imitators had brought Europe to the brink of war, the Russian historian Simon Dubnov refused to be pessimistic, arguing that the Jews of Europe would be free once Europe itself was liberated. But this was not to be. By the time Europe was liberated, six million Jews had been murdered in what has come to be known as the Holocaust, and the majority of these were from eastern Europe. In September 1939 there were approximately seven million Jews in eastern Europe; by May 1945 the total was less than two and a quarter million. The area had been transformed into a vast Jewish graveyard.

It was in Poland, in particular, that the Germans chose to locate their extermination camps, at places such as Auschwitz, Treblinka, Chelmno and Sobibor. Poland was chosen not because of the long-standing anti-Semitism of the Poles but for essentially pragmatic reasons: millions of Jews lived there, the area was under total German occupation, and furthermore it was sufficiently remote to prevent information about the atrocities reaching the outside world.

The reaction of east European Jews to Nazi policy was conditioned by two factors: first, initial ignorance of the ultimate aim of the policy, for although there were localized massacres from the first days of the invasion, mass extermination did not begin until early in 1942; secondly, the Jews were very isolated in much of eastern Europe because of the general hostility of the local populace – most especially in Poland where rampant anti-Semitism meant that there was already, in effect, a war against the Jews.

Nevertheless, the resistance of the Jews in eastern Europe to Nazi oppression was vigorous, equalling that of other conquered peoples. The Warsaw ghetto revolt

Life and death in the Warsaw ghetto, summer 1941. Jews were confined to the ghetto by the Nazis and died of starvation and disease. Preferring to risk their lives rather than endure slavery, the inmates rose in armed rebellion in April 1943. These photographs are from an extraordinary collection taken by a German soldier, Willy Georg, who was also a professional photographer.

in April 1943, for example, was the first urban revolt against the Germans in all of Europe. By November 1939 the Germans had herded about half a million Jews from Warsaw and other Polish cities into the Warsaw ghetto, where they were used as a pool of forced labour. In 1942 those who had survived the dreadful conditions of the ghetto began to be deported to the extermination camp at Treblinka, about fifty miles away. The revolt took place when only some 60,000–70,000 Jews still remained in the city. Despite the enormous odds against them, the Jews in the ghetto, fighting with only small arms and grenades, held off the Nazis for forty-two days before being overcome. The symbolic value of the uprising was great, and it provided the inspiration for other revolts, notably in the concentration camps of Czestochova, Treblinka and Auschwitz. Some Jews managed to escape in the final days of the Warsaw ghetto, often by making their way through an intricate maze of passages from house to house or through the sewers, and many of these survivors were instrumental in the formation of Jewish partisan and guerrilla groups.

Throughout occupied eastern Europe, Jews were active in various resistance groups, some of which were specifically Jewish while others were more broadly based. Although it is not possible to establish the precise extent of Jewish involvement in the partisan and guerrilla movement, all the evidence suggests that it was considerable. For instance, it is known that Jewish partisan groups in Lithuania and the Ukraine disrupted German supply lines and protected those Jews who managed to escape the invading armies.

In the Soviet Union (and elsewhere in eastern Europe before the German occupation), Jews also participated in the struggle against the Germans as members of their country's armed forces. From the earliest days of the Red Army, Jews had been prominent in its ranks, and during the war a large number received awards and decorations – their record compares favourably with that of more numerous minorities, such as Uzbeks, Tatars and Kazakhs. Obviously, these men and women were fighting as Soviet citizens and not just as Jews, but their record suggests that they identified strongly with the battle against the Nazis.

The advent of war had caused the Soviet government to change its repressive attitude to the Jews and other minorities, and to become much more concilliatory: the need was for a united front against the aggressor, so discriminatory policies were set aside in order to ensure the support of the entire population. In the cause of unity, the Soviet government also played down the particular fate that awaited the Jews at the hands of the Nazis. The intention was to avoid implying that the Nazi threat was directed against just one section of the population, as that could have proved divisive. Rather, the Soviet authorities wanted to demonstrate that the Nazis directed their terror against the Soviet population as a whole so that all the Soviet peoples would fight together in the 'Great Patriotic War' to save the motherland.

There was one partial exception to this strategy of de-emphasizing the plight of the Jews – the formation, with official backing, of the Jewish Anti-Fascist Committee (*Antifashistskii Komitet Evreev*) in mid-1942. Its objectives were to enlist the financial and moral support of foreign Jews, mainly American, for the Soviet war effort and to win worldwide Jewish sympathy for that effort. The Committee was headed by prominent Soviet Jews, among them leading generals, academicians and artists (for example, the novelist and journalist Ilia Erenburg, and the violinist David Oistrakh), with Yiddish cultural figures to the fore (in particular, the actor and producer Solomon Mikhoels, the novelist David Bergelson, and the poets Itsik Fefer and Perets Markish). Because the Jewish Anti-Fascist Committee was the only central representative organization of Soviet Jewry, it became something of a rallying point and the focus for Jewish identification. Furthermore, during the later war years and after, the Committee was active in dealing with manifestations of anti-Semitism and in helping evacuees and survivors of the war to resettle in their former communities. Despite originally receiving strong support from the Soviet Bureau of Information, the Committee quickly fell from favour once the objective of defeating Nazi Germany had been attained. Indeed, after the war the Soviet government returned to its discriminatory policies toward the Jews and other minorities.

After the Second World War

The experience of war affected the outlook of the east European Communist governments and that of east European Jewry in contrasting ways. The period of Soviet expansion inaugurated by the war was accompanied by growing state xenophobia and intellectual isolationism at home. Soviet Jews, on the other hand, because of the shared Jewish ordeal of Nazi persecution, had an increased sense of their Jewish identity and a heightened feeling of kinship with co-religionists throughout the world. In eastern Europe generally, repressive government policies and the resurgence of anti-Semitism tended to foster a sense of solidarity among the Jews. These sentiments were highlighted in the Yiddish literature of the war and immediate post-war years, where some of the principal themes were the heroism and suffering of the Jews, their solidarity, and the part the Jewish people had played in the victory over the Nazis. Perceiving this Jewish awareness as a threat, the authorities attempted to suppress it, but suppression only served to make it stronger.

The contradictory nature of the Soviet government's policy on Jewish matters became apparent to the outside world shortly after the war, with the Soviet Union's attitude toward the establishment of a Jewish state in Palestine. Since the Bolshevik Revolution, Zionist organizations had been suppressed by the Soviet government; nevertheless, in 1947 the Soviet Union and its satellite states gave full diplomatic support to the partition resolution at the United Nations whereby the Jewish state came into existence. Moreover, the Soviet Union, through its Czech allies, made arms supplies available to Israel for defence against Arab attack – this policy did not signify a conversion to Zionism, but rather a desire to strengthen the position of the Soviet bloc in the Middle East and, correspondingly, weaken the West's position.

Thus a short-term convergence of interest emerged between the Soviet Union and Israel. Unfortunately, this accord did not affect the status of Jews inside the Soviet Union. On the contrary, the creation of the state of Israel may well have increased the tensions between Soviet Jews and the Communist regime, and intensified the divisions among Soviet Jews themselves. These tensions and divisions were all too evident in a notorious article by Ilia Erenburg, the eminent Jewish writer, which appeared in *Pravda* on 21 September 1948. Erenburg condemned the Zionists as 'mystics' and rejected any notion of Jewish solidarity. However, while scorning the Zionists, he deftly justified Soviet support for Zionism by arguing that the Soviet Union supported the Jewish aspiration to statehood, but that it condemned Israel's government as 'bourgeois': Soviet Jews, then, should have no more attachment to Israel than to any other capitalist country. Erenburg went on to contend that the workers of Israel should fight not only against the Arab invaders but also against their own bourgeois rulers. The *Pravda* article illustrates the great paradox of Soviet policy toward the Jews in the immediate post-war years. On the one hand, in order to bolster its own position internationally, the regime supported Israel's right to exist; on the other hand, Stalin – fearing the rise of nationalist sentiments among the Soviet Union's many national minorities – clamped down on Jewish activity within the Soviet state.

Erenburg's article was especially significant because of its timing – it appeared shortly before a huge and entirely spontaneous pro-Israel demonstration greeted the first Israeli envoy to Moscow, Golda Meir, when she attended the Jewish New Year service at Moscow's central synagogue on 16 October 1948. The article may well have been intended as an official warning, through the mouthpiece of the often politically pliable Erenburg, against the overt expression of Jewish national sentiments. Taken together, these conflicting events in the autumn of 1948 illustrate the wide range of feelings within the Soviet Jewish community on the subject of the state of Israel.

The year 1948 marked the inception of a period that has come to be known as 'the black years' of east European Jewry. Thousands of Jews fled from Poland in the aftermath of pogroms carried out by the reactionary National Armed Forces (*Narodowe Sily Zbrojne*), an organization reminiscent of the 'Black Hundreds' in late tsarist Russia. In the Soviet Union, Solomon Mikhoels, head of the Jewish Anti-Fascist Committee and director of the Yiddish-language Jewish State Theatre, was murdered in January 1948; in November, the Committee itself was disbanded and most of its members arrested. Also in 1948, Jewish theatres began to be closed down all over the Soviet Union, and in 1952, twenty-three Jewish writers, artists and poets were executed on the allegation that they were 'agents of American imperialism'. In Poland, Zionist parties and the Bund were banned, all Jewish schools were nationalized, and the teaching of Hebrew was virtually eliminated. Meanwhile, the press in eastern Europe waged a campaign against 'rootless cosmopolitans', a code name for Jews, who were depicted as traitors, swindlers, exploiters and cowards. Jews were dismissed from both government and Communist Party positions, and bizarre show trials of 'Zionist conspirators' were staged in Czechoslovakia, Bulgaria and Hungary. In January 1953 the campaign reached its zenith when the Soviet news agency Tass reported the discovery of the 'Doctors' Plot' and accused six Jewish physicians of murdering two prominent Communist Party officials by deliberately giving incorrect medical treatment; they were also accused of plotting to kill the leaders of the Red Army. The six were alleged to be 'Zionist spies' and in league with British and American intelligence agencies. There is some evidence to suggest that Stalin planned to use these allegations as a pretext for initiating the mass expulsion of Jews to Siberia. Only Stalin's death in March 1953 brought a halt to the trial of the doctors and to the plans for mass expulsion. A month later, Moscow Radio revealed that the Doctors' Plot had been a complete fabrication.

Although the worst excesses of the anti-Semitic campaign of the Stalinist period were not repeated, relations between the Soviet state and the Jewish minority continued to be troubled. Evidence abounds that anti-Semitism persisted at government level; for instance, in the late 1950s and the early 1960s the rate of synagogue closures accelerated. In 1961 the young Soviet poet Evgenii Evtushenko brought the subject of anti-Semitism into the open with his poem 'Babi Yar', named after the ravine near Kiev where at least 30,000 Jews had been killed by the Nazis in 1941. Not only did Evtushenko emphasize the notion of a continuously existing Jewish people, but he also referred to ongoing anti-Semitism in Soviet lands. The poem won widespread sympathy among liberal intellectuals, and the composer Dmitrii Shostakovich included its words in his Thirteenth Symphony, composed and first performed in 1962. Yet even this public exposure was not enough to halt the government's anti-Semitic campaign.

As the 1960s progressed, and particularly after the Six-Day War in 1967, a number of anti-Semitic and anti-Israeli ideas, some of them quite fantastic, were given currency in the Soviet media: Jewish and Israeli leaders were represented as erstwhile collaborators with Nazi Germany and as allies of the neo-Nazis; Israel was depicted as an imperialist state; Zionists were portrayed as akin to a 'fifth column' inside socialist countries; and international Jewish organizations were alleged to be reactionary, all-powerful occult forces. According to the media, Judaism was itself a religion that called for genocide and for the enslavement of all other peoples by the Jews. Two notorious works added substantially to these perversions – Trofim Kichko's *Judaism and Zionism (Iudaizm i sionizm)*, published in 1968, and Iurii Ivanov's *Beware: Zionism! (Ostorozhno sionizm)*, published in 1969.

In the face of such anti-Semitism, Jews had two possible responses: they could either remain in the Soviet Union and take advantage of any opportunities offered by the state, or they could seek to emigrate to Israel or the West. Many Jews chose to accept the regime, and a large proportion made their mark in the professions and in intellectual life. In fact, the majority of Soviet Jews enjoyed a relatively high standard of living: more than half of them had university degrees or vocational qualifications, and it is noteworthy that the Jews constituted the second largest ethnic group (after the Russians) of scientific workers holding doctorates – the Soviet Union's highest academic degree. Linguistically, Soviet Jewry was becoming increasingly integrated in the 1970s, with more Jews giving Russian rather than Yiddish as their native language. This, then, was the response of a number of Soviet Jews to the repressive regime – an increasing conformity to the norms and aspirations of Soviet society. Even so, the state remained profoundly suspicious of Jews, and the degree of official mistrust was demonstrated by the fact that they were still excluded from positions in political life and the security services.

While many Jews were reconciled to the regime, others were not and endeavoured to leave – the atmosphere created by the anti-Zionism of official propaganda (barely distinguishable from anti-Semitism) providing a spur to emigration. However, Soviet emigration policy was, by and large, very restrictive, as indeed it had been since the Second World War and most evidently since the founding of the state of Israel. From 1948 until the end of Stalin's regime in 1953, virtually no Soviet Jews had been allowed to emigrate to Israel (the preferred destination) or to any other country, though there were ongoing schemes under which Jews and others who had been displaced by the war were repatriated to Soviet bloc countries, especially to Poland. With the 'thaw' after the death of Stalin in 1953, there began a trickle of Jewish emigration under the provisions of a family reunification scheme whereby some Soviet citizens were allowed to leave the Soviet Union to settle with relatives abroad; thus a number of mainly elderly or infirm Soviet Jews were permitted to go to Israel. By the early 1960s, some younger Jews were also allowed to leave under this scheme, and the numbers emigrating began to increase, but there was still no general Jewish emigration. Most would-be Jewish emigrants continued to be frustrated as in the past. Despite many thousands of applications over the years for exit permits for Jews to join relatives in Israel, only a small number were granted: an average of just a few hundred permits a year were issued in the 1950s (and only seven in 1959), with the numbers rising to over a thousand a year in the early 1960s.

Those Jews who wanted to emigrate often found themselves the victims of international politics. For example, the Six-Day War in 1967 led to the severing of diplomatic relations with Israel and to a clampdown on emigration, so in 1968 only 379 Soviet Jews were given permission to leave for Israel (compared with 1444 in 1965, 1892 in 1966, and 1162 in the first half of 1967). Through the 1970s, Soviet emigration policy continued to reflect developments in international relations: the emigration of all minority groups from the Soviet Union increased after the announcement of US-Soviet detente, decreased in the wake of international tensions created by the Yom Kippur War of 1973, and increased again after the 1975 Helsinki Conference on Human Rights. Jewish emigration peaked in 1979, with over 100,000 Jews leaving for all destinations in the period 1976–9, but fell off after the rise in tension resulting from the Soviet invasion of Afghanistan in late 1979, only to increase dramatically with the coming of Mikhail Gorbachev and glasnost in 1985.

The cutback in emigration following the Six-Day War gave impetus to the emigration movement in the Soviet Union, which became a significant social force in its own right after 1967. Andrei Sakharov, the leading Soviet human rights campaigner and founding member of the unofficial Committee for Human Rights, wrote to the Presidium of the Supreme Soviet in 1971: 'the freedom to emigrate . . . is an essential condition of spiritual freedom for all'.[15] Although help, pressure and encouragement came from Jews in Israel and in the West, this freedom had to be won by the Soviet Jews themselves. From the late 1960s until the 1980s, Soviet Jews used every means available to them – sit-ins, demonstrations, hunger-strikes and petitions – to force the hand of the leadership. The authorities retaliated with imprisonment, exile, dismissal and often the violent treatment of demonstrators.

Soviet 'refusenik' Anatolii Shcharanskii and his wife Avital after his arrival in Israel in 1986. Shcharanskii's release after years of official harassment and imprisonment was an early result of Gorbachev's policy of allowing greater freedom of emigration for Soviet Jews.

The case of the mathematician, Anatolii Shcharanskii, exemplified the plight of many 'refuseniks' – Soviet Jews who were refused the right to emigrate. In 1973, Shcharanskii's wife was allowed to leave for Israel, but he was denied an exit permit. He was then dismissed from his job, harassed by the Soviet secret police and eventually charged with treason as an American agent and imprisoned; he was held in solitary confinement for a long period and was not released until 1986 – even then he was ignominiously traded with the West as part of a 'spy swap'. But Shcharanskii's endurance was instrumental in establishing the right to emigrate.

The profiles of Soviet Jewish emigrants and their destinations have changed considerably since the Second World War. Initially, the emigrants were mostly traditional, Zionist-minded Jews from Central Asia, the Caucasus and the western territories of the Soviet Union (Lithuania, Latvia, Moldavia etc.). Almost all these Jews made Israel their destination. However, as the emigration movement gained momentum and the economic situation in the Soviet Union worsened in the 1970s – all in an atmosphere of official anti-Jewish policies – Jews from the urban centres of Moscow, Leningrad and Kiev increasingly tried to leave. While the majority of these urbanized Jews followed earlier emigrants in resettling in Israel, one in three now chose other countries, mainly the USA. Along with a steady decrease in overall Soviet Jewish emigration, the period 1981–5 saw a further reduction in the number of Jews settling in Israel, with the majority preferring the USA, Canada, western Europe, Australia and New Zealand.

It was not only in the Soviet Union that emigration was the response to repression: the pattern was repeated in other countries of eastern Europe. Thus Jewish emigration from Poland remained high in the post-war period as Jews tried, by legal and illegal channels, to escape the repressive regimes of Wladyslaw

Gomulka and Edward Gierek. From a starting point of over 200,000 in the immediate post-war years, the Jewish population of Poland fell to roughly 50,000 by 1950, and by the early 1980s, Poland – once the great centre of east European Jewry – was the home of only 6000 Jews.

Gorbachev and post-communist eastern Europe

Soon after he came to power in the Soviet Union in 1985, Mikhail Gorbachev introduced the associated policies of glasnost and perestroika; the former, aimed at creating a more liberal, open society, was a necessary prerequisite to the restructuring of the stagnant Soviet economy envisioned by the latter. These reforms had mixed effects on Soviet Jews. On the positive side, they allowed greater expression of Jewish religion and culture inside the Soviet Union, for example by permitting the establishment of various Jewish centres, the teaching of Hebrew and Yiddish, the importation of religious books and objects, and the initiation of contacts between Soviet Jews and international Jewish organizations. Official anti-Semitism was condemned, and the Jewish communists who had been victims of Stalin's purges (Zinoviev, Kamenev, Radek and others) were rehabilitated.

Furthermore, restrictions on Jewish emigration were relaxed – a result of a general warming in Soviet-Israeli relations, as well as the United States linking trade agreements to Soviet human rights policy. The improvement in relations was demonstrated when the Soviet government established a permanent diplomatic mission in Tel Aviv in 1987, the first since 1967, and Israel dispatched a similar mission to Moscow a year later. In December 1990 the two countries raised the status of their diplomatic missions to the level of consulate, an important step toward the re-establishment of full diplomatic ties. Also in December 1990, trade credits worth nearly $1 billion were opened to the Soviet Union when the United States administration waived a 1974 act prohibiting aid to communist countries that engaged in the suppression of dissidents. With the easing of restrictions on emigration, the number of Jews leaving the Soviet Union rose dramatically from around 10,000 in 1988 to over 150,000 in 1990, though paradoxically the need for Jews to emigrate was lessened by the more liberal climate.

On the negative side, Gorbachev's policies allowed the re-emergence of popular anti-Semitism. The Anti-Zionist Committee (*Antisionistskii Komitet Sovetskoi Obshchestvennosti*), founded in 1983, worked to refute charges of anti-Semitism made against nationalist groups and, at times, argued that Soviet Jews were fundamentally anti-Zionist. The most vocal right-wing groups, Memory (*Pamiat*), and the related organization, Fatherland (*Otechestvo*), proclaimed a policy of 'Russia for the Russians' and inveighed against 'cosmopolitan and international Zionist capital'. Perhaps one of the most alarming indications of rising anti-Semitism was the announcement in 1990 by the *Military-Historical Journal* (*Voenno-Istoricheskii Zhurnal*), a monthly journal with a circulation of nearly 300,000, that it intended to publish the *Protocols of the Elders of Zion*.[16] The reasons for republishing the *Protocols* were unclear, but their appearance in an official journal would be an ominous development, possibly signalling a shift to the right in policy toward the

Jews. Although official Soviet sources tended to attribute anti-Semitic activity to various small, far-right political groups, anti-Semitic sentiment is, in fact, a much more widespread phenomenon and persists in much of eastern Europe.

It would, therefore, seem that the collapse of communist regimes in the former Soviet bloc may be both a blessing and a curse for east European Jews. With the rise of new political systems from the Baltic to the Black Sea, and the dissolution of the Soviet Union in December 1991 following an abortive military coup in August of that year, decades of anti-Jewish policies have come to an end. But the resurgence of latent nationalisms and the sporadic desecration of Jewish graves and monuments may point to a period of renewed popular anti-Semitism. So the present situation is one of uncertainty: it remains to be seen whether the new cultural and political freedoms will restore east European Jewry to the pre-eminence it once enjoyed in the Jewish world.

5 North American Jewry

Leon Jick

New beginnings – the colonial and early national period

During the age of discovery, exploration and colonization of the Americas, almost all Jews lived in eastern Europe, the eastern Mediterranean and North Africa. These areas remained unaffected by the new developments in commerce and technology that were taking place in central and western Europe, and played little part in the colonization and settlement of the New World. In 1492, the year in which Columbus discovered America, the Jews were expelled from Spain, and in 1497 Portugal followed suit, marking the end of the last Jewish communities in western Europe. Most of the Spanish and Portuguese Jews (Sephardim) fled to North Africa and to the Ottoman Empire. Those who remained after the expulsions were forced to convert to Catholicism. However, many of these 'converts' continued to practise their Jewish religion secretly – they came to be known as Marranos. According to the records of the Inquisition, a large number of Marranos settled in the New World, where they hoped to be able to practise their religion openly. However, they were subjected to harassment and periodic trials for heresy in Central and South America, and this continuous persecution made it impossible for any Jewish communities to be established in the Spanish or Portuguese domains until the nineteenth century.

A small number of Jewish refugees from Spain and Portugal settled in Holland, which had declared its independence from Spain in 1579. In Protestant Holland, commercial capitalism replaced feudalism as the predominant social and economic pattern, and Amsterdam emerged as the freest and most tolerant city in Europe. Though subject to residual discrimination, the Jewish community of Amsterdam was able to participate in the economic and intellectual life of Holland. The philosopher Baruch Spinoza, who was excommunicated for his 'heretical' writings, was a member of this community. Jews became shareholders in the Dutch West India Company, which financed settlement in the New World, and were also among the settlers in Dutch colonies in the Americas.

In 1630, the Dutch captured the settlement at Recife in Brazil, which soon had a thriving Jewish community. At the peak of its prosperity, the community is reported to have numbered almost 1500, supporting two synagogues as well as a number of schools. In 1654, the Portuguese recaptured the city and gave the Dutch and Jewish inhabitants three months in which to depart. Most returned to Amsterdam, but some Jews moved to the islands in the West Indies, where they joined existing groups of Jewish settlers.

In September of the same year, one band of twenty-three Jews landed in the Dutch settlement of New Amsterdam and established the first Jewish community on the North American continent. With the assistance of their fellow Jews in Amsterdam, the refugees overcame initial opposition and won grudging permission from the local authorities to remain, on condition that 'the poor among them shall not become a burden to the [Dutch West India] Company or to the community but be supported by their own nation'.[1] Subsequently the right of Jews to settle, trade in real estate and practise their religion 'in all quietness within their homes'[2] was granted. In 1656, a group of Jewish petitioners received permission to establish 'a burying ground for their nation'.[3] The acquisition of property for a cemetery confirmed the existence of a community of practising Jews. At the same time, the Jewish community of New Amsterdam won the right to serve in the militia rather than pay a special tax, and were admitted to burghership (citizenship of the town).

In 1664, New Amsterdam was captured by the British. They renamed the city New York and confirmed the atmosphere of toleration in what was already a mosaic of religious and ethnic diversity. Some restrictions on the right to trade and to worship remained in effect, but in general these were not stringently enforced.

During the century that followed, a small but steady trickle of Jewish immigrants led to the establishment of Sephardi Jewish congregations in the British colonies along the eastern seaboard in Newport, Philadelphia, Charleston and Savannah as well as in New York, and in Montreal. However, throughout the colonial era no ordained rabbi served in America, no Jewish journal or publication of any kind was established and, as a result, no instrument existed for the exchange of Jewish ideas or information. Consequently, colonial American Jewry left only a meagre documentary record of their communal development and religious practices.

Despite difficulties and shortcomings, Jewish religious life sustained itself, conducted by devoted but often poorly educated laymen. In 1682, a Dutch cleric recorded that the Jews 'hold their separate meetings in New York'.[4] In the same year, the Jewish community purchased its second cemetery – a burial ground that exists in lower New York to this day (now known as Chatham Square cemetery) and is one of the oldest historical sights of the city. In 1695, the memoirs of an English clergyman reported that among the approximately 855 families in New York, twenty were Jewish. On a map of the city that he drew, he marked a site as 'The Jews' Synagogue'. A real estate document of the period describes a house on Mill Street as 'commonly known by the name of Jews' Synagogue'.[5] Although these references offer no details concerning the life of the community, they do testify to the existence of a small congregation that had confirmed its right to public worship, secured a building for this purpose and made its presence felt in the city. In 1728, the Jewish citizens of New York purchased a plot of land and erected a building specifically intended for use as a synagogue.

Any uncertainty about the right of Jews to citizenship in the colonies was resolved in 1740 when the British parliament passed a law granting naturalization throughout the colonial Empire after seven years' residence. In taking the oath of citizenship, Jews were permitted to omit the words 'upon the true faith of a Christian'. By this time, Jews enjoyed more freedom in the British colonies than anywhere else in the world.

Throughout the eighteenth century, Jewish immigrants were few in number. In 1790, when the first population census was taken, it was estimated that no more than 2000 to 2500 Jews resided in the United States. The Jewish masses of the Old World lived in areas that had not yet awakened to the possibility of migration to America. However, an increasing number of those who did come were Ashkenazim – Jews of north European origin who were natives of German-speaking states. Without exception, they joined the established Sephardi congregations and colonial American Jewry remained Sephardi in its formal religious practice.

At the same time, the lifestyle of the small community underwent significant changes. Encouraged by the atmosphere of toleration and openness, colonial Jews became 'Americanized' and entered into general social life to a degree that would have been inconceivable in Europe. For example, Jacob Franks, a wealthy merchant and president of Shearith Israel Congregation of New York, and his wife Abigail were very prominent in New York society in the 1740s (see Plates 5 and 6). While ritual practices were preserved in the synagogue without change, Jewish knowledge became increasingly attenuated. In the traditional community, the all-pervasive pattern of Jewish thought, action, outlook and association had been punctuated by occasional excursions into general society – primarily in pursuit of economic ends. In the newly developing American Jewish mode, a distinctively American pattern of thought, action, outlook and association was punctuated by occasional excursions to the synagogues for the performance of increasingly marginal ceremonial functions.

In 1760, Isaac Pinto, hazan (cantor) of Shearith Israel Congregation of New York, published the first Jewish book to be printed in the western hemisphere – a translation of the Hebrew prayer book into English. In his introduction, Pinto explained that Hebrew was 'imperfectly understood by many, by some not at all' and expressed the hope that an English translation would 'tend to the improvement of many of my brethren in their devotion'. In 1785, a report from Philadelphia to Amsterdam concluded that 'most of the sons of this province are not devoted to Torah and do not understand our holy tongue [Hebrew]'. The fact that this small, isolated group was able to maintain itself and preserve its identity is remarkable. At the same time it is clear that the American Jewry that emerged in the early decades of American independence was highly acculturated, integrated into the general society and substantially transformed.

By the time the American Revolution began in 1775, Jews were actively involved not only in the economic life of the colonies, but in social and political affairs as well. Like the population at large, Jews were divided in their loyalties between the causes of the Patriots (the Americans fighting for independence) and the Tories (the British colonists). The majority were Patriots and, in fact, the Jewish communities of Newport and New York disbanded during the British occupation of those cities during the war. Jews participated in the revolutionary armies and a number, such as David Salisbury Franks, Benjamin Nones and Isaac Franks, served as officers: Nones and Isaac Franks were on George Washington's staff. One of South Carolina's contributions to the revolutionary cause was a 'Jews' company' – so designated because twenty-six Jews served in its ranks. The involvement of colonial Jews in the revolutionary effort demonstrates the degree of their acceptance by fellow citizens and their integration into colonial society.

In the years following independence, any additional barriers to full equality were eliminated. The state constitution of Virginia, the Northwest Ordinance of 1787, the United States Constitution and the Bill of Rights all guaranteed political and religious liberty. All the states with significant Jewish populations followed soon after with such guarantees. As a result, Jews in America never faced the struggle for 'emancipation' that confronted all European Jewish communities. Equality before the law was given in a society which from the outset encompassed religious and ethnic pluralism.

When George Washington was inaugurated as president in 1789, the Jewish community, small as it was, was unable to agree on sending one letter of felicitations to the newly elected president. Consequently, three letters were dispatched. In a gracious response to the letter from the congregation in Newport, Rhode Island, President Washington reciprocated the good wishes of the 'Children of the stock of Abraham' and expressed his confidence in their continued well-being in a society that 'happily gives to bigotry no sanction, to persecution no assistance, and requires only that they who live under its protection should demean themselves as good

A portrait of Colonel David Salisbury Franks (c. 1743–93) by Charles Willson Peale. Born in Philadelphia, Franks espoused the revolutionary cause of America. He became an aide to General Benedict Arnold who, when tried for treason, cleared Franks in a statement to George Washington. Franks was later promoted and sent on important diplomatic missions to France.

Plate 1 *'Jeremiah mourning the destruction of Jerusalem' by Jacob van Rijn Rembrandt (1630). The prophet sits with objects rescued from the Temple, while Jerusalem and the Temple itself can be seen burning in the background.*

Plate 2 *Ezekiel prophesying to the Elders of Israel in Babylon, from a sixteenth-century Turkish manuscript. Unlike Jeremiah, Ezekiel accompanied Nebuchadnezzar's Jewish captives into exile in 597 BCE. As Ezekiel is regarded as a prophet by Muslims, his face is partially obscured in accordance with the Islamic convention for representing prophets.*

Plate 3 *The first panel from the altar painting 'The profanation of the host' by Paolo Uccello (c. 1465). Christians in the medieval and Renaissance periods accused Jews of destroying the host, or consecrated wafer, eaten during Mass. In this panel, a woman gives a Jewish moneylender a stolen host to redeem her cloak which was security for a loan. The scorpion on the wall, because of its deadly sting, symbolizes Judas Iscariot and, by extension, the Jews.*

Plate 4 *The second panel of Uccello's 'The profanation of the host'. A Jew is heating the host in a pan over the fire. Blood flows from the desecrated wafer across the floor and out into the street, where Christian soldiers are breaking down the door to retrieve the host and arrest the Jew.*

Plates 5 and 6 *Jacob Franks and his wife Abigail Bilhah Levy Franks by an unknown artist (c. 1740). London-born Franks emigrated to New York around 1708 and established a successful mercantile business, serving as the British Crown's sole fiscal agent for the northern colonies and acting as civilian commissary during the French and Indian War. Abigail Franks' affluence and social prominence attest to the considerable freedom and social integration of Jews in the American colonies.*

Plate 7 *'Portuguese synagogue in Amsterdam' by Emanuel de Witte (c. 1680). In the seventeenth century, Jewish emigres found enough toleration in the Protestant countries of northern Europe to return to open religious observance. The Portuguese Jewish community in Amsterdam, formally established in 1619, was sufficiently prosperous by 1675 to erect this imposing synagogue.*

Plate 8 *The fortress of Masada, overlooking the Dead Sea, where Herod the Great (reigned 37–4 BCE) constructed a magnificent Judeo-Hellenic palace. After the Roman conquest of Jerusalem and the destruction of the Second Temple in 70 CE, Jewish rebels held Masada against the Romans for three years before a mass suicide in the face of imminent defeat.*

citizens'.[6] American Jewry was recognized as a component in the mosaic of American pluralism.

One of the 'clergymen' reported to have been in attendance at George Washington's inauguration was Gershom Mendes Seixas, hazan of Shearith Israel Congregation in New York. Seixas was not a rabbi. He was American born and bred, and by the standards of classical Judaism his training was minimal and his competence in matters of Jewish law was limited. However, he was energetic and devoted and soon began to assume functions that had never been the responsibility of the European rabbi but which were expected of an American minister. He regularly delivered sermons, he officiated at life-cycle ceremonies and performed pastoral duties, he engaged in ecumenical activities and in 1800 even delivered a sermon from the pulpit of St. Paul's Episcopal Church in New York – probably the first such address by a Jew in history. Seixas was the first Jewish example of the type of religious leadership that was more characteristic of Protestantism in the American setting.

In the last years of the eighteenth century and the early years of the nineteenth, revolution and war in Europe reduced immigration to a trickle. American Jewry, small in numbers and weak in intellectual resources, entered a phase of steady attrition. The new American version of Judaism was viable, but it never succeeded in becoming vital. 'Alas,' wrote Rebecca Gratz, a prominent member of the influential Gratz family of Philadelphia, 'it is thought among our degenerate sons and daughters of Israel that only its women and priests acknowledge the force of patriotism and zeal for Judaism.'[7]

A community grows – the German migration, 1820–60

Large-scale immigration to America resumed after 1815, when the return of peace to Europe at the end of the Napoleonic Wars restored normal transportation across the Atlantic. A large proportion of these immigrants originated in central Europe and an increasing number of Jews were among them. In 1818, Mordecai Manuel Noah, a New York journalist, playwright and politician, estimated the Jewish population of the United States to be 3000. By 1826, Isaac Harby, a Charleston schoolmaster, put the number at 6000. The presence of immigrants and the prospect of further immigration stirred signs of life in the near moribund American Jewish community.

In 1823, the first Jewish periodical to be published in North America appeared – a monthly journal called *The Jew*. It was devoted solely to reporting the conversionist polemics of Christian missionary societies, especially the so-called 'Society for Ameliorating the Condition of the Jews'. In its two years of publication, *The Jew* did not include a single reference to events occurring in the Jewish community of its time. The circumscribed content of the journal simply reflected the meagreness of Jewish life. However, the very existence of this publication was an indication of awakening enterprise and growing awareness of need and opportunity.

In the years between 1815 and 1830, grandiose schemes for encouraging immigration proliferated in America. English, German, Swiss and French groups attempted to establish national settlements in what was then called the 'west', the area between the Allegheny Mountains and the Mississippi River. In 1825, shortly after the opening of the Erie Canal, Mordecai Noah proposed the establishment of a Jewish settlement on Grand Island in the Niagara River, proclaiming himself to be 'Judge and Governor of Israel'. Nothing came of the proposal – after a flurry of publicity, it was dropped without Noah ever having set foot on Grand Island. The proposal indicates that there was an awareness of the Jewish immigration that was in progress and of the likelihood of it increasing in the future.

The new Jewish immigrants were almost all poor and usually minimally educated in both Jewish and secular learning. Almost all came from hamlets and villages in Bavaria, south-eastern Germany and Posen. Their previous occupations were either petty trade or a craft – most commonly tailoring or shoemaking. Like all other immigrants, Jews moved to places where economic opportunity beckoned, which at this time were the newly developing regions of the mid-continent (Ohio, Indiana, Illinois, Michigan, Wisconsin, Alabama, Kentucky and Tennessee). Here their skills were needed. With the population expanding into new areas of settlement, it became essential that a means of distributing manufactured wares developed. As a result, many immigrants became pedlars and took supplies to isolated farmers in the countryside. The work was difficult and sometimes even dangerous, but it could be undertaken with little or no capital and it enabled poor immigrants to establish a foothold in the new land.

In these new areas of settlement, as well as in old-established centres, Jewish immigrants formed congregations according to their own mode of worship. This was inevitable in the light of the increase in numbers and diversity of the Jewish population. The first synagogue to follow the Ashkenazi rite in worship was established in Philadelphia, possibly as early as 1795. However, the congregation did not succeed in maintaining itself on a sound footing until the late 1820s, when the influx of new immigrants reinforced its ranks. At the same time, two new Ashkenazi congregations were established – one in New York and one in Cincinnati. In 1828, a third synagogue was established in New York.

The number of new congregations proliferated. The most common explanation for their growth was a preference for the Ashkenazi manner of conducting the ritual, but the situation was actually far more complex. Acculturated native American Jews – many of Sephardi origin – found the newcomers alien, abrasive and uncouth; whilst new immigrants from central Europe found their Americanized fellow Jews haughty, aloof and lax in religious observance. Established American burghers wanted an orderly and undemanding 'Jewish church' that would affirm their respectability. Insecure newcomers sought an environment of involvement and interaction reminiscent of the intimate village gathering place they had known – a place where they could pray in their accustomed way, which involved all individuals praying aloud for themselves, giving rise to a cacophony of voices, and where they could be among sympathetic peers and find acceptance by God and other people. As the immigrants became acculturated and their economic circumstances improved, they too aspired to respectability and decorum, which required the adoption of more orderly, Protestant-like responsive prayer. The bewildered newcomers of one decade became the solid and settled gentry of the next. Each succeeding wave of immigration brought a repetition of this same pattern.

By 1840, before the largest influx of immigrants had begun and when not a single rabbi had yet arrived, the number of congregations in New York had risen to six. The pace of institutional growth accelerated sharply in the 1840s and congregations burgeoned in cities from Boston to San Francisco. In 1848, Isaac Leeser (hazan of the Sephardi Mikveh Israel congregation in Philadelphia) observed that 'synagogues are springing up as if by magic . . . From the newly gotten Santa Fe to the confines of New Brunswick and from the Atlantic to the shores of the Western sea, the wandering sons of Israel are seeking homes and freedom.'[8] By 1850, there were at least seventy-six formally organized synagogues, and by 1877, two hundred and seventy-seven. Before the end of the decade, cities with substantial Jewish populations such as Albany, Baltimore, Cincinnati, New Orleans, Philadelphia, Richmond and St. Louis had two or more congregations, and New York boasted (or endured) the existence of fifteen, with more in the process of formation.

The openness of America, the lack of a Jewish communal structure and the absence of religious or intellectual leadership combined to foster an atmosphere of chaos in American Jewish life. Well-intentioned but poorly educated laymen assumed leadership and tried to establish the rudiments of a Jewish community. Authority was absent, and unity in dealing with common concerns seemed unattainable.

Not surprisingly, the earliest manifestations of any national Jewish communal consciousness came in response to a perceived threat from the outside. In 1840, the ancient blood libel, which accused Jews of murdering Christians and using their blood in rituals, was revived in Damascus. This spectre of medieval bigotry, even in far away Damascus, startled both native-born and immigrant Jews. The president of the Sephardi Mikveh Israel congregation in Philadelphia wrote, 'If such calumny is not nipped in the bud, its effect will not be limited to any particular place but will be extended to every part of the globe.'[9] Disparate Jewish groups in major urban centres joined together with each other, with Jews in other American cities and with communities in Europe to express their mutual concern – a response signifying an awakening of group consciousness.

The rapidly growing sense of mutual concern led to the first proposals for a permanent link between Jews in various cities and for an attempt to deal with the quality of Jewish religious life. Isaac Leeser took the initiative in July 1841 and circulated a detailed plan for a national union of American Jewish congregations. Leeser came from a German Jewish background and migrated to the United States as a young man in the 1820s. His formal European educational background was modest and in his homeland would have qualified him to be no more than an elementary school teacher. However, because he was bright, ambitious and energetic, he was soon elected to serve as hazan of the oldest established Sephardi congregation. The absence of any other religious officers with more impressive credentials enabled Leeser to assume a national leadership role. His proposed 'Union for the Sake of Judaism' projected the establishment of a 'Central Religious Council' to be elected by congregational representatives. The Council was to 'watch

over the state of religion', certify the competence of cantors and of ritual slaughter-
ers (who were responsible for the preparation of kosher meat), and oversee the
quality of religious schools (for both sexes) which 'were to be established in every
town where Israelites reside' but 'not interfere directly or indirectly in the internal
affairs of the congregations'.[10] The proposal, modest as it was, did not elicit a single
positive response. The voluntary nature of religious institutions in America and
Jewish congregational autonomy combined to subvert any attempt to establish
authority or achieve unity.

Leeser may have been disheartened but he was not deterred, and he proceeded
at once with other ventures. The following year he announced plans for publishing
a monthly journal in English and, in April 1843, the *Occident and American Jewish
Advocate* appeared. In this journal, Leeser proposed 'to give circulation to everything which can be interesting to the Jewish inhabitants of the Western Hemisphere'. American Jewry not only had a spokesman, it now had a forum for the
exchange of information and ideas.

In 1844, Leeser contributed an article on 'The Jews and their religion' to a
publication dealing with 'the religious denominations of the United States'. In it,
Leeser is described as 'pastor of the Hebrew Portuguese Congregation of Philadelphia' and the 'most prominent divine' among American Jews. In his essay, Leeser
states: 'We have no ecclesiastical authorities in America other than the congregations themselves. Each congregation makes its own rules for its government, and
elects its own minister, who is appointed without any ordination, induction in office
being made through his election.'[11] The role of the traditional scholar-rabbi in
American Judaism, as experienced and explained by Leeser, was at best marginal.

At the time Leeser was writing, the first ordained rabbis had arrived in America
from the German-speaking states of central Europe, but they had not yet found a
recognized place or function for themselves in the new environment. Abraham
Rice, who arrived in 1840 and served for a time as rabbi of the Baltimore Hebrew
Congregation, wrote to his teacher in Germany: 'I dwell in complete darkness,
without a teacher or a companion . . . The religious life in this land is on the lowest
level. I wonder whether it is even permissible for a Jew to live in this land.'[12] Rice's
gloom was not shared by Isaac Leeser who wrote: 'In America, where the Constitution secures to every person the enjoyment of life, liberty, and the pursuit of
happiness without anyone having the right to question him concerning his religious
opinion or acts, the Children of Jacob have received a new home.'[13] In 1845, Leeser
proceeded to establish an American Jewish publication society to publish material
on Jewish subjects in English and to make it possible 'to obtain a knowledge of the
faith and to defend it against the assaults of the proselytemakers on the one side and
of infidels on the other'.[14] Among its first publications was an edition of the
Pentateuch with an English translation printed in parallel to the Hebrew text.

In that same year, Rabbi Max Lilienthal arrived in America from Bavaria – the
first rabbi with unquestioned credentials and an excellent prior reputation to settle
in America. In his earliest endeavours, he sought to introduce traditional Jewish
practices and to promote 'decorum' in worship. Lilienthal also attempted to
organize a bet din – a rabbinic court – to 'render beneficial service to the Jewish

congregations of America'. In deference to the autonomy of American congregations, Lilienthal stipulated that the *Bet Din* would not assume any 'hierarchical authority', but would act 'only in an advisory capacity'.[15] His effort proved unsuccessful and Lilienthal soon withdrew from congregational life and established, and ran for several years, a Jewish all-day school, which taught secular as well as religious subjects. This differed from most Jewish education, which was conducted in supplementary schools that tended to meet in the afternoons and on Sundays.

A year after Lilienthal settled in America, another rabbi arrived who was to assume a significant leadership role – Isaac Mayer Wise. Wise had served as a rabbi in a provincial town in Bohemia but, unlike Lilienthal, lacked reputation or credentials. Nevertheless, he was determined, hard-working and ideologically flexible as well as an effective orator and a competent organizer. He secured a position in Albany, New York, and began at once to project himself on to the national scene, establishing himself as an aspirant to leadership.

In December 1848, Wise published a paper in the *Occident*, addressed 'To Ministers and other Israelites', calling for a union of congregations. Although both Leeser and Lilienthal associated themselves with this call, and nine congregations responded favourably, no meeting was held. Wise was not discouraged. Five years later, he was elected rabbi of a synagogue in Cincinnati, referred to at the time as 'the Queen City of the West'. He promptly set about convening a conference to organize a 'Union of American Israel' whose aim would be to establish a regular synod consisting of delegates chosen by Jewish congregations and societies.

At the same time, Wise began publication of an English-language newspaper, *The Israelite*, and established the first Hebrew college in the United States, which he called Zion College. The college closed after one year and Wise concluded that American Jewry was not ripe for such an undertaking. However, the newspaper flourished and the conference did take place in Cleveland in October 1855. A series of resolutions were adopted which attempted to bridge the growing ideological conflict between traditionalist and reformist factions. Unfortunately, personal rivalries, sectional antagonisms between the eastern 'elite' and midwestern provincials, and residual hostility between the older native 'aristocracy' and newer immigrant 'upstarts' proved more intractable and less amenable to compromise than ideology. A second conference was scheduled but never convened.

Jewish religious reform

During the early decades of immigration from central Europe, there was little evidence of the struggle over religious reform that was stirring in German Jewry during these years. In the German states, conferences were held in 1844, 1845 and 1846 to discuss reformation of traditional Judaism by eliminating many practices regarded as not in keeping with the spirit of the times. However, of the scores of synagogues established in America between 1825 and 1860, only three had the avowed intention of introducing reforms, and even in these congregations, any real changes introduced were relatively modest. On the contrary, in the period immediately following their arrival, most immigrants seemed more interested in preserving the status quo of the synagogue as a refuge from the compromises made in their private lives because of economic necessity.

In central Europe, Jewish religious reformism had radical overtones and consequences, challenging not only the traditional Jewish communal order, but also the established social and political order. Religious reform was associated with the struggle for political emancipation. Precisely the opposite dynamics were at work in America. When Jewish reformism emerged, it reflected a desire not to change the established social and political order, but rather to join it. In nineteenth-century America, Jewish religious reform began with a series of modest ritual changes and shifts in emphasis that were primarily concerned with appearances and social conformity. Ideology in the European sense played a minimal role. In central and western Europe, reform was viewed as a precursor of acculturation and integration. In America, acculturation and integration proved to be precursors of reform.

The earliest attempt at reform was made in 1825 in Charleston, South Carolina, by a native-born, thoroughly Americanized group. Their proposal stressed decorum and intelligibility, rather than substantive revisions of either faith or practice. The effort expired after a few years and had no influence on subsequent developments. When 'reform' emerged again as an issue in the 1850s, it was once more primarily concerned with issues of decorum and the use of English rather than with principles. The people most interested in reform were the upwardly mobile immigrants whose economic advance and Americanization were rapidly progressing.

In 1855, Rabbi David Einhorn arrived in America and took up a post in Baltimore at the reform Har Sinai congregation. Einhorn had been a leader of the radical faction at the German rabbinical conferences of the 1840s. In *Sinai*, the German-language monthly magazine which he established, Einhorn espoused intellectually consistent reform and ridiculed piecemeal efforts to achieve decorum. He denounced both Wise and Leeser and expressed his contempt for the level of intellectual life in America, which he called 'a land of humbug'. But Einhorn was never at home in America. His continued stress on the use of the German language (which he called the 'carrying case of reform') was disregarded by his eagerly Americanized congregants. Ultimately, many of Einhorn's ideas were accepted, not because of the intellectually rigorous reform he advocated, but, rather, because they provided a convincing justification for the patchwork of practices that had been accepted for pragmatic reasons.

As the decade of the 1850s drew to a close, American Jewry grew in vigour and self-confidence. Many immigrants who had begun their American careers as pedlars prospered and became shopkeepers. In one Pennsylvania town, the proportion of Jews engaged in peddling fell from 70 per cent in 1845 to 39 per cent in 1860. By 1870, the number would decrease to 12 per cent. In addition to economic stability, American Jewry was acquiring organizational competence and political confidence. This was demonstrated by their response to the infamous Mortara case of 1858, when a Jewish child living in Rome was allegedly baptized by his nurse during an illness without the knowledge or consent of his parents. When the nurse confessed this act to her priest, the papal authorities sent police to the child's home and seized him on the grounds that he was now a Catholic. As a result, there was a flood of petitions of protest from Jewish communities throughout America urging the American Secretary of State to intercede. In 1859, twenty-four congregations joined in establishing the Board of Delegates of American Israelites whose primary goal was to keep a watchful eye on occurrences in the USA and abroad to ensure that the civil and religious rights of Jews were not encroached upon.

Jewish religious life and practice was also evolving. Without a formal change in ideology, ritual practice or institutional structure, a basic transformation of image and outlook was taking place. As Isaac Mayer Wise wrote in 1859: 'We are Jews in the synagogue and Americans everywhere.'[16] Formal commitment to reform was still minimal. A German Jewish traveller who completed his tour of America in 1861 reported that 'in a land that numbers more than two hundred orthodox congregations, the reform congregations number eight'.[17] A decade later, however, there were few congregations in which substantial reforms had *not* been introduced.

American Jewry, the Civil War and its aftermath

On the eve of the Civil War, American Jewry was not intensely involved in the issues of slavery and abolition. The majority of Jews were recent immigrants still struggling to establish themselves and were not immersed in the issues and problems of American politics. On 4 January 1861, one congregational leader, Morris Raphall of Bnai Jeshurun in New York, delivered a widely circulated sermon that defended slavery as being in accord with biblical precepts. He was denounced by Rabbi David Einhorn and other abolitionists. Isaac Mayer Wise and Isaac Leeser, who had the largest popular following, were generally neutral on the issues of slavery and abolition, and did not devote any space to these controversies in the newspapers that they published. In its annual report of 1853, the Anti-Slavery Society observed: 'It cannot be said that the Jews have formed any denominational opinion on the subject of slavery.' Once the Civil War had begun, Jews generally acted and reacted in the same ways as their neighbours – the Jews in the north supported the Union (i.e. the Federal government) and those in the south supported the Confederacy.

Two issues arose during the Civil War that directly affected Jewish interests. The first concerned a clause in the law providing for the appointment of chaplains in the Union army which required that a chaplain 'must be a regularly ordained minister of some Christian denomination'. Jewish protesters appealed directly to President Abraham Lincoln and the discriminatory clause was amended by Congress in July 1862 to read 'some religious denomination'. In 1863, Rabbi Jacob Frankel became the first Jewish chaplain to be appointed as a result of this amendment. The acceptance of Jews as an American religious denomination was thus achieved.

The second issue involved General Order Number 11 – this was issued by General Ulysses S. Grant of the Union army on 17 December 1862, and ordered the evacuation of all Jews from the area known as the Department of Tennessee, on the grounds that they were engaged in smuggling and illegal trade, especially in cotton. While some Jews were involved, it is clear that they were a small minority

Rabbi Jacob Frankel (left), *the first Jewish chaplain in the Union Army, and his commission* (right) *signed by Abraham Lincoln in 1863.*

among the chief offenders, whose ranks included numerous well-placed military officers. Once again appeals were directed to President Lincoln, and the order was cancelled on 4 January. Disquieting as this latter episode was, its speedy resolution strengthened the conviction of Jews that in America any obstacle to their full acceptance could be overcome.

The Civil War experience accelerated the Americanization of all immigrant groups, and the economic growth that followed stimulated general upward mobility. The vast fortunes of the Rockefellers, the Carnegies and the Vanderbilts were established during the booming war and post-war economy, and while no Jews achieved that level of success, many did acquire great wealth. For example, the Seligmans, who had begun as pedlars, became investment bankers. The dry goods stores of the Gimbels and the Bloomingdales grew to become department stores. The manufacture of ready-made clothing – from Levi Strauss's copper-riveted blue jeans to Hart Schaffner and Marx's well-tailored suits – became virtually a German Jewish monopoly. Although the number of individuals who became millionaires was small, relative affluence was widespread.

American Jewry was moving forward into the mainstream of American life. Isaac Mayer Wise became a member of the board of directors of the Free Religious Association, alongside Ralph Waldo Emerson. Sumptuous new edifices, such as the

(Left) *The interior of Beth Elohim Synagogue in Charleston, South Carolina, in the late eighteenth century. The second synagogue built in the United States, it was dedicated in 1794 and, until destroyed by fire in 1838, served Charleston's flourishing community of Jewish merchants and traders.* (Right) *The dedication ceremony at Temple Emanu-El, New York on 11 September 1868. This elaborate edifice houses the leading Reform congregation of New York City.*

Temple Emanu-El in New York, were built in all the major cities to house wealthy congregations now eager to perpetuate an elegant, decorous style of worship compatible with their new status. According to the United States 1870 census of religious bodies, the value of synagogue buildings increased from $1,135,500 in 1860 to $5,155,235 in 1870.

In 1869, David Einhorn convened a conference of rabbis in Philadelphia to formulate a statement of principles that would serve as a platform for the reformation of Judaism in America. Twelve rabbis, most of whom had only recently arrived in America, participated. The brief creed that was adopted stressed the Jewish people's 'universal mission' and the goal of a Messianic Age that would 'realize the unity of all rational creatures and their call to moral sanctification';[18] it disavowed the hope for the restoration of Zion or for a personal Messiah. The statement was issued in German and, not surprisingly, it had little discernible impact.

Four years later, in 1873, the pragmatist Isaac Mayer Wise succeeded in organizing a 'Union of American Hebrew Congregations' in Cincinnati with thirty-four congregations participating. In 1875, this Union became the sponsoring organization of the Hebrew Union College, a seminary for training rabbis in American Jewry. In the late 1870s, the Union absorbed the old Board of Delegates of American Israelites and became the one constituent body that represented virtually all Jews.

With the exception of the old-line Sephardi synagogues, most of the well-established congregations in the country became affiliates of the Union. Reform had carried the day. Without any formal action or specific reformulation, Jewish doctrine was redefined to conform to the presumed dictates of reason. Jewish ritual practice was modified to reflect the tastes of an affluent, acculturated constituency with more concern for respectability and decorum than for piety and fervour. For a brief period, it seemed as though an increasingly homogeneous American Jewry of 250,000 had achieved what it regarded as a generally accepted 'American Jewish' pattern.

The formal platform of American reform Judaism was adopted after the reformation had been achieved. In 1885, a conference of rabbis in Pittsburgh adopted a platform 'broad, compassionate, enlightened, and liberal enough to impress and win all hearts and also firm and positive enough to dispel suspicion of agnostic tendencies or of discontinuing the historic thread of the past'. An eight-point resolution was adopted by the seventeen participating rabbis which hailed 'the modern era of the universal culture of heart and intellect and the approach of the realization of Israel's great Messianic hope for the establishment of the kingdom of truth, justice, and peace among all men'. All ceremonies regarded as 'not adapted to the views and habits of modern civilization' were rejected. The traditional hope for return to Zion was repudiated: 'We consider ourselves no longer a nation but a religious community.' Judaism emerged as a 'progressive religion ever striving to be in accord with the postulates of reason'.[19]

Flood tide – the east European migration, 1880–1914

By the time the platform of American reform Judaism was adopted, American Jewry was being radically altered by the influx of east European Jews that began in 1881, as a result of the pogroms and anti-Semitic legislation that followed the assassination of Tsar Alexander II. Worsening social, political and economic circumstances in eastern Europe provided the push, whilst America's need of a workforce for its growing industries provided the pull.

Economic opportunity drew the new immigrants to New York and other large cities, where working and living conditions in the teeming urban slums were atrocious. But the attractions of freedom and opportunity proved irresistible to the immigrants; and the availability of improved cheap transportation placed the option of immigration within the reach of millions. By 1900, more than 500,000 Jews had entered the United States, and between 1900 and 1924, another 1.25 million arrived. The Jewish population grew from an estimated 250,000 in 1880 to 2,933,000 in 1914. The established Americanized German Jewish community was

A cartoon from Judge *(1892) portraying the effects of Jewish immigration. Jews fleeing from persecution in Russia are shown taking over New York, forcing old-established Americans to move westwards.*

swamped by the influx of newcomers, who were separated from them by social, cultural and economic barriers as well as by religious differences. Reform Judaism was reduced to a marginal position, representing only that fraction of American Jews who were on an upper economic level.

The new immigrants were poor, Yiddish-speaking and orthodox in their religious practices; only a few were highly educated in their religious training. They were mostly ordinary people from small towns and villages, whose folk religion and simple piety were not easily transplanted to the turbulent industrial urban environment of America. In 1885, the surviving representatives of traditional orthodox Judaism in the established American Jewish community organized the Jewish Theological Seminary to train rabbis from the new immigrant constituency. But the gap between the dignified, English-speaking orthodoxy of the acculturated and the rustic, Yiddish-speaking orthodoxy of the new immigrants proved to be too great to permit communication, and the Seminary failed to gain a following among the new immigrants.

In 1888, an attempt was made to transplant the European religious pattern to the New World – a group of east European synagogues in New York joined forces to bring Rabbi Jacob Joseph, a well-known scholar from Vilna, to New York to serve as chief rabbi. However, their effort was undermined by a number of factors: the majority of orthodox congregations were not involved in the project and so were rather indifferent to it, reform rabbis and the Americanized orthodox community opposed the move, and secular and radical immigrants were also antagonistic. Rabbi Jacob Joseph, confused and disheartened, was never able to assert rabbinic authority in the fragmented and increasingly heterogeneous American Jewish community.

Traditional Judaism remained weak and disorganized in the years around the turn of the century. The few attempts to raise the level of religious study, to maintain standards of observance and to exercise authority met with little success. The Rabbi Isaac Elhanan Theological Seminary – the first *yeshivah* to be established in America – was founded in 1897. Decades later, it would become the basis for the development of Yeshivah University, but at the time, it remained small and exercised little influence. In 1898, Rabbi Henry Pereira Mendes of the Sephardi Sherith Israel Congregation in New York organized a Union of Orthodox Jewish Congregations; and in 1902, a Union of Orthodox Rabbis was formed. Both remained marginal and their influence at the time was negligible. No institution emerged to serve as a centre for the religious life of east European Jewry in America. An impoverished immigrant community, struggling to establish itself and to deal with the problem of poverty, social dislocation and linguistic adjustment could not yet deal with the challenge of a new and radically religious environment.

In addition, a substantial proportion of the new Jewish immigrants, especially after 1900, were not religious at all but were secularist and socialist. They neglected traditional Jewish religious observance, but did not abandon their ethnic characteristics. They promoted the idea of secular Jewish culture and fostered the use of the Yiddish language.

Despite poverty and privation, a vigorous cultural and artistic life developed in the immigrant ghettos. The Yiddish press flourished and each of the larger cities saw the publication of Yiddish daily newspapers. New York City had as many as four Yiddish dailies at one time. The newspapers served not only to disseminate news, but also as an outlet for Yiddish literature. Popular and intellectual Yiddish-theatre flourished. The market-place of ideas and ideologies bustled.

Secular Jewish culture had its strongest base in the American Jewish labour movement. Trade unions organized along ethnic immigrant lines were common in turn-of-the-century America, and Jewish immigrants followed this example. As early as 1888, the United Hebrew Trades was formed as an umbrella organization for struggling immigrant Jewish craft unions. After 1900, union organizations, especially in the garment industries, achieved stability and effectiveness, and were able to organize strikes that led to substantial improvements in wages and working conditions. At the same time, a Jewish socialist fraternal order – the Arbiter Ring (Workmen's Circle) – was formed and became an important educational force in the immigrant community.

The waning years of the nineteenth century also witnessed the birth of the Zionist movement. In its early years, Zionism gained little support in America. The acculturated German Jewish community almost unanimously opposed Zionism as antithetical to the 'universalism' of reform Judaism. As for the recent east European immigrants, they were too busy struggling to establish themselves in America to think of becoming involved with a movement designed to encourage emigration to Palestine. Moreover, the socialists among them were hostile to the very idea of

Zionism. During the early years of immigration, the primary concerns of the new arrivals were survival and adjustment.

After the turn of the century, leaders of the Americanized and largely native-born community adopted increasingly effective measures to deal with the problems experienced by the immigrants. A network of social institutions was created to cope with these problems and also to respond to the worsening travails of Jews overseas. Men like the investment banker Jacob Schiff and the distinguished constitutional lawyer Louis Marshall exercised leadership in organizing charitable and educational agencies that dealt with social welfare and civil rights. In 1906, they led a group that formed the American Jewish Committee, whose stated goal was 'to prevent the infraction of the civil and religious rights of Jews in any part of the world'. Among their endeavours was the reorganization of the Jewish Theological Seminary in 1901 to serve as a centre for the creation of an American version of traditional Judaism. Their financial support made it possible to bring Solomon Schechter, an eminent Jewish scholar, from England to serve as president of the Seminary.

Schechter possessed both east European rabbinic training and German university education; and, in addition, he served as Reader in Rabbinics at Cambridge University in England. Schechter created a seminary in which traditional Jewish learning was combined with critical scholarship and use of the English language. Like the pragmatic reformers of fifty years earlier, he emphasized decorum and dignity in religious worship.

Schechter and his associates accepted the idea that Judaism would change in response to modern conditions, but believed that the necessary changes must be made within the framework of the Jewish legal tradition. The type of modified Americanized traditionalism espoused at the Jewish Theological Seminary came to be known as 'conservative' – a halfway position between reform and orthodoxy. In 1909, a Teachers' Institute was established at the Seminary. By 1913, Schechter was able to form the United Synagogue of America with sixteen congregations identified as conservative and with the participation of the association of conservative rabbis called the Rabbinic Assembly. In that year, Rabbi Joseph Hertz, a graduate of the Seminary, became Chief Rabbi of the United Kingdom, a post that he held until his death in 1946.

The failure of the Revolution of 1905 in Russia brought a number of Zionist leaders to America and infused the movement with new energy. As the situation of Jews in eastern Europe continued to deteriorate and the Jewish community in Palestine began to develop, interest in and support for Zionism grew. The movement won its most important convert in 1914, when Louis D. Brandeis, a prominent lawyer and political reformer of German Jewish origin, agreed to become chairman of the Provisional Committee for General Zionist Affairs. He was an adviser to President Woodrow Wilson who had served as arbitrator in the garment industry strike of 1910 and was responsible for the Protocol of Peace that settled the strike. Brandeis provided both organizational and ideological fibre to the American Zionist movement. He claimed that Zionism was consistent with American patriotism and declared that 'every American Jew who aids in advancing the Jewish settlement in Palestine, though he feels that neither he nor his descendants will ever live there, will likewise be a better man and a better American for doing so'.[20] American Zionism as defined by Brandeis implied support for the national Jewish idea, but not personal participation in the task of building the homeland.

The First World War

The outbreak of the First World War interrupted the mass immigration to the United States and, at the same time, thrust American Jewry into the role of leadership of the Jewish world. American Jewry's first response was to form the Joint Distribution Committee to coordinate relief and general assistance to beleaguered European Jewish communities, especially in eastern Europe. The second response was to prepare to represent Jewish concerns at the peace conference. However, a struggle ensued between the leaders of the American Jewish Committee, who saw themselves as the appropriate representatives of American Jewry, and the Zionist leaders. The former group opposed the idea of a Jewish national homeland, whilst the Zionists favoured democratic elections for representatives and wanted the homeland provision included in the peace treaty. A congress was convened whose duration was limited to the war emergency and a compromise was reached in which a platform encompassed minority rights and support for a homeland. The Versailles peace treaty included both provisions and Louis Marshall, who had been the head of the Jewish delegation, announced on his return that Jewish rights had been secured and that the 'nightmare of the past' had ended. 'Let it be swallowed up by the dawning of a new day,' he declared.[21] Unfortunately, the promise was not fulfilled and the traumas to come were worse than any conceivable nightmare.

The inter-war years

After the war, immigration to the United States was only briefly resumed before being permanently reduced by the adoption of stringent immigration quotas in 1921 and 1924. The process of Americanization was accelerated as Jews moved out of immigrant ghettos into other settlements and into middle-class areas. Of the 353,000 Jews in the Lower East Side of New York City in 1916, only 121,000 remained in 1930. By the mid-1920s, the Jewish population of the United States was estimated to be approximately four million.

The 'roaring 20s' was a decade of frantic instability. In the immediate post-war period, economic depression, general disillusionment and the anxiety created by the Bolshevik Revolution precipitated a wave of xenophobia and an outburst of anti-Semitism. The post-Civil War Ku Klux Klan was revived and won considerable support for its anti-Semitic, anti-Negro and anti-Catholic platform. The industrialist Henry Ford sponsored the publication of an anti-Semitic newspaper, the *Dearborn Independent*, which reprinted the notorious forgery, the *Protocols of the Elders of Zion*, which allegedly were the minutes of meetings held by powerful Jews who aimed to take over the world. But when the economy recovered in the mid-1920s, anti-Semitism retreated to the margins of society, the Klan dwindled to insignificance, and Jews, along with all other Americans, were again able to pursue their private interests. The words of President Calvin Coolidge characterized the spirit of the time: 'The business of America is business.'

However, one area in which anti-Semitic bias persisted was in university admissions, especially in professional and medical schools. Harvard and Columbia Universities took the lead in introducing stringent quotas for the admission of Jewish students – a philosophy that was emulated in all leading universities. The existence of publicly supported colleges and universities and the large number of privately sponsored institutions in America made it possible for many Jews to gain admission somewhere, but the quota system proved to be a handicap and a barrier that was not removed until after the Second World War.

In other walks of life there were greater opportunities for Jews, particularly in the newly emerging entertainment and communications industries. Jewish producers and entrepreneurs played a key role in the development of the motion picture industry in the 1920s. Their enterprise, willingness to take risks and their responsiveness to complex tasks made it possible for them to succeed where older, more established investors were loath to venture. The same was true for the new medium of commercial radio, which emerged in the mid-1920s.

At the same time, Jewish composers, playwrights and entertainers, most of whom were the children of immigrants, played a significant part in the cultural revival that was taking place. The American musical theatre was virtually the creation of Jewish talent: Jerome Kern, George Gershwin, Irving Berlin and Richard Rodgers being the most outstanding of a roster that included many other contributors. Elmer Rice and Clifford Odets were among the playwrights who contributed to the creation of a vigorous American theatre. Al Jolson, Jack Benny, Eddie Cantor and Fanny Brice gained popularity as entertainers. The areas open to Jewish participation were circumscribed, but Jewish visibility in public life was growing.

The participation of Jews in political life during the 1920s was minimal. There were exceptions: President Theodore Roosevelt had earlier named Oscar Straus secretary of commerce, the first Jew appointed to a cabinet post; Louis D. Brandeis was proposed as a judge to the Supreme Court by Woodrow Wilson in 1916, and after a prolonged debate was confirmed by a narrow margin; and in the 1920s, a handful of representatives of predominantly Jewish districts in New York and Chicago held seats in the House of Representatives. But for the most part, Jewish political influence was negligible and Jews were timid about exercising whatever influence they had.

During this period, religious development continued in some sectors but stagnated in others. The increase in affluence and acculturation resulted in a rash of synagogue building, especially in areas of new settlement. New structures were often elaborate and contained classrooms, auditoriums and occasionally gymnasiums. Mordecai Kaplan, a conservative rabbi and dean of the Teachers' Institute of the Jewish Theological Seminary, developed the idea of a 'synagogue-centre' and established such an institution in New York.

The United Synagogue, an organization of conservative congregations that was formed in 1913, grew rapidly during the 1920s and 1930s. Conservative Judaism provided a combination of traditional ambience with English-language readings and sermons. This appealed to the acculturated immigrant and the second-generation burgher, who felt reform Judaism was too cold and the old-fashioned orthodox Judaism rather idiosyncratic. Men and women sat together in synagogues, the lengthy prayers were slightly abbreviated and individuals whose attachment was directed to Jewish peoplehood rather than to ritual observance could feel at home.

On the other hand, the reform movement was at a virtual standstill in the 1920s. Its institutions were located in Cincinnati, far from the centres of Jewish life, and its mode of worship attracted few Jews of east European origin. Moreover, the prevailing anti-Zionism of the movement antagonized secularists with Zionist sentiments. To counter this trend, in 1922, Rabbi Stephen Wise, a reform rabbi and a leading Zionist, established the Jewish Institute of Religion in New York. Later, in 1947, the Institute was united with the Hebrew Union College and maintained as the New York branch of the combined reform seminary.

The state of orthodoxy in the 1920s is less clear. On the one hand, American-ized immigrants and their children were becoming less and less observant, and many were abandoning religious practice and affiliation altogether. At the same time, small but significant steps were taken to develop an American form of orthodoxy to counteract the challenge. In 1915, Bernard Revel became head of the Rabbi Isaac Elehanan Theological Seminary, which merged with Yeshivat Etz Chaim and introduced secular studies. In 1923, the Rabbinical Council of America was formed in which alumni of American *yeshivot* predominated. In 1928, Yeshivah College was established as the first general education institution of higher education under Jewish sponsorship.

In the 1930s, the rise of Hitler and the resurgence of anti-Semitism brought a radical change in the outlook and orientation of American Jewry. Zionism won increasing acceptance in all circles. Even the reform movement reassessed its attitude towards Zionism and traditional practices. In 1937, the Reform Central Conference of American Rabbis adopted a new platform embracing these changes and the Union of American Hebrew Congregations unanimously passed a resolu-tion urging the restoration of traditional symbols and customs. In 1940, a revised version of the reform Union Prayer Book appeared which reinstated some cere-monies, and moved closer to the traditional prayer book. By 1941, Zionists were in the majority in the Central Conference of American Rabbis.

The conservative movement was energized by the ideas of Mordecai Kaplan, who described Judaism as a 'religious civilization' and stressed the concept of 'peoplehood' and the totality of Jewish culture. In 1935, Kaplan founded the reconstructionist movement to disseminate his ideas. He rejected the option of establishing a new denomination and sought to influence American Jewry in general. His theological emphasis on religious naturalism was less influential than his sociological emphasis on Jewish communality, but his ideas did exert significant influence, especially within the conservative movement.

Orthodoxy in America was strengthened by the arrival of distinguished European scholars and rabbinic leaders. Rabbi Joseph Soloveitchik became the leading figure among the 'modern orthodox' associated with Yeshivah College and the religious Zionists. Rabbi Moses Feinstein, one of the leading authorities in halakhah (Jewish law), became a prominent figure in right-wing orthodoxy. The presence of these and other rabbinic leaders, together with numbers of *yeshivah* students who had come to America as wartime refugees, paved the way for a revival of orthodoxy in the post-war period.

During the depression era, Jews participated actively in conceptualizing and implementing the social programme of the New Deal. Many entered government as mid-level bureaucrats and advisers to government agencies. However, pervasive isolationism and the resurgence of anti-Semitism in the 1930s created a climate of insecurity that made it difficult for Jews to assert themselves in the political arena, particularly where specifically Jewish interests were involved. Jewish political behaviour continued to be characterized by timidity and what has been described as 'the cult of gratitude'.

Jewish immigration to Canada

The restriction of immigration to the United States in the 1920s diverted a significant number of immigrants to Canada. Prior to 1900, the Jewish population of Canada numbered less than 16,000, and most of these were recent immigrants. By 1930, the population had increased to 140,000. The predominance of east European Jews, who were the recent immigrants, and the multilingual nature of Canadian society resulted in the establishment of a stronghold of Yiddish language and Jewish secular culture. Canadian multinational and multilingual society made educational separation a more attractive option than in the United States. The progress of both the orthodox and the reform movements was slow, but the conservative movement made rapid strides. Orthodox, conservative and reform congregations and their rabbis were all affiliated with the movements in the United States.

Holocaust and revival – 1941–60

Throughout the Hitler period, the wall of immigration restriction was not breached in either the United States or Canada. The great depression of the 1930s caused massive unemployment in both countries, and the general social unrest, further exacerbated by Nazi propaganda, led to rising anti-Semitism and virulent opposition to the admission of refugees. American and Canadian Jewish communities, finding themselves under attack, were cautious in their response. They feared that their support for so unpopular a cause would jeopardize their own position without succeeding in changing government policy. However, despite hesitations, protest meetings were held, an anti-Nazi boycott of goods imported from Germany was organized and appeals for help were addressed to the President and other government authorities – but all without significant result. Even after America entered the war in December 1941, and after information concerning the destruction of

European Jewry came to light in the autumn of 1942, the desperate plight of
European Jewry still received little government attention. The pleas of American
Jewish leaders were not heeded and the proposals they advanced were ignored. By
the time the War Refugee Board was established in 1944, on the initiative of
Secretary of the Treasury Henry Morganthau, the effort was too little and too late.
Whether or not American Jewry should or could have been more aggressive in
demanding a greater effort from the American government to rescue the Jews in
Europe remains an unresolved question. Given the circumstances of the war and
the climate of opinion in America, it is doubtful whether an even more vigorous
protest would have significantly changed the tragic situation in which six million
Jews perished.

As a consequence of the decimation of European Jewry, the centre of gravity of
Jewish life shifted to the United States and to the embattled Jewish communities in
Palestine. The hideous revelations of the catastrophe in Europe and the struggle for
the establishment of the state of Israel drew hundreds of thousands of Jews into
fund raising and rescue activities. The ranks of Zionist organizations swelled and
groups such as Bnai Brith, which had previously been non-Zionist, became supporters of Zionism. A new vigour and militancy characterized Jewish political
behaviour in the struggle to help the survivors of the Holocaust and to establish a
Jewish state.

American Zionist leaders such as Rabbi Abba Hillel Silver took their place
alongside the leaders of the Jewish Agency from Palestine in advocating the Zionist
cause before the United Nations and in Washington. Though the number of
American Jews who migrated to Israel remained small, American Jewry was
involved in the struggle for the establishment of the state. Some thousands even
fought as volunteers in the Israeli War of Independence.

American Jewry emerged from the Second World War with increased energy,
self-confidence and opportunities. The heightened sense of Jewishness combined
with rapid suburbanization and the general religious revival in America to fuel an
unprecedented growth in Jewish religious institutions. Reform Judaism, which
claimed 290 temples and 50,000 families in 1937, reported 520 congregations and
255,000 families in 1956. The conservative movement, which claimed 250 synagogues and 75,000 member families in 1937, claimed over 500 congregations and
200,000 families in 1956. Both reform and conservative seminaries opened
branches on the west coast. Synagogue affiliation – not personal piety – had become
a central element in Jewish identification in America.

Orthodoxy, which suffered numerical losses in the large-scale movements from
city to suburbs, none the less showed remarkable vigour. In 1945, Yeshivah College
became Yeshivah University and in subsequent years expanded to include Stern
College for Women, Revel Graduate School and Einstein Medical College. Jewish
all-day schools at both elementary and high school level proliferated, primarily
under Orthodox auspices.

Immigration after the Second World War greatly strengthened the ultra-
orthodox segment of American Jewry, especially its Hasidic branch. Survivors of
Hasidic Jewish communities of Europe, uprooted by Hitler, emigrated together

with their rabbinic leaders and settled in enclaves primarily in New York City and its vicinity. The branch of Hasidism known as Lubavich, after its town of origin, established a network of schools and centres and adopted a policy of 'outreach' to secular and non-Hasidic Jews. The extremist Satmar Hasidic sect (also named after its town of origin) maintained its isolation and its vigorous opposition to Zionism and the state of Israel, but still succeeded in establishing a base. From the left wing of reform to the most extreme right wing of orthodoxy, Judaism in the United States and Canada grew in institutional strength and in vitality.

New influences exerted themselves on Jewish religious life. Rabbis such as Joshua Loth Liebman led the way in harmonizing the principles of religion with the insights of psychology. Will Herberg, a sociologist, philosopher and convert from Marxism to Judaism, set about redefining Judaism in terms of religious existentialism. Abraham Joshua Heschel, a refugee rabbi and scholar from Poland who became an influential member of the faculty of the Jewish Theological Seminary, espoused a neo-orthodox, neo-mystical approach to Judaism that proved to be extremely appealing to rabbis and laypeople alike.

In the immediate post-war years and during the 1950s, barriers of legal segregation and discrimination were attacked and reduced. The 1954 Supreme Court decision outlawing segregation in the public schools was the most dramatic and most significant advance. Prior to that time, the quota system, which limited the admission of Jews and other minorities to universities and professional schools, had been virtually abrogated. Jews joined the faculties of expanding universities in unprecedented numbers. Numerous professions and areas of employment were open to all. Jews and Jewish community relations organizations took the lead in supporting laws to end discrimination in employment, housing and civil rights.

The increased openness of American life was manifested in cultural life as well. For the first time, Jewish writers (especially those who dealt with Jewish themes and subjects) took their places in the front ranks of American literature. Novelists Norman Mailer, Saul Bellow, Bernard Malamud and (somewhat later) Phillip Roth, playwright Arthur Miller and poets Karl Shapiro and Allen Ginsburg were the most prominent representatives of a larger group of what was called the 'American Jewish school'. Most surprisingly, Isaac Bashevis Singer, who still wrote in Yiddish and whose works were set in the vanished Jewish world of eastern Europe, was elected to the American Academy of Arts and Letters and hailed as an American writer. In the 1930s, *Call It Sleep*, a novel by Henry Roth about the experiences of an immigrant Jewish child, was ignored and forgotten. Rediscovered in the late 1950s by the critic Alfred Kazin, it became a best-seller and was hailed as a classic. Jewish subject matter had taken its place on the American literary agenda.

Crises and responses – 1960 to the present

The Jewish religious revival of the 1950s seemed to wane in the early 1960s when the Jewish community, like society in general, was swept up in a wave of social action. While the 'God is dead' movement never exercised any influence within Judaism, there was a noticeable lessening of involvement in religious institutions and religious leaders began to lose their influence. This tendency was sharply reversed in the late 1960s when the emergence of militant Black nationalism changed the tone and the direction of the civil rights movement and stimulated a revival of ethnicity that affected the whole of American society. The changed atmosphere stimulated Jewish secular and cultural identification and motivated increased Jewish communal involvement.

At the same time, the threat to the existence of the state of Israel in the weeks prior to the Six-Day War in 1967 evoked astonishingly strong emotions of commitment and solidarity. It was as though the spectre of another Holocaust had arisen, and this time American Jewry was determined not to be found wanting. The reminder of the precariousness of the state of Israel and the centrality of that state to the identity and security of Jews everywhere galvanized the community into action. The vigorous and outspoken response demonstrated that the timidity and self-consciousness that had characterized American Jewry in earlier decades had disappeared.

In the years following the establishment of the state of Israel, the organized Zionist movement had dwindled in numbers and in influence, partly because support for the state was taken up by the community as a whole. In every city federations of Jewish charities were organized and became the central instruments for supporting both local Jewish agencies and overseas needs. In responding to the emergency of June 1967, these federations consolidated their role as the central agencies in American Jewish life and as the focus of what has been called 'Jewish civil religion'.

The events of June 1967 also energized Jewish life behind the Iron Curtain, where a national movement emerged among Soviet Jews, long denied access to Jewish culture or contact with other Jewish communities. The primary demand of the movement was 'repatriation' – the right to 'return' to the homeland of the Jews. The plight of Soviet Jewry captured the hearts of American Jews and the right of Soviet Jews to emigrate became the major item on the agenda of American Jewry. In the late 1960s, American Jewry mobilized itself effectively for political action, primarily on behalf of Israel and Soviet Jewry. The success of these efforts was evidenced by the passage in 1974 of the Jackson–Vanick bill, which tied American trade with the Soviet Union to Soviet policy regarding emigration.

Jewish participation in general political life also increased significantly. Several Jews served in the Senate and the House of Representatives, including such outstanding figures as Herbert Lehman (1949–56), Jacob Javits (1956–74) and Abraham Ribicoff (who held various political offices, 1954–81). Arthur Goldberg served in the cabinet (1961–2), on the Supreme Court (1962–5) and as a US representative to the United Nations (1965–8). Henry Kissinger, serving as assistant to the President for national security affairs (1969–75) and secretary of state (1973–7) and Harold Brown, who served as secretary of defense (1977–80), were two of the many Jews who held cabinet positions. The presence of Jews in the political mainstream was clearly demonstrated in 1984 when Diane Feinstein, a Jewish woman who was mayor of San Francisco, was seriously considered as a candidate for vice-president on the Democratic ticket.

Golda Meir, Prime Minister of Israel at a United Jewish Appeal dinner in 1974, after the Yom Kippur War of October 1973.

The late 1960s also witnessed a revival of interest in the Holocaust as a subject for study, publication and commemoration. In the years immediately following the Second World War, there seemed to be a general reluctance to confront the facts of the Holocaust. However, the Eichmann trial in Jerusalem in 1961 reopened the issue and the threat to the state of Israel in 1967 gave the study of the Holocaust renewed relevance. The crisis of the Yom Kippur War in 1973 intensified this mood and further stimulated interest.

The energies generated by all of these developments led to new initiatives within all the religious movements of Judaism. One result of this revival was a significant increase in the number and quality of Jewish all-day schools under conservative and reform as well as orthodox auspices. A new form of religious fellowship called the *Havurah* emerged as a significant factor. These self-generated, intimate groups of intensely committed Jews were sometimes independent and sometimes to be found within large synagogues. At the same time, the study of Judaism and Jewish subjects on college campuses expanded rapidly, often stimulated by student interest and by communal support. Together with these formal developments, a movement of *baalei teshuvah* – penitent returners – who might be characterized as 'born again' Jews, gained strength. They were to be found in all of the movements, but were most visible among the orthodox.

The 1970s saw an amalgamation of numerous developments denoting a strengthening of Jewish communal life and the invigoration of Jewish identity on the part of large numbers of individuals. The general tendency within all branches of Judaism was towards increased observance.

However, there are two recent trends that run counter to these developments and raise problems for the unity of the Jewish people in the future. Perhaps the most serious is the growing rate of intermarriage. Given the integration of Jews into every phase of American life, the dispersal of compact Jewish neighbourhoods and the increasing social openness and freedom of association in society, the number of intermarriages has inevitably increased. One response by the reform movement has been a programme of outreach to non-Jewish spouses, encouraging them to become 'Jews by choice'. An increasing number of converts has been accepted by all three of the movements (although only the reform movement has an outreach programme) and efforts to integrate them into the community are developing. Unfortunately, conversions performed by reform or conservative rabbis are not recognized by the orthodox community or by the rabbinate in Israel; the result may be the emergence of two classes of Jews.

The second trend is a declining birthrate, brought about by the improved status and increasing career orientation of women. This is particularly marked among American Jews, whose level of education is generally high. Recent statistics indicate that child-bearing has not been rejected by working women, but merely postponed, and that the decline in the birthrate is not as precipitous as was once thought. Nevertheless, it is clear that except for the orthodox group, the demographic issue of population maintenance is a concern. The conflict between orthodox and non-orthodox over the role and rights of women has intensified in recent years with no solution in sight. The orthodox movement has resisted demands for changes in the status of women in its own ranks and has maintained the traditional role of women. In contrast, the reform movement has ordained women as rabbis and cantors. The conservative movement has recently sanctioned the ordination of women as rabbis, but its cantorial group has not yet accepted women. Like intermarriage, this issue creates a gap between two types of Judaism and two types of Jews that will not be easily bridged.

These difficulties have led some scholars and critics to predict the decline or even the ultimate demise of American Jewry. Others, pointing to the active organizational life and the increase in commitment and practice in numerous areas, express confidence in the future of American Jewry. Throughout history, predictions of decline and disappearance of the Jews have been a permanent feature of the Jewish landscape. One scholar called the Jews 'the ever-dying people' because of the continuity of such predictions. On the other hand, American Jewry in the 1980s proved to be more vigorous, more dynamic, more creative, more committed than anyone could have predicted in any previous period. So, it is impossible to say how American Jewry will fare in the future. What is clear is that American Jewry entered the 1990s as a vigorous, highly organized, diverse community that encompasses a wide variety of institutional and ideological options.

6 *The Origins of Religious and Racial Anti-Semitism and the Jewish Response*

Philip S. Alexander

The origins of the term: 'anti-Semitism'

The term 'anti-Semitic' was probably introduced into modern usage by the German political pamphleteer Wilhelm Marr who, in 1879, founded the League of Anti-Semites. The aim of the league was to promote extreme anti-Jewish views and to create a popular political movement based on anti-Semitism, using pamphlets and public lectures to spread its message. The nature of Marr's anti-Semitism is abundantly clear from his writings, notably his tract *The Victory of Judaism over Germandom: Regarded from a Non-Denominational Point of View*. Marr's views may be summed up in three propositions:

- The Jews as a race are evil and so is the culture they have created (the 'Jewish spirit')
- The Jews act in concert to foist their culture on other nations with a view to controlling them
- It is imperative for other nations to take appropriate practical measures in self-defence against the Jews and their culture and to reassert their own nationhood.

Marr wrote: 'We have among us a flexible, tenacious, intelligent, foreign tribe that knows how to bring abstract reality into play in many different ways. Not individual Jews, but the Jewish spirit and consciousness have overpowered the world.'[1]

Marr's position represents classic anti-Semitism and may be taken as a convenient benchmark for defining it. Anyone asserting the truth of these three propositions – which may be expressed in different ways in different contexts – is unquestionably anti-Semitic. But what is the relationship between the three propositions of the anti-Semitic credo? What if, for example, only one (or two) of them is affirmed? Clearly the first proposition is fundamental: an anti-Semite is first and foremost someone hostile to the Jews and Jewish culture. That hostility is implicitly (if not explicitly) racist: it is directed against Jews as a group or as a people, stereotyping them and defining the essence of their culture in a certain way. But does endorsing the first proposition inevitably lead to an assertion of the other two? In principle, the answer would appear to be 'no'; in practice, however, the answer is far from clear. If one propagates anti-Jewish views, one may be guilty of providing others less fastidious than oneself with grounds for taking anti-Jewish action. Moreover, one's motives may fairly be called into question. Views are usually publicized with the aim of influencing public opinion. They can affect, however obliquely, the course of events – a point recognized by modern race-relations legislation. Propaganda advocating even a generalized, unspecific hatred of a given race or group may be actionable in law because it can so easily lead to a breach of the peace. Implicit in all anti-Jewish propaganda is an anti-Jewish programme, however much the promoters of that propaganda may deny the logic of their position. It is, therefore, reasonable to describe those who assert the first proposition alone as anti-Semitic.

Marr may have popularized the term 'anti-Semite', but he did not invent anti-Semitism as such. The ideas which he labelled 'anti-Semitic' were already widespread in Germany and Austria in the nineteenth century, particularly among the anti-liberal, anti-modern, nationalist political parties and movements which were growing in influence at this time. Moreover, similar ideas can be found much earlier in history, and there are distinctive features of modern anti-Semitism that relate to underlying continuities with the anti-Judaism of earlier ages. Marr and other anti-Semites of the late nineteenth century did their best to exploit these continuities.

This chapter will trace the development of anti-Semitism from the first century CE to modern times, focusing in particular on the late nineteenth and early twentieth centuries. A restricted, rather precise definition of anti-Semitism, derived from Marr's statements, is employed throughout to avoid the trap of labelling all opposition to the Jews and Judaism as anti-Semitic.

Pagan anti-Judaism in late antiquity

In late antiquity, there were Jewish communities scattered throughout the Mediterranean world and, as a result, Jews and Judaism were frequently referred to by Greek and Roman writers. These references are, for the most part, highly unfavourable, and there are a number of recurrent themes. For example:

- Jews are 'atheists' who despise the gods of the city and the state which other men worship
- Jews are 'misanthropists' whose law teaches them to show common human decency only to their co-religionists
- Jews flout the laws of the state and engage in many absurd and dubious practices and rites.

The Roman satirist Juvenal (c. 60–130 CE) wrote:

Some [Jews] who have had a father who reveres the Sabbath, worship nothing but the clouds, and the divinity of the heavens, and see no difference between eating swine's flesh, from which their father abstained, and that of a man; and in time they take to circumcision. Having been wont to flout the laws of Rome, they learn and practise and revere the Jewish law, and all that Moses handed down in his rites, and conducting none but the circumcised to the desired fountain.[2]

Juvenal's contemporary, the historian Tacitus (c. 56–120 CE), in similar vein, condemned the customs of the Jews as 'base and abominable', and blamed the persistence of these customs on the Jews' 'depravity'. He wrote:

> [Converts to Judaism are] the worst rascals among other peoples, renouncing their ancestral religions, always keep sending tribute and contributing to Jerusalem, thereby increasing the wealth of the Jews. Again, the Jews are extremely loyal toward one another, and always ready to show compassion, but toward every other people they feel only hate and enmity. They sit apart at meals and they sleep apart, and although as a race, they are prone to lust, they abstain from intercourse with foreign women; yet among themselves nothing is unlawful. They adopted circumcision to distinguish themselves from other peoples by this difference. Those who are converted to their ways follow the same practice, and the earliest lesson they receive is to despise the gods, to disown their country, and to regard their parents, children, and brothers as of little account.[3]

Why were writers such as Juvenal and Tacitus so contemptuous and hostile towards Jews and Judaism? Part of their opposition may be attributed to xenophobia – because the Jews formed one of the most cohesive, non-conformist groups of the Mediterranean, they were subjected to the same kind of suspicion and hostility that most foreigners suffered at the time. Indeed, some anti-Jewish writers also atacked other foreigners in rather similar ways. However, there was more to it than that. Juvenal and Tacitus both reflected the prevalent fear that Rome might cease to be a Roman city characterized by Roman customs and manners: owing to the influx of foreigners from the east, it ran the risk of being orientalized. In addition, the Jews rejected the Roman gods: an attitude that the authorities viewed as disloyal and likely to undermine the state. There was, therefore, an element of what today would be regarded as old-fashioned conservative nationalism in Rome's hostility.

However, not all Romans and Greeks were hostile to the Jews or Judaism. Many Gentiles, some of high social standing, were attracted by the simplicity of Jewish worship and by the philosophical nature of the Jewish view of God. A number of those who did not actually convert to Judaism attended a synagogue as 'God fearers' and sent gifts to the Temple in Jerusalem. Juvenal and Tacitus regarded such people as traitors to their cities and ancestral gods. The Jews, therefore, were a menace because they attracted proselytes.

Anti-Judaism in the Mediterranean region was fuelled by yet another factor – anti-Jewish propaganda, originating in Egypt, but circulated widely. Jews lived in very considerable numbers in Egypt, especially in Alexandria. Their relations with the local population were often strained and occasionally there were anti-Jewish riots. It is difficult to determine whether the causes of this tension were economic, political, religious or a mix of all three, but anti-Jewish feeling undoubtedly ran high. Local Egyptian writers appear to have added to the problem by producing a considerable amount of anti-Jewish propaganda – for example, an alternative account of the biblical story of the Exodus which claimed that the Egyptians had driven the Jews out of Egypt as an act of self-defence because the Jews had been infected with plague. This material spread throughout the Mediterranean (indeed, there is evidence that Tacitus knew the alternative version of the Exodus), and it probably affected attitudes towards Jews even in areas where there was little grounds for social tension. Despite unrest and rebellion among the Jews of Palestine and the diaspora, the Roman state did not treat the Jews so badly. Judaism was recognized as a legal religion and concessions were made to accommodate Jewish religious sensibilities. However, among some pagans in late antiquity, a definite hostility existed towards the Jews and Judaism which displayed many of the hallmarks of anti-Semitism.

Anti-Judaism in early Christianity

The Christian Church has undoubtedly played a major role in the development and dissemination of anti-Semitism. The roots of the church's anti-Semitism can be traced right back to its origins in the first century CE. Two major factors shaped early Christian anti-Judaism: the church's view of itself as the new Israel and the Jewish rejection of Jesus.

It was a central tenet of Christianity that the church was the new, authentic Israel. Although Christianity began as a religious movement within Second Temple Judaism, from the outset it displayed a deep ambivalence towards Jewish law and tradition. Christianity recognized the Hebrew Scriptures as the Word of God, but claimed that they had been superseded by a newer, fuller revelation in Jesus Christ – the Sinai Covenant had been replaced by a New Covenant in Christ. However, the early church did not simply discard the Hebrew Scriptures, and for a very good reason: it needed those Scriptures to validate its claims that Jesus of Nazareth was indeed the prophesied Messiah and that the new order which he had inaugurated was that foretold by the Hebrew Scriptures. Early Christian writers confidently predicted the imminent demise of the old order, perhaps encouraged by the Roman destruction of the Second Temple in Jerusalem in 70 CE. Thus, after quoting Jeremiah's promise of a new covenant, the writer of the Epistle to the Hebrews concluded:

> By speaking of a new covenant He [God] has pronounced the first one old; and anything that is growing old and ageing will shortly disappear.[4]

According to this view, the religion of the Old Covenant could persist after the inauguration of the New Covenant, but only as a fossilized anachronism, lacking any continuing validity.

The second factor that shaped early Christian anti-Judaism was the Jewish rejection of Jesus. The fact was that Jewish religious leaders, and indeed the majority of ordinary Jews, did not acknowledge Jesus as the long-awaited Messiah, nor did they embrace Christian doctrine. Paradoxically, Christianity did make considerable headway among Gentiles, particularly among the 'God fearers' on the fringes of the synagogue.

The Jewish rejection of Jesus raised acute theological problems for early Christianity, and these were dealt with in a variety of ways. One explanation was to argue that the Hebrew Scriptures had predicted the rejection and disbelief. Jesus was identified with the 'stone of offence' and 'rock of stumbling to both houses of Israel' mentioned in Isaiah.[5] Another explanation focused on the Old Testament Prophets' frequent and often fierce denunciations of the sinfulness and wayward-ness of the people, and argued that in rejecting Jesus the Jews were acting totally in character and displaying their perverse and wicked nature. This line of argument was developed with great consistency in the Book of Acts, particularly in the speeches. For example, the long and impressive speech of Stephen (the first Christian martyr) in Acts 7 is largely devoted to arguing that at every significant juncture in the sacred history, Jews had rejected God's messengers. The speech concludes:

> How stubborn you are, heathen still at heart and deaf to the truth. You always fight against the Holy Spirit. Like fathers, like sons. Was there ever a prophet whom your fathers did not persecute. They killed those who foretold the coming of the Righteous One, and now you have betrayed him and murdered him, you who received the Law as God's angels gave it to you and yet have not kept it.[6]

As Stephen appears to be talking about ingrained traits of the people as a whole, it seems that he is suggesting a blanket condemnation of the Jews.

For Stephen, the supreme proof of the Jews' depravity is the fact that they murdered the 'Righteous One'. At various points in the New Testament, the Jews are held responsible for the death of Jesus. The accusation is made with particular force in the Gospel of Matthew, which depicts Pilate as actually wanting to release Jesus, but being frustrated by the crowd who were egged on by the chief priests and elders.

> Pilate could see that nothing was being gained and a riot was starting; so he took water and washed his hands in full view of the people, saying 'My hands are clean of this man's blood; see to that yourselves.' And with one voice they answered 'His blood be on us and on our children.' He then released Barabbas to them; but he had Jesus flogged and handed over to be crucified.[7]

The notion of the basic wickedness of the Jews, manifested in their rejection of Jesus, takes on a darker colouring in the context of the sharply dualistic world view of the Gospel of John. When the Jews remind Jesus that Abraham is their father, he savagely retorts:

> Your father is the Devil, and you choose to carry out your father's desires. He was a murderer from the beginning, and is not rooted in the truth; there is no truth in him. When he tells a lie, he is speaking his own language, for he is a liar and the father of lies. But I speak the truth and therefore you do not believe me.[8]

It is sometimes argued in mitigation of such passages that they reflect what is essentially an internal Jewish debate. After all, the early Christians were mostly

Jews, so they can hardly have intended such condemnation to be absolute or all-embracing. If all Jews were irredeemably wicked, they themselves could never have been saved. The strength of their language may to some extent be put down to rhetoric and may reflect the passion typical of internal religious controversy. This defence, however, is not entirely convincing. Certain early Christian writers, faced with the question of why some Jews had believed whereas many others had not, appear to argue that those who did not believe were in some sense not true Jews – the promises of the Old Covenant never really applied to them. This idea may lie behind the passage found in John in which Jesus denies that his opponents are 'sons of Abraham'. This line of argument is also developed by Paul who discriminates sharply among those who say they belong to 'Israel':

> Not all descendants of Israel are truly Israel nor, because they are Abraham's offspring, are they all his true children.[9]

This suggests that God was separating out the true Israel from the false. The former, who constituted only a 'remnant', were destined for salvation and would join together with the redeemed Gentiles to form the Israel of God; the latter, who made up the majority, were predestined to damnation and were, in Paul's own words, 'vessels of wrath made for destruction'.[10] Paul, therefore, seems to have written off the majority of the Jews as beyond salvation. From his harsh perspective the debate between Christians and Jews was definitely not an internal matter, since for him it had now become clear that the majority of Jews had *never* been within the true community of Israel.

Other Church Fathers, though less hostile, were equally as negative. St Jerome, for example, readily acknowledged his indebtedness to Jewish learning, but was otherwise critical of the old faith. The more tolerant St Augustine was curious about the destiny of the Jews. The contrast between what the Jewish people might have been (had they not rebelled against God and rejected Jesus) and what they had become prompted him to speculate on the reasons for the continued existence of the Jews:

> And if they had not sinned against Him, led astray by unholy curiosity as by some magic acts, falling away to worship idols and finally murdering the Christ, they would have remained in the same kingdom, and if it did not grow in size, it would have grown in happiness. As for their present dispersion through almost all the lands and people, it is by the provenance of the true God, to the end that when the images, altars, groves, and temples of the false gods are everywhere overthrown, and the sacrifices forbidden, it may be demonstrated by the Jewish scriptures how this was prophesied long ago. Thus the possibility is avoided that, if read only in our books, the prophecy might be taken for our invention.[11]

St Augustine's statement, as given above, not only indicates a period in which Judaism, Christianity and paganism were still engaging each other but also supplied the basis for the idea, that was to be widely applied in the Middle Ages, that Jews were to be suffered in Christian society on condition that they were humiliated and isolated.

Christian anti-Judaism after Constantine

In the first century, Christianity was a small, frequently persecuted sect within Judaism whose strong views about other Jews and their religious beliefs and practices carried little weight. However, Christianity spread rapidly through the Roman world. By the fourth century, it had become the official religion of the Empire and was in a position to translate its anti-Judaism into concrete legislation and action. The church saw its triumph as irrefutable proof of divine favour, and it was not prepared to countenance any opposition. It regarded Judaism as an anachronism sustained only by the stubbornness of the Jews. It demanded that Jews be isolated socially, that the practice of Judaism be circumscribed. Jewish communities were to be kept in the position of humility, subservience and powerlessness to which God had condemned them as a punishment for rejecting the Messiah. These broad demands were the roots of a whole series of vexatious anti-Jewish laws which began in the reign of Constantine the Great (312–337). The most comprehensive early set of these measures was enacted by the Emperor Theodosius II in 439. The feast of Purim, believed to be the occasion when Jews burned images of the cross, was attacked; the construction of new synagogues was prohibited and existing ones destroyed; the office of patriarch was abolished and fresh taxation imposed. A statute of 438 defined Jews as 'enemies of the Roman laws and of the supreme majesty'. In consequence, Jews were excluded from civil and military offices; denied jurisdiction over Christians, but not exempted from onerous curial offices. Jewish inferiority was thus sanctioned by law. The Theodosian Code became the model for much subsequent anti-Jewish legislation, of both church and state.

The Theodosian Code was taken to extreme lengths by the Visigoth kings of seventh-century Spain, who not only introduced legislation to punish the Jews for professing their faith, but also took measures to ensure that the Jews behaved as good Christians, including the authority to remove Jewish children so as to give them a Christian upbringing. Severe punishment was reserved for those who declined to comply.

The Jews of the Carolingian Empire of the eighth and ninth centuries were rather more fortunate than their Spanish co-religionists. Louis the Pious and his counsellors looked favourably upon the Jews as traders and their status rose. Jews were granted 'letters of protection', permitting them to live according to their own laws; their slaves were safeguarded against baptism; and they were even allowed to proselytize among the Christians. This was all too much for Archbishop Abogard of Lyons who repeatedly urged the prince to curb Jewish influence. 'No matter how kindly we treat them,' he wrote, 'we do not succeed in drawing them to the purity of our spiritual faith. On the contrary, several among us, willingly sharing with them the food of the body, have also allowed themselves to be seduced by their spiritual nourishment ... Some Christians even celebrate the Sabbath with the Jews and violate the blessed day of rest. Many women live as domestics or paid labourers of the Jews, who lure some from their faith. Labourers and peasants are inveigled into such a sea of errors that they regard the Jews as the only people of God ...'[12] Worse, Abogard informed the king, Jews were flaunting their persons and their faith. 'They display the dresses that their wives, they claim, have received from your family, and from the ladies of the palace; they boast of having received from you, contrary to the law, the right to build new synagogues.'[13] Measures to segregate Christians and Jews, he argued, were necessary to protect the people from Jewish contagion. Trade requirements held sway, however, and for the moment the temporal powers did little. Others, though, would prove more accommodating.

How did Judaism respond to the Christian challenge and to Christianity's triumphant rise to power? This can best be assessed in terms of the responses of the rabbis. Rabbinic Judaism, which became orthodox Judaism, had its roots in the sect of the Pharisees which, like early Christianity, was one of the religious movements within the Second Temple period of Judaism. Like early Christians, the Pharisees also promoted their own distinct form of Judaism and struggled to win the hearts and minds of all Jews. That struggle is echoed in the numerous Gospel stories that show Jesus and the Pharisees in bitter conflict. Eventually, Pharisaic-rabbinic Judaism emerged from the struggle victorious. By the fourth century, when Christianity was dominant in the Gentile world, the rabbis were celebrating the effective victory of rabbinism within the Jewish world, at least in Palestine and Babylonia. Jewish Christianity had all but disappeared; the church had abandoned attempts to persuade the Jews to convert and had moved on to a more aggressive policy of direct confrontation.

The reasons for the success of rabbinism are complex. Compared with the radicalism of Christianity, rabbinism was conservative. This enabled the rabbis to argue more plausibly that they represented continuity with the past and to claim that their message was derived from the Hebrew Scriptures. The rabbis stressed fidelity to the Sinai Covenant, and resisted any attempt to suggest that it had been abrogated or the election of the Jews as chosen people rescinded. They adopted a series of measures aimed at isolating Jewish Christians within the Jewish communities and neutralizing their influence. They tried to exclude them from the synagogues; they denied the authority of their sacred books; they urged rabbinic Jews to avoid social and business contacts with Jewish Christians; and they attacked, often in satirical and scurrilous terms, Christian claims about Jesus, asserting that he was nothing more than a magician who had led Jews astray and deceived them. The policies adopted so successfully by the rabbis in the Talmudic period were to remain down to modern times the central element of their strategy to keep the Jewish communities loyal to the Torah of Moses and to ward off Christian attacks.

The Jew in the Medieval Christian world

The Church passed on its accumulated legacy of anti-Semitism to the Middle Ages when, magnified by the lens of a new, intense religiosity, it took on more terrible, even bizarre, forms. The position of the Jew worsened markedly in medieval Christian society in Europe. Because Jews were an easily identifiable non-conformist element in a conformist world, they became the focus of the irrational fears of a very superstitious society.

The medieval world-view was haunted by the Devil and by demons, so the early

Christian belief that Jews were in league with the powers of evil was readily accepted. In the mystery plays the Jews are regularly depicted as the agents of the Devil – for example, in the French drama *Le Mystère de la Passion*, devils hover in the background inciting the Jews to reject Pilate's offer to release Jesus. Jews were also widely regarded as sorcerers working black magic through the assistance of dark powers. Some held that the Jews had so given themselves over to Satan that they had taken on the physical characteristics of the Devil – they had horns and a tail, and gave off a bad smell (the so-called *foetor Judaicus*) – in contrast to the saints, whose bodies exuded a sweet odour of sanctity! Some medieval texts even implied that the Jews were devils incarnate and were not human at all.

As discussed in Chapter 1, the main accusations made against the Jews fell into three categories:

- The 'blood libel' – Jews were accused of abducting and killing children and then using their blood for ritual purposes.
- The desecration of the host – Jews were accused of stealing the consecrated wafers that represented Christ's body in the Mass and of destroying them in a frenzied attempt to kill Christ.
- The poisoning of wells – Jews were said to have caused the spread of the Black Death by poisoning wells.

The blood libel was a variant on the theme of the Jews recrucifying Jesus. A version of this accusation has been immortalized as the Prioress's Tale in Chaucer's *Canterbury Tales*. The story is set in a city in Asia, apparently at some time in the past. It tells of how a pious little boy was murdered by the Jews because they were affronted by his singing of the hymn 'Alma Redemptoris Mater' as he passed through the ghetto on his way to and from school. To conceal the body, they threw it into a cesspit. When the boy does not return home, his mother goes looking for him. As she approaches the cesspit, a miracle occurs: the boy, although his throat is cut, begins to sing the 'Alma Redemptoris Mater'. The Jews are rounded up, tortured and put to death. But the unquiet spirit still does not leave the boy's body and he eerily continues to sing. A holy abbot asks him what they must do to stop the singing; the boy tells him that the Blessed Virgin has put a 'grain' beneath his tongue and, so long as it is there, he will continue to sing. The abbot removes the grain, the spirit leaves the body peacefully and everyone is amazed at the miracle. They take the 'fair and sweet' body of the 'little martyr' and entomb it in a 'marble sepulchre' – doubtless to be venerated as the body of a saint. The Prioress's Tale is relatively restrained, only hinting at the analogy between the death of the Blessed Virgin's little devotee and the death of her Son. Other versions of the story are more explicit and dwell in lurid detail on how the boy is tortured and crucified in mockery of the death of Christ. It was also widely believed that the Jews drew blood from the body of the innocent victims and used it for various nefarious purposes and rituals.

These irrational beliefs were not the only reason for the unpopularity of the Jews: they were also hated and resented for their money-lending activities. The Third Lateran Church Council of 1179 had forbidden Christians to lend money at interest. Article LXVII of the Decrees of the Fourth Lateran Church Council

A woodcut showing Jews worshipping the Devil. In the background, three Jews kneel and worship the Devil. In the foreground, two affronted Christians seek the help of a lord who holds a whip and a sword as symbols of justice.

(1215) also expressed the Church's disapproval of the practice, although it did allow Jews to engage in usury, provided the interest they charged was not excessive:

> The more the Christian religion refrains from exacting interest (usura), the more does the perfidy of the Jews in this practice increase, so that, in a short time, they exhaust the wealth of Christians. Desiring, therefore, to protect the Christians in this matter from being immoderately burdened by the Jews, we ordain by synodal decree that if, on any pretext, Jews extort heavy and excessive interest from Christians, all relationships with Christians shall be withdrawn from them, until they make adequate restitution for their exorbitant exactions. The Christians also shall be compelled, if need be, by ecclesiastical punishment against which no appeal will be heard, to abstain from business dealings with the Jews.
>
> Moreover, we enjoin princes not to be hostile to the Christians on this account, but rather to endeavour to restrain the Jews from so great an oppression. And under threat of the same penalty we decree that the Jews shall be compelled to make good the tithes and offerings owed to the Churches, which

the Churches were accustomed to receive from the houses and other possessions of the Christians, before these came, by whatever entitlement, into the
hands of the Jews, in order that the Churches may be preserved against loss.[14]

The charge of usury was, of course, well founded. Jews were widely involved in
money-lending in the Middle Ages, mainly because many other professions or
means of livelihood were not open to them. The various trades and crafts were
dominated by Christian guilds which were fiercely anti-Jewish, so it was difficult for
a Jew to become, for example, a carpenter or a stonemason. The guilds appear to
have functioned like medieval trade-unions, running 'closed shops'. Few Jews seem
to have cultivated the land on any considerable scale. Under the feudal system, they
could only hold the land as a fief for services rendered to some lord; and, on the
whole, lords were reluctant to grant Jews such fiefs. Moreover, given the basic
insecurity of the Jews' position, it was not advisable for them to tie up too much
wealth in land as they ran the risk of losing it if they were expelled or forced to flee.
The only two ways of earning a livelihood readily open to Jews were trading (that is,
buying and selling) and money-lending, in which they put to use some of the
surplus money they acquired through trading.

As the financial systems of the medieval world were extremely primitive, the
state actually encouraged Jewish money-lending. There was only a rudimentary
bureaucracy to help collect taxes and few sources of ready cash from which one
could get a loan to finance a project or to tide one over in a financial crisis. This
chronic shortage of ready cash and credit particularly affected rulers. Although
potentially rich, they lacked hard cash. If they needed money to wage a war or build
a castle, there were very few sources of finance to which they could turn. Consequently, Jews were encouraged to perform the functions both of substitute tax
collectors and bankers. Through various tax concessions and privileges, the state
promoted their wealth but then creamed off a proportion of it into the state coffers.
Thus, the Jews were encouraged to fleece the people so that the state could, in turn,
fleece the Jews. This put the Jews in an invidious position socially, and exacerbated
their already fraught relations with the Christian population.

Throughout the Middle Ages, hostility towards the Jews sometimes flared up
into open riots. At times, the riots resulted from religious hysteria, as in 1096 when
thousands of Jews were massacred in the Rhineland towns of Speyer, Worms,
Mainz and Cologne by Crusaders heading towards the Holy Land. At other times,
more mundane factors seemed to have come into play, as in the York riots of 1190
when the Jews committed mass suicide (*kiddush ha-Shem*) in a castle where they had
taken refuge. One of the first acts of the rioters was to burn the records of debt to
the Jews.

While the general populace took to the streets to vent its feelings against the
Jews, other elements within medieval society held rather different attitudes.
Because the state benefited from the Jews, it could be protective and, in any case,
could not tolerate the public disorder resulting from anti-Jewish riots. The higher
echelons of the Church also tended to be less actively hostile toward the Jews than
the lower clergy. Pope Innocent IV (in 1245) and Pope Gregory X (in 1274) issued

papal bulls denying the charge that Jews indulged in ritual murder. However, the two preaching orders, the Franciscans and Dominicans, were extremely anti-Jewish. They regularly played upon the fears of the ignorant masses and roused them to a fever pitch of anti-Semitic fury.

Those who upheld the Augustinian conception, that Jews should exist on sufferance within Christian society, protested. Bernard of Clairvaux restated the older policy which humiliated the Jews but defended their lives and property against monkish incitement. In a letter addressed to senior churchmen and others, he wrote:

> The Jews are not to be persecuted, killed, or even put to flight . . . The Jews are for us the living words of Scripture, for they remind us always of what our Lord suffered. They are dispersed all over the world so that by expiating their crime they may be everywhere the living witness of our redemption . . . Under Christian princes they endure a hard captivity, but 'they only wait for the time of their deliverance' . . .[15]

The Jews, then, fulfilled an important Christian purpose.

> Is it not a far better triumph for the Church to convince and convert the Jews than to put them all to the sword? Has that prayer which the Church offers for the Jews, from the rising up of the sun to the going down thereof, that the veil may be taken from their hearts so that they may be led from the darkness of error into the light of truth, been instituted in vain?[16]

In 1146 it was difficult to go further.

The religious enthusiasm unleashed by the Crusades affected Jews as well as their oppressors. As in the past, *kiddush ha-Shem*, the tradition of martyrdom, which had served to sustain Jewish identity in extreme situations, was fully aroused. Thousands chose death rather than slavery or submission. If they could not live freely as Jews, they would rather not live at all. From the wars of the Maccabees to the failure of the revolts against the Romans, Jews had been willing to make the supreme sacrifice in defence of their faith, and their successors were like-minded. The ideology of *kiddush ha-Shem*, fortified by the bloody onslaught of the Crusades, found an awesome re-affirmation in the mass suicides of 1096.

In general, attitudes were so prejudiced against the Jews that there was little they could do to defend themselves. They were seldom given a fair hearing in public. Occasionally Jews were ordered to defend their religion in public, but these disputations were hardly fair debates. In the most famous disputation, held in Barcelona in 1263, the great Jewish protagonist Nachmanides seemed to have thoroughly defeated his Christian opponent, the apostate Pablo Christiani.[17]

The debate lasted for four days and took place in the presence of the king, the court and numerous ecclesiastical dignitaries. Christiani, relying on his opponent's need for circumspection, had undertaken to prove the Messianic claims of Jesus from the Talmud. The areas of debate encompassed the appearance of the Messiah, his status (divine or human), and whether the Jews or Christians were in possession of the true faith. Christiani, who had relied upon haggadic texts, was quickly disarmed by Nachmanides' distinction between the Bible, which all were bound to believe, and revered but not authoritative sources. The Jewish Messiah, he also argued, was not divine and of less importance to Jews than to Christians, on the grounds that it is more worthy for Jews to observe the precepts in exile under a Christian prince, than under the rule of the Messiah, when all would act in accordance with the Law. Shortly after his daring 'victory', Nachmanides was thrown out of Spain.

For the most part, the Jews seem to have resorted to the oldest of arts, 'behind-the-scenes diplomacy', to try to protect themselves and their interests. Particularly in the later part of the Middle Ages and in early modern times, some Jews acquired influence with the authorities – perhaps as a banker or trusted physician to a Christian ruler. These Court Jews (*Hofjuden*) often played the dangerous role of intercessors on behalf of their communities, and doubtless there were times when, like Esther in the Bible, they were able to avert disaster.

The Reformation of the sixteenth century, in shattering the unity of Christendom, altered the situation in which the Jewish minority found itself and, in the long run, created the framework for a more tolerable Jewish existence. In the short run, though, it brought more suffering in its wake. The clash between Christian Humanists and traditionalists in Germany at the start of the century gave a foretaste of troubles ahead. Once again, it was an apostate, Johannes Pfefferkorn, whose proposed destruction of the Talmud provoked controversy. Pfefferkorn was supported by the Dominicans. Emperor Maximilian, when pressed to sanction the burning of the books, sought the advice of scholars. The counter-argument, advanced by the philologist and jurist Johannes Reuchlin, was that both the Talmud and Kabbalistic writings contained much that was pertinent to Christianity – including the confirmation of its claim to truth. Reuchlin enjoyed the support of many great humanist scholars. Erasmus, though he despised Jews, spoke up for Jewish learning. Luther, too, was supportive at first, but subsequently changed his mind and turned on the 'accursed' minority with a savagery that even contemporaries found startling. As a result, popular animosity against the Jews of Reformation Germany increased and the fear of violence, whether Catholic or Protestant, became part of the fabric of everyday life.

Modern anti-Semitism

The modern era in Europe has been marked by a steady decline of Christianity and the emergence of a post-Christian culture. The beginnings of that decline may be traced back to the Renaissance, which reasserted humanist values against the traditional teachings of the Church, and to the Reformation, which split Christendom and damaged the Church's authority. The Enlightenment of the seventeenth and eighteenth centuries also played a part by stressing the primacy of reason and by subjecting revelation itself to rational critique. The Enlightenment provided the ideological underpinning for the French Revolution, which set in motion the process of Jewish emancipation, first in France and then in other states of western Europe.

The Industrial Revolution accelerated the decline of traditional Christianity: it broke up the social patterns on which traditional Christianity was based and encouraged new, radical ways of thinking. At the same time, the enormous progress of scientific discovery brought about a conflict between the Bible and science, exposing the literal truth of the Bible as untenable.

With all these developments, it might have been expected that anti-Semitism would simply wither away: people's attitudes would be coloured less and less by Christian anti-Jewish prejudice, and emancipated Jews would be fully integrated into a new tolerant and pluralistic society. That, however, is not what actually happened. Instead, anti-Semitism simply mutated into a modern, pseudo-scientific form more appropriate to the spirit of the age. Its language became largely non-religious, but the substance of its allegations remained the same.

Modern anti-Semitism may be classified into two main types: the racial and the conspiratorial.

Houston Stewart Chamberlain (1855–1927) was one influential exponent of racialist anti-Semitism. English by birth, Chamberlain developed a strong dislike of his native land, feeling himself instead increasingly drawn to Germany as his spiritual home. He deeply admired Richard Wagner and promoted both his operas and his aesthetic theories. He finally became a member of the inner circle at Bayreuth and married Wagner's only daughter, Eva, in 1907. In his magnum opus *The Foundations of the Nineteenth Century*, first published in 1899 in German, Chamberlain argued that race was the key to history. He believed that 'humanity was nothing more than a linguistic makeshift', composed of quite distinct races, each with its own physical, moral and mental capacities – culture and civilization, he claimed, lie in the genes. Using a panoramic sketch of history, Chamberlain tried to prove that it was the Germanic or Teutonic (or, as he occasionally called it, the Aryan) race that had been responsible for creating European civilization, which he believed to be the highest form of civilization to have existed. Chamberlain's beliefs, however, included a profoundly pessimistic streak: he was haunted by the fear that Germanic culture was going into decline and showing signs of degeneracy. Like the rest of the Bayreuth circle, he saw himself as engaged in a crusade to regenerate German art along the lines laid down by Wagner, and to rescue German civilization from the assaults of a number of foes, chief among them being the Jews.

Chamberlain had total contempt for Jewish culture which he saw as a bizarre mixture of contradictory elements drawn from both capitalism and Marxism, and encompassing 'red-hot fanaticism' and political liberalism. The Jew was a chameleon, ever changing his position to achieve the best advantage:

> His physiognomy and form change. He conceals himself, he slips through the fingers like an eel. Today he wears Court livery and tomorrow drapes himself in a red flag; servant of princes and apostle of freedom, banker, parliamentary spokesman, professor, journalist – anything you like; like the priest in his cowl, one does not recognize him; unnoticed he invades all circles.[18]

Chamberlain tried to explain the characteristics of Jewish culture by arguing that the Jews were 'mongrels' – the result of cross-breeding between three different racial types: the Semitic Bedouin, the Syrian Hittite and the Amorite. The Semitic Bedouin contributed 'the basic human material' of the present Jewish race. Bred of the monotonous life of the desert, their narrow-minded, unimaginative, materialistic outlook manifested itself in the Jews' shallow, fanatical religious fervour and insatiable desire for power. The second racial component was the Syrian Hittite, who, though physically strong, was intellectually and morally inferior. This strain was responsible for the Jews' business acumen and their spiritual poverty. The third racial component was the Amorites who, Chamberlain believed, were Aryans from the north. The injection of their blood did little to redeem the basic faults of the Jews, but the Amorite strain did help to explain why they were formidable adversaries and a threat to the superior Germanic race. Chamberlain saw little hope for European civilization if interbreeding with the Jews was allowed to continue: Europe would end up inhabited by 'a herd of pseudo-Hebraic mestizos, a people beyond all doubt degenerate physically, mentally and morally'.

Chamberlain showed a certain coyness about drawing direct political conclusions from his ideas. He denied any 'personal animus against individuals belonging to the Jewish nation', and he dedicated *The Foundations of the Nineteenth Century* to a Jew, Julius Wiesner, Rector of the University of Vienna, with whom he had studied. Others, however, were less squeamish about translating his views into concrete political action. Chamberlain lived long enough to witness the arrival of Hitler on the German scene, and in 1923 hailed the Führer of the Nazi Party as the future saviour of Germany.

Conspiratorial anti-Semitism is founded on the allegation that the Jews have hatched a conspiracy to take over the world and to subjugate all other peoples. The classic expression of this 'conspiracy' is to be found in the *Protocols of the Learned Elders of Zion*. A short version of the *Protocols* first appeared in 1903 in the Russian newspaper *Znamya* ('The Banner'), and a longer version appeared in 1905 in the second edition of a religious tract by a tsarist civil servant, S. A. Nilus. The *Protocols* purport to be the minutes of secret meetings held by a group of powerful Jews (the 'Learned Elders of Zion'), in which they outline their aim to take over the world and decide on ways and means of achieving this objective. The basic strategy was quite clear: to destabilize existing governments, mainly by promoting liberalism and socialism, and then, when disorder had set in, to use their financial control to seize power. According to the First Protocol:

> In our day, the power which has replaced that of the rulers who were liberal is the power of Gold. Time was when Faith ruled. The idea of freedom is impossible of realization because no one knows how to use it with moderation. It is enough to hand over a people to self-government for a certain length of time for that people to be turned into a disorganized mob. From that moment on we get internecine strife which soon develops into battles between classes, in the midst of which States burn down and their importance is reduced to that of a heap of ashes. Whether a state exhausts itself in its own convulsions, whether its internal discord brings it under the power of external foes – in any case it can

be counted irretrievably lost: it is in our power. The despotism of Capital, which is entirely in our hands, reaches to it a straw that the State willy-nilly must take hold of: if not – it goes to the bottom.[19]

In 1920, the *Protocols* were exposed as a clumsy forgery. They were almost certainly concocted by the *Okhrana*, the tsarist secret police, in order to discredit liberalism and socialism by claiming that both movements were controlled by Jews, and to divert public unrest from the tsar's rule onto the Jews. Nevertheless, the *Protocols* have been astonishingly successful: they have been translated into nearly every major language in the world and are still widely believed. In 1921, Henry Ford, the American industrialist who promoted the *Protocols* in America, expressed his faith in them: 'The only statement I care to make about the *Protocols* is that they fit in with what is going on. They are sixteen years old, and they have fitted the world situation up to this time. They fit it now.'[20]

It is very difficult to change the opinions of anyone who believes in a conspiracy theory such as that advocated by the *Protocols*. Critics are liable to find themselves discounted as agents of the conspirators sent to sow disinformation. The very lack of evidence can feed the theory: it can be seen as proof of how well the conspirators have covered their tracks!

The racial and the conspiratorial types of anti-Semitism are not mutually exclusive. They can easily be integrated and, in fact, most modern anti-Semitic literature mixes them together. The rise of the modern varieties of anti-Semitism did not, however, mean the end of traditional religious anti-Semitism, which continued in the more conservative religious circles, particularly in the more backward parts of Europe. Racial anti-Semitism arguably marks an intensification of anti-Semitism. In principle, medieval anti-Semitism left open the possibility of escape through conversion to Christianity. Some Jews did convert and rose to positions of power and influence within the Church. But modern anti-Semitism seems to offer no escape: there is no way of altering one's genetic make-up. The Jews as a race are saddled with an ineluctable destiny.

The origins of modern anti-Semitism

Modern anti-Semitism emerged as a clear response to certain intellectual and social developments of the nineteenth century. Explorers and anthropologists had begun to document the life and culture of non-European societies, and to depict the immense variety of people making up the human race. This naturally raised questions about how this diversity could be explained – why certain societies were classed 'advanced' and others 'primitive'. One answer to such questions was to attribute the diversity to innate racial factors. The existence of different races appeared to be supported by other scientific discoveries. In the nineteenth century, philology (the historical study of the languages of the world) clearly demonstrated the existence of two great, unrelated families of languages: the Indo-European family (or, as it was sometimes called in the nineteenth century, the Indo–Germanic or Aryan family) and the Semitic family (which included Hebrew and Arabic). Philologians tended to trace the origins of each of these families back to an ancestral language spoken in the remote past by the forebears of the Europeans and the Semites. The question then arose as to how these two ancestral groups could possibly have been genetically related if their languages were so distinct. Darwinism, which so deeply affected the nineteenth-century intellectual world view, suggested the possibility that some societies, and indeed some races, might be more evolved socially and genetically than others. 'Race' and 'racialism' thus became intellectually respectable concepts.

Modern anti-Semitism was also responding to profound political and social changes in the nineteenth century. From the late eighteenth century onwards, a mood of romantic nationalism (epitomized by the writings of Johann Gottfried Herder and Johann Gottlieb Fichte) began to emerge in certain intellectual circles in Europe. It was particularly strong in the German states which were moving towards national unity and whose people were seeking a national identity. Certain German thinkers provided that identity by appealing to a mythical Teutonic past and by using the Teutonic myth to define the essence of being German. Such an approach led naturally to chauvinism and boded ill for any identifiable non-German groups living on German soil.

Social factors also played an important role in the rise of modern anti-Semitism. The social upheavals of the nineteenth century, particularly those related to the Industrial Revolution, which created a new, menacing proletariat, were deeply disturbing to many of the bourgeoisie. They found it all too easy to focus their neuroses and paranoia on the Jews, who became a 'scapegoat' for all society's ills. On the one hand, Jews were seen as being the driving force behind the liberal and socialist movements which many in the middle class considered to be so threatening. On the other hand, Jews were envied for their success in business and in the traditional middle-class professions, and for the wealth that some of them managed to acquire. Jews thus found themselves caught in an impossible dilemma: they came to be identified in the minds of significant sections of the European bourgeoisie with both revolutionary socialism and international capitalism. As Theodor Herzl, the father of modern political Zionism, put it: 'When we [Jews] sink [socially], we become a revolutionary proletariat, the corporals of every revolutionary party; on the other hand, when we rise, there rises with us our terrifying financial power.'[21]

All these factors help to explain the advent of modern anti-Semitism, but they do not explain the persistence of anti-Semitism. In this context, it is necessary to stress the continuity between medieval and modern anti-Semitism.

Modern racial anti-Semitism arguably represents the modernization of the medieval concept of the Jew as innately evil and in league with the Devil; modern conspiracy theories represent the modernization of the medieval notion of the malevolent Jew bent on dominating or destroying Christendom. This suggests that anti-Semitism is so deeply rooted in European society, and, indeed, in the European 'psyche', that it simply cannot disappear: it can only mutate. Anti-Semitism has behaved like a fundamental religious belief, its development running parallel to the development of Christianity. Christianity, faced with modernism, tried to redefine itself in modern terms; anti-Semitism has done the same.

The Jewish response to modern Anti-Semitism

The Jewish response to the emergence of new forms of anti-Semitism in the nineteenth century was complex. In the eighteenth and early nineteenth centuries, European Jews had responded positively to emancipation and seized the social and economic opportunities it offered. Many had become acculturated or even assimilated into the host societies, and most looked forward to integration and acceptance. The *Haskalah* movement and reform Judaism tried, in various ways, to modernize Judaism. Reform Judaism de-emphasized Jewish nationalism and modified or abolished those aspects of traditional practice (for example, the dietary laws) that had made social integration difficult.

In the second half of the nineteenth century, however, a nationalist emphasis began to re-emerge strongly in Jewish intellectual circles. Symptomatic of the new mood were the writings of the *maskil* Perez Smolenskin who used his influential journal *Ha-Shahar* to stress a new fidelity to Jewish tradition. Opinion is divided over the extent to which this return to tradition was influenced by the new anti-Semitism and the discovery by emancipated Jews that European society was still in many ways hostile towards the Jews.

In one very important episode, however, the connection between Jewish nationalism and anti-Semitism can hardly be denied. Theodor Herzl, in response to his experience of French anti-Semitism at the beginning of the Dreyfus Affair, proposed the re-creation of a Jewish state and founded the Zionist Organization. Herzl's essay *The Jewish State* (subtitled 'A modern solution to the Jewish question') was totally dominated by the problem of anti-Semitism; indeed, the only argument he put forward for establishing a new Jewish state was that it would solve the problem of anti-Semitism. His one-sided position was severely criticized by some Zionist thinkers. For example, Ahad Ha'am, the acknowledged philosopher of cultural Zionism, attacked Herzl's proposals for their lack of Jewish cultural content. Ahad Ha'am placed much greater emphasis on the need to create a Jewish cultural renaissance appropriate to the modern age; he argued that the political independence of the Jewish state was less important than its role as a cultural centre for world Jewry. Herzl, however, clearly demonstrated how many Jews, faced with modern anti-Semitism, had turned their backs on European society and sought their destiny outside Europe in their own sovereign national state.

But even in eastern Europe, where Jews were most oppressed and such appeals strongest, there was no uniform programme. Debate about the probable future of the Jewish people was intense and many-sided. The series of pogroms in Russia after the assassination of Tsar Alexander II (1881) transformed the situation. The Jews of Russia were the victims of three large-scale waves of pogroms. These occurred in the years between 1881 and 1884, 1903 and 1906 and 1917 and 1921. In these furious outbursts, the Jews were massacred, often with the encouragement of the authorities. The conclusion seemed irresistible: neither Enlightenment nor Emancipation were sufficient to create a world fit for Jews to live in. It was not merely official reaction that rendered liberalism hopeless. What was so demoralizing for many Jews was that some radical critics, so far from defending the oppressed

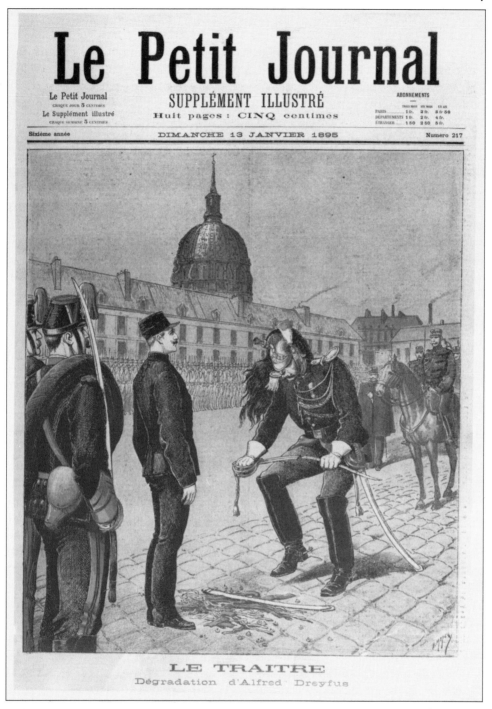

The public humiliation of Alfred Dreyfus as depicted in a popular newspaper of the time. In 1894, a Jewish captain in the French army, Alfred Dreyfus, was accused of selling military secrets to the Germans and imprisoned. The Dreyfus Affair led to violent outbursts of anti-Semitism throughout France. A group of French intellectuals, including Emile Zola, campaigned for his release. Dreyfus was found to be innocent and was exonerated in 1906.

minority, viewed the outbreaks as the harbinger of a positive revolt against exploitation on the part of peasants and labourers. There seemed no future for the Jews in
Tsarist Russia. Some turned to revolutionary socialism; others turned towards the
United States where between 1881 and 1914 more than 2.5 million Jews settled.
Those who did not believe that anti-Semitism was a Russian peculiarity, or thought
of emigration as a permanent solution, looked increasingly towards the restoration
of Jewish nationhood as the only way forward.

Best known among them was Perez Smolenskin (1842–85) who edited and
published the Hebrew journal *Ha-Shahar* (The Dawn) in the Pale of Settlement.
Equally significant was Leon Pinsker, whose pamphlet *Autoemancipation*, published
in German in 1882, argued that anti-Semitism or Judophobia, as he called it, was
rooted in the minority's disembodied, abnormal existence. Only through the return
of the Jews to a country of their own could normality be restored and Gentile hatred
eradicated. Pinsker's voice, though, was one of many. Socialist Zionism, as formulated by Nachman Syrkin, identified the position of the Jew in the class struggle as
the heart of the matter and argued for a Socialist Jewish state in Palestine. Labour
Zionists, though less determinist in outlook, saw in the Jewish homeland the
opportunity to create a new man in place of the alienated denizens of the diaspora.
The Jewish nationalist awakening, stimulated by the pogroms, found expression in
the formation of a movement in which territorialist and non-territorialist, Marxist
and non-Marxist, and political and cultural Zionists vied for position.

Revolutionary socialism also remained significant. Jewish socialists, organized
in their own section of the Russian Social Democratic Party, the Jewish Bund,
looked to a future in which national differences, including those between Jew and
Gentile, would disappear, and in which the only significant distinctions would be
those between one class and another, until, on the morrow of the victorious
revolution, classlessness would replace Jewishness. Such people, and there were
many of them, argued that the segregation of the Jewish masses in the ghetto was
the cause of Russian anti-Semitism. It was, so they argued, the 'alien' national
characteristics of the Jews that made them easy targets for the Tsarist regime. Rapid
assimilation was the only progressive solution to the Jewish national problem.
Anything which impaired the fusion of Jewish and non-Jewish workers in the
socialist movement was deplorable. Zionism and Bundism were, from this perspective, little more than twin forms of 'Jewish separatism'. Assimilated Jews like
Martov, Trotsky or Rosa Luxembourg misunderstood the nature of anti-Semitism
and repeatedly failed to see the danger it presented. Lenin summarized their
position thus:

> Whoever, directly or indirectly, puts forward the slogan of a Jewish 'national
> culture' is (whatever his good intentions may be) an enemy of the proletariat, a
> supporter of the *old* and of the *caste* position of the Jews, an accomplice of the
> rabbis and the bourgeoisie. On the other hand those Jewish Marxists who join
> international Marxist organizations, together with the Russian, Lithuanian,
> Ukrainian and other workers doing their bit (in Russian and in Yiddish) towards
> the creation of an international culture of the working class movement – such

Jews, despite the separatism of the Bund, uphold the best traditions of the race, by fighting the slogan of 'national culture'.[22]

Of such are tragedies made.

The Holocaust

From its inception, the Nazi Party made anti-Semitism a major plank of its political platform. Its Programme of 1920, which was declared to be irrevocable, maintained that race was the basis of the German state and denied Jews the right to German citizenship:

> Only he who is a folk-comrade [*Volkgenosse*] can be a citizen. Only he who is of German blood regardless of his Church can be a folk-comrade. No Jew, therefore, can be a folk-comrade.[23]

The same Programme pledged the Party to opposition against 'the Jewish spirit within and around us'. The anti-Semitism of Hitler, who became Führer of the Party in 1921, amounted to extreme paranoia: *Mein Kampf* (1925–7), his political testament and the Nazi Party's 'gospel', contains anti-Semitism of the crudest and most virulent kind.

In the 1920s and early 1930s, Nazi anti-Semitism was expressed in propaganda and in isolated acts of violence against Jewish individuals and their property. However, the situation changed dramatically in 1933 when Hitler became Chancellor of Germany. He immediately set about eliminating all political opposition and turning Germany into a one-party state. The Nazis were then able to implement an anti-Semitic policy backed by the powers and resources of a major, modern industrial state.

The Nazi onslaught on the Jews can be divided into two main phases. The first phase extended from Hitler's accession to power in 1933 until about 1941; the second phase lasted from 1941 to the end of the war in 1945.

In the first phase, the Nazis concentrated principally on forcing the Jews to leave Germany. Their aim was to make Germany free of Jews (*Judenrein*), and to accomplish this they partly used 'legal' means. Laws, such as the Reich Citizenship Law of 1935, were passed to deprive Jews of German citizenship, exclude them from universities, public office, the civil service, the professions and artistic life, and to confiscate and 'Aryanize' their businesses. The result was that the livelihoods of Jews in Germany were destroyed and their survival in Germany became virtually impossible.

At the same time, the Nazis orchestrated an unrelenting round of acts of thuggery against the Jews, which they often represented as spontaneous uprisings of the 'Aryan' masses against their Jewish oppressors. These culminated in the so-called *Kristallnacht* ('night of broken glass') of 9–10 November 1938, when Jewish houses, shops, warehouses and synagogues were attacked throughout Germany, allegedly in retaliation for the murder by a Polish Jew of Ernst Vom Rath, third secretary of the German embassy in Paris. These attacks took place in a climate created by a constant barrage of anti-Semitic propaganda aimed at vilifying the Jews and justifying the measures taken against them. To a large extent, the Nazis achieved their objective: life became intolerable for the Jews and many left Germany.

The second phase of the Nazi onslaught on the Jews was even more extreme, and included the notorious 'Final Solution'. This phase was given impetus by a number of factors. First, after the outbreak of war in 1939, Jewish emigration became increasingly impractical and, in 1941, the Nazis themselves put an end to it. Second, the Nazi victories in the early part of the war brought vast numbers of Jews under German control. This was most marked during the eastward thrust of the German armies into Poland (1939) and Russia (1941), the two main centres of Jewish population in Europe. These victories magnified the 'Jewish problem' for the Nazis and prompted more radical solutions. Finally, in the 1930s, the attacks on the Jews had been carried out in full view of the world. During the war, however, with the media tightly controlled and with armies and civilians on the move, atrocities could be committed without attracting much attention.

From around 1941, a new policy began to emerge within the Nazi bureaucracy. A letter dated July 1941 from Reichsmarshal Hermann Goering to Reinhard Heydrich, deputy chief of the SS, clearly signalled the change of direction:

> Complementing the task already assigned to you in the decree of 24 January 1939 to undertake, by emigration or evacuation, a solution of the Jewish question as advantageous as possible under the conditions at the time, I hereby

The beginning of the Nazi boycott of Jewish businesses on 1 April 1933. The placards read: (top) The Jews have until 10 o'clock on Saturday to consider. Then the fight begins! (bottom) All the Jews in the world want to destroy Germany! German people! Defend yourselves! Don't buy from Jews!

charge you with making all necessary organizational, functional and material preparations for a complete solution of the Jewish question in the Jewish sphere of influence in Europe.[24]

Six months later, in January 1942, a number of leading Nazis met at Wannsee, a suburb of Berlin, to plan and co-ordinate the 'Final Solution', which involved nothing less than the extermination of the Jews in Europe.

The Nazis carefully guarded the secrecy of the operation. All documents relating to it were classified as top secret, and even within these documents, coded language was used to conceal what was really happening. Aspects of the operation itself were referred to by innocuous and up-beat expressions: for example, gassed Jews were recorded as having been 'appropriately dealt with' (*entsprechend behandelt*).

The genocide of the Jews was effected in two main ways. First, special mobile units (*Einsatzgruppen*) followed the advancing German armies and shot all the Jews they could find. These units operated with particular efficiency in Russia. Second, Jews were herded into camps (such as Bergen–Belsen, Treblinka, Maidanek and Auschwitz–Birkenau) where they were either worked to death, starved or gassed. These camps were death factories in which the Nazis applied the industrial techniques of mass production to the destruction of human beings – with ruthless efficiency.

During the war, the Jews made occasional attempts to resist. The supreme example of this resistance was the Warsaw ghetto uprising, which the Nazis only managed to put down at considerable cost to themselves. There were also uprisings in the camps. But such acts of defiance were the exception. The Nazis managed to deceive, disorientate and terrorize their victims to effectively that most went unresisting to their deaths.

Intervention from outside Nazi-controlled Europe was largely ineffectual, especially after the outbreak of war. It took some time for news of the extermination programme to leak out, and even when it did it tended to be met with incredulity at first. However, some rescue operations were successfully mounted, though on a pitifully small scale. After the war, various organizations, both Jewish and non-Jewish, moved into Europe to help the survivors, many of whom expressed the understandable wish to emigrate and leave behind the trauma of their life in Europe.

It is not easy to penetrate the mentality of the Nazis, nor to fathom their reasons for committing such acts of unparalleled barbarism. There was, undoubtedly, an element of opportunism and expediency in their policy. Anti-Semitism was endemic in German society, and the Jew was a popular 'bogeyman' against whom everyone could unite. This, however, cannot be the whole story, as the Nazis continued killing Jews almost to the very end of the war – long after, on any rational calculation, this policy could have yielded any possible 'benefits'. Almost to the end, transport and materials desperately needed for the war effort were diverted to keep the camps running. This suggests that the Nazis were labouring under the delusion that it was the Jews, and not the Allies, who were their main enemy, a delusion which makes sense only in the context of some bizarre apocalyptic vision of the world.

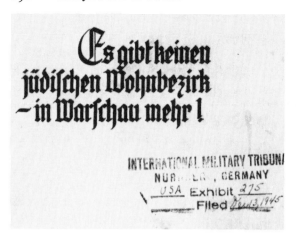

Part of the title page (above) and a photograph from the 'Stroop Report'. The words announce 'There is no longer a Jewish Quarter in Warsaw!' Jürgen Stroop was the general in charge of the destruction of the Warsaw ghetto. His report, presented to Heinrich Himmler, and later found by American soldiers was used at the Nuremburg trials.

Dieter Wisliceny, an SS officer writing in 1946 while awaiting trial for war crimes, provides some insight into that vision:

Anti-Semitism constituted one of the basic elements of the Nazi Party's programme. Essentially it was the product of two ideas: (1) ... pseudo-scientific biological theories ... and (2) a mystical religious notion that the world is ruled by good and evil powers. According to this view the Jews represented the evil principle, aided and abetted by the Church (the Jesuit Order), Freemasonry and Bolshevism. The literature of this viewpoint is well known; the older writings of the Nazi Party teem with such ideas. A straight line leads from the *Protocols of the Elders of Zion* to Rosenberg's *Myth* ... It is absolutely impossible to make any impression on this outlook by means of logical or rational argument; it is a sort of religiosity which compels men to form themselves into a sect. Under the influence of this literature millions of people believed these things – an event which can only be compared with similar phenomena of the Middle Ages such as witch mania. Against this world of evil the race-mystics set the world of good, of light, embodied in blond, blue-eyed people who alone were supposed to possess the capacity for creating civilization or building a state. Now these two worlds were allegedly locked together in constant strife, and the war of 1939, which Hitler started, represented only the final battle between these two powers.[25]

In his political last will and testament, dictated in his bunker as Berlin collapsed in flames around him, Hitler wrote: 'Above all, I bind the leadership of the nation and its subordinates to the painful observance of the racial laws and to merciless resistance against the world-poisoner of all nations, international Jewry.'[26] This monstrous vision of the world fused together with deadly clarity all the disparate elements of one thousand years of theological and racial anti-Semitism and Judeophobia in Europe.

The Nazis and their collaborators murdered around six million Jews, totally destroying the great Jewish communities of Germany and of central and eastern Europe. As a result, the centre of gravity in Jewish culture moved irrevocably from Europe to Israel and the USA. Thus, the Holocaust was a pivotal element of twentieth-century Jewish history, an event that would soon have a profound impact on Jewish life and thought.

The legacy of the Holocaust

Since the war, it has been very important for most Jews that the victims of the Holocaust should be remembered and the criminals responsible brought to justice. A Holocaust remembrance day (*Yom ha-Sho'ah*) is observed by many communities throughout the world on 27 Nisan and Holocaust memorials have been erected in various countries, the most impressive being Yad Vashem in Jerusalem. Another form of remembrance can be seen in the work of the Jewish and non-Jewish scholars who have documented every aspect of the Holocaust in meticulous detail, and who have struggled to record the story of every community, however small, that the Nazis wiped out.

Jewish organizations such as the Simon Wiesenthal Centre have continued to hunt down war criminals long after the Allied governments apparently lost interest. Israel claims the right, as the representative of the Jewish people, to try Nazi war criminals in its own courts. It exercised that right most dramatically when an Israeli court tried and ordered the execution of Adolf Eichmann, who had played a prominent role in the 'Final Solution', after he had been traced to Argentina, kidnapped and taken to Israel by Israeli agents.

The Holocaust has raised profound questions for traditional theism in general and for Judaism in particular. After Auschwitz, how can the traditional theistic view of a benevolent, omnipotent God be maintained? Why did God allow such a triumph of evil? Where does Auschwitz leave the Sinai Covenant and the election of the Jews as the chosen people? Traditional Jewish theodicy has regarded disasters such as the destruction of the Temple in 586 BCE and the massacres of the First Crusade as punishments for sin and violations of the terms of the Sinai Covenant. But such an explanation seems rather inadequate to address the evil of the Holocaust. To suggest that Hitler and the SS were instruments of God's will would, to put it mildly, be a startling proposition. What sins could have possibly merited such appalling 'punishment'? And if the Holocaust was in any sense a 'punishment' for sin, why did the blow fall so heavily on the traditional, largely pious communities of eastern Europe?

The Jewish response to the religious challenge of the Holocaust has been very diverse. Despite the problems involved, some Jewish thinkers have tried to accom-

The Yad Vashem Memorial in Jerusalem. Yad Vashem is dedicated to documenting the Nazi persecution of the Jews and preserving the memory of the victims of the Holocaust. The ashes of murdered Jews are interred in front of the eternal flame.

modate the Holocaust within the framework of traditional theodicy. They have argued that the Holocaust represents an event which differs in degree, but not in kind, from earlier disasters that have befallen the Jewish people. Others, however, have argued that Auschwitz has shattered the traditional Judaic world view – this is the line taken by Richard Rubenstein:

> We live in the time of the death of God . . . the thread uniting God and man, heaven and earth has been broken. We stand in a cold, silent, unfeeling cosmos, unaided by any purposeful power beyond our own resources. After Auschwitz what else can a Jew say about God?[27]

Rubenstein does not, however, conclude that religion must be thrown out as a sham or a delusion. Instead, he argues that Jews still need at least the rituals of religion to give life meaning and to help individuals cope with the tragic necessities of existence. The theologian Emil Fackenheim offers a third response: the Holocaust has provided the Jews with an imperative which, in fact, they have largely recognized – not to give 'posthumous victories to Hitler'. Hitler tried to destroy both Jews and Judaism. If Jews abandon Judaism after Auschwitz, they will be completing Hitler's work for him. Jews must obey the 'commanding voice' of Auschwitz to remain faithful to Judaism – each in his or her own way.

Conclusion

This chapter has tried to cover a complex and highly emotive subject within a brief compass. It has deliberately worked within a restricted, rather precise definition of anti-Semitism in order to avoid classifying all opposition of Jews and Judaism as 'anti-Semitic'. It has traced the development of this anti-Semitism in European intellectual history in the late nineteenth and early twentieth centuries and described how it provided the ideological underpinning for the Nazi persecution of the Jews.

The chapter has explored the thesis that modern anti-Semitism in its outward formulation is secular and scientific and has its roots in much earlier Christian and pagan attitudes towards the Jews. It found reasons to conclude that the modern anti-Semitic credo was expressed in certain earlier Christian and pagan texts in language appropriate to its time. This suggested that one should not make too sharp a distinction between modern 'secular' anti-Semitism and pre-modern 'religious' anti-Semitism. The former is arguably simply a modernization of the latter, a mutation which has responded to the spirit of the modern age.

This chapter has also raised many questions about the origin and nature of anti-Semitism and its effects on the historical evolution of Judaism. However, the chapter has provided few answers because the issues are so complex that the answers cannot be simple or obvious.

7 Zionism and the Palestine Question

Joseph Heller

The development of Jewish nationalism in nineteenth-century Europe

The concept of 'the Jewish people' is organically linked to two other concepts: that the Jews were chosen by God, and that they have an unmediated relationship with the land of Israel. The unbroken bond of the people with the land was proclaimed through a divine commandment to Abraham, the first Patriarch: 'Go forth from your native land and from your father's house to the land that I will show you' (Genesis 12:1). Thus was the land of Canaan transformed into the land of Israel in the nation's consciousness. The synthesis of the people and the land is not autochthonous; it is a product of the divine will. The most salient expression of the Children of Israel's transformation into a people was inherent in the religious revelation at Mount Sinai. There the covenant between the united nation and the divine Torah (Law) was forged. When the nation violated the covenant and caused the union to dissolve, it was punished by exile from the land.

Within the land promised to the nation Jerusalem is the place designated for the shrine of the Divine Presence. The first exile followed the destruction of the First Temple. But within no more than half a century the people began the return to Zion, an act inherently tinged with messianic overtones because of the indissoluble bond between the nation, its God and its land. The need to realize the return to Zion stemmed from the messianic urge to end the punishment of exile.

The tradition of the return to Zion has its origins in a proclamation by Cyrus (538 BCE) and in the 'ascension' to the land of Zerubavel, Ezra and Nehemiah. This proclamation is the source of the term *aliyah* (literally going up, ascending, and still used to denote Jewish immigration to Israel): 'Anyone of you of all His people – may his God be with him, and let him go up to Jerusalem that is in Judah' (Ezra 1:3). It was imperative to go up to the land in order first to fulfil the commandment to settle the land of Israel and the precepts dependent on one's being in the land, and secondly to visit and worship at the holy places (pilgrimage).

An individual *aliyah* that assumed a symbolic significance in the nation's consciousness was that of Rabbi Yehuda Halevi (1141 CE), whose famous poem 'My heart is in the East and I am at the edge of the West' gave voice to the feeling that the exile was vitiating Jewish life. The first organized *aliyah* since Cyrus's proclamation was by English and French rabbis in the year 1211. A new chapter in the history of Jewish settlement in the land of Israel began with the arrival, in the year 1700, of some 1300 religious students led by Rabbi Judah Hasid (who was not connected with the Hasidic movement, but preceded it). At the end of the eighteenth century came the disciples of Israel Ba'al Shem Tov (1699–1760), the founder of the Hasidic movement, and of another renowned rabbi, the Gaon of Vilna (Elijah ben Shlomo Salman, 1720–1797), who established the Old (Ashkenazi) Community in Palestine. However, in 1882, immigration began to draw its momentum from the rise of modern, secular Jewish nationalism.

Two developments – the European Enlightenment on the one hand, and the emancipation which gave Jews legal equality after the French Revolution on the other – led the Jewish people to begin to define themselves less in religious and more in secular national terms. But disillusionment set in when the universal ideals propounded by the Enlightenment failed and led cultured Jews in Hebrew literature and scholarship, who were advocates of the Enlightenment, to seek a new path. At the same time, the failure of emancipation brought about the rise of nationalism. In fact, the *roots* of Jewish nationalism had been planted beforehand. A series of dramatic events – the Polish uprisings of 1830–1831 and 1863, the Greek war of liberation, the struggle for national independence in the Balkans and the wars for union in Italy and Germany – stirred European Jewry, although not sufficiently to produce more than a budding national movement. Three major figures exemplify the new mode of thought: Rabbi Judah Alkalai (1798–1878), Rabbi Zvi Hirsch Kalischer (1795–1874), and Moses Hess (1812–1875).

Alkalai was active in the cultural realm among Sephardi Jewry as the rabbi of Semlin, a town near Sarajevo. The Greeks' war against the Turks and the Balkan independence struggles in general influenced him powerfully. However, he did not think in terms of a Jewish war of liberation, believing (as he explained in his book, *The Offering of Judah*, 1841), that a special fund could be created in order to buy the Holy Land from the Turkish sultan. More pertinently, he saw the importance of the role played by language in the national revival of the Balkan peoples as a condition for the crystallization of a national consciousness.

Kalischer was influenced by the national liberation struggles of the Poles in the province of Posen; though they formed the majority here, it was under German rule. He served here as a rabbi. In 1836 he first expressed his hope that redemption would come about more through the willingness of the European states to enable the dispersed Jewish people to assemble in the Holy Land than through a divine miracle. In his book *Seeking Zion* (1862) he explained systematically what the Jewish people should learn from the liberated nations of Europe about the basic rationale of European nationalism. Two examples were the Hungarians' uprising against the Austrians in 1848 and the Italians' war for independence and national unity: 'Why do the people of Italy and of other countries sacrifice their lives for the land of their fathers, while we, like men bereft of strength and courage, do nothing?'[1]

Moses Hess, who was born in the Rhineland, came to inhabit a world very different from that of Alkalai and Kalischer. He drifted from a traditional environment to a more secular background; his influences were Hegel and Marx, and he was at home in left-wing Hegelian circles. At first he proposed assimilation within the framework of a socialist solution. He pointed to the absence of a Jewish national consciousness as demonstrated in the Damascus blood libel of 1840 (when the Jewish community of Damascus was charged with the ritual murder of a monk but was rescued by leading Jewish figures from abroad). In 1862, against the background of the Italians' war of independence, Hess underwent a radical intellectual transformation and began advocating a national solution. That year also saw the publication of his book *Rome and Jerusalem* in which, as its title suggests, he contrasted the liberation of Rome, the Eternal City of Christendom, with the Eternal City of the Jewish people.

Of all the intellectual founders of modern European nationalism, Hess was the most influenced by the Italian patriot and revolutionist Giuseppe Mazzini (1805–1872), who fused national particularism with a universalist vision. Hess was also impressed by the crucial role played by France in the unification and liberation of Italy. France, he thought, should take up the cause of the Jewish and Arab national movements alike, and he foresaw a harmonious relationship developing between them along the lines espoused by Mazzini. However, it took a double cataclysm to ignite the Jewish national movement: an outbreak of Russian anti-Semitism in 1881, which produced a mass national movement on a country-wide scale (the Hibbat Zion movement), and the appearance of anti-Semitism in France, which generated a full-fledged thrust for national liberation.

Conditions in Palestine and revived European interest in the Levant

From the late nineteenth century, administrative control in Palestine, which had been conquered by the Turks in 1517, was divided between the two *vilavets* (provinces) of Damascus and Beirut, while the *sanjak* of Jerusalem was directly controlled by Istanbul. Most of the governors were Turks, who found Palestine difficult to rule because of the heterogeneous population and the intervention of foreign powers. The Ottoman administration did little to further economic development, and private entrepreneurs were not encouraged as this would have caused an expansion of foreign interests under the system of European Capitulations, which guaranteed resident European nationals special financial privileges.

Amidst this stagnation the development of the transportation system stood out as an exception. A railway line from Jaffa to Jerusalem was built in 1892, and a Haifa–Damascus line in 1905. Their purpose was to enable the control of a country which had become a frontier region since the conquest of Egypt by Britain in 1882. However, internal security remained poor owing to insufficient security forces and a constant tension between the Muslim and non-Muslim communities. The situation was further exacerbated by disputes amongst the various Christian sects. The Armenians, the Greek Orthodox and the Jews had the status of *millets*, or autonomous religious communities. The modernization processes, which were intended to strengthen the central government, brought about greater co-operation and unity within the Arab population, highlighting its separate character.

The Sephardi community was officially recognized by the authorities, unlike the Old Community (of Ashkanazi Jews), which was composed of foreign nationals. In the 1870s the population of western Palestine stood at 375,000, of whom no more than 30,000 were Jews – although this was a considerable increase from the 6500 at the turn of the century.

European interest in the Levant dates from Napoleon's conquest in 1799, and was heightened by Muhammad Ali's subsequent intervention in Palestine and Syria (1832 to 1840). Britain's concern for the integrity of the Turkish Empire guaranteed a continuing European involvement. In addition, the holy places in Palestine were a major attraction for foreigners. The pilgrims, researchers, missionaries and settlers established a ramified system of institutions: houses of worship, monasteries, convents, hostels and hospitals. In 1833, seven years after arriving in Jerusalem, John Nicolayson, a Church of England missionary, was able to establish a church in the city thanks to the Egyptians' tolerant and orderly administrative apparatus.

Growing activity in the Holy Land by France and the Russian Empire prompted Britain to open the first foreign consulate in Jerusalem in 1838.[2] The British move gave rise to escalating European activity in Palestine, which was marked by competition and rivalry among both the great powers and the various church sects. Indeed, the activities of the two were often interwoven, with inter-power relations being affected by disputes over the control of the holy places. The theft of the Latin 'Silver Star' from the Church of the Nativity in Bethlehem and an imbroglio over the maintenance of the Church of the Holy Sepulchre in Jerusalem were direct causes of the Crimean War (1853–1856), in which the Russian Empire was pitted against the allied powers of the Ottoman Empire, Britain, France and Sardinia. The war gave the Ottomans another breather but they were forced to extend the rights of non-Muslims in Palestine. France, which opened a consulate in 1843, showed it would stop at nothing to guarantee Catholic interests, though the establishment of additional consulates reduced its influence as the exclusive protective power of Christians.

Britain's interest in Palestine stemmed from its desire to prevent a hostile power turning it into a base for operations. At the same time a favourable attitude manifested itself in Britain – at the highest levels of government, in millenarian circles and in the public at large – toward the Jewish people's bond with Palestine, although the hope was that the Jews would take up Christianity. The Foreign Secretary, Lord Palmerston, ordered the British Consul in Jerusalem to extend his protection to the Jews. Political and religious interests dovetailed. In 1878, when the Congress of Berlin placed Cyprus under British occupation, Prime Minister Disraeli expressed the hope that Palestine would also become part of the British Empire, though this became less feasible following Britain's occupation of Egypt.

The efforts of the Scot, Laurence Oliphant, to initiate Jewish settlement in the Gilead region, east of the Jordan River (see *The Land of Gilead*, 1889), attest to a Zionist frame of mind in Britain, although Oliphant was told at the highest levels of government that his plans would not receive official support. Until World War I

Britain sought to maintain the integrity of the Ottoman Empire, despite its growing enmity with it (aggravated by the Anglo–Russian alliance). Relations deteriorated sharply in 1906, when Britain issued an ultimatum to the Sultan, who had laid claim to the entire Sinai Peninsula, to retract the declaration.

Russia had maintained a consulate in Jerusalem since 1858, but neither its extensive educational activity nor the many Russian pilgrims who visited the Holy Land were enough to enable Russia to compete with Britain and France as the possible successor to the Ottomans. There were also some 2200 German settlers in the country, from the Templar sect, and the Germans also wielded church influence, as was shown during Kaiser Wilhelm II's visit in 1898. However, Palestine was not within Germany's sphere of interest in the crumbling Ottoman Empire. The Jewish community, which numbered some 85,000 on the eve of World War I, was not an instrument in the hands of any of the powers, nor indeed was Palestine the focus of their rivalries.

The forerunners of Jewish nationalism and modern anti-Semitism

The forerunners of Zionism appear around the middle of the nineteenth century. Their motivation was not a pessimistic assessment of the Jewish situation; they wished to establish an exemplary nation in Palestine, not to bring western Jewry there. Kalischer adduced a traditional Jewish–messianic conception: his idea was to gather part of the Jewish people in the Holy Land with the sanction of the great powers, offer sacrifices at the site of the Temple and settle the land. The next stage: a war of Gog and Magog, and finally the full ingathering of the exiles.

Kalischer's innovation lay in his notion of an 'inhabited land' brought about by man, not God. Yet his nationalism was steeped in the old Judaism. The fulfilment of the precepts which entailed residence in the land of Israel, he argued, could be the augury of redemption. Kalischer castigated the Old Yishuv (community) in Palestine, which lived mainly off the systematic collection of donations from Jews abroad. He ascribed its non-productivity to its small population, which precluded a self-sustaining economy. His solution was to found the Society for the Colonization of the Land of Israel in order to improve Palestine's socio-economic situation. Another plan called for the creation of a fund to 'redeem' the land, to be supported by affluent Jews such as the Rothschilds and Sir Moses Montefiore. Kalischer believed that agricultural settlement in Palestine was essential.

The world view of Rabbi Alkalai was also grounded in religious tradition, although he emphasized modern nationalistic principles such as the revival of a national language and land purchases. To dispel all possibility of false messianism, Alkalai proposed a natural redemption; a first Messiah, the son of Joseph, would take part in the war of Gog and Magog and the land of Israel would be conquered by force of arms. Disappointed that the 1840 blood libel was not followed by events adumbrating the advent of the Messiah – the rescue of the Damascus community had triggered messianic expectations – Rabbi Alkalai turned to a new concept of redemption. Jewish notables, he wrote, could without limit solicit the 'kings of the earth' to permit the Jews to return to the land of their forefathers. Every Jewish family would send one of its sons to the Holy Land. The diaspora would support the settlers, and they would earn their own livelihood in the fields and vineyards. A 'Great Assembly' of world Jewry would prepare the political steps for the appeal to the kings of Europe and the sultan.

Moses Hess rejected emancipation as a solution on the grounds that the Jews were not a religious sect. Indeed, he argued, emancipation only heightened tensions between the Jews and the surrounding national community. This perception led him to discern the incipient rise of racist anti-Semitism. His vision of a Jewish socialist community in Palestine, including public ownership of the land and the means of production, was not meant for the Jewish bourgeoisie but for the masses in eastern Europe and the Islamic countries.

However, the appearance of the forerunners, with all their importance, did not herald the emergence of an organized mass movement.[3]

Modern racial anti-Semitism was an important stimulus to the development of Jewish nationalism. In contrast to classic anti-Semitism, in which the religious element was dominant (the Jews as Christ-killers), the new anti-Semitism focused on the alien character of the 'Jewish spirit' which was said to derive from disparities between the Jewish and Aryan races. The new anti-Semitism also spawned a plethora of anti-Jewish organizations and political parties. Hatred of Jews became a salient expression of national loyalty.

A milestone in the development of race theory was a book by the French diplomat and essayist Comte de Gobineau, *Essay on the Inequality of Human Races* (1853/6). Although Gobineau did not single out Jews as an inferior race, his work enhanced the credibility of the concept that defines race as a factor in the interpretation of historical and social phenomena. Charles Darwin's famous *On the Origin of Species* (1859) was also pressed into service for this purpose. A significant contribution to the growing belief that race explained historical and social developments was made by the French historian of religions, Ernst Renan (1823–1892). In his *The Life of Jesus* (1863) he castigated the Jewish intolerance that had led to Jesus' death; instead of the divine curse said to afflict the Jews, he cites cultural–racial attributes as decisive. Renan, who engaged in historical and linguistic research, did not invest the concept of race with biological–deterministic meaning, but already in 1848 he hypothesized the existence of a fundamental dissimilarity between the Aryan race, with its manifold natural talents, and the Semitic race, which was devoid of positive traits.

The turning point in the history of modern anti-Semitism came in 1879, with the emergence of political anti-Semitism, an idea linked with the names of the Berlin court preacher, Adolph Stoecker, and the leading German historian Heinrich von Treitschke. The same year saw the publication of *The Victory of Jewry over Germandom* by the German agitator Wilhelm Marr. Nor were they the first to disseminate anti-Semitic literature in Germany. The well-known tract *The Jews in Music*, by the composer Richard Wagner, had appeared in 1869 (it was anonymously published in 1850).

Yet these disseminators of Jew-hatred still did not place the racial element at the centre of their treatises. The critical year for the crystallization of racial anti-Semitism was 1880 when Eugen Dühring, an economics and philosophy lecturer at Berlin University, published his *The Jewish Question as a Question of Race, Morals and Civilization*. He traced the inferiority of the Jewish race back to the Bible and discerned the same inferiority in everyone of Jewish origin, from Spinoza to Marx. He wanted Jews everywhere expelled. As Jewish traits were indelible, he claimed, Christian baptism could make no difference.[4]

A highly influential book was Edouard Drumont's *La France Juive* (1886), in which the author, drawing on the work of Renan, asserted that the Jews were an inferior race and that their religion was an inferior faith. Drumont laid the groundwork for the incitement against the French officer Alfred Dreyfus a decade later, and had a crucial influence on the decision by Theodor Herzl, the founder of political Zionism, to discard assimilation in favour of the national solution. But the best-selling of these anti-Semitic books was Houston Stewart Chamberlain's *The Foundations of the Nineteenth Century* (1899). Chamberlain, an Englishman who adopted German nationality and became Wagner's son-in-law, maintained that racial attributes were the result of a blending of the racial elements: a successful blending led to positive achievements, as among the Germans, whereas the Jews were characterized by degeneration and moral corruption.

To those Jews who, until the 1880s, had pinned their hopes on assimilation, as urged by Treitschke, racial anti-Semitism demonstrated that emancipation had failed and that their only recourse was to seek a national–territorial solution to the problem of their national identity.

Zionism's multi-faceted character and the diverse opposition encountered by the movement

Auguries of a Jewish national movement existed before the advent of Hibbat Zion (Love of Zion), not only in the guise of the forerunners but also in the form of Hebrew-language papers such as Perez Smolenskin's *Hashahar* in Vienna and David Gordon's *Hamaggid* in Prussia, and in the articles of Eliezer Ben-Yehuda ('the reviver of the Hebrew language') in the 1870s about a spiritual centre in the land of Israel. However, the thrust for the emergence of Hibbat Zion as a popular national movement came from a series of savage pogroms perpetrated against Russian Jewry, notably in 1881. They were triggered by the assassination of Tsar Alexander II on 1 March 1881 by members of the Narodnaya Volya (People's Will). The murders, rapes and looting, the impotence of the authorities and the silence of the intelligentsia made it clear that the solution lay in a territory where a separate national existence could be maintained. The aftermath of the attacks saw the establishment in the Russian Empire of Jewish nationalist associations such as the Bilu society (the name was an acrostic from the biblical 'House of Jacob, let us arise and go', Isaiah 2:5), whose charter stated: 'The society's goal is the political, economic and national–spiritual revival of the Jewish people in Syria and the land of Israel.' The society opened an office in Istanbul in order to obtain from the sultan a *firman* (a writ of title) for Jewish settlement in Palestine.

The philologist-lexicographer Eliezer Ben-Yehuda and his daughter at work on his Hebrew dictionary in 1920. The revival of the Hebrew language was an integral part of the growth of the Zionist movement.

Most of the new societies sent emissaries to tour Palestine or purchase land. Few of them thought in terms of immediate settlement; their main achievement was to articulate an ideology. Few, indeed, settled in Palestine, and most of those who did later left. The personal careers of Hibbat Zion's leaders encapsulate the movement's fate. Before the wave of pogroms, M. L. Lilienblum (1843–1910) had thought that the Enlightenment movement was the answer to the division between Jews and Christians. But the emergence of anti-Semitism led him to conclude that the Jew had become the universal enemy: 'The cosmopolitans see us as unbending nationalists with a nationalist God and a nationalist Torah; the nationalists see us as cosmopolitans, whose homeland is wherever we are well off.'[5]

Like Lilienblum, Leon Pinsker (1821–1891) also believed, before the pogroms, that the solution lay in Russification. Immediately afterwards, however, in his famous essay *Autoemancipation* (1882), he argued that the main cause of Jew-hatred was the fear of the Jews' wraithlike existence, a fear he called 'Judophobia'. Pinsker proposed the establishment of a national directorate to purchase land for persecuted Jews and that a general Jewish congress be convened. The Jewish people, he contended, needed a safe haven, though not necessarily in Palestine, perhaps in the United States.

Hibbat Zion held its first conference in the Upper Silesian town of Kattowitz in 1884. One of the movement's problems was its lack of a charismatic leadership.

The main programme called for agricultural settlement in Palestine, to be facilitated through an organization set up by the conference and named after Moses
Montefiore. The movement's centre remained in Odessa, despite efforts to move it
to western Europe. Hibbat Zion did not succeed in inspiriting the settlement
movement in Palestine and showed itself powerless to support newly established
villages such as Gedera and Petah Tikva, which were ultimately saved from
abandonment by the largesse of Baron Edmond de Rothschild.

Zionism's great breakthrough occurred in 1897 with the convening of the First
Zionist Congress at the initiative of Theodor Herzl (1860–1904). Herzl was the
Paris correspondent of the leading Viennese daily *Neue Freie Presse*. His stay in the
French capital taught him that anti-Semitism would prevent the Jews from enjoying
the fruits of emancipation, even in a socially advanced country like France. He
reached this conclusion during the Dreyfus trial of 1895, in which an innocent
French–Jewish officer was sentenced to life imprisonment on trumped-up
espionage charges. In 1896 Herzl had published Zionism's most famous manifesto,
The Jewish State, although in it he did not express a definite opinion about the
location of the future state, suggesting Argentina as a possible alternative to
Palestine. However, by the time he wrote his Utopian novel, *Altneuland* ('Old–
New Land', 1902), there was no longer any doubt that the Jews' state would be in
Palestine.

Herzl was the first to place the Jewish question on the international agenda.
Using tactics of modern diplomacy, albeit without the backing of an actual state, he
lobbied rulers and statesmen to obtain a charter for Jewish settlement in Palestine.
To the sultan he pledged that, as a quid pro quo for a charter, the financial situation
of the Ottoman Empire would improve. He even met with Kaiser Wilhelm II in a
futile effort to secure his support and get him to use his influence with the sultan.
Nor did other meetings, such as that with the Russian Interior Minister, Count von
Plehve, advance the Zionist movement's immediate interests. Herzl's only successes came in talks with British leaders. They could not deliver Palestine, but they
did offer alternatives in Sinai (El Arish), Cyprus and, in 1903, Uganda. This last
offer sparked the first great controversy in the history of Zionism; it ended with a
Zionist expression of eternal loyalty to the land of Israel, with Herzl, too, proclaiming: 'If I forget thee, O Jerusalem, let my right hand forget her cunning.' Uganda
was also rejected as a possible 'night haven' where Jews could find shelter until
Palestine could be obtained: the offer had come as a new wave of pogroms,
including the Kishinev atrocity of 1903, swept the Russian Empire.

By the time of Herzl's untimely death in 1904 at the age of 44, Zionism had not
yet registered any political achievements, but the Zionist movement had established
itself as a permanent institution, which was becoming a powerful force among Jews
in both the east and west.[6] The coming stage required a change in the international
status of Palestine.

Early Zionist 'streams': spiritual, labour and religious Zionism

The idea of 'spiritual Zionism' was propounded by the Ukrainian-born Ahad Ha'am (Hebrew for 'one of the people', pen-name of Asher Ginsberg, 1856–1927). It originated in the period of Hibbat Zion, whose settlement activities in Palestine seemed to Ahad Ha'am a poor substitute for what he considered far more important, 'preparing the [people's] hearts'. Spiritual revival, he maintained, must precede practical action; to this end, what the Jewish people needed was a spiritual centre of the elect. In 1892 Ahad Ha'am launched an elite group, B'nei Moshe (Sons of Moses), which lasted a few years; it was a kind of order of devoted activists whose goal was to revive and disseminate Hebrew culture.

Ahad Ha'am's central thesis was that a Jewish state would be incapable of alleviating the material distress of all the Jews in the diaspora, as it could not absorb ten million Jews. On the other hand, a Jewish state *could* alleviate the spiritual distress of western Jews by imbuing them with a sense of national identity. In eastern Europe, however, the malaise encompassed the whole of Jewry and not only individuals. Only after the establishment of a model centre embracing all aspects of national culture, from working the land to the cultivation of literature, would a political government be feasible. This was Ahad Ha'am's response to the complete absence of Jewish culture in Herzl's *Jewish State*. Herzl's imagined state, in which the citizens spoke German and French, and Italian opera was performed, would never materialize, Ahad Ha'am argued; the absence of a spiritual side would alienate it from the diaspora.

The foundations of socialist Zionism were laid by three thinkers: Nahman Syrkin (1867–1924), Dov Ber Borochov (1881–1917) and A. D. Gordon (1856–1922). Syrkin was the originator of the idea. The premise of his pamphlet, *The Jewish Problem and the Socialist–Jewish State*, published in 1898, the year after the First Zionist Congress, was that as long as the Jews lacked a material base – a state of their own and political power – they would remain an anomaly. However, only a socialist state would do, since large-scale settlement required comprehensive social planning and this would be unavailable in a capitalist market economy. Moreover, a Jewish state based on private property would not address itself to the Jewish proletariat in the diaspora.

Whereas Syrkin rejected the necessity of a class war to bring about a social solution, as this would only exacerbate the Jews' plight by generating class-based anti-Semitism, Ber Borochov plunged ahead in an attempt to reconcile Marxism and Zionism. Marxism's rejection of nationalism could be remedied through 'Austro-Marxism' which took into account the separate national existence of the various peoples comprising the Habsburg Empire. In the diaspora the class struggle was artificial, since Jewish workers suffered from both anti-Semitism and class oppression, hence national liberation would enable a more successful class struggle (*The National Question and the Class Struggle*, 1905). Only a territorial concentration in Palestine would relieve the plight of the Jewish proletariat. Emigration to America would aggravate the conflict with the non-Jewish society and, moreover, the means of production there were already taken.

A. D. Gordon argued that only by doing its own manual labour would the Jewish people reacquire its independence. Only labour could create the necessary economic infrastructure for the Yishuv (pre-state Jewish community in Palestine). Labour created a nation's bond with its homeland; conversely, a severance from labour cut one off from the homeland ('Labour', 1911). Culture, science, art – none of them can flourish without a return to labour and work, which are the foundations of civilization, Gordon insisted ('The Religion of Labour'). In sum, Gordon linked the concept of labour with the cultivation of the soil.

The ideas of Gordon and Syrkin became the main intellectual underpinning of social–democratic Zionism, while Borochov is considered the founding father of the minority Marxist–Zionist orientation.

The synthesis of religion and Zionism may also usefully be presented by three of its major exponents: Rabbi Shmuel Mohilever (1824–1898), Y. M. Pinnes (1843–1912) and Rabbi Abraham Isaac Kook (1865–1935). Mohilever, the rabbi of Bialystok in Byelorussia, was the first of the rabbis and religious officials who were not unwilling to cooperate with the secular majority in the Zionist movement. His guiding principle was that the Jewish people were in danger and that anyone able to help should be welcomed with joy and understanding. Nevertheless, his differences with the main office of Hibbat Zion in Odessa led him to establish a separate centre to promote Zionism among the religious public. The new organization was called Mizrahi (an abbreviation of *merkaz ruhani*, Hebrew for spiritual centre).

Pinnes, who was born in Grodno, Poland, settled in Palestine in 1878 and headed a fund named after Sir Moses Montefiore. He became a leading ideologue of the concept that the Jewish people and the Jewish religion were identical and, in particular, that a secular Jewish nation was a contradiction in terms. At the same time, he dismissed the idea, adduced by Reform Judaism, that the Jewish religion lacked a national element.

Rabbi Kook accepted modern Jewish nationalism in its secular version, viewing it as an expression of the divine spark within the Jewish soul and a harbinger of the Messiah. He believed that the first generation of the British Mandate in Palestine was the generation referred to in the prophetic writings, the generation of the Messiah. Therefore preparations should begin in earnest for the renewal of worship in the Temple in Jerusalem. Rabbi Kook, who served as the first Ashkenazi Chief Rabbi of Palestine, from 1921 until his death, saw the secular public as the unwitting tool of the redemptive process.

Zionism's Jewish opponents were primarily the ultra-Orthodox, the socialists and the 'territorialists'. Ultra-Orthodox groups who objected to Zionism, outraged by a resolution of the 10th Zionist Congress in 1911 to launch cultural and educational activity, convened at Kattowitz in the following year and founded the World Union of Agudat Israel. The new organization was joined by some Mizrahi members who had left the Zionist Organization. The guiding principle of Agudat Israel was summed up by the group's founders: 'The Jewish people is outside the framework of the political nations and differs from them in its essence. The sovereign of the Jewish people is God, His Torah is the ruling law of the people and the Holy Land is destined for the Jewish people in all times. Therefore the Torah is decisive in all the activities of Agudat Israel.' (The movement nevertheless took part in the Zionist struggle to create the Jewish state, always ensuring that its ultra-Orthodox interests were met.)

Jewish socialist opposition to Zionism came mainly from the Bund (the General Union of Jewish Workers in Lithuania, Poland and Russia, formed in 1897). At first the Bund was part of the Russian Social-Democratic party but in 1901 it demanded that the party be organized as a federation of fully autonomous nationalities. In the revolution of 1905 in Russia, at which time it had 35,000 members, and in inter-war Poland, the Bund became the leading party amongst Jewish workers. It dismissed Zionist promises to bring the Jewish people to Palestine, arguing that in one year more Jewish children were born in Europe than the Zionists had been able to absorb into Palestine in a generation.

The Jewish Territorialist Association (JTA) was founded in 1905, in the wake of the Uganda controversy, by radical Zionists such as the British writer Israel Zangwill and Nahman Syrkin. Its slogan was 'Zionism without Zion is better than Zion without Zionism.' The group examined proposals for Jewish settlement in Angola, Cyrenaica, Mesopotamia and South Africa. All its efforts ended in failure. Zangwill, who had left the Zionist movement, returned following the announcement of the Balfour Declaration in 1917, while Syrkin, who had despaired of the territorialists by 1909, joined the left-wing Poalei Zion.

Christian opposition to Zionism dates from the movement's very inception. Some of its causes were spiritual while others reflected a concern that Christian interests in Palestine would suffer. The idea that Jerusalem would become the centre of a revivified Jewish state clashed with the prophecy of Jesus, notwithstanding that Herzl had said the holy places would be extraterritorial. Pope Pius X, in his meeting with Herzl in January 1904, refused to support Zionism because the Jews did not recognize Jesus Christ as the Messiah. Christian opposition to Zionism intensified following World War I because the priority given Zionism in the Mandate charter would enable the Jews to seize control of the Holy Land. The Vatican claimed that the Zionists were anti-religious, were therefore not realizing the biblical prophecies and indeed had nothing to do with the promised return to the Holy Land.

Islamic opposition dates from 1891, spurred by Jewish land purchases and the fear of economic competition. The Ottoman authorities had prohibited land purchases and the entry of Jewish immigrants, but these restrictions were relaxed under pressure from the great powers. In 1899 Yusuf Zia Pasha, a member of the political elite in Jerusalem, wrote to the Chief Rabbi of France that although the Zionist idea was natural and just, Palestine was part of the Ottoman Empire and was already inhabited by non-Jews. Despite their wealth, without guns and gunboats the Jews could not gain possession of the holy places. In 1905 a former Ottoman official, Naguib Azouri (a Maronite Christian by origin), published a book in Paris called *Le Réveil de la Nation Arab* in which he warned that the Jews' purpose was to occupy the country as far as its natural borders. Azouri, who founded an anti-Semitic and anti-Dreyfus society in Paris, predicted that the two national movements, the Jewish and the Arab, would fight each other until one of them emerged victorious. Following the 'Young Turks' revolution of 1908 the Jaffa and Jerusalem representatives to the Ottoman parliament pointed to the political and economic dangers of Zionism. However, before 1914 Arab opposition was not entirely a function of nationalism but was often based on local patriotism and loyalty to the Ottoman Empire.

Great Britain and the Balfour Declaration

The reasons which prompted Britain to issue the Balfour Declaration in 1917 – a document stating that Britain 'view[ed] with favour the establishment in Palestine of a national home for the Jewish people' – must be sought in the new situation created by World War I. Underlying the decision was the Ottoman Empire's affiliation with the Central Powers (Germany and Austria–Hungary) in October 1914. From that moment, Britain, forming with France, Russia and others, the Entente that was fighting the Central Powers, ceased to support the integrity of the Ottoman Empire. Here was Zionism's great opportunity to find a place in the emerging new Middle East order.

The first ranking Briton to raise the idea of Anglo-Zionist cooperation was Herbert Samuel, who held a Cabinet seat from 1914 to 1916. Appalled by the possibility that Germany or France, Britain's rivals in the region, might gain control of Palestine, Samuel proposed that Britain should support Jewish autonomy there.

At the same time Dr Chaim Weizmann (1874–1952), a leader of British Zionism, Russian-born (though he had been a British subject since 1910), decided to seize the moment. In September 1914 he attracted the interest of Charles P. Scott, editor of the *Manchester Guardian*. The following February Scott arranged for Weizmann to meet his friend David Lloyd George, the Chancellor of the Exchequer. Arthur Balfour, a former prime minister, who had met Weizmann in 1906 when the latter was teaching chemistry at the University of Manchester, was also sympathetic towards Zionism. Weizmann assisted the British war effort by developing a synthetic acetone for the production of explosives. (Lloyd George was appointed Minister of Munitions in the spring of 1915 and shortly afterwards Balfour became First Lord of the Admiralty.)

Weizmann also enlisted the support of Lord Robert Cecil, the Undersecretary of Foreign Affairs, while Samuel recruited Sir Mark Sykes, the Prime Minister's chief adviser on near eastern policy in 1916. Sykes was convinced that the Zionists could help Britain buttress its position in Palestine through joint rule with France. In May 1916 Sykes and a French representative, Georges Picot, signed a secret agreement (whose existence was only revealed by Trotsky after the Bolshevik Revolution in Russia) dividing the Middle East into spheres of influence. Under the accord, the middle of Palestine was to be an international area (the 'Brown Zone'). It was to include everything between (in the north) a line running from the northern tip of the Sea of Galilee to north of Acre on the Mediterranean and (in the south) a line running from the middle of the Dead Sea to the Mediterranean, south of Hebron and Gaza. The area to the north (the 'Blue Zone'), including Lebanon,

Lebanon, Syria and parts of Turkey and Iraq, would be under French control or influence, and the areas to the south and east (the 'Red Zone') would go to the British. The issue was made even more complicated by the correspondence between Sharif Hussein of Mecca and the British High Commissioner in Egypt, Sir Henry MacMahon, in October 1915; this excluded the area west of the Damascus–Aleppo line. A sharp and protracted controversy arose as to whether Palestine was also excluded.

The Zionist cause was strengthened when Lord Milner and South Africa's Jan Christian Smuts joined the War Cabinet formed in 1916 under Prime Minister Lloyd George and in which Balfour was the Foreign Secretary. A decision was taken to have British forces advance on Palestine from Egypt. Negotiations between Sykes and Weizmann got under way in January 1917, focusing on concrete matters directly relevant to the granting of a pro-Zionist declaration: first, the assistance that a future national home for the Jews, or Jewish commonwealth, would render to Britain in order to push the French out of the 'Brown Zone'; secondly, the need to obtain the assistance of the Russian Zionists, and through them the support of the new government established in Petrograd following the revolution in March 1917, to further British ambitions in the Middle East.

However, British policy-makers overestimated the ability of the Russian Zionists to overcome the anti-war sentiment in their country. Indeed, Russia's failure in the war and the possibility that it might pull out of the war altogether immediately raised the spectre of a German victory on the western front. For the Entente states, this presented a frightening scenario in which German forces, no longer needed in the east, could be transferred westward and decide the result of the war. A pro-Zionist declaration, it was thought, would induce Russian Jewry to wield its influence to persuade Russia to remain in the war.

At the same time the chief opponents of a pro-Zionist statement within Anglo-Jewry – the assimilationists and the anti-Zionists led by Claude Montefiore, one of the heads of the Reform movement and the 'Conjoint-Foreign Committee' – dropped their antagonism. In a crucial vote (56:51) held in June 1917, the Board of Deputies, the representative body of British Jewry, decided in favour of a pro-Zionist orientation. In the same month Balfour requested that a draft proposal should be drawn up for a pro-Zionist proclamation. The draft text was presented to the Cabinet in September but it encountered vigorous opposition from the Secretary of State for India, Sir Edwin Montagu, himself a Jew. Such a statement, he asserted, would derail his contacts with the representatives of the Indian national movement and would, moreover, thrust him back into the ghetto from which he had endeavoured his whole life to extricate himself.

To buttress the pro-Zionist camp, the Government sought the support of President Woodrow Wilson. But the American leader was cool to the idea, relying solely on the advice of his foreign affairs advisor, Colonel House, who looked askance at growing Jewish influence. Nevertheless, in early October, with the situation on the front deteriorating and Weizmann pressing for a decision, the Cabinet discussed the matter further. Finally, under the prodding of the Jewish Supreme Court Justice Louis D. Brandeis, Wilson agreed to support the Zionist cause.

The half-hearted talks held by a few German Zionists with the authorities in Berlin concerning a possible pro-Zionist declaration by Germany were blown up out of all proportion. As Turkey's ally in the war, Germany was in no position to issue a pro-Zionist proclamation, which the Ottomans would have regarded as clearly detrimental to their interests. Equally ineffectual were attempts by German Zionists to convince Turkish politicians that such a proclamation would be useful.

The Cabinet members who supported the proclamation when it was put to the vote on 3 October 1917 were aware of its urgent propaganda value and did not consider it binding at a future peace conference. Not only did constraints on the Government preclude a more binding declaration; the Zionist leadership also believed that no foundation as yet existed for more sweeping claims. For this reason the demographically large Arab presence in Palestine was not considered a crucial factor, although Lord Curzon, the Lord President of the Council, objected to the declaration because it ignored the possibility that it could turn the local Arabs into 'hewers of wood and drawers of water'. However, he did not press the matter, being persuaded by the general assumption that the declaration had propaganda value only.[7]

So the Balfour Declaration (issued on 2 November 1917 in the form of a letter to Lord Rothschild, President of the British Zionist Federation) was the result of the harsh war constraints in which Britain found itself in 1917, although the Zionists hardly played a passive role. They took full advantage of the unique conjunction of their interests with Britain's aims to ensure British support for the Zionist idea. The decision-makers in Britain believed that the vague promise of a national home for the Jews in Palestine, provided it was not prejudicial to either the status of non-Zionist Jews or the civil and religious rights of existing non-Jewish communities in Palestine, would suffice to change the balance of forces between the Entente states and the central powers. No one in the Cabinet could foresee that Britain was thus providing the first stimulus to a fierce and protracted conflict between the Arab and Jewish national movements. This would not become apparent until the post-war era, when a permanent settlement was sought.

Palestine during the British Mandate

The military administration that ruled in Palestine from 1918 to 1920 was hostile to Zionism, notwithstanding the view of the Lloyd George Government that Zionism was compatible with British interests in the Middle East, particularly in helping to undercut the French position. Jewish settlement activity pushed the northern border as far as the Dan River, although this was not far enough to include all the water sources, as the Zionists had requested at the peace conference.

British rule in Palestine meant that they controlled an unbroken expanse of territory from the Suez Canal to the Persian Gulf. Safe passage could thus be guaranteed from Britain via the Suez Canal to India and the British spheres of influence in the Far East and Australia. Palestine on both sides of the Jordan River was crucial for Britain's strategy in the Middle East. That strategy was further underpinned by the building of various facilities in Palestine: a deep-water port in

Haifa Bay (1933); refineries, also in Haifa, for incoming oil from Iraq (1939); military air fields; roads linking Palestine with the neighbouring countries.

In April 1920 the victorious powers, meeting at San Remo, ratified the British Mandates for Palestine and Iraq and the French Mandate for Syria and Lebanon. The Palestine Mandate recognized the relatively high level of development of the existing population and was therefore given as a temporary trust until the granting of independence. The two crucial features of the Palestine Mandate were, first, that it gave legal sanction to the Balfour Declaration, which was incorporated in the preamble of the Mandate charter and, secondly, that it included saliently pro-Zionist clauses such as Article 2, which spoke of 'political, administrative and economic conditions as will secure the establishment of the Jewish national home', although the same article also called for 'the development of self-governing institutions'. Article 6 assured the facilitation of Jewish immigration, without prejudicing other sections of the population, and 'close settlement by Jews on . . . State lands and waste lands' in cooperation with the Jewish Agency. And Article 11 referred to

Dr Chaim Weizmann with Emir Feisal in Palestine in 1918. Together they prepared a short-lived friendship treaty, signed on 3 January 1919, in which Feisal accepted large-scale Jewish immigration and the establishment of a Jewish 'National Home'. In return, the interests of the Palestinian Arab population were to be maintained and Arab nationalism advanced in Iraq and Syria.

public works and the development of the country's natural resources, once more in cooperation with the Jewish Agency, even though the Jews constituted only 10 per cent of the population when the Mandate took effect. Thus the roots of the conflict were embedded in the Mandate document itself.

No sooner had the British consolidated their rule than the Palestinian Arabs showed their hostility towards Zionism. True, in 1919 Weizmann and Emir Feisal, the leader of the Arab thrust for independence, signed an agreement in which Feisal accepted the presence of a Jewish entity in Palestine. However, it soon emerged that the accord was not worth the paper it was written on because of the opposition it aroused among Feisal's Palestinian associates. Severe riots erupted in Jerusalem when the French ejected Feisal from Damascus in April 1920. Sir Herbert Samuel, who was appointed Britain's first High Commissioner for Palestine in July 1920, granted amnesty to those responsible for the disturbances. The most prominent among the Arab agitators was Haj Amin al-Husseini, whom Samuel soon appointed Mufti of Jerusalem and president of the Arab Higher Committee, in the hope of appeasing the Arabs.

A second major outbreak of unrest occurred in May 1921, triggered by Arab opposition to Jewish immigration; the first attack was on an immigrants hostel in Jaffa. The Palestinians objected to the newcomers for nationalist reasons, because of the modernization schemes they wanted to introduce and because of a rumour that the incoming Jews were Bolsheviks. Samuel now sought to effect a more just balance between Jews and Arabs. First, in a British Government White Paper issued in 1922, the phrase 'Palestine as a national home' was altered to 'a Jewish National Home in Palestine'. Secondly, immigration was linked to the country's 'economic capacity . . . to absorb new arrivals'. Thirdly, the area of Trans-Jordan was separated from western Palestine when the applicability of the Mandate's Zionist clauses was concerned.

In the short term Samuel got the calm he wanted, but he failed in his attempts to form self-governing institutions because of the Arabs' refusal to recognize any body that might imply recognition of the Mandate itself. Throughout the 1920s the Arabs appealed repeatedly to London to revoke the Mandate. However, the second half of the decade saw opposition to Zionism decline owing to a drastic decline in Jewish immigration: in 1928, for instance, Jewish emigrants outnumbered immigrants by more than two to one (5071 to 2178).

Large-scale troubles erupted once more in 1929, this time sparked by a dispute over the Jews' right to bring ritual objects to the Western (Wailing) Wall in the Old City of Jerusalem and to set up a screen separating men and women during Jewish worship at the site (which had been part of the ancient Holy Temple). Incitement by the Mufti of Jerusalem, in reaction to the Zionists' supposed intention to seize control of the holy places, was the initial cause of the rioting. Throughout the country, in six days of assaults on the Yishuv (23–28 August) 133 Jews were killed and hundreds wounded. Britain now despatched considerably larger numbers of army and police personnel to maintain law and order. The new policy represented a further retreat from London's pro-Zionist policy: it was set forth in a 1930 White Paper issued by Lord Passfield, the Colonial Secretary, following the reports of a

The Western (Wailing) Wall in Jerusalem at the beginning of the twentieth century. A supporting wall of the Temple Mount, the Western Wall has remained intact since the destruction of the Second Temple in 70 CE and is the focus of Jewish religious and national consciousness.

parliamentary commission of inquiry headed by Sir Walter Shaw, which held hearings in Palestine, and of Sir John Hope Simpson, who conducted a one-man investigation. The Passfield White Paper called for local self-government and imposed additional restrictions on Jewish immigration and land purchases in order to take into account Arab needs and feelings.

However, in February 1931, under Jewish pressure, Prime Minister Ramsay MacDonald sent a letter to Weizmann that effectively annulled the prohibitions of the Passfield White Paper. The MacDonald Letter was the main turning point in the history of Zionism in general and of Palestine in particular. It enabled widespread Jewish immigration to take place (between 1931 and 1935 the Jewish population in Palestine doubled, from 174,606 to 355,157) and thus transformed the Yishuv into an embryonic Jewish state.

The rise of Hitler, growing Jewish immigration, the Arab Revolt and the 1939 White Paper

Arab disappointment with the MacDonald Letter gave rise to a new wave of nationalism in the 1930s, culminating in the Arab Revolt of 1936–1939. The test of British rule measured its ability to cope with three cardinal issues: Jewish immigration, land rights and the institutions of self-government. To a large degree, decision-making was left to the new High Commissioner, Sir Arthur Wauchope, whom Zionist leaders persuaded to permit massive Jewish immigration: from 9553 arrivals in 1931 the figure leaped to 30,327 in 1933, 42,359 in 1934 and, the highest yearly figure in the whole period of the Mandate, 61,854 in 1935. All told, 186,097 Jewish immigrants arrived in Palestine between 1932 and 1939. However, immigration from Germany (35,980) was a distant second behind the arrivals from Poland (83,847). It was the troubled political and economic situation of Polish Jewry on the one hand, and their Zionist awareness on the other, that led them to emigrate to Palestine in such numbers.

The authorities in London and Jerusalem allowed Jews to enter on the assumption that numerical parity between Jews and Arabs would help defuse the conflict and that a parallel concession to the Arabs on self-rule would bring about a balance in the relations of the two peoples. This policy was shown to have failed at the end of 1935 when the Arabs' outcry against the huge influx of Jewish immigrants reached a new climax. The Arabs indeed now gave the British an ultimatum to halt Jewish immigration and land purchases and to grant them independence.

In early 1936 the British parliament scotched the idea, proposed by High Commissioner Wauchope, of establishing a Jewish–Arab legislative council in Palestine; the Arab Revolt began soon after.[8] Its first stage, which continued until October 1936, was marked by acts of terror and a general strike. The British, seeking a more comprehensive solution to the problem, appointed a Royal Com-

Arab insurgents during the Arab Revolt. This photograph was found on the body of an Arab rebel killed by a British army patrol in November 1938.

mission of Inquiry, headed by Lord Peel, a former Secretary of State for India. The six-man commission arrived in Palestine in November 1936 and published its findings the following summer.

Basically, the Peel Commission concluded that the Mandate had failed and that the solution lay in partitioning the country between the two peoples. Alternatively, political restrictions could be placed on Jewish immigration and land acquisitions. However, partition drew the most attention. Even though the commission recommended giving the Jews only 20 per cent of Palestine (Galilee and the coastal plain), the idea incensed the Arabs and they reacted by intensifying the revolt. The British, their empire under threat from Germany, Italy and Japan, moved forcefully to quell the insurrection in order to maintain their credibility. More than 600 Jews died during the three years of the Arab Revolt, hundreds more were wounded, and property damage was immense. On the other hand, British–Jewish cooperation in security affairs helped the Jews to build up their military strength. To compensate the Arabs politically, London sent out a new commission, headed by Sir John Woodhead, whose report, submitted to Parliament in November 1938, tore the Peel Commission Report to shreds and effectively acknowledged the impact of the Arab Revolt, with all the political ramifications this position entailed.

Given the deterioration in the international arena caused by Hitler's invasion of Czechoslovakia in March 1939, *realpolitik* made the carrot-and-stick policy on Palestine adopted by the Government of Neville Chamberlain, in the form of a White Paper issued in May of that year, a virtual necessity. With war all but inevitable, the decisive factor for Britain became the need to preserve its strategic interests in the Middle East. Arab control of strategic resources, from the Suez Canal to the oil fields in Iraq, dictated a policy of conciliation toward the Arab states, particularly because of their involvement in the Arab Revolt. From this point of view, the Cabinet's support for the Peel Commission's recommendations was no more than a passing episode. The establishment of a Jewish state was now perceived as being absolutely inimical to British regional interests. At the same time, the Cabinet could not possibly ignore the presence in Palestine of nearly half a million Jews with powerful national aspirations who saw themselves as the vanguard of the persecuted Jewish people. Clearly, the Jews would fight rather than accept a situation in which Palestine was handed over to the Arabs. Hence the Government's need to find a solution acceptable to both sides.

The 1939 White Paper placed a limit of 100,000 Jewish immigrants to Palestine in the coming five years, and required Arab consent for any additional immigration. The country would be divided into three regions for land purchases, which would be prohibited outright in most areas, and an 'independent Palestinian state' was pledged within ten years (with the first steps towards that goal to be taken within five).

To Britain, an Axis-backed Arab insurrection seemed far more probable than a rebellion by the Jews. In any event, Hitler's radical anti-Jewish policy left the Zionists with no choice but to support the British. With the exception, indeed, of the tiny extreme right in the Yishuv, led by Avraham Stern,[9] the majority supported the stand expressed by David Ben-Gurion, Chairman of the Jewish Agency and the ranking Jewish leader. The Yishuv, Ben-Gurion asserted, must fight Hitler as though the White Paper did not exist, and fight the White Paper as though Hitler did not exist. In practice, the Yishuv, and the entire Jewish people, mobilized to combat the Nazis. The war against the White Paper would have to be deferred until after the war.

The impact of the Holocaust

We must distinguish between the period before it was known that the Germans were engaged in genocide against the Jewish people and the period, beginning in November 1942, when the evidence became clear-cut. In both periods the Jewish Agency made desperate efforts to rescue Jews by both legal and illegal means. At the same time, the British Government strictly enforced the White Paper, fearing an Arab uprising on the one hand and the inundation of Palestine with pro-German Jewish spies on the other. British sensitivity was particularly high while Palestine was threatened by a German invasion from Syria (until June 1941) and from Egypt (until autumn 1942): hence Britain's uncompromising attitude to illegal Jewish immigration and the tragic events that ensued, such as the scuttling in November 1940, by the *Haganah* – the Jewish Agency's underground military arm – of the refugee ship *Patria* (which the British were about to expel to Mauritius) with a loss of 267 people. In February 1942 another refugee ship, the *Struma*, was sunk on the Black Sea with 769 people aboard, after the High Commissioner, Sir Harold MacMichael, refused to give its passengers entry visas for Palestine.[10]

On a far larger scale, the Jews were also unable to save Hungarian Jewry. In 1944 the Germans proposed a 'blood for merchandise' deal but the Allies were unwilling to assist Hitler's logistic effort. The Jews were also unable to induce the Allies to bomb the Auschwitz death camp or the railway line leading to it.[11] Pressure to establish a Jewish army was also unavailing until 1944, and even then it was implemented only on a small scale, thanks to Churchill. The Yishuv co-operated with British intelligence against the German war effort, and 33 parachutists from the Yishuv were dropped into occupied Europe in a symbolic attempt to rescue Jews.

All that the Zionist leadership could do was point to the Holocaust and hope to convince the great powers that the only solution to the Jewish problem was a Jewish state. Had such a state existed before the war, many Jews could have been rescued.

Bitterly frustrated by their inability to rescue Jews during World War II, the Zionists were now determined to establish a Jewish state. It fell to a Labour Government in Britain to try to resolve the Palestine issue. The party had a strong pro-Zionist record, including a declared readiness to transfer Arabs out of a Jewish state and make border adjustments favourable to the Jews. However, after its return to power in July 1945 the party was compelled to bring its policy into line with the pro-Arab stance of the Foreign Office. In the immediate post-war situation there was concern about possible Arab sympathy for the Soviet Union and the dangers this would pose for Britain's regional interests.

Britain, weakened by its wartime effort, sought to have the United States share some of the responsibility for dealing with Palestine: hence the formation, in late 1945, of an Anglo-American Committee of Inquiry. Foreign Secretary Ernest Bevin and his advisors had no qualms about their anti-Zionist line and gave short shrift to American pressure (under Jewish influence), which posited a crucial linkage between the Palestine question and the Jewish refugees who had survived the Holocaust. The committee's report, issued at the end of April 1946, called for the immigration to Palestine of 100,000 Jewish DPs (displaced persons) then housed in refugee camps in Europe and the retraction of the 1939 White Paper. However, the committee did not advocate the establishment of a state in Palestine, either Jewish or Arab. In general the report, which leaned towards the Americans' support for a humanitarian (Zionist) solution, was a setback for the policy espoused by the British Government of Prime Minister Clement Attlee.

However, London did not let the matter rest there and initiated another Anglo-American committee, the Morrison–Grady Committee. In July 1946 this committee of experts proposed a direct connection between the humanitarian and political aspects of a solution in the form of a plan for 'provincial autonomy' in Palestine. The territory of the Jewish autonomous province would be limited to areas of current Jewish settlement; Jerusalem and the southern Negev desert would be under British control; the remainder would become an autonomous Arab province. After five years a choice would be made between partition and a united state.

This idea was rejected by all sides, including the United States Administration under President Harry Truman, which agreed to a compromise between the Jewish programme for a state in two-thirds of Palestine and the British plan. In the London Conference (September 1946 to February 1947) Attlee's Government made a final futile effort to persuade Arabs and Jews to accept British proposals. The unbending line taken by the Arab states at the conference led the Government to drop the option of partition (in a plan drawn up by Bevin and Harold Beeley, the Foreign Office's chief expert on Palestine). The British were no more successful in suppressing illegal Jewish immigration into Palestine and Jewish terrorism. This triple failure finally induced London to dump the whole Palestine question into the lap of the United Nations, without any recommendations of its own.

The United Nations resolution on Palestine

Acting quickly, the United Nations General Assembly in May 1947 set up yet another inquiry body, the United Nations Special Commission on Palestine (UNSCOP). At the same time the Soviet Union announced its preference for a binational state, but said that if this were not feasible it would support partition. Stalin changed his line on the Jews and Palestine because he thought that he could split the Anglo-American alliance, a view which was fully reflected in Gromyko's speech of 14 May 1947. The great powers were deliberately left unrepresented on UNSCOP, which was to submit its report within 120 days. It comprised two members of the British Commonwealth, Canada and Australia; two from the Eastern Bloc, Yugoslavia and Czechoslovakia; a Muslim state, Iran, and a state with

The ruins of the King David Hotel which was bombed on 22 July 1946 by the Irgun, a terrorist offshoot of the Haganah. The destruction of Britain's administrative headquarters and military command in Palestine ended the Labour Government's attempts to resolve the crisis, and prompted London to pass the Palestinian question to the United Nations.

a substantial Muslim population, India; two western European countries, Sweden and The Netherlands; three from Latin America, Peru, Guatemala and Uruguay. Following fierce infighting, the Latin American representatives were persuaded to support Palestine's partition into two states in return for the internationalization of Jerusalem and a single economic structure.

UNSCOP reported on 31 August 1947. Seven states backed a solution giving the Jewish state 62 per cent of the area of Palestine (later reduced to 55 per cent), with the rest designated for a Palestinian state. Three countries (Iran, India and Yugoslavia) recommended a federal plan in which most of the land would go to the Arab state with Jerusalem as its capital. Australia abstained.

On 29 November 1947 the General Assembly approved the two-state plan by a vote of 33 to 13 with ten abstentions. Britain abstained but objected strongly to the plan, contending that the Arabs to be included within the Jewish state – more than 400,000 – would become an irredentist element like the Sudeten Germans in pre-war Czechoslovakia. Similar irredentist tendencies would eventually emerge on the Jewish side.[12] To the Arabs the United Nations vote was tantamount to a declaration of war; for the Jews it was a final opportunity to create a state of their own.

Israel and the Arab World

The continuous intrusion of the Islamic factor into political life in the Arab states, in non-Arab Muslim states such as Iran, and among the Arabs in Israel and in the occupied territories is a source of concern to those striving for peace in Israel and elsewhere. The root cause lies in the Quran (B58/61), which relegates Jewry to eternal abasement and poverty; the Jews are also said to possess despicable traits and to be treacherous cheats. In addition, the Holy Land and Jerusalem are sacred in Islam. The mosque of al-Aqsa, the site of the miraculous ascent of the Prophet Muhammad to heaven, is in Jerusalem.

A striking illustration of the Islamic resurgence is the Islamic Resistance Front, or Hamas (an Arabic acronym also meaning courage and ardour). It was formed in 1986. Its charter uncompromisingly refuses to accept Israel's existence. Hamas believes that it is the personal duty of every Muslim to partake in a *jihad* (holy war) against Israel because of the Jews' 'plunder' of Palestine. Article 11 of the charter

V8/A/159/Rev.7
1 October 1947

GENERAL ASSEMBLY
SESSION 49
ROLL-CALL FORM

PLENARY MEETING 128   DATE Nov 29

COMMITTEE   TIME

Question at issue: Palestine Partition

Country	YES	NO	ABSTAIN	Country	YES	NO	ABSTAIN
AFGHANISTAN		x		LEBANON		x	
ARGENTINA			x	LIBERIA	x		
AUSTRALIA	x			LUXEMBOURG	x		
BELGIUM	x			MEXICO			x
BOLIVIA	x			NETHERLANDS	x		
BRAZIL	x			NEW ZEALAND	x		
BYELORUSSIAN S.S.R.	x			NICARAGUA	x		
CANADA	x			NORWAY	x		
CHILE			x	PAKISTAN		x	
CHINA			x	PANAMA	x		
COLOMBIA			x	PARAGUAY	x		
COSTA RICA	x			PERU	x		
CUBA		x		PHILIPPINES	x		
CZECHOSLOVAKIA	x			POLAND	x		
DENMARK	x			SAUDI ARABIA		x	
DOMINICAN REPUBLIC	x			SIAM			—
ECUADOR	x			SWEDEN	x		
EGYPT		x		SYRIA		x	
EL SALVADOR			x	TURKEY		x	
ETHIOPIA			x	UKRAINIAN S.S.R.	x		
FRANCE	x			UNION OF SOUTH AFRICA	x		
GREECE		x		UNION OF SOVIET SOCIALIST REPUBLICS	x		
GUATEMALA	x			UNITED KINGDOM			x
HAITI	x			U.S.A.	x		
HONDURAS			x	URUGUAY	x		
ICELAND	x			VENEZUELA	x		
INDIA		x		YEMEN		x	
IRAN		x		YUGOSLAVIA			x
IRAQ		x					
TOTAL 1st Column:				TOTAL:	33	13	10

The chart showing the result of the vote on the partition of Palestine at the United Nations General Assembly on 29 November 1947. The partition plan for separate Jewish and Arab states was passed by 33 votes to 13 with ten abstentions.

states: 'Palestine is Islamic *waqf* [religious trust] land of the Muslims for all time. It is forbidden to give up any or all of it. No state or all the Arab states, no king or president or all the Arab kings and presidents, nor any organization, Palestinian or Arab, has the right to [give up land].' Neither the 'Communist East' nor the 'infidel imperialist West' can be trusted. All international conferences and peace initiatives are unacceptable because they imply legitimacy for the Jewish state.

The image of the Jew in Hamas literature resembles that of the international Jewish conspirator in *The Protocols of the Elders of Zion* (the basic document of modern anti-Semitism). The Jews are said to be behind all the major revolutions and wars, acting through secret organizations. Their control of the world's finances will help them achieve world domination.

Hamas's attitude towards the Palestine Liberation Organization is ambivalent. On the one hand, the PLO is like a part of the family, its secular character due only to the penetration of western ideas into Islam since the period of the Crusades. On the other hand, Hamas's rejection of secular notions is absolute.

The key to a full understanding of the conflict between the Jewish and Palestinian national movements lies in the asymmetry of the two sides' claims.

The Jews stated their readiness for a territorial compromise as early as 1937 and repeated it in 1947 (with opposition only from a small fundamentalist minority). The central Jewish *historical* claim is simultaneously a religious imperative: 'To your offspring I give this land, from the river of Egypt to the great river, the river Euphrates' (Genesis 15:18). The conquest of the land by the Israelites in the thirteenth century BCE long predated the Muslim conquest. And despite the protracted exile of most of the Jewish people, Jewish settlement in the Holy Land remained unbroken. Their *legal* claim was based on the endorsement of the British Mandate, with its pro-Zionist clauses, by the fifty-two League of Nations member-states in 1922, and on the United Nations resolution of 1947. The primary *moral* argument stemmed from the murderous depths to which European anti-Semitism plunged in the period framed by Herzl and the Holocaust. Moreover, Zionism's gains (until 1948) did not come at the expense of the local Arab population; the Yishuv, rather, developed barren areas. Beyond this, there were many independent Arab states while the Jews were asking for only one, and it was only natural to establish it in their historic homeland. The Jewish state, Zionist leaders pledged, including those on the right (other than a handful who supported a population transfer), would be founded on political, civil and religious equality of rights irrespective of creed, race or sex.

The Arab case began with the contention that the Canaanites, who inhabited the land before the Jews, were the Arabs' ancestors, hence the Muslim conquest in the seventh century CE was not the first by the Arabs. The Jews had ruled in the land for only 400 years, the Arabs for 1300. The Arabs assailed the legality of the Mandate, arguing that only Article 22 of the League of Nations charter, which assured independence to the nations of the Ottoman Empire, was relevant. The *religious* claim was based on Palestine's sanctity for Muslims and held that foreign claims adduced by infidel nations were inapplicable to the Holy Land. In any event, the Jews were not a nation but a community or a sect. They numbered only 15 million, against 750 million Christians and 350 million Muslims (this in the 1920s).[13] The Arabs' primary *moral* argument was that the persecution of the Jews in Europe did not give them the right to create a homeland at the expense of another people.

These polarized stands have consistently prevented the two national movements from finding a *modus vivendi*.

The establishment of the State of Israel and Arab–Israeli conflict

Israel's creation was not just the result of an international political and diplomatic struggle. (The State of Israel, founded on 14 May 1948, was recognized immediately by the United States and three days later by the Soviet Union.) Jews and Arabs also fought a bitter war, triggered by the United Nations partition resolution. In the first part of the war, from 29 November 1947 (the resolution) until 14 May 1948 (the declaration of the state), Haganah forces engaged local Arab irregulars and volunteers from neighbouring states. In the second stage, from 15 May, the date of the final British withdrawal from Palestine and of the Arab states' invasion, until the armistice agreements of 1949, the Jews achieved victory but at a heavy cost.

The Yishuv's victory was made possible by the enhancement of the Haganah forces through the formation of well-trained units such as the Field Corps and the Palmach shock troops, and thanks to the experience gained by 30,000 Yishuv residents who fought in the British Army. Equally important, however, was an arms deal with Czechoslovakia (undertaken with Soviet consent) which provided the Yishuv with badly needed materials and munitions. The Arab forces were equipped with modern weapons but lacked co-ordination, as the various states that took part in the fighting were unable to agree on the goals of the war. The principal Arab state, Egypt, was defeated by October 1948, and the first armistice agreement was signed with that country.

A serious Arab refugee problem was created from the start of the fighting. There was no master-plan for the expulsion of Arabs, but Jewish officers took local initiatives with the blessing of both politicians and the army high command.[14] Evacuated houses were often occupied by newly arrived immigrants. News of a massacre perpetrated on 9 April 1948 at Deir Yassin, a village on the outskirts of Jerusalem, in which 250 Arabs were killed, spread quickly and persuaded large numbers of Palestinians to flee: they feared that this was the fate lying in store for the entire Arab population. Arabs left or were expelled from the large towns of Jaffa, Haifa, Tiberias, Beit She'an, Beersheba, Ashdod and Ashkelon and dozens of villages. The exact number of Arabs who became refugees in the 1948–1949 war has been in dispute ever since, but it was between 600,000 and 766,000 – slightly more than half the Arab population of Palestine in 1947.

Israeli policy-makers believed that the armistice accords would be a corridor to peace, which would, in turn, generate a political, social and economic revolution throughout the Middle East. However, the scale of the defeat soon gave rise to the fear that the Arabs would seek a war of revenge.[15] In the Arab states the war's stunning outcome undermined the old feudal regimes; but the radical regimes which supplanted them would adopt an anti-Israeli stance quite as intense as their predecessors.

The Jews did not exploit their momentum to conquer all of western Palestine; parts of Judea and Samaria were controlled by Jordan and (temporarily) by Iraq, while the Gaza Strip was occupied by Egypt. Following the war the fledgling state set out to build a nation through widespread immigration and intensive settlement. Overseeing this policy was David Ben-Gurion, who became Israel's first prime minister when his social-democratic party, Mapai, obtained 35.7 per cent of the votes in the elections to the first Knesset (parliament) in January 1949. Ben-Gurion introduced proportional representation, believing that this was the highest embodiment of the democratic ideal; but the effect of the system has been to put too much power in the hands of small political parties, enabling them to act as king-makers for Israel's governments.

The ink was hardly dry on the armistice agreements when Israel had to cope with terrorism and armed clashes with the Arab states. On the Syrian border the fighting was over water sources and the disputed demilitarized zones between the two countries. On the Jordanian border the clashes were caused by terrorist infiltrations and the subsequent deterioration of the internal situation in Israel; on the Egyptian border Israel had to deal with *fedayun* (guerrilla) squads and press its case for the use of the Suez Canal, a right denied it by Cairo.

Escalation towards full-scale war began in 1954 with the signing of the Anglo-Egyptian agreement for Britain's evacuation of the Suez Canal zone. Israel tried to scuttle the agreement (and prevent the British withdrawal) through the use of *agents provocateurs* in Egypt, but failed and caused a serious crisis in Ben-Gurion's party. Another factor was an important Egyptian–Czech arms agreement made in 1955, which was facilitated by Cairo's close ties with Moscow. Israel, feeling that the balance of forces was tilting in the Arabs' favour, sought an alliance with France, which was in a willing mood because of the secret aid Egypt's militant ruler Gamal Abd al-Nasser was offering the Algerian insurgents trying to oust the French from their country. At the same time, Anglo-Israeli ties improved considerably as Anglo-Egyptian ties worsened. Egypt also felt threatened by the Baghdad Pact between Iraq and Turkey, which was engineered by the British in 1955. Tension peaked in the summer of 1956 when Egypt nationalized the Suez Canal.

Throughout the period terrorist incursions directed from Egypt into Israel from the Gaza Strip increased. So did infiltrations from Jordan. Israel countered with reprisal raids of which the most famous was carried out against Egyptian forces in Gaza in February 1955; the scale of the attack was seen by the Egyptians as a turning point and drove Nasser into the arms of the Soviets. Under Ben-Gurion's leadership Israel manœuvred itself into a war with Egypt. Still, there would have been no war had not a combination of circumstances enabled Israel to form an alliance with Britain and France. The French also provided Israel with military aid and air cover in the Suez War of October 1956. Israel captured the entire Sinai Peninsula and the Gaza Strip, and Ben-Gurion declared the 'Third Jewish Commonwealth', but was forced to retract within twenty-four hours under joint United

States–Soviet pressure, which brought about a full Israeli withdrawal by March 1957. Nevertheless, ten years of relative quiet followed, although in that decade the seeds of the next war were sown.[16]

All the basic elements that had fed the Arabs' implacable hostility to Israel remained in place, particularly the ranking Arab ruler, Egypt's Nasser. Escalating conflict with the Syrians over the control of the water sources led to a heightened tension on the Egyptian border as well; in May 1967 Nasser ordered that the Straits of Tiran should be closed to Israeli vessels, an act considered a *casus belli* by Israel. The maritime powers promised to break the blockade but their foot-dragging compelled the Israeli political leadership under Prime Minister Levy Eshkol to yield to pressure by the General Staff and let the Israel Defence Forces (IDF) do the job.

The outcome of the war that broke out on 5 June 1967 was a milestone in the modern history of the Middle East, second in importance only to the establishment of Israel itself nineteen years earlier. Israel dealt the Arab forces a stunning and unprecedented defeat. Within six days it captured Judea and Samaria (the West Bank) from Jordan, the Gaza Strip and the Sinai Peninsula from Egypt, and the Golan Heights from Syria. As a result the conflict with the Arab world entered a new stage of intensification: on 1 September 1967 an Arab League summit conference held at Khartoum, Sudan, adopted a resolution asserting that there would be no peace, no recognition of and no negotiations with Israel, and recognizing the Palestinian people's right to its homeland.[17]

Poster produced by a leading Palestinian resistance organization after the Six-Day War. The territorial gains made by the Israeli army has led to heightened conflict between Palestinian Arabs and Jews, and has been the source of deep internal division in Israeli society.

The Israeli occupation unleashed a new wave of Arab terror, and wars of attrition flared up along the Suez Canal and the Jordanian border. Security Council Resolution 242 (22 November 1967), calling for the 'withdrawal of Israeli armed forces from territories occupied' in the June war, remained a controversial document, with Israel demanding a territorial compromise and the Arabs insisting on a total withdrawal. The only compromise Israel, still under Labour Party leadership, was willing to consider was a plan drawn up by Minister Yigal Allon, a senior figure in the party. Under the Allon Plan, Israel would retain the Jordan Rift Valley and the heights to its west, but cede those densely populated Arab areas that would be connected by Jordanian link roads.

The PLO was ruled out as a negotiating partner because of its terrorism and its Palestinian Covenant, whose revised version (1968) reinforced the thrust for Israel's annihilation by force of arms. Opposition by the PLO and the Arab states prevented Jordan's King Hussein from reaching a compromise with Israel. This process culminated in a resolution adopted at an Arab summit conference in Rabat, Morocco (October 1974), declaring the PLO the 'sole, legitimate representative of the Palestinian people'. In the meantime, United Nations and United States mediation efforts had failed, and Israel (led by Golda Meir, prime minister from 1969 to 1974) refused to pull back from the Suez Canal on the basis of a partial peace agreement.

Anwar al-Sadat took power in Egypt following Nasser's death in September 1970, and declared his intention of regaining the land occupied by Israel. On 6 October 1973, the Jewish fast-day of Yom Kippur (Day of Atonement), he launched a war that caught Israel unprepared. As Egyptian troops stormed across the Suez Canal in the south, Syrian forces attacked on the Golan Heights in the north. Jordan did not participate. The three-week campaign that ensued, known in Israel as the Yom Kippur War and in the Arab world as the October War, marks the third milestone in modern Middle East history. Israel was plunged into its most difficult war. Under Minister of Defence Moshe Dayan, the hero of the Six Day War, Israel barely managed a tactical victory, in which it retained its 1967 territorial conquests on two fronts. But its deterrent posture was undermined and Palestinian terror was stepped up, resulting in atrocities such as the attack in 1974 on a school in the Upper Galilee town of Ma'alot, which claimed the lives of eighteen children and the hijacking of a bus on the Coastal Road near Tel Aviv (1978), in which a large number of Israeli civilians were killed. On the Egyptian front, disengagement agreements, involving Israeli retirements in Sinai, were concluded in 1974 and 1975, through the mediation of US Secretary of State Henry Kissinger.[18]

On 19 November 1977 President Sadat made a historic visit to Jerusalem at the invitation of the right-wing Government led by Prime Minister Menachem Begin whose Likud Party had won the general election six months earlier. Under the tutelage of US President Jimmy Carter a 'framework for peace in the Middle East' was signed by Begin and Sadat at Camp David, the presidential retreat, on 17 September 1978, followed by the signing of an Israeli–Egyptian peace treaty on 26 March 1979.

However, no progress was made on the other fronts, and the autonomous regime that, under the Camp David Accords, was supposed to be implemented for the Palestinians in the occupied territories, remained a dead letter. But the situation in the territories was far from stagnant. The shooting had hardly stopped in the 1967 Six-Day War when a growing number of rightist elements, centred around the messianic Gush Emunim (Bloc of Fidelity) group, insisted that it had been a war of liberation and not of occupation. Against the background of a regional political deadlock, the exponents of this view now dragged the Government into increasing settlement activity in the occupied territories. With the Palestinian question unresolved following the breakdown of the autonomy talks, there was a new surge of terrorism, particularly from Lebanon, where the PLO, expelled from Jordan a decade earlier, had entrenched itself as a virtual state within a state.

In June 1982 Israel launched what was billed as a limited campaign to remove the terrorist threat from southern Lebanon but under Defence Minister Ariel Sharon it became the three-year Lebanon War. Sharon wanted to impose a new order in the region by installing a pro-Israeli government in Beirut under a Maronite Christian leadership and expelling the Palestinian refugees in Lebanon to Jordan, which would become the 'Palestinian state'. The plan failed completely and Israel was finally forced to withdraw its troops from Lebanon under heavy terrorist pressure wielded by Shi'ite organizations affiliated with Iran and Syria.

Israel and the Palestinians after 1967

Although the Palestinian problem was not the cause of the Six-Day War, that war resulted in the PLO's becoming the main representative organization of the Palestinian Arabs. It had been created three years earlier, under the auspices of the Arab League. However, it was the Israeli occupation that gave it the momentum it had previously lacked. Israel was not alone in viewing the PLO as a ruthless enemy; Jordan also had good reason for doing so.

Israel views the PLO as an organization bent on its eradication. Article 6 of the Palestinian Covenant states that only Jews who had resided in Palestine before 1917 would be considered citizens of the independent Palestinian state. Articles 8 and 9 deal directly with the liberation of Palestine through an armed struggle. It suggests (Article 10, for example) that one means to achieve this is through a 'popular liberation war', i.e. guerrilla warfare, on the Algerian model.

The PLO's claim to the West Bank also made it a serious rival to Jordan's ambitions to reassert itself there. Jordanian–PLO tension erupted into fighting in 1970, resulting in the elimination of the PLO stronghold in Jordan. Israel's Labour governments tried to reach a territorial compromise with Jordan in order to neutralize the PLO, but King Hussein was too weak to take such a step on his own.

Meanwhile, the PLO went from strength to strength. In 1974, as already noted, the Arab League summit recognized it as the Palestinian people's exclusive representative. Internationally its standing soared in 1974 and 1975, when the United Nations adopted most of its platform (though not the plank calling for Israel's annihilation) and the General Assembly passed a resolution equating Zionism with racism (10 November 1975).

Israeli attempts in the 1970s to counter the PLO by encouraging local figures in the territories and creating the Village Leagues failed abysmally. PLO influence in the territories was an unassailable fact. The Camp David Accords ignored the organization, and the proposed autonomy plan also fell by the wayside owing to Israeli fears. The main difference between the two main Israeli parties was that the left-leaning Labour bloc was ready for a territorial compromise with Jordan (the Allon Plan); Jordan would then form a federation or confederation with the Palestinians. The rightist Likud, however, was unwilling to countenance the idea of a territorial compromise for both ideological ('Greater Israel') and strategic reasons. A Palestinian state, it was thought, would serve as the springboard for a new Arab war against Israel. At the same time, not even the Likud dared to annex the territories (other than the Golan Heights in 1981, East Jerusalem having been annexed immediately after the June 1967 war).

The PLO's extreme ideological posture, as expressed in the Palestinian Covenant (Article 22, for example, views Zionism as racist), nourished the extremists in Israel. But the PLO was unable to achieve a breakthrough and in the 1980s its standing declined, owing in large measure to the strong support shown for Israel by the United States under President Ronald Reagan. Finally, on 15 November 1988, PLO Chairman Yasser Arafat declared the organization's acceptance of the two-state principle, according to which Israel and an independent Palestinian state in the West Bank and Gaza would co-exist. Israel did not greet the announcement rapturously as it was not accompanied by the revocation of the Palestinian Covenant. Suspicion that the whole matter was little more than a publicity stunt grew because of the opacity that remained regarding the issue of the 'right of return': this principle, which Israel absolutely rejects, holds that the Palestinian refugees have the right to return to the former Palestine. Arafat's announcement came at the height of the Intifadah, the uprising in the occupied territories, which erupted in December 1987 and further intensified the enmity between Israelis and Palestinians.

In short, nearly a quarter of a century after the Six-Day War, Jordan remains the only partner with which a compromise agreement can be reached, given the PLO's refusal to modify its ideological tenets. The PLO's dialogue with the United States, which began after Arafat's November 1988 announcement, was also terminated because of an abortive terrorist attack on the Israeli coast in May 1990 by a group affiliated to the PLO. During the Gulf War in 1991 the PLO identified totally with Iraq; this move bolstered Israel's principled and operative assertion that the PLO is not a partner for peace. The root causes of the Israeli–Palestinian confrontation remain unresolved.

The complexity of Israel: political, cultural and psychological

The external pressures that make it so difficult for Israel to play a positive role in the international system may be traced to the circumstances of its birth in 1948. Israel's isolation in the region is due to the opposition of the Arab states and the Muslim world to its very establishment. Over the years, the United Nations has undergone a radical change, as the Third World countries that have freed themselves from colonial rule have become the dominant force in the world body. In their view, Israel itself is effectively a colonial state because it deprives the Palestinians of their homeland. Israel, they contend, is the South Africa of the Middle East, its policy towards the Palestinians a form of apartheid. Moreover, in the 1950s the Soviet Union and the Communist Bloc shifted their support from Israel to the Arab states. Having no one else to turn to – American support not yet being all-embracing – Israel was forced to appeal to France, thus reinforcing its colonialist image. Nor did that image change after the 1967 war, when the United States replaced France as Israel's superpower patron; indeed, it was strengthened because the United States was marked with the stigma of imperialism in the Cold War era, giving the Soviets and their Arab allies a powerful propaganda weapon.

The situation began to improve, and Israel gradually began to emerge from its isolation, when the Camp David Accords and the Israeli–Egyptian peace treaty were signed and Soviet influence in the region waned. Internationally, the change came in the aftermath of Soviet President Mikhail Gorbachev's introduction of glasnost and perestroika. On the one hand, the Arab–Israeli conflict was no longer an element in superpower rivalry, so that the pressures on Israel were reduced. On the other hand, the United States, as part of its effort to bring about a new world order, is determined to engineer an Arab–Israeli peace. Such a peace, even if it initially takes the form of interim accords – for example non-belligerency agreements with countries like Syria whose ideologies prevent them from accepting Israel's existence – would be preferable to the status quo, which constantly harbours the potential for war.

Israel will face harsh new trials entailing territorial and functional concessions. The era now emerging is characterized by renewed national self-determination everywhere; this will be realized within independent frameworks – if these nations can demonstrate economic and political viability – or in federative or confederative structures. American pressures on Israel, which are essentially pragmatic in nature, in contrast to the ideological or religious pressures exerted by Arabs, Muslims and Communists, may produce a solution because of America's fundamental commitment to Israel's independence and security. The new Pax Americana will be inherently constructive, not destructive.

Israel is also coming under pressure from the European Community. The EC is increasingly a crystallized power bloc wanting just as much as the United States to terminate the Arab–Israeli conflict, in order to help stabilize the international economic and political system. Japan, a rising international power broker, has a similar role to play, although its dependence on Arab oil and its weak relations with Israel make it unlikely that Tokyo will adopt a staunchly pro-Israeli position. Ultimately, Japan will follow the lead dictated by the Americans. Balancing Israeli and Arab needs will be the responsibility of the superpowers but, once the process is complete, Israel will be able to free itself from its intolerable dependence on American loans and grants and produce a more balanced budget in which social welfare will take pride of place and the burden of security will be reduced to a minimum. When that happens, Israel will also become a magnet for western Jewry.

Israel and the Holocaust

It is only natural that the impact of the Holocaust is felt more intensely in Israel than in any other country. True, Israel did not exist at the time of the Holocaust, but the Yishuv then considered itself a 'state on the way' and the vanguard of the Jewish people. Moreover, in Zionist consciousness the Holocaust is considered the ultimate moral and historical justification for the Jews to be allowed a state of their own.

The result of these perceptions was that between 1945 and 1948 the symbols of the desperate Jewish heroism in the ghettos and the resistance movements became models for emulation among the young people who were fighting the British (in the Haganah as well as in the extremist Irgun and Lehi groups). After the creation of the state these symbols, and especially the manifestations of Jewish heroism, were transformed into national rituals. In 1951 the Knesset set aside a 'Holocaust and Heroism Memorial Day' close to Remembrance Day for Israelis who fell in battle. Another law (1953) provided for the establishment of an institute in Jerusalem – Yad Vashem – to commemorate the martyrs and heroes of the Holocaust. Holocaust studies became a separate discipline in Israeli institutions of higher learning.

Israel also undertook to bring Nazi war criminals to trial. The most famous case was that of Adolf Eichmann, who was responsible for deporting Jews in Europe to the death camps at the height of the extermination process (1942–1944). Eichmann was kidnapped in Buenos Aires by Israeli agents, tried and convicted in 1961, and hanged in 1962. The dramatic nature of the events spread an awareness of the Holocaust world-wide and allowed the young generation in Israel for the first time to grasp the magnitude of the Holocaust. Notwithstanding the efforts of some observers to depict the trial as an exploitation of the Holocaust for indoctrination purposes (see especially Hannah Arendt's *Eichmann in Jerusalem: A Report on the Banality of Evil*), the Israeli prosecution, led by the Attorney General, Gideon Hausner, did in fact succeed in making it the trial of the Jewish people against the Nazi regime.

Trenchant proof that the preoccupation with the Holocaust in this period was genuine and not manipulative is the fact that the entire question of Jewish collaboration with the Nazis had already been put on the public agenda in the sensational Kasztner trial in the mid-1950s.*

Cultivation of the memory of the Holocaust and its central place in the national consciousness is part of the Israeli ethos; at its centre is the conviction that never again will the Jewish people be led 'like sheep to slaughter'. Such feelings are heightened by the myth that if the state of Israel had existed during World War II

*Rezsö Rudolf Kasztner, journalist and lawyer, was a leader of the Zionist movement in Romania and Hungary. During World War II he negotiated with the Germans to save Jewish lives. Kasztner settled in Israel after the war and, in 1953, was accused of having collaborated with the Nazis. He was shot dead by Ze'ev Eckstein in 1957 and posthumously cleared of all charges by the Supreme Court a year later.

there would not have been a Holocaust. From the moment of its creation Israel saw itself entitled to speak for the millions who perished. Hence its demand for reparations from Germany in 1951, a demand that triggered a fierce national controversy, with the opposition on both the right and the left charging that the reparations claim violated the memory of the Holocaust. Prime Minister Ben-Gurion saw the matter differently, distinguishing between the pragmatic need for reparations (in order to consolidate the Israeli economy) and the moral, educational aspect.

Israel and the diaspora

Israel's relations with the diaspora have changed radically since the pre-state period. Prior to 1948 the negation of the diaspora was a central tenet of Zionist ideology. But Israel's huge security and financial needs turned the picture upside down; relations with the major Jewish communities in the West, first and foremost with the five million Jews in the United States, but also with those in France, Britain, Canada and South Africa, underwent a complete change. Although the wealthy American Jewish community has been particularly active on behalf of Israel in the economic sphere, its true clout derives from the powerful lobby it has created to influence United States policy toward the Middle East in general and Israel in particular. (AIPAC, the America Israel Public Affairs Committee, is unparalleled in any other ethnic minority.)

True, there are limits to the ability of Jewish influence to affect American foreign policy, owing mainly to the question of dual loyalty, the clash between American and Israeli interests. This conflict does not arise with issues in which the human rights element is clear, such as the emigration of Soviet Jews to Israel. However, the Arab–Israeli conflict has become a central issue since the gates of the Soviet Union were opened. The regional nature of the conflict leads to American concern about ensuring a continuous supply of critical energy resources, such as oil, and protecting the pro-American feudal regimes that control those resources. The Conference of Presidents of Major Jewish Organizations, which encompasses the leading American Jewish groups, generally coordinates its stands with the Israeli Government.

However, it was the unprecedented strength of the American Jewish community that exempted it from the basic Zionist precept, immigration to Israel. In the early days of the state Ben-Gurion felt he could not forgo this potential, so he forged an alliance with the non-Zionists among American Jewry, through an agreement in 1951 with the President of the American Jewish Committee, Jacob Blaustein. This led to the cooperation of the powerful AJC with Israel, in certain defined areas. However, the pressures faced by Israel, largely caused by the conflict with the Arabs, effectively forced Ben-Gurion to give up the notion of Israel's becoming a magnet and spiritual centre for the Jewish people. Instead, it became a focus for national, cultural and religious identification. Thus the relations between Israel and the diaspora were changed.

Experience has shown that the asymmetry between the sense of a common

Jewish destiny and the national interests of the State of Israel can make these relations turbulent: Argentina and South Africa are two notable examples.* Israel is compelled to accept its status as a haven for persecuted Jews only, such as the communities in the Soviet Union or Ethiopia. But these developments have also proved the validity of the central Zionist thesis that Israel needs to exist as a haven for all Jews. As for western Jewry, they have not needed a haven. As a result, Israeli relations with Jewish communities in the West are not those between a centre and a periphery but between two separate centres. In many ways Israel has given legitimacy to the existence of an exilic centre, akin to a new Babylon, in North America.

A cultural background: Europeanization vs Orientalization vs Americanization

At the time of Israel's birth in 1948 oriental Jewry accounted for 20 per cent of its Jewish population. But the Yishuv never had to cope with a culture clash between different ethnic communities such as developed when a million new immigrants, who arrived within a decade, half of them from Middle-Eastern and North African countries, quickly developed an antipathy with the Israeli national identity as encapsulated in the sabra (native-born Israeli). The largest and most critical group from the standpoint of the clash of cultures were the North Africans. In the Yishuv period new arrivals needed to adapt themselves to the native culture and they sought a part in shaping the embryonic entity. In contrast, the post-1948 North African communities could do neither as they were uneducated, unemployed and underpaid. They perceived the dominant European–Ashkenazi culture as overbearing and arrogant.

The Israeli establishment abandoned its paternalistic policy following the violent protest movement that jolted Haifa's Wadi Salib section in 1959 and the appearance of the social-protest group known as the 'Black Panthers' in 1970. In the former case the protest was symptomatic of a phenomenon the establishment found particularly serious: a massive protest vote in favour of the saliently radical right-wing party Herut threatened the ruling party, Mapai, which to the deprived oriental communities was the very incarnation of the European–Ashkenazi establishment. In the latter case the protesters identified with the left and the establishment coped with the social-protest phenomenon, with some success, by diverting resources to housing, welfare and education.[19] The fact is that ethnic parties are part of the Israeli political scene to this day, although nowadays the major party of this kind (Shas, the Sephardi Torah Guardians) speaks of religious rather than socio-economic discrimination.

To the oriental communities, the Zionist revolution is a wholly European phenomenon. Their revolt against western culture will end only with their full and permanent integration into all spheres of life in Israel, but particularly in education and politics. The solution to the problem is now being implemented: (i) in politics

---

*The State of Israel's relations with Argentina and South Africa have sometimes had an adverse effect on local Jews.

by the growing participation of these communities at every level, including the Knesset and the government; (ii) in the realm of employment and income, through which the oriental communities have raised their status significantly. In education the proportion of university students from these groups is still low, but considerable progress has been achieved at the high-school level. Equally crucially, oriental cultural traditions have acquired legitimacy in Israeli society.

The process of Americanization, especially since 1967, helps blur the gap between Europeanization and orientalization. In other words, the hallmarks of an affluent society that characterize Israel have brought about, among other results, a dramatic improvement in the living standards and the social performance of the oriental communities. This form of Americanization, which does not necessarily demand outstanding achievements in higher education (except of the Israeli elite) and is satisfied with financial success and social status not necessarily linked to a university degree, can act as a bridge between the European and oriental heritages. The proof lies in the shared popular culture of the young generation, in film, music and dress. The current wave of Soviet immigration will have a profound impact on the cultural battlefield within a generation or two.

Israel's future prospects

Israel has three options for its future development. It can maintain the post-1967 status quo by continuing to rule one and a half million Palestinians who reject Israel with every means at their disposal and who are demanding the right to self-determination. It can go on trying to promote the combined solution of a Jordanian–Palestinian confederation. Or it can seek a direct solution with the Palestinians themselves.

The first option, espoused by the radical right, is ultimately unworkable because of international and regional opposition, including the objections of Israel's best friends in the United States. The Israelis may elect another radical-right government, but its policy would be a certain recipe for another war and for Egypt's revocation of its separate peace with Israel. This option would continue to shackle Israel with the image of a state under siege and bring about considerable emigration.

The third option is feasible only through the strict de-militarization of a Palestinian state in the West Bank and Gaza Strip. For this option to be workable the Palestinian leadership would have to show a willingness to change ideologically and politically far greater than it has shown so far.

Arguably, it is the second option which holds out the best hope for a secure future for Israel since, if adopted, it might moderate Palestinian extremism and facilitate Israel's integration into the region. It is also acceptable to the free world and in particular to the Americans.

In all three options the commitment of the superpowers is necessary but not sufficient. Much depends on the readiness of the region's peoples to discard the inflexible positions they have maintained in the recent past. However, the sacrifice Israel would be called to make far outweighs that of its many adversaries, with their greater potential. Israel has much to lose if the Palestinians' national passions, fed by the 'rejection front' Arab states, are not reined in but generate immediate irredentism. Israel's reluctance is understandable given its past experience with the Palestinians. It was Moshe Dayan who said that it is impossible to raise the social-welfare banner and the security banner at the same time.[20]

CHRONOLOGY

JEWISH HISTORY		GENERAL HISTORY
	BCE	
Abraham; Isaac; Jacob; Family of Jacob; Patriarchs develop earliest form of monotheism; settlement in Israel; migration to Egypt; Joseph and the Children of Israel.	2000–1500	Mesopotamian civilization; Minoan Golden Age in Greece; Middle Kingdom in Egypt; Bronze Age in Europe; river valley civilizations in India and China.
Moses; ten plagues of Egypt; liberation from slavery and Exodus; forty years wandering in the desert; Moses receives Tablets of the Law on Mt Sinai; the Covenant or Mosaic Law; conquest of Israel by Joshua; the Philistines.	1500–1000	Assyrians overthrow Babylonian rule in Mesopotamia; peak of Mycenaean power in Greece; Trojan War; Shang Dynasty in China; Kingdom of Kush in Africa.
Kingdom of David with capital in Jerusalem; King Solomon and building of First Temple; Kingdom divided into Israel and Judah; Assyrian conquest; Babylonian conquest and destruction of First Temple; Babylonian exile; Babylonian Empire overthrown by Persians; return from exile and construction of Second Temple.	1000–500	Assyrian Empire in Mesopotamia; Golden Age of Classical Greece; Phoenician colonization of Mediterranean; Etruscan period followed by birth of Roman Empire; Egypt falls to Persia; Hindu society established in India; Mayan and Aztec civilizations in Americas.
Macedonian conquest of Israel and Egypt; Hellenism; Seleucid rule; Maccabeean revolt; restoration of Jewish autonomy; Hasmonean Jewish Kingdom; Pharisees and Sadducees; Roman conquest.	500–1	Parthian Empire in Persia; Macedonian conquests; Alexander the Great; Rome annexes Greece; Roman conquest of Egypt; Buddha in India; Confucius in China; Kingdom of Nok in Africa.
	CE	
Herodian rule; Jewish revolts against Rome; Zealots; destruction of Second Temple; Masada; Patriarchy established; Babylonia becomes centre of Jewish learning; compilation of the *Mishnah* and *Gemara* – Jerusalem and Babylonian Talmuds; St Augustine's Doctrine.	1–500	Jesus of Nazareth; spread of Christianity; decline of Roman Empire; Constantine the Great founds Byzantine Empire and converts to Christianity; Visigoths and Celts in Europe.
Arab conquest of Jerusalem; much of Jewry under Islamic rule; rise of Karaism; Khazar Jewish	500–1100	Byzantine Empire of Justinian; Muhammad; spread of Islam; Vikings in Europe; feudalism in

	500–1100 cont.	

Kingdom; Arab conquest of Visigoth Spain; Golden Age of Spanish Jewry; Jewish settlement in England, India, China; First Crusade.

500–1100 *cont.*

medieval Europe; Tang and Sung Dynasties in China.

Crusader Kingdom of Jerusalem; blood libels and increasing anti-Jewish activity; Mameluke rule in Jerusalem; Jews expelled from England, France, Spain and Portugal; spread of Ashkenazi and Sephardi traditions; Jews from central Europe migrate to Poland to escape persecution.

1100–1500

Crusades; Magna Carta; Black Death; Mongol conquests under Genghis Khan; Ming China; end of Byzantium; Aztecs in Mexico; Columbus reaches the Americas.

Ottoman Empire rules Jerusalem and Palestine; Council of the Four Lands; Khmelnitskii Massacre; Jews readmitted to England; Jews settle in South and North America; Hasidism.

1500–1800

Renaissance in Europe; Martin Luther and the Reformation; the Enlightenment; partitioning of Poland; American and French revolutions; Industrial Revolution.

Jewish Enlightenment; Pale of Settlement; Napoleon's Sanhedrin; Jews emancipated in England; pogroms in Russia; mass emigrations from Russia to North America; early Zionist settlements; Dreyfus affair; the Bund; rise of modern anti-Semitism; First Zionist Congress.

1800–1900

Napoleonic Wars; Congress of Vienna; 1848 revolutions; American Civil War; emancipation of serfs in Russia; Karl Marx; unification of Germany and Italy; colonization of Asia and Africa.

Emancipation in Russia; Zionism; Balfour Declaration; British Mandate in Palestine; rise of Arab nationalism; *Kristallnacht* and Nazi persecution of the Jews; Holocaust; Ben Gurion; State of Israel proclaimed; United Nations recognises Israel; Arab-Israeli War; large-scale emigration to Israel.

1900–1950

Russo-Japanese War; First World War; Russian Revolution; Treaty of Versailles; League of Nations; Great Depression; Second World War; Stalinism in the Soviet Union; United Nations; Gandhi in India; Mao in China; apartheid in South Africa.

Masada excavations; Eichmann trial; Six-Day War; reunification of Jerusalem; Golda Meir; Yom Kippur War; Camp David Accords; Israel withdraws from Sinai; Israel invades Lebanon; further large-scale (mainly Soviet) emigration to Israel; Jewish population in USA exceeds six million; Gulf War.

1950–1990

Korean War; Suez; independence in Asia and Africa; Cold War; Vietnam War; space race; third world famine and debt; glasnost and perestroika; collapse of communist states in eastern Europe; Iraq invades Kuwait leading to Gulf War.

Biographical Notes

AHAD HA-AM (ASHER HIRSCH GINSBERG): (1856–1927)
Russian-born Zionist intellectual and writer, he was the founder of 'spiritual Zionism' – the idea of creating a cultural–spiritual centre in Palestine rather than establishing a Jewish state – and one of the first Zionists to anticipate Arab resistance to 'political Zionism'.

AKIVA: (c. 50–135 CE)
Born in Judea, Akiva was a prominent scholar, patriot and martyr, and an important influence upon rabbinic Judaism. He was significant in developing and systematizing the *Halakha* and was imprisoned for openly teaching the Torah in defiance of Rome. He was one of the ten leading rabbis martyred by the Emperor Hadrian.

ALEXANDER I: (Tsar of Russia 1801–1825)
Relatively liberal by comparison with his father Paul I (1796–1801), his Jewish Statute of 1804 encouraged the productive employment, secular education and cultural assimilation of the Jews. It also included limitations on Jewish residence and land tenure, limiting the power of the Jewish *kahal*, and requiring Jewish students to study Russian, Polish or German.

ALEXANDER II: (Tsar of Russia 1855–1881)
He was known as the 'Tsar-Liberator' following his emancipation of the Russian serfs in 1861. Towards the Jews he was less accommodating. Apart from the abolition of the juvenile conscription of Jews and measures to facilitate the movement of some Jews from the Pale of Settlement, his assimilation policies reflected traditional anti-Jewish pronouncements.

AL-HUSSEINI, AL-HAJJ (MUHAMMAD) AMIN: (1895[?]–1974)
Leader of the Palestinian-Arab nationalist movement during the British Mandate from 1929, he was Grand Mufti of Jerusalem (1921), President of the Supreme Muslim Council (1922), President of the Arab Higher Committee (1936) and instigator of the Arab Rebellion of 1936–39. He inspired anti-British nationalism whilst a refugee in Iraq (1939–41). Barred from returning to Palestine after the Second World War, he remained in Egypt and then Lebanon. The Palestinian Liberation Organization is considered his political heir. (See chapter 7.)

ALKALAI, JUDAH BEN SOLOMON HAI: (1798–1878)
Sephardi rabbi and precursor of modern Zionism, he was born in Bosnia and brought up in Jerusalem. He had little faith in emancipation, insisting that settlement in Palestine was the only solution for Jews in Europe. He called for a tithe to finance settlement and for the

revival of spoken Hebrew. He worked towards an international recognition of a Jewish homeland in Palestine and his pamphlet, *Mevasser Tov*, was translated into English as *Harbinger of Good Tidings: An Address to the Jewish Nation on the Propriety of Organizing an Association to Provide the Regaining of Their Fatherland* in 1852.

ANAN, BEN DAVID: (eighth century)
He was the founder of the Ananite Sect in Babylonia and was embraced by the Karaites as their spiritual founder. His teachings included a rejection of the Talmudic tradition and the authority of the rabbinical academies. Instead he advocated a return to the Scriptures as the source of God's Law.

ST AUGUSTINE: (354–430)
Bishop of Hippo in North Africa and leading ecclesiastical scholar, unlike many Christian theologians of the time he studied the Old Testament extensively, emphasized the unity of God and adopted a missionary attitude toward the Jews. St Augustine's doctrine argued that the Jews should not be destroyed but allowed to exist in order to fulfil their ultimate destiny within the fullness of the Christian church.

BIRNBAUM, NATHAN: (1864–1937)
Distinguished intellectual personality in Austria and Germany, he founded and edited the first Jewish nationalist journal in German, *Selbstemanzipation*, in which he coined the term 'Zionism' from Leo Pinsker's pamphlet *Autoemancipation*. He developed a cultural rather than political conception of Zionism, so as not to alienate the Jews of the diaspora. At first he demanded the cultural autonomy of the Jews, but his atheism and secular nationalism gradually gave way to religious conviction, evidenced in his works *Um die Ewigkeit* (1920) and *Et La'asot* (1938).

CATHERINE II (THE GREAT): (Empress of Russia 1762–1796)
A devotee of the Enlightenment and appreciative of the commercial role played by Jews, she was nevertheless dependant on the support of the nobility and the Church. Hence she confined Jewish trade and settlement to the area known as the Pale of Settlement which came to include 'New Russia' on the shores of the Black Sea, captured from Turkey, and the new territories deriving from the partition of Poland in 1792.

CHAMBERLAIN, HOUSTON STEWART: (1855–1927)
The influential exponent of racist anti-Semitism was English by birth but Germany became his adopted home. Friend of Richard Wagner whose daughter he married, he was part of the Bayreuth Circle which saw the Teutonic race as the born leaders of civilization and Jews as a mongrel race whose existence was a crime against humanity. Hitler's Nationalist-Socialist ideology was largely founded on his *Die Grundlagen des 19. Jahrhunderts* (*The Foundations of the Nineteenth Century*, 1899).

DREYFUS, ALFRED: (1859–1935)
A captain in the French army, he was falsely accused of treason and sentenced to life imprisonment in 1894. A celebrated and practical campaign brought his eventual release, and in the First World War Dreyfus re-enlisted and was promoted to the rank of lieutenant-colonel. The Dreyfus Affair rocked the Third Republic; Jews were shocked that it could take place in France, the home of liberty, equality and fraternity.

EICHMANN, ADOLF OTTO: (1906–1962)
From March 1941 Eichmann, a Nazi official and SS officer, headed Nazi operations to expel and exterminate European Jewry. Obsessed with the 'final solution of the Jewish

question', he personally supervised many aspects of the extermination and expulsion processes, answering only to Heydrich (q.v.) and Heinrich Himmler. At the end of the war he escaped to Argentina where he lived until a world-wide search for him ended in May 1960. He was abducted to Israel where he stood trial and was sentenced to death for his crimes.

EINHORN, DAVID: (1809–1879)
He was a controversial German Reform rabbi and theologian. He went to the United States in 1855, and was a significant contributor at the Philadelphia Rabbinical Conference in 1869, which adopted a Reform platform.

EZRA
A priest and scribe, he rose to prominence in Babylonia as a religious and community leader and as a Persian functionary in charge of Jewish affairs. He played an important role in the rebuilding of the Temple after the return from Babylonian Exile to Jerusalem. In his instruction on Mosaic Law he emphasized democracy in education and the exclusivity of the Jewish people.

GERSHOM BEN JUDAH ME'OR HA-GOLAH: (906–1028)
He was an early German Talmudic scholar who introduced a structure and cohesion into Ashkenazi life; he was a spiritual model for German Jewry. The *piyutim* he composed reflect the attacks and troubles suffered by his generation and are noted for their emotion and simplicity.

GOERING, HERMANN WILHELM: (1893–1946)
A Nazi leader, he formed the Gestapo and was responsible for the policy of financing German rearmanent by the expropriation of Jewish property, symbolized in all its brutality by the *Kristallnacht* in 1938. He was a fanatical anti-Semite, and when he was condemned to death by the Nuremberg International Military Tribunal following the Second World War specific mention was made of his role in the extermination of the Jews.

GORDON, MIKHEL: (1823–1890)
Gordon was a Hebrew and Yiddish poet born in Vilna; he rose to prominence with his Yiddish songs, of which *Shtey oyf Mayn Folk* ('Awake My People') composed in 1869 is the most famous. It is widely regarded as the classical poetic expression of the spirit of the Russian Jewish enlightenment.

HANOKH BEN MOSES: (d. 1014)
Spanish Talmudist, he was appointed rabbi of Cordoba on the death of his father around 965 and, as such, was virtually chief rabbi of all Muslim Spain. As his father did, he sought to provide the Jews of Andalusia with a Torah centre independent of Babylonian influence. His most important disciple was Samuel ha-Nagid (q.v.).

HERZL, THEODOR (BENJAMIN ZE'EV): (1860–1904)
First leader of the Zionist movement and founder of 'political Zionism', he was born in Budapest, later moving to Vienna, where he studied law. As a journalist he witnessed the anti-Semitism of the Dreyfus Affair, which convinced him that the only solution was a Jewish national territory. Setting out his ideas in *Der Judenstaat* ('The Jew's State') in 1896, he devoted his life to the Zionist cause, negotiating with European statesmen and the Ottoman Empire for territory, primarily in Palestine but also in Cyprus, the Sinai Peninsula and by the controversial 'Uganda Scheme'. He founded the World Zionist Organization and became its life president.

HEYDRICH, REINHARD TRISTAN: (1904–1942)
Nazi SS leader, Himmler's assistant and sometime chief of the Gestapo, he played an important role in the design and execution of the 'final solution', with Jewish affairs concentrated in his hands by 1938. With the help of Eichmann he organized the mass deportation and extermination of Jews. He was killed by Czech resistance fighters in 1942.

HILLEL (THE ELDER): (end first century BCE)
He was one of the greatest sages of the Second Temple period; he was a native of Babylonia, spending his early days in Jerusalem. He emphasized the study of the Torah and for this he has been compared with Ezra. His ethical and religious teachings have been preserved in a series of proverbs in both Hebrew and Aramaic and his simple and humble manner became a model of conduct for subsequent generations.

HIRSCH, SAMSON (BEN) RAPHAEL: (1808–1888)
His views, as a leading exponent of Orthodoxy in Germany in the nineteenth century, were elaborated in his written works, notably *Neunzehn Briefe ueber Judentum* (1836), *Choreb, oder Versuche ueber Jissroels Pflichten in der Zerstreuung* (1837) and the pamphlet *Die Religion im Bunde mit dem Fortschritt* (1854). He challenged the Reformers, arguing that Jews rather than Judaism were in need of reform. He opposed organizational separation between Orthodox and Reform Judaism, used the concept of 'national Jewish consciousness' and believed in the Hebrew language as an important means of communication amongst Jews in the diaspora.

JABOTINSKY, VLADIMIR (ZE'EV): (1880–1940)
A Russian-born Zionist writer, soldier and orator, Jabotinsky became a Zionist after witnessing the pogroms. He founded the Jewish Legion during the First World War and created Jewish Battalions to assist the British war effort. In 1920 he and others were jailed then given amnesty by the British in Palestine for their part in the Jerusalem riots of that year. He became the leading opposition figure against the mainstream Zionist leadership (Weizmann and Ben-Gurion), spiritual leader of the Irgun Zeva'i Le'ummi (IZL) and the main ideologue of the Herut Party, at present the leading party in the Likud.

JEREMIAH
Beginning his preaching in 627 BCE, the prophet persuaded the Jews to accept foreign domination by the more powerful Babylonians under King Nebuchadnezzar, who had destroyed the Temple. He regarded the Babylonian conquest as Divine punishment for the unfaithfulness of his people and insisted on submission to no God other than the unique God of Israel. The building of the Second Temple from 516 BCE was seen as proof of God's protection and fulfilment of his prophecy.

JUDAH HA-NASI: (late second and early third century CE)
Became Patriarch of Judea when the Romans re-established a Jewish leadership in Palestine at the end of the second century CE. Referred to as rabbi or 'the Prince' he descended from Hillel and was regarded as a saviour of Israel by his contemporaries and later generations. He spread knowledge of the Torah and committed the law to writing in the *Mishnah*.

KAPLAN, MORDECAI MENAHEM: (1881–1983)
Kaplan was Lithuanian-born; his family emigrated to the United States, where he developed the idea of and founded the first synagogue-centre that would serve cultural and social needs as well as religious functions. His philosophy of reconstructionism, influential in both the Reform and Orthodox movements, defined Judaism as an evolving religious civilization.

In support of his ideas he founded the magazine *The Reconstructionist*, the Society for the Advancement of Judaism and the Jewish Reconstructionist Foundation. A rabbinic seminary that followed his ideas was established in Philadelphia in 1968.

LENIN, VLADIMIR ILYICH: (1870–1924)
The Russian revolutionary leader of the Bolsheviks and founder of the former Soviet State, Lenin adopted a consistently positive attitude to the Jewish question. Despite his belief that the separate cultural and social existence of the Jews was a corollary of anti-Jewish discrimination and persecution and that its disappearance was inevitable, he recognized Yiddish as the national language of the Jews, endorsed the establishment of departments for Jewish affairs and campaigned vigorously against anti-Semitism.

LEVINSOHN, ISAAC BAER: (1788–1860)
He was a Hebrew author, known as the 'Father of the Haskalah' in Russia. His *Te'udah be Yisrael* (*Testimony in Israel*) was written in 1823 but not published till 1828 owing to Orthodox opposition. In it he criticized traditional Hebrew schools and advocated a complete reform of the Jewish educational system, placing special emphasis on trades, crafts and agriculture. His ideas generally enjoyed tsarist support and protected him from the fury of his fanatical opponents.

LILLIENBLUM, MOSES LEIB: (1843–1910)
He was a Hebrew writer, critic and political journalist. From Odessa he published his political satire, *Kehal Refa'im* (1870) and edited the Yiddish journal *Kol Mevasser* (1871), challenging contemporaries and calling for the normalization of Jewish life through agricultural labour and work in industry, crafts and commerce. Following the pogroms of 1881 he became a nationalist leader of the Hibbat Zion movement and an exponent of the ideology of 'practical Zionism'.

MAIMONIDES, MOSES (MOSES BEN MAIMON): (1135–1204)
A Jewish philosopher, he and his family accepted Islam while still remaining Jews under Muslim rule in Spain and Morocco. In 1165 he moved to Egypt, reverted to Judaism and became the physician to Sultan Saladin. As head of the Jewish community he advocated tolerance of the Karaites whilst ensuring the supremacy of the Rabbanites. The works on which his fame chiefly rests are the *Mishneh Torah* (1180) and the *Guide of the Perplexed* (1189). His influence on Judaism was, and is, vast.

MARR, WILHELM: (1818–1904)
Marr was a German anti-Semite, who began his political career during the revolution of 1848 in his native Hamburg. In 1862 he published an anti-Semitic pamphlet *Der Judenspiegel* ('Jews' Mirror'). In 1879 he founded the League of Anti-Semites and thus introduced the word anti-Semite into the political vocabulary. His was the first effort at creating a popular political movement based on anti-Semitism.

MENDELSSOHN, MOSES: (1729–1786)
Prominent spokesman of the Haskalah and spiritual leader of German Jewry, he argued in his *Jerusalem: oder, Ueber Religioese Macht und Jedenthum* (*Jerusalem: or On Religious Power and Judaism*) in 1783, for a rationalist approach to Judaism. Actively involved in the struggle for the protection and civil rights of the Jews, he also stressed the need for young Jews to draw closer to German thought and culture.

MONTEFIORE, SIR MOSES: (1784–1885)
He was an Italian-born British philanthropist. The best known of British Jews, he played a

leading role in the struggle for Jewish emancipation. Sheriff of London in 1837–1838, he was knighted by Queen Victoria and in 1846 received a baronetcy in recognition of his humanitarian efforts on behalf of his oppressed co-religionists in Poland, Russia, Romania and Damascus.

NICHOLAS II: (Tsar of Russia 1894–1917)
He considered Jews resonsible for much of the revolutionary unrest that marked his reign. Despite advice from Witte and Stolypin, he refused to change the anti-Jewish laws and gave support to the violent anti-Semitic movement, the 'Union of Russian People' (the 'Black Hundreds'), while his police and army were wilfully ineffective during the pogroms.

PINSKER, LEON: (1821–1891)
Leader of the Hibbat Zion movement in Russia and author of the pamphlet *Autoemanzipation* (*Autoemancipation*) in 1882, he was originally a supporter of the Haskalah arguing in the first Russian Jewish weekly *Razsvet* ('Dawn') and its successor *Sion*, for acquaintance with the Russian culture and language. The pogroms of 1871 and 1881 led him to doubt the value of the emancipation of Russian Jewry and to call for the establishment of a Jewish state either in Palestine or elsewhere.

RIESSER, GABRIEL: (1806–1963)
Champion of Jewish emancipation in Germany, Riesser campaigned for Jewish rights by way of pamphlets, petitions, the press and participation in liberal politics. He distinguished himself in the Frankfort Vorparlament and the National Assembly and played a prominent role in the 1848 revolution.

RUPPIN, ARTHUR: (1876–1943)
Ruppin was a German-born and educated Zionist economist and sociologist; he published *Die Juden der Gegenwart* in 1904, which laid the foundations for the descriptive sociology of the Jews. A member of the Zionist Commission and the Jewish Agency Executive, he founded and directed the Institute for Economic Research in Palestine from 1935. From the 1920s his research influenced the creation of new forms of rural and urban settlements. He worked towards the establishment of a bi-national state in Palestine, whilst advocating a strengthening of the Jewish position economically and politically.

SAADIAH GAON: (882–942)
Scholar, author and leader of Babylonian Jewry, he was learned in the Torah, a devotee of Hebrew, and a dominant figure in the development of Judaism and its literature.

SAKHAROV, ANDREY DMITRIYEVICH: (1921–1989)
A nuclear physicist and outspoken advocate of civil liberties and political reform in the Soviet Union as well as of Soviet-American cooperation, he was awarded the Nobel Peace Prize in 1975 but was internally exiled to the city of Gorky by the Soviet government in 1980. He was allowed to return to Moscow in early 1987 and was subsequently elected to the Congress of People's Deputies as a representative of the Soviet Academy of Sciences.

SAMUEL HA-NAGID (ISMAIL IBN NAGREL'A): (993–1055)
A refugee from the Berber conquest of Cordoba, he settled in Granada where his political and military career as a vizier represents the highest achievement of a Jew in medieval Muslim Spain. In addition to his successes as a warrior-statesman, he was a communal leader and poet. He is credited with having introduced the poetry of battle into Hebrew literature.

SCHECHTER, SOLOMON: (1847–1915)
Schechter was the chief architect of Conservative Judaism in the United States; he was born in Romania, educated in Vienna and Berlin and came to England in 1882. In 1890 he served as a rabbinic scholar at Cambridge and in 1899 became Professor of Hebrew at University College, London. In 1902 he went to America where he assumed the presidency of the Jewish Theological Seminary in New York. Amongst his most important works are *Avot de-Rabbi Nathan* (1887), *Studies in Judaism* (three volumes, 1896–1924) and *Some Aspects of Rabbinic Theology* (1909).

SEIXAS, GERSHOM MENDES: (1746–1816)
The first native-born Jewish minister in the United States, he was appointed to the Shearith Israel Congregation of New York in 1768. During the upheaval of the American Revolution he moved first to Connecticut and then to Philadelphia, returning to his congregation in New York in 1784, where he stayed until his death.

SILVER, ABBA HILLEL: (1893–1963)
He was a reform Rabbi and Zionist leader, born in Lithuania and taken to the United States at the age of nine. He was ordained in 1915, becoming rabbi of the Tifereth Israel Congregation in Cleveland, Ohio, where he served until his death. A liberal leader, he was an early organizer of the anti-Nazi boycott in the 1930s and supported organized labour. As a Zionist he chaired both the United Palestine Appeal and the American section of the Jewish Agency, presenting the case for an independent Jewish State before the United Nations in 1947.

SMOLENSKIN, PEREZ: (1840 or 1842–1885)
Smolenskin was a Hebrew writer, an editor and leading exponent of the Haskalah in eastern Europe. He was born in Russia and settled in Vienna. He wrote many novels, the most important of which is *Ha-To'eh be- Darkhei ha-Hayyim* ('The Wanderer in the Paths of Life') (1868–71), but he is best known for his founding and editing of the Hebrew monthly *Ha-Shahar* in 1868, which provided a literary platform for the Haskalah in its later period and the early nationalist movement. He believed that the Hebrew language was the real foundation of Jewish nationalism, providing a substitute for a national territory.

SPINOZA, BARUCH (BENEDICTUS): (1632–1677)
A Dutch-born dissident Jewish philosopher and member of the Amsterdam Jewish community, Spinoza devoted his simple and moral life to rational enquiry, rejecting supernatural religion, scriptural authority and ceremonial Judaism in favour of religious tenets based on reason. Variously described as a 'God-intoxicated man' and a 'systematic atheist', he was excommunicated from the Nation of Israel in 1656 for his heretical views. His major works are *Tractatus Theologico-Politicus* (1670) and *Ethics* (1674).

WESSELY, NAPHTALI HERZ: (1725–1805)
As a Haskalah poet and linguist, Wessely collaborated in Berlin with Moses Mendelssohn and pioneered the revival of biblical Hebrew. He is best known for his poetry and his *Shirei Tiferet* (1789–1802) is the major literary work of the German Haskalah. A pioneer in education, he sought to mobilize the Jewish community to support the Edict of Tolerance of Joseph II of Austria, which proposed opening schools to Jewish children.

WISE, ISAAC MAYER: (1819–1900)
He was a pioneer of Reform Judaism in the United States. Born in Bohemia he emigrated to America in 1846 where he served as a rabbi at first in Albany, New York and then in

Cincinnati. There he organized the Union of American Hebrew Congregations from 1873 and the Hebrew Union College from 1875, both of which became central institutions of Reform Judaism.

WISE, STEPHEN SAMUEL: (1874–1949)
This rabbi and Zionist leader in the United States was born in Hungary. His parents emigrated to America. He studied at Columbia University and in Vienna, becoming rabbi of the N'nai Jeshurun Congregation in New York in 1893. He served a number of congregations as rabbi until 1907 when he founded the Free Synagogue in New York, which he headed till his death. He was an early supporter of Zionism, founded the New York Federation of Zionist Societies in 1897 and the following year served as the American secretary of the World Zionist movement.

Glossary

ALIYAH: 'Going up', that is, emigrating to Israel.

ARENDA: A Polish term to describe the lease of fixed assets or of prerogatives such as land, mills or the collection of taxes. The arenda system was widespread in the economy of Poland–Lithuania from the Middle Ages. The agricultural arenda were of central importance to Jewish economic life in the sixteenth and seventeenth centuries.

ARK OF THE COVENANT (ARON HA-KODESH): Originally referred to the chest containing the two stone tablets given by God to Moses at Sinai; it was carried by the wandering Israelites until it was permanently installed in the First Temple. The term now refers to the shrine containing the scrolls of the Torah in the synagogue.

ASHKENAZI (*plural* ASHKENAZIM): The biblical name for descendants of Ashkenaz (Genesis 10:3). From medieval times it referred to Jews of east and central European origins. They comprise over 80 per cent of world Jewry and have a ritual and Hebrew pronunciation distinct from the Sephardim.

ST AUGUSTINE'S DOCTRINE: Adopted by the Roman Catholic Church, the doctrine that 'protected' Jews in the Eastern Roman Empire. A leading church theologian in the fourth century CE, St Augustine insisted that Jews should not be destroyed but scattered to exist as a living testimony to the truth of Christianity.

BABYLONIAN TALMUD: *See* Talmud.

BAR MITZVAH: The ceremony in the synagogue that marks the attainment of religious maturity by a Jewish boy at the age of thirteen. He is then called up for the reading of the Law.

BCE: An abbreviation of 'Before the Common Era' equating exactly with BC in Christian usage.

BET DIN: A rabbinical court which has jurisdiction in civil, criminal and religious cases. In contemporary Israel it is also authorized to deal with marriage, divorce and (if all parties agree) inheritance. (The court of the British Chief Rabbi is called the Beth Din.)

BILUIM: Adherents of *Beit Ya'akov Lechu Venelcha* (BILU), one of the first modern Zionist pioneering groups, founded by Jewish students in Russia in 1882 in reaction to the pogroms. Its members were among the earliest Zionist agricultural settlers in Palestine.

BUND: A Jewish Marxist party formed in Russia in 1897, which organized strikes and demonstrations amongst Jewish workers and called for equal rights for Jews in the future socialist era. It was suppressed and its leaders forced into exile in 1922.

CALIPH: The head of the Muslim community, as successor of Muhammad.

CE: An abbreviation of 'Common Era' equating exactly with AD in Christian usage.

COURT JEWS (HOFJUDEN): Wealthy Jews used by rulers in the promotion of commerce and industry. Through their link to the state they exerted undue influence over fellow Jews and undermined the autonomy and cohesion of the community.

DHIMMI: A person belonging to the category of 'protected people' in the Islamic state. These were the recognized monotheists, Jews, Christians and Sabians, with divinely-revealed scriptures, who were tolerated if they paid a head tax and abided by certain rules.

ESSENES: Jewish mystics and devotees of the Torah from the second century BCE to the second century CE. They often separated themselves in communities as at Qumran near the Dead Sea. Entrance to the order was by a novitiate and a strict period of probation.

EXILARCH: One of a line of Jewish rulers in Babylonia who exercised authority over, and received tribute from, Jews in all countries from the third to the tenth century CE.

FIRST TEMPLE: Jerusalem and the First Temple were destroyed by the Babylonian conquest of the Kingdom of Judah in 586 BCE. The captive tribes of Judah and Benjamin endured a seventy-year period of exile in which they created the concept of a national homeland existing together with a diaspora.

FISCUS JUDAICUS: A Roman law stringently enforced in the second century CE to prevent the revival of a Jewish national centre. It required every Jew to contribute an annual sum for the upkeep of the Temple of Jupiter in Rome to replace contributions to the Temple in Jerusalem.

GAON (*plural* GEONIM): The head of one of the great Babylonian Jewish academies.

GEMARA: A body of work based on biblical verses to supplement and explain the *Mishnah*.

GENTILES: Non-Jews.

HABAD HASIDISM: Known too as Lubavitch Hasidism, it placed more emphasis on intellectual striving than on emotions, compared with the broader Hasidic movement.

HALAKHA: That part of traditional oral Jewish Law that deals with rules for living, both legal and ethical.

HANUKKAH: The Feast of Dedication in celebration of the achievement of Judas Macca-baeus in regaining possession of the Temple from the Syrian Greeks in 165 BCE. It is also known as the Feast of Lights.

HASIDISM: Chiefly (although the term has an older history) the mystical and revivalist religious movement which arose in eighteenth-century Poland and attracted the vast majority of east European Jews. Emphasizing simplicity, sincerity and joyful emotion, it was a reaction to the dominance of the scholarly elite.

HASKALAH: The Jewish Enlightenment of the late eighteenth century led by Moses Men-delssohn (1729–1786) and others. It resulted in a new emphasis on education and a resurgence of the study of Hebrew and the Jewish scriptures in a modern context. Its adherents were known as *maskilim*.

HASMONEANS: An independent Jewish kingdom which grew out of armed resistance to the Syrian Greeks and established itself from 164 BCE. It soon occupied as wide an area as had King David eight centuries earlier.

HAZANUT: The cantorial art which includes the correct chanting of the service in a synagogue by cantors.

HOFJUDEN: *See* Court Jews.

INTIFADAH: The large-scale, unarmed but violent uprising dating from late 1987 and carried out by young Palestinian nationalists inspired by the ideologies of both the Palestinian Liberation Organization and Islamic fundamentalist movements.

JIZYAH: A tax once levied on such non-Muslim adult males as were able to pay it, provided that they belonged to a religion recognized as divinely revealed, that is, provided they were 'people of the Book'.

KABBALAH: An esoteric theosophical system which reached its peak in thirteenth-century Spain, involving mystical methods of studying Jewish texts. It influenced Hasidism and the popular Judaism of North Africa and the Yemen but was challenged in Europe during the Haskalah.

KAHAL: A traditional form of Jewish self-government which, apart from religious requirements, provided for semi-secular needs including education, the judiciary and social welfare. Under Polish rule it also served as a tax-collecting agency for the government.

KARAISM (KARAITES): From the Hebrew for 'to read', a religious movement rejecting the rabbinical tradition of the authority of the Oral Law and basing its teaching on an almost literal interpretation of Scripture alone.

KASHRUT: Jewish dietary laws. *See also* Kosher.

KEHILLAH: In common usage this now refers to a Jewish community or organized congregation.

KIBBUTZ (*plural* KIBBUTZIM): In Israel, a voluntary, collective community, mainly agricultural, in which there is no private wealth, the community being responsible for the needs of the members and their families.

KIDDUSH: A blessing recited at the beginning of the Jewish Sabbath and on other holy days.

KIDDUSH HA-SHEM: A principle in which, in times of persecution, every Jewish man, woman or child was expected to accept death rather than abandon his or her religious faith.

KNESSET: The parliament of the state of Israel, located in Jerusalem.

KOSHER: Meaning 'ritually acceptable', the term most commonly applied to those categories of food that Jews are permitted by their faith to eat, and also to the preparation of such food in accordance with dietary laws.

MAGGIDIM: Itinerant preachers who frequently followed and encouraged an ascetic way of life. They were partly responsible for the spread of Hasidism in Europe during the eighteenth century.

MARRANOS: From the Spanish for 'swine', a pejorative term for Spanish and Portuguese Jews and their descendants, forcibly converted to Christianity, who practised their Jewish faith in secret. Many settled in the New World.

MASADA: The excavated site of the Zealot fortress where around a thousand Jewish rebels held out against the Romans before a mass suicide as an act of *Kiddush ha-shem*. It has become a shrine for national pilgrimage and a powerful symbol for Israelis.

MASKIL (*plural* MASKILIM): Jewish intellectuals who emerged under emancipation in Europe during the eighteenth century and developed a tradition of internal criticism informed by the efforts of Moses Mendelssohn (1729–1786).

MATZAH (*plural* MATZOT): The unleavened bread used during the Jewish Passover Festival to commemorate the Exodus from Egypt.

MIDRASH (*plural* MIDRASHIM): The teaching and commentary of Jewish rabbis. *Halakhic Midrash* deals with the Law, and *Aggadic Midrash* deals with the narrative of scripture.

MISHNAH: The codification of rabbinical or oral law by which all Jews should live, compiled *circa* 200 CE. It forms the basis of the Palestinian and Babylonian Talmuds.

MITNAGDIM: Opponents of Hasidism who adhered to traditional authoritarian Judaism.

MITZVAH (*plural* MITZVOTH): A central concept of Judaism that literally means 'commandment', but it can also mean an obligation or good deed required of the Jews by God.

MOSAIC LAW: God's laws, including the Ten Commandments, brought by Moses from Mount Sinai.

NUMERUS CLAUSUS: Literally 'closed number', that is, the fixing of a quota on the admission of Jews to institutions of higher learning, the professions, public office and so on. It was widespread in Europe, being applied in the nineteenth century and extended in the twentieth.

PALE OF SETTLEMENT: A term that came into use in the nineteenth century for a large area in the western and south-western provinces of the Russian Empire open to Jewish settlement under Empress Catherine the Great. During the nineteenth century Jews were confined exclusively to this area.

PATRIARCH: The official title given to the head of the Jewish population by the Romans from the second century CE, an office that was granted wide-ranging powers.

PENTATEUCH: The first five books of the Bible, described by the Jews as the Torah, and believed by them to have been dictated by God to Moses on Mount Sinai.

PESACH (PASSOVER): A festival of the Jewish year celebrated in the spring (14 Nisan Hebrew Calendar) for eight days, commemorating the Exodus from Egypt.

PHARISEES: An Aramaic word describing scribes and scholars who were distinguished in the second century BCE for their strict observance of the Torah, and their study and development of the Oral Law. They were the founders of rabbinic Judaism and were opposed by the Sadducees.

PILPUL: A dialectical technique for reconciling contradictory texts; it was challenged during the Haskalah by radical reformers who favoured a more literal approach to the scriptures.

PIYUTIM: The liturgical poetry of the Jewish service that was eliminated by the reforms introduced under the Haskalah.

POGROM: Originally describing the anti-Jewish outbreaks during the last decades of Tsarist Russia in the nineteenth century, a term now used for any organized massacre or expulsion of Jews.

PRACTICAL KABBALAH: A means of trying to achieve divine communication, for example by juggling with biblical words and letters, originally developed by Spanish exiles in the Galilee hill town of Safed but adopted by the Jewish masses in Poland during the eighteenth century under the impact of Hasidism.

REFORM JUDAISM: A religious movement, originating in Germany in the nineteenth century, aimed at adapting Judaism and its traditional customs to modern conditions (for example, by modifying dietary laws).

RESPONSA: Replies from Babylonian rabbinical authorities in the eighth century CE to questions from far-flung Jewish communities throughout the diaspora. The questions and *responsa* were delivered by caravans of international Jewish traders.

ROSH HASHANAH: The Jewish New Year, recalling God's act of creating the world. This day inaugurates Ten Days of Penitence, which culminate in Yom Kippur, the Day of Atonement.

SADDUCEES: Jewish priests of conservative outlook who became prominent in the first centuries BCE and CE in opposition to the principle of a binding Oral Law as developed and promoted by the Pharisees. They recognized only the Written Law and denied resurrection and the after life. They died out after the destruction of Jerusalem in 70 CE.

SANHEDRIN: The highest Jewish tribunal, consisting of seventy members, which met in Jerusalem. Julius Caesar gave it authority over all Judea. Its functions ceased about 425 CE. The name is also associated with the rabbinical assembly summoned by Napoleon in 1807 to endorse his reforms.

SECOND TEMPLE: The period between the Babylonian exile and the Roman destruction of the Second Temple in 70 CE; it was a formative period for Jewish religion and culture.

SEPHARDI (*plural* SEPHARDIM): Originally Jews from Spain and Portugal, the term that came to loosely describe Jews from various oriental countries. In Israel the term is frequently applied to all non-Ashkenazi Jews.

SIDDUR: The Jewish daily prayer book.

TALMUD: The most important source of Jewish Law, a body of literature written in Hebrew and Aramaic, which represents the definitive codification and interpretation of the Oral Law. It comprises the *Mishnah*, the Oral Law collected by the second century CE, and the *Gemara*, rabbinic commentaries on the *Mishnah* dated 200–500 CE. It exists in two distinct compilations, the Palestinian Talmud and the Babylonian Talmud.

TORAH: The Pentateuch (the Five Books of Moses) or Written Law of Judaism contained in the Bible, and, in a more general sense, the whole body of Jewish religious teaching, including the 'oral Torah' contained in the Talmud and other non-biblical compilations.

YESHIVAH (*plural* YESHIVOT): A religious academy devoted largely to the study of the Talmud.

YISHUV: A collective term for the Jewish population of Mandatory Palestine.

YOM HA-SHO'AH: The holocaust remembrance day observed by many communities throughout the world on 27 Nisan (Hebrew calendar).

YOM KIPPUR: The most solemn holy day, the Day of Atonement, a fast day which brings to an end the Ten Days of Penitence, which begin with Rosh Hashanah.

ZADDIKIM: Hasidic leaders deriving their authority from an especially close relationship to God as well as from miraculous and charismatic powers. Followers owed them spiritual and temporal obedience and financial support.

ZEALOTS: An early fanatical Jewish sect originating in Galilee, noted for their resistance to foreign occupation.

Notes

1 Post-Biblical Jewish History – The Long Vista

1   Jeremiah 29: 4–14.
2   Ezekiel 37: 11–14.
3   Isaiah 44: 24, 28.
4   Ezra 4: 4–5.
5   Ezra 10: 10–11.
6   Nehemiah 8: 2, 7–8.
7   II Maccabees IV, *The Apocrypha A.D. 1611* (London: Oxford University Press) p. 389.
8   Ibid., p. 312.
9   Josephus. Cited in *Letters of Jews Through the Ages* (London: East and West Library, 1952) p. 50.
10   Josephus. *The Jewish War*, Book II (Grand Rapids, MI: Zondarvan, 1982) pp. 184–5.
11   Seneca, 'On Superstition'. In M. Whittaker *Jews and Christians* (Cambridge: Cambridge University Press, 1984) p. 88.
12   The Jewish calendar comprises twelve months and, unlike the Gregorian calendar, is based on the phases of the moon. To ensure that the months always fall within the same seasons, an adjustment must be made to reconcile the lunar year of 354 days with the solar year of 365¼ days. This is done by adding an extra month to seven out of every nineteen years. The names of the Hebrew months are of Babylonian origin.
13   Jerusalem Talmud, Succah 5.
14   Simon Bar Kochba's real name was Simon Bar Koziba. He was renamed Bar Kochba ('A star has risen from Jacob') by Rabbi Akiva.
15   *The Middrash Rabbah*, New Compact Edition, Vol. 4, *Lamentations* (Oxford: Oxford University Press, 1977) Proem II, p. 2.
16   Exodus 21: 24.
17   (*Mishnah*).
18   *Gemara* (Babylonian Talmud). Tractate Baba Kamma VIII – First Gate, 83b/84a.
19   Matthew 5: 17–19.
20   Matthew 15: 22–28.
21   I Thessalonians 2: 14–16.
22   John 8: 44–47.
23   In Aramaic, *Resh Galuta* (the Head of the Exiles). At the time the Talmud was being edited, the heads of Babylonian Jewry were known as the Heads of Yeshivot (*Rosh Yeshivah* or, in Aramaic, *Roshei Yeshivot*). The title Gaon was introduced in 590 CE, after the Talmud had been finished.
24   Al Masudi, tenth-century Arab diplomat and traveller. Cited in A. Koestler, *The Thirteenth Tribe* (London: Hutchinson, 1976) p. 60.
25   A. Koestler, *The Thirteenth Tribe* (London: Hutchinson, 1976) p. 13.
26   Abn Ishak Al-Elviri, eleventh-century Muslim poet, writing in a Muslim report on Jewish

power. Cited in H. Graetz, *History of the Jews* (Philadelphia: Jewish Publication Society of America, 1948) p. 278.

27   Jacob von Königshofen. Cited in A. A. Rogow (ed.) *The Jew in a Gentile World* (New York: Macmillan, 1961) pp. 94–5.

28   Letter from Pope Innocent IV to King Louis IX of France (1244). Cited in R. Chazan (ed.) *Church, State and Jew in the Middle Ages* (New York: Behrman House, 1980) pp. 231–2

29   Jacob von Königshofen. Cited in A. A. Rogow (ed.) *The Jew in a Gentile World* (New York: Macmillan, 1961) p. 95.

30   Martin Luther, 'That Jesus was Born a Jew' (1523). In A. A. Rogow (ed.) *The Jew in a Gentile World* (New York: Macmillan, 1961) pp. 100–1.

31   Martin Luther, 'Of the Jews and Their Lies' (1543). In A. A. Rogow (ed.) *The Jew in a Gentile World* (New York: Macmillan, 1961) pp. 101–2.

32   Cited in P. R. Mendes-Flohr and J. Reinharz, *The Jew in the Modern World: A Documentary History* (Oxford: Oxford University Press, 1980) pp. 20–4.

33   Nathan of Hanover. Cited in *Source Book of Jewish History and Literature* (London: Shapiro Valentine, 1938) p. 195.

34   Kabbalah represents the most important stream of the Jewish mystical tradition. Its central text, the Zohar, written down in thirteenth-century Spain, reinterprets the principal beliefs and rituals of Judaism in terms of esoteric theology. The development of the ideas in the Zohar by Isaac Luria (1534–1572) introduced a pronounced Messianic element which found dramatic expression in the Shabbatean movement.

35   Jewish population statistics derived from *Encyclopaedia Judaica* Vol. 13 (Jerusalem: Keter, 1972) pp. 869, 877–8, 889–90. General population statistics derived from McEvedy and Jones, *Atlas of World Population History* (Harmondsworth: Penguin, 1978).

36   Psalm 115: 17.

2   Jews in Islamic Lands

1   Terminology for the region is complex and has changed over time. In this book the usage varies with context. However, the following points should be noted: in the Middle Ages, Iraq was the Arabic name for an area comprising Babylonia (essentially a Jewish term) plus some adjoining territory. Medieval Iraq was, in fact, smaller than modern-day Iraq. The toponym 'Mesopotamia', which may be encountered, is a European term for the region bounded by the Tigris and the Euphrates, encompassing Babylonia to the south.

2   The Sasanian Empire was established in the third century under the Sasanian dynasty of Iran. Its territory consisted mainly of what is now Iran and part of Iraq. The Empire came to an end in the middle of the seventh century as a result of Arab conquest.

3   The term 'Palestine' has had various meanings over the centuries. Ancient Palestine, in other words Palestine in biblical times and up to the advent of Islam, is referred to by Jews as the Land of Israel (Erez Israel). For most of the period dealt with in this chapter, Arabic Palestine, or 'Filastin', was at most a small subsection of that area. With the British Mandate following the First World War, 'Palestine' took on a different meaning. Mandated Palestine consisted of regions which had, in Islamic times, been part of a larger geographical entity known as al-Sham, that is Syria. It did not include all of the geographical area that had been ancient Palestine. Nowadays the term 'Palestine' has a specific political application. In this chapter the term is used in those instances where it is necessary to make clear that the region concerned corresponds to the area defined by biblical and pre-Islamic usage.

4   In N. A. Stillman (compiler), *The Jews of Arab Lands: A history and source book* (Philadelphia: Jewish Publication Society of America, 1979) p. xv.

5   See, for example, B. Lewis, *The Jews of Islam* (Princeton: Princeton University Press, 1987).

6   See D. Z. H. Baneth, 'What did Muhammad mean when he called his religion "Islam"? The original meaning of *aslama* and its derivatives', in *Israel Oriental Studies*, Vol. 1 (1971) pp. 183–90.

7   Originally formulated by M. G. S. Hodgson in *The Venture of Islam: Conscience and history in a*

world civilization, Vol. 1, *The Classical Age of Islam* (Chicago: University of Chicago Press, 1974) pp. 56–60.

8 In Stillman, *The Jews of Arab Lands, op. cit.*, p. 64. This timespan obviously necessitates making certain choices, and so I have laid aside the original manuscript of 400 pages and have chosen instead to speak only of the Jewish sources by way of a reading of certain representative texts.

3   Jewish Emancipation in Central and Western Europe in the Eighteenth and Nineteenth Centuries

1 Alexander Pope, 'Epitaph. Intended for Sir Isaac Newton, In Westminster-Abbey' (1730).
2 Immanuel Kant, 'What is Enlightenment', *Berlinische Monatsschrift* IV (1784).
3 Voltaire, *Lettres Philosophiques*, Vol. 1, ed. G. Lanson (Paris, 1924) p. 74.
4 *Transactions of the Parisian Sanhedrin*, trans. Tama (London, 1807) p. 132.

4   East European Jewry Since 1770

1 The term 'eastern Europe' is generally taken to mean all the countries of the old Soviet bloc. However, in the context of Jewish history, the focus is primarily on Poland and the western part of the former Soviet Union – historically the great centres of east European Jewry.
2 Under the Union of Lublin in 1569, the Kingdom of Poland and the Grand Duchy of Lithuania united to form the Polish Commonwealth (sometimes colloquially referred to just as Poland). The Polish Commonwealth controlled a sizeable portion of northeastern Europe, with lands stretching from modern-day Frankfurt, east nearly to Moscow, and south almost to the Black Sea. But through a series of wars with Russia, Turkey and Sweden in the late sixteenth and seventeenth centuries, the Commonwealth's economic and military strength dwindled. By the late eighteenth century, the Polish Commonwealth was so weak that it was carved up by the three great central European powers – Russia, Austria and Prussia. After the third partition of 1795, the Polish Commonwealth ceased to exist as an independent political entity. It was not until 1918 that an independent Poland would again appear on the map of Europe.
3 From Gordon's well-known poem, 'Awake, my people' (*'Hakizah Ammi'*), 1863.
4 Hessia Helfman came from a 'bourgeois' Jewish family and joined *Narodnaia Volia* in late 1879, participating in preparations for the assassination of Alexander II. After the Tsar's assassination, she was sentenced to death along with other conspirators, but her sentence was commuted to 'indefinite imprisonment' since she was pregnant. Helfman died while in prison and, in the former USSR, is considered to be one of the 'first martyrs' of the Russian revolutionary movement.
5 L. Pinsker, *Autoemancipation* (London: Rita Searl, 1947) pp. 33–4. Originally published as *Autoemanzipation, ein Mahnruf on seine Stammesgenossen von einen russischen Juden* (Berlin, 1882).
6 Ibid., p. 25.
7 Naphtali Friedman. Cited in J. Frumkin, G. Aronson and A. Goldenweiser (eds), *Russian Jewry (1860–1917)*, M. Ginsburg (trans.), (London: Thomas Yoseloff, 1966) p. 58.
8 Prince Shcherbatov. Cited in J. Frumkin, G. Aronson and A. Goldenweiser (eds), *Russian Jewry (1860–1917)* p. 114.
9 In a wave of anti-German fervour during the First World War, the name of St Petersburg was 'russified', becoming Petrograd. After Lenin's death in 1924 the city's name was again changed, this time to Leningrad, in honour of the founder of the Soviet state. In 1991, after a referendum, the city returned to its original name, St Petersburg.

   Moscow was the historic capital of Russia, but with the founding of St Petersburg by Peter the Great in 1703, most of the imperial administration was moved to this new capital city. After the Bolshevik Revolution the centre of government returned to Moscow.
10 Provisional Government decree, 1917. Cited in J. Frumkin, G. Aronson and A. Goldenweiser (eds), *Russian Jewry (1860–1917)* p. 117.

11   Until the Bolshevik Revolution, dates in the Russian Empire were reckoned according to the Julian calendar which was, by then, thirteen days behind the Western, or Gregorian, system. On 31 January 1918, Lenin's government officially adopted the Western calendar. According to the Western system, the February Revolution began on 8 March 1917 and the October Revolution on 7 November 1917.

Unless otherwise indicated, dates in the text relating to Russia before 31 January 1918 are given according to the Julian calendar, and thereafter according to the Western, or Gregorian, system.

12   Summons to an all-Russian Jewish congress, 1917. Cited in S. W. Baron, *The Russian Jew under Tsars and Soviets* (New York: Macmillan, 1976) pp. 168–9.

13   I. Babel, 'Gedali' in *Chetyre rasskaza* (Letchworth: Bradda Books, 1965) p. 17. (Quotation translated by C. E. King.)

14   J. V. Stalin, 'Marksizm i natsionalnyi vopros' in *Sochineniia*, Vol. 2 (Moscow: Izdatelstvo politicheskoi literatury, 1946) p. 340.

15   A. Sakharov, *Memoirs*, R. Lourie (trans.) (London: Hutchinson, 1990) p. 343.

16   *International Herald Tribune*, 8 January 1991, p. 5.

5   North American Jewry

1   Letter from the Amsterdam Chamber of the Dutch West India Company to Peter Stuyvesant, 26 April 1655. Cited in M. U. Schappes (ed.), *A Documentary History of the Jews in the United States, 1654–1875* (New York: Schocken Books, 1971) p. 5.

2   Letter from the Directors of the Dutch West India Company to Peter Stuyvesant, 14 June 1656. Cited in M. U. Schappes (ed.), *A Documentary History of the Jews in the United States, 1654–1875*, p. 12.

3   Resolution of burgomasters, 22 February 1656. Cited in D. de Sola Pool, *Portraits Etched in Stone* (New York: Columbia University Press, 1952) p. 8.

4   Letter from Domine Henricus Selyns. Cited in D. de Sola Pool, *Old Faith in the New World* (New York: Columbia University Press, 1955) p. 34.

5   Cited in D. de Sola Pool, *Old Faith in the New World*, p. 35.

6   George Washington's reply to the Hebrew Congregation of Newport, Rhode Island. In J. L. Blau and S. W. Baron (eds), *The Jews of the United States 1790–1840 – A Documentary History*, Vol. 1 (New York: Columbia University Press, 1963) p. 9.

7   Letter from Rebecca Gratz to Solomon Cohen. In Blau and Baron, *The Jews of the United States*, Vol. 3, p. 955.

8   *The Occident and American Jewish Advocate*, Vol. 6 (Philadelphia, 1848) p. 366.

9   Abraham Hart. Cited in Blau and Baron, *The Jews of the United States*, Vol. 3, p. 934.

10   Cited in J. Buchler, 'The Struggle for Unity – Attempts at Union in American Jewish Life: 1654–1848', *American Jewish Archives*, Vol. 2 (1949) pp. 39–44.

11   In D. I. Rapp (ed.), *An Original History of the Religious Denominations in the United States* (Philadelphia: J.Y. Humphreys, 1844) p. 368.

12   Cited in I. M. Fein, *The Making of an American Jewish Community* (Philadelphia: Jewish Publication Society of America, 1971) pp. 56–7.

13   *The Occident and American Jewish Advocate*, Vol. 3 (Philadelphia, 1846) p. 265.

14   *Address of the Jewish Publication Committee to the Israelites of America* (Philadelphia, 1845).

15   In D. Philipson, *Max Lilienthal, American Rabbi: Life and Writings* (New York: Block Publishing, 1915) p. 55.

16   Cited in L. Jick, *The Americanization of the Synagogue 1820–1870* (Hanover, NH: University Press of New England, 1976) p. 162.

17   I. J. Benjamin, *Three Years in America, 1859–1862*, Vol. 1 (Philadelphia: Jewish Publication Society of America, 1956) p. 310.

18   Cited in D. Philipson, *The Reform Movement in Judaism*, rev. ed. (New York: Macmillan, 1931) p. 354.

19   Cited in B. Levy, *Reform Judaism in America* (New York: Block Publishing, 1933) p. 61.

20 Cited in M. I. Urofsky, *American Zionism from Herzl to the Holocaust* (New York: Doubleday, 1975) p. 121.

21 Address of Louis Marshall on his return from the Versailles Peace Conference, 28 July 1919. In C. Reznicoff (ed.), *Louis Marshall Champion of Liberty, Selected Papers and Addresses* (Philadelphia: Jewish Publication Society, 1957) p. 545.

6   The Origins of Religions and Racial Anti-Semitism and the Jewish Response

1   Quoted from P. R. Mendes-Flohr and J. Reinharz, *The Jew in the Modern World: A Documentary History* (Oxford: Oxford University Press, 1980) p. 272.

2   Juvenal, *Satire* xiv, 96–106.

3   Tacitus, *Histories* V, v, 1–2.

4   Hebrews 8: 13.

5   See 1 Peter 2: 8 and Romans 9: 33.

6   Acts 7: 51–3.

7   Matthew 27: 20, 24–6.

8   John 8: 44–6.

9   Romans 9: 6–7.

10 Romans 9: 22.

11 W. C. Greene (ed. and trans.), *City of God*, Book 4, 34 (London: Heinemann, 1963), p. 129.

12 Quoted by Leon Poliakov, Vol. 1, *The History of Anti-Semitism* (London: Routledge and Kegan Paul, 1974) pp. 29–32.

13 Ibid.

14 See P. S. Alexander, *Textual Sources for the Study of Judaism* (Manchester: Manchester University Press, 1984) p. 173.

15 B. S. James (trans.), *The Letters of St Bernard of Clairvaux* (London, Burne Oates, 1953) no. 391.

16 B. S. James (trans.), *The Letters of St Bernard of Clairvaux*, no. 393.

17 It should be noted that polemics between Christians and Jews have a long pedigree. The Christian side goes back to the First Century CE; the Jewish polemic started some centuries later. The role of Jewish converts in these controversies is particularly noteworthy.

18 See G. G. Field, *Evangelist of Race: The Germanic Vision of Houston Stewart Chamberlain* (New York: Columbia University Press, 1981) p. 193.

19 See V. E. Marsden (trans.), *Protocols of the Meetings of the Learned Elders of Zion* (London: The Britons Publishing Society, 1925) p. 12.

20 From an interview with Henry Ford in *New York World*, 17 February 1921. Quoted in Marsden, *Protocols of the Meetings of the Learned Elders of Zion*.

21 See P. S. Alexander, *Textual Sources for the Study of Judaism*, p. 158.

22 Quoted by R. S. Wistrich, *Revolutionary Jews from Marx to Trotsky* (London: Harrap, 1976) p. 11.

23 See B. M. Lane and L. J. Rupp (eds), *Nazi Ideology Before 1933: A Documentation* (Manchester: Manchester University Press, 1978) p. 41.

24 See P. S. Alexander, *Textual Sources for the Study of Judaism*, pp. 179–80.

25 Ibid., pp. 178–9.

26 See G. Boldt, *Hitler – Die letzen zehn Tage* (Frankfurt-am-Main: Verlag Ullstein) p. 201. Translated by P. S. Alexander.

27 R. Rubenstein in *The Condition of Jewish Belief: A Symposium Compiled by the Editors of Commentary Magazine* (New York: Macmillan, 1966) p. 200.

7   Zionism and the Palestine Question

1   S. Avineri, *The Making of Modern Zionism* (New York: Basic Books, 1981) p. 52.

2   See M. Verete, 'Why was a British Consulate established in Jerusalem?', *English Historical Review* (1970) pp. 316–45.

3   See J. Katz, 'The Jewish National Movement: A Sociological Analysis', *Journal of World History* (1968) p. 278.

4   J. Katz, *Antisemitism. From Religious Hatred to Racial Rejection* (Tel Aviv, 1979) p. 250. Hebrew edition.

5   Quoted by A. Hertzberg in *The Zionist Idea* (New York, 1959) p. 173.

6   The best assessment of Herzl is in D. Vital, *Zionism. The Formative Years* (Oxford: Oxford University Press, 1982).

7   L. Stein, *The Balfour Declaration* (London: Valentine Mitchell, 1961) pp. 544–66. See also I. Friedman, *The Palestine Question 1914–1918* (London, 1973).

8   Y. Porath, *The Emergence of the Palestine Arab National Movement. From Riots to Rebellion* Vol. 2, 1929–39 (London: Cass, 1977) pp. 178–95, 233–73.

9   J. Heller, 'Avraham Stern – Myth and Reality', *The Jerusalem Quarterly* (January, 1989) pp. 121–44.

10   B. Wasserstein, *Britain and the Jews of Europe 1939–1945* (Oxford: Oxford University Press, 1979) pp. 60–74, 143–56.

11   M. Gilbert, *Auschwitz and the Allies* (London: Michael Joseph, 1981) pp. 303–5.

12   Palestine. CP(47)259. CAB129/21. Foreign Secretary's Memorandum to the Cabinet, 18.9.1947, Public Record Office, London. See also M. Cohen, *Palestine and the Great Powers 1945–1948* (Princeton, 1982) pp. 274–6.

13   Y. Porath, *The Emergence of the Palestinian Arab National Movement, Vol. 1 1918–1929* (London: Cass, 1974) pp. 39–63.

14   B. Morris, *The Birth of the Palestinian Arab Refugee Problem* (Cambridge: Cambridge University Press, 1987) p. 292.

15   D. Ben-Gurion, *War of Independence Diary*, eds G. Rivlin and E. Orren (Tel Aviv, 1982) Vol. 3 p. 853.

16   M. Dayan, *The Story of My Life* (New York, 1977) pp. 361–457.

17   M. Shemesh, *The Palestinian Entity 1959–1974. Arab Politics and the PLO* (London: Cass, 1988) pp. 95–7.

18   H. Kissinger, *Years of Upheaval* (London: Weidenfeld and Nicolson, 1982) pp. 838–46.

19   D. Horowitz and M. Lissak, *Trouble in Utopia. The Overburdened Polity of Israel* (Albany: State University of New York Press, 1989) pp. 77–83.

20   Ibid., p. 239.

Notes on Contributors

PHILIP S. ALEXANDER is Head of the Department of Middle Eastern Studies, University of Manchester. His published works include *Textual Sources in the Study of Judaism* (Manchester: Manchester University Press, 1984).

DAVID ENGLANDER is Senior Lecturer in European Humanities Studies at the Open University. He is the author of *Landlord and Tenant in Urban Britain 1838–1918* (Oxford: Clarendon Press, 1983), co-editor of *Culture and Belief in Europe 1450–1600* (Oxford: Blackwell, 1990) and co-author of *Mr Charles Booth's Inquiry: Life and Labour of The People in London Reconsidered* (London: Hambledon Press, 1992).

JOSEPH HELLER is Associate Professor in the Department of International Studies and the Department of Jewish History at the Hebrew University of Jerusalem. His Hebrew-language publications include book-length studies on Zionist politics and the Stern Gang, and he is the author of *British Policy towards the Ottoman Empire 1908–1914* (London: Frank Cass, 1983).

LEON JICK is Chair of the Department of Near Eastern and Judaic Studies, Brandeis University, USA. He is the author of *The Americanization of the Synagogue 1820–1870* (Hanover, New Hampshire: University Press of New England, 1976) and other works.

LIONEL KOCHAN, formerly Bearsted Reader in Jewish History at the University of Warwick, is the author of *The Making of Modern Russia* (London: Jonathan Cape, 1962) and editor of *The Jews in Soviet Russia since 1917* (Oxford: Oxford University Press, 3rd edn. 1978).

JACOB LASSNER, Chair of the Department of Near Eastern Studies and Director of the Centre for Judaic Studies, Wayne State University, USA. His published works include *The Topography of Baghdad in the Early Middle Ages* (Detroit: Wayne State University Press, 1970).

RONALD NETTLER is a Fellow in Muslim–Jewish Relations at the Oxford Centre for Postgraduate Hebrew Studies and Hebrew Centre Lecturer in Oriental Studies at the University of Oxford. He is the author of *Past Trials and Present Tribulations: A Muslim Fundamentalist's View of the Jews* (Oxford: Pergamon Press, 1987).

DAVID SORKIN is Leslie Painter Research Fellow, St Antony's College, Oxford and Clore Fellow at the Oxford Centre for Postgraduate Hebrew Studies. He is the author of *The Transformation of German Jewry 1780–1840* (Oxford: Clarendon Press, 1987) and co-editor of *From East and West: Jews in a Changing Europe 1750–1840* (Oxford: Blackwell, 1990).

ROBIN SPIRO, founder and Director of the Spiro Institute for the Study of Jewish History and Culture, is a respected educationalist and a specialist in Jewish Studies.

Illustration Acknowledgements

Grateful acknowledgement is made for permission to reproduce the following illustrations, in printed order:

Colour Plates: Rijksmuseum, Amsterdam; Turkish and Islamic Arts Museum, Istanbul; Urbino, Palazzo Ducale, photo: Scala, Florence; as preceding plate; American Jewish Historical Society; as preceding plate; Israel Museum, Jerusalem; Magnum, London, photo: Fred Mayer.

Black and White Illustrations:
Chapter 1
A Pictorial History of the Jewish People by Nathan Ausubel, Crown Publishers, New York, 1953; Bibliotheque Nationale, Paris; *The Jewish People: 4000 years of survival* by Max Wurmbrand and Cecil Roth, Macmillan Publishing Co. 1974, North American © Massada Press, Israel; by permission of the British Library Board, London; Judisches Museum, Frankfurt am Main; Public Record Office, London; Ronald Sheridan, The Art and Architecture Collection; Judisches Museum, Frankfurt am Main.

Chapter 2
Ara Guler, Istanbul; by permission of the British Library Board, London; by permission of the Syndics of Cambridge University Library; by permission of the British Library Board; Israel Museum, Jerusalem; as preceding illus.

Chapter 3
Mansell collection, London; Frontispiece of *Les Juifs d'Alsace* (1790); Bibliotheque Nationale, Paris; Historisches Museum, Frankfurt am Main; *Illustrated London News*, 28 July 1858.

Chapter 4
Crown Publishing Group, New York; by permission of the British Library Board; Roger-Viollet, Paris; Camera Press, London; R. F. Scharf, London; as preceding illus.; Associated Press, London.

Chapter 5
American Jewish Archives, Cincinnati; as preceding illus.; as preceding illus.; American Jewish Historical Society; Library of Congress; by permission of the British Library Board; United Jewish Appeal, New York.

Chapter 6
Stadtarchiv, Freiburg im Breisgau; Mansell Collection, London; Bildarchiv Preussischer Kulturbesitz, Berlin; Luchterhand Literaturverlag, Hamburg and Zurich; Bildarchiv Preussischer Kulturbesitz, Berlin; Israel Museum, Jerusalem.

Chapter 7
Israel Museum, Jerusalem; Central Zionist Archives, Jerusalem; Israel Museum, Jerusalem; Popperfoto, London; as previous illus.; United Nations Public Information Service; Harry S Truman Research Institute, Hebrew University of Jerusalem.

Index